From top left to right

1. Don E. Lester Sr.
2. Leland Lester
3. Vernon J. Main Jr.
4. William Persky
5. Robert B. Ruffato
6. John A. Morrill Jr.
7. Edwin Price Ramsey
8. Austin L. Andrews
9. Raymond L. Richmond
10. William G. Roy
11. Bert Stolier
12. W. V. "Bud" Taylor
13. Lester I. Tenney
14. Eugene Wallace
15. Edward E. Wise
16. Angelo Borruano

WAR
STORIES

WORLD WAR II
FIRST HAND

WEIDER HISTORY
PUBLICATIONS

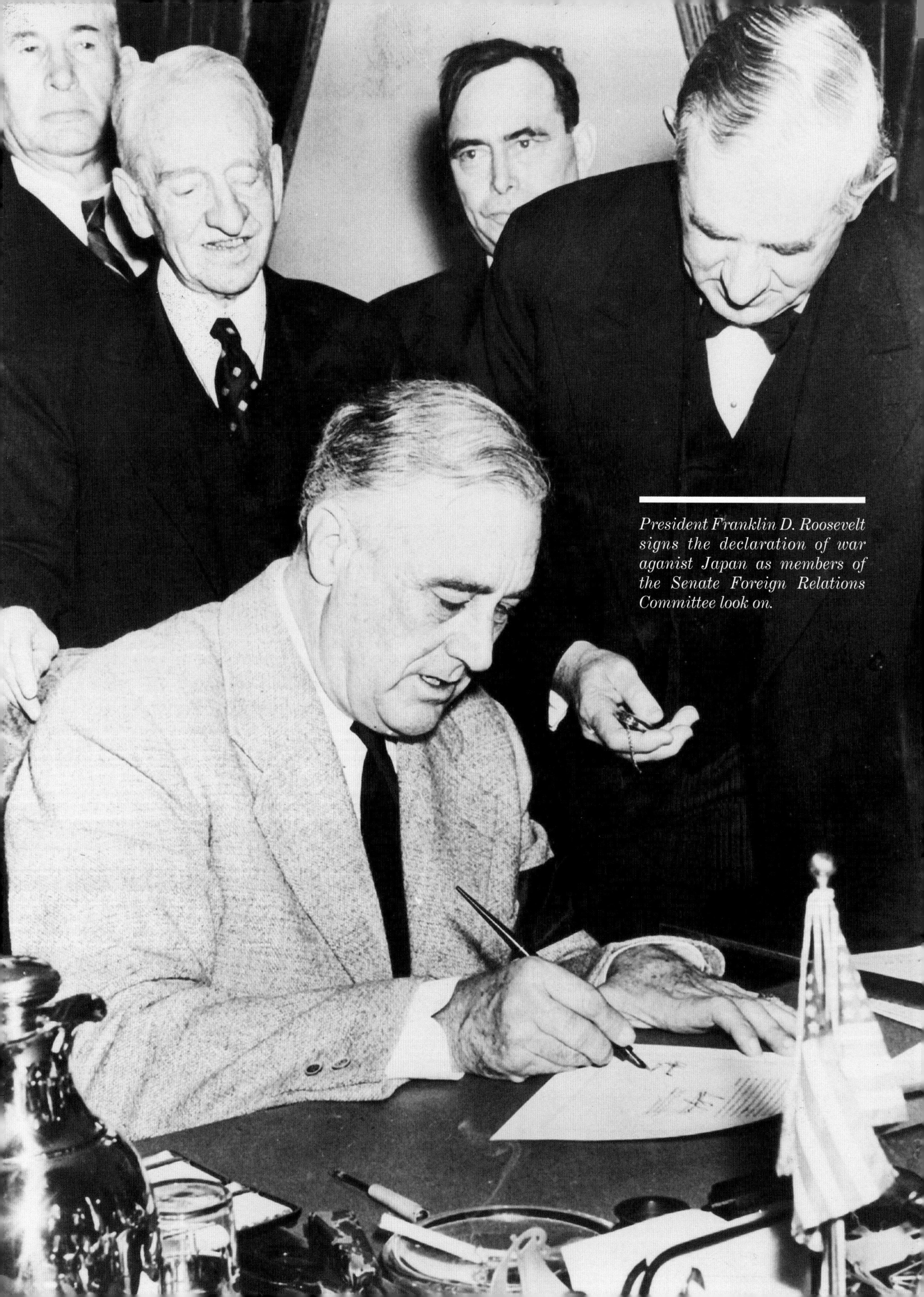

President Franklin D. Roosevelt signs the declaration of war aganist Japan as members of the Senate Foreign Relations Committee look on.

WAR STORIES
WORLD WAR II FIRSTHAND

The Pacific

VOLUME ONE
Pearl Harbor to Guadalcanal

JAY WERTZ

WEIDER HISTORY PUBLICATIONS

To Gerald, Vester, Paul, Herbert,
Edwin, William, Herbert, Harry and Bill
– A few among millions who served their
country in World War II.

Weider History Publications
An imprint of Weider History Group, Inc.
19300 Promenade Drive
Leesburg, VA 20176
www.HistoryNet.com

PRINTED IN THE UNITED STATES OF AMERICA

ISBN 10: 0-9842127-0-1
ISBN 13: 978-0-9842127-0-5

For more information about this book please visit:
www.HistoryNetShop.com
or call: 1-800-358-6327

Table of Contents

Foreword

More than twenty months ago long time friend and colleague Jay Wertz and I met for supper near my Arlington, Virginia home. We had met nearly a score of years ago and had collaborated on *Smithsonian's Great Battles of the Civil War,* winner of the prestigious Telly Award for a documentary television series and on the companion guidebook.

When Wertz invited me to join his team for his latest project, my answer was a resounding 'Yes!" My task would be easy and consisted of reading the draft manuscript of *War Stories: World War II Firsthand – The Pacific – Volume One: Pearl Harbor to Guadalcanal.* The core of the book to be the War as seen and experienced by the veterans. After reviewing the manuscript I would write the foreword.

This work I saw as a labor of love. It was an opportunity to turn back the clock to my youth and relive my most memorable years. I have always considered I was fortunate to be born on June 26, 1923, and to grow up on a cattle ranch in Sarpy, Montana. It was two and one-half miles over a two-rut dirt road to the nearest neighbor and a 12-mile round trip horseback ride to and from a one-room frame schoolhouse. We did not have a telephone and used an outdoor toilet, both at school and at home. In winter the torture of that icy seat reminded us of James Whitcomb Riley's poem "Ode to an Outhouse."

We, however, always possessed an Atwater-Kent battery-powered radio with a half-mile aerial with which my father – a sports fanatic – could pick up WGN in Chicago, WHO in Des Moines, etc., and I would listen to news broadcasts by H. R. Gross, H. V. Kaltenborn, Gabriel Heater, Edward R. Morrow, William L. Shirer, etc. Possessing an excellent retentive memory and an all abiding interest in current events, I honed these listening skills and absorbed most of what I heard. For my 12th birthday an aunt gave me a year's subscription to *Newsweek* and she renewed this every year until I left for the U. S. Marine Corps. My parents subscribed to *Life* Magazine beginning with the inaugural issue in November 1935. My father subscribed to Col. Bertie McCormick's *Chicago Tribune* which came by RFD via the Sarpy post office twice a week – four daily editions on Tuesdays and three on Thursdays.

More than a year before the Civil War first drew my attention when my father read to me John W. Thomason's *Jeb Stuart,* my interest was drawn to the Horn of Africa, the Suez Canal, the Mediterranean Sea, and the failure of collective security and economic sanctions imposed on an aggressor nation by the League of Nations. For the first time on a large scale map I plotted the ebb and flow of armies as Benito Mussolini's Fascist legions invaded Ethiopia on October 3, 1935. That war ended May 5, 1936, when Italian troops entered Ethiopia's capital, Addis Ababa, and sent Emperor Haile Selassie on a futile mission to Geneva. Two weeks later the League rejected Selassie's appeal for justice and refused to continue its economic sanctions against Italy.

My interest in the dictators' rise and the triumph of aggression was next whetted by the outbreak of the long and bloody Spanish Civil War. This conflict erupted on July 18, 1936, and lasted 33 months before Gen. Francisco Franco and his Nationalists, backed by Adolph Hitler and Mussolini's Italy, emerged victorious over the forces of the Republic supported by the Soviet Union. This war had a significance far beyond the Iberian Peninsula. It afforded a testing ground for new weaponry and tactics particularly for members of Germany's Condor Legion who honed the skills that characterized the blitzkrieg.

Less than a year later war returned to the Far East. On July 7, 1937, a company of the Japanese Imperial Army on a training mission near Marco Polo Bridge, a short distance southeast of Beijing, clashed with Chinese troops. This led to a resumption of war between General Chiang Kai-shek's Nationalist China and Japan. Fortunately the living room of my parents' log house had much wall space to affix additional plywood backboards to which I secured the maps on which I now traced troop movements in both Europe and China.

There are certain dates that stand out in my memory and even today my day-to-day conduct. In the autumn of 1938 I was a sophomore in high school and attending St. John's Military School at Delafield, Wisconsin. At that time the crisis over the Sudetenland border region of Czechoslovakia, the majority of whose inhabitants were Germans, had brought Europe to the brink of war. Our Modern European History teacher was Capt. Leon W. McFee and he brought a radio to class to enable his students to track the crisis. Well do I recall Prime Minister Neville Chamberlain's September 30 return from Munich to London, to declare after having caved in, "I believe it is peace for our time." The symbol for this appeasement of Hitler and his lackey Mussolini and the sacrifice of Czechoslovakia became Chamberlain's umbrella. Since that day I have never carried or used an umbrella and on occasions wear a T-shirt depicting Chamberlain and his umbrella on their arrival at No. 10 Downing Street.

Beginning on September 1, 1939, upon the German invasion of Poland and the introduction of blitzkrieg warfare, I secured the largest-scale map of Europe vended by the National Geographic Society (NGS), mounted it appropriately and continued to track the armies. Following the Japanese December 7, 1941 sneak attack on Pearl Harbor and our involvement in the Pacific War, I took up additional footage on my parents' living room wall with a special map the NGS printed of the Pacific, with insets along its margins depicting the islands and atolls destined to become household words during the next four years.

Of far more importance than tracking what had now become a World War, was what I would do with my life. It was a grim and thoughtful supper at the Bearss' ranch on the evening before President Franklin D. Roosevelt's most memorable address to the American people. In unforgettable words he described the events of December 7 as, "Yesterday…a date which will live in infamy…." he asked for a declaration of war on the Japanese Empire.

As we listened to an onsite broadcast from Manila telling of the disastrous attack on Gen. Douglas MacArthur's Far East Air Force, I informed my folks that I planned to join the U. S. Marine Corps now! Although the Congress by a one-vote majority in the House had enacted and President Roosevelt had signed into law on September 16, 1941 the nation's first peacetime conscription law, it only applied to single men between 21 and 27. At 18 I needed parental consent to enlist. My folks said that they would sign the needed consent papers if I would tend to the ranch until they returned from a long-planned vacation to New Orleans and the Gulf Coast. Thus held hostage, I deferred my enlistment until April 28, 1942. Two days later I arrived at the Corps' San Diego Recruit Depot and was assigned to Boot Camp Platoon 369.

The nearly five months that I looked after the ranch and plotted the progress of the war on my maps were among my life's most frustrating experiences. The few people I saw were on my twice a week visits to the Sarpy post office involving

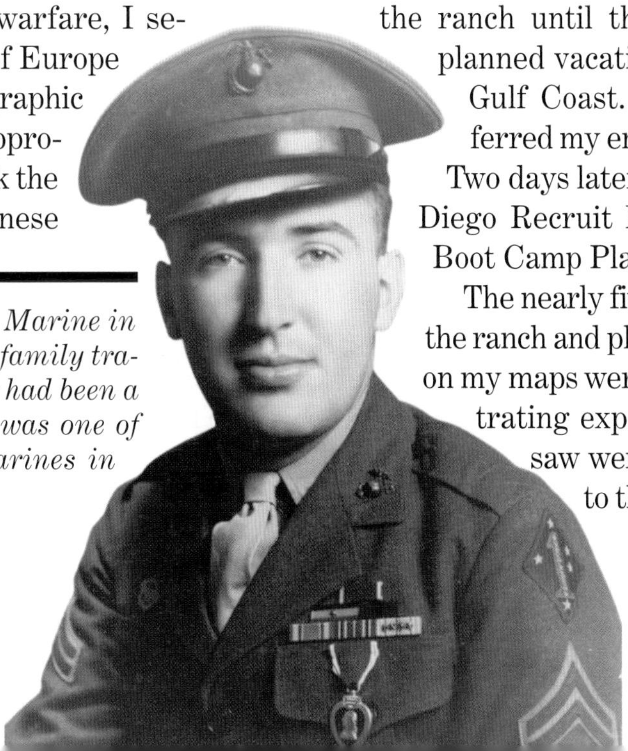

Edwin Cole Bearss as a young Marine in World War II. He continued a family tradition in the Corps. His father had been a Marine and his cousin Mike was one of the most highly decorated Marines in World War I.

a 10-mile roundtrip horseback ride through a snow-covered landscape. News from the Far East was grim as the Kido Butai, the Japanese carrier task force that had struck Pearl Harbor, continued to run amuck in the Western Pacific, the Java Sea and deep into the Bay of Bengal. The Japanese, demonstrating a mastery of amphibious warfare, jungle fighting and aerial combat captured Singapore, overran the Netherlands East Indies and on April 9 compelled the Battling Bastards of Bataan to lay down their arms. All this while I was saddled with my commitment to my parents to watch the Ranch.

Now thanks to Jay Wertz and Weider History Publications I can relive these grim days through the eyes and memories of veterans who stood tall at Pearl Harbor and fought the Japanese at Clark Field, on the shores of Lingayen Gulf and in the fetid jungles of Bataan. Among those who were at Pearl on December 7 whom I came to know well were men I served with in Company C, 3rd Raider Battalion. One was Lt. Bud Tinker, a Marine's Marine who at Pearl was a platoon sergeant in the battleship *West Virginia*'s Marine detachment. The other was James W. Coupe who was in the brig but was released and manned a .50 caliber machine gun by the time the second attack wave arrived. Coupe was fated as a sergeant on November 1, 1943 in the fight for Puruata Island, off Bougainville's Cape Torokina to be KIA [killed in action].

More fortunate than Coupe were two members of the Harden High School Class of 1940 who graduated a year ahead of me. They were John McLoud and Lyle "Porky" Dillon. They enlisted in the U. S. Army Air Corps and were at Clark Field on December 8. Good fortune smiled on the duo, veterans of Bataan, the Death March, a trip to Japan on a Hell ship, and laborers in a Home Islands coal mine. They survived.

The Pacific – Volume One: Pearl Harbor to Guadalcanal underscores Jay Wertz's multifaceted talents both in historical research and in identifying veterans who have and are willing to share their stories. He has tirelessly attended veterans' reunions to find those who will share their recollections. Jay has identified and made use of oral histories compiled by the defense agencies, parks and universities. When spliced together they form the grist of a montage that is relevant to the story and enrich his readers' appreciation of what Tom Brokaw called "The Greatest Generation." With World War II veterans dying at a rate, according to the Veterans Administration, of 1200 per day, the clock is ticking on an undertaking of this sort.

Wertz, after getting the needed oral histories, then does what no one with whom I have worked is his master. He sets the stage with a concise but informative narrative that bridges gaps between his talking heads. This requires a keen understanding of World War II minutia as well as the big picture.

I have been keenly interested with a good recall of events leading from the Ethiopian-Italian war and Germany's remilitarization of the Rhineland in the spring of 1935-36 through V-J Day. In addition I served as a combat Marine in World War II. Both in college and since then I have continued to read extensively on the subject. In addition I have led six battlefield tours to Europe and one to the Southwest Pacific. With this background I am proud to endorse and call to readers' attention *War Stories: World War II Firsthand – The Pacific – Volume One: Pearl Harbor to Guadalcanal.*

Edwin Cole Bearss
Arlington, Virginia
September 3, 2010

Emperor Hirohito was crowned in 1926 during a return to traditional ways in Japan. He is pictured in this wartime photograph reviewing Japanese troops.

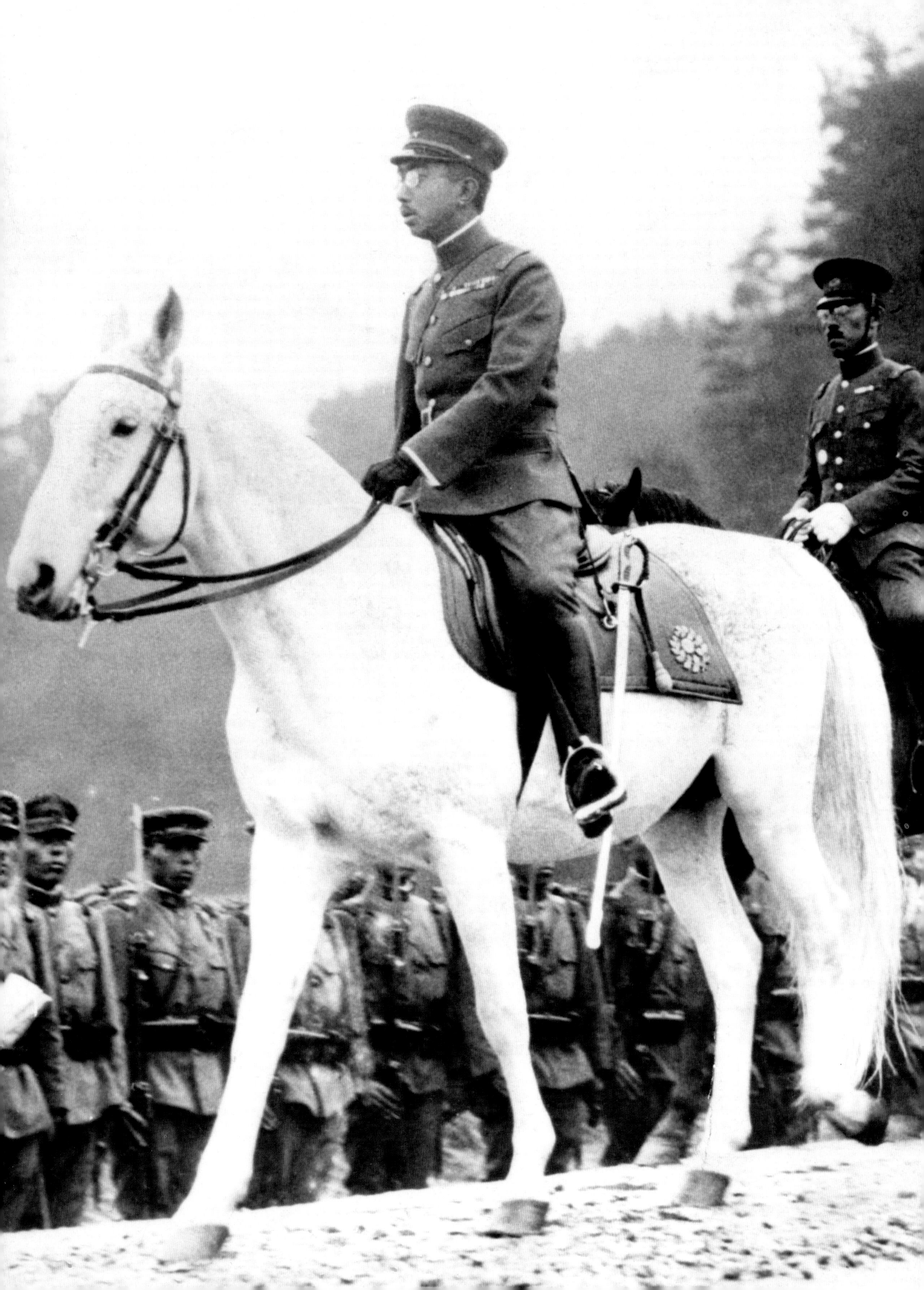

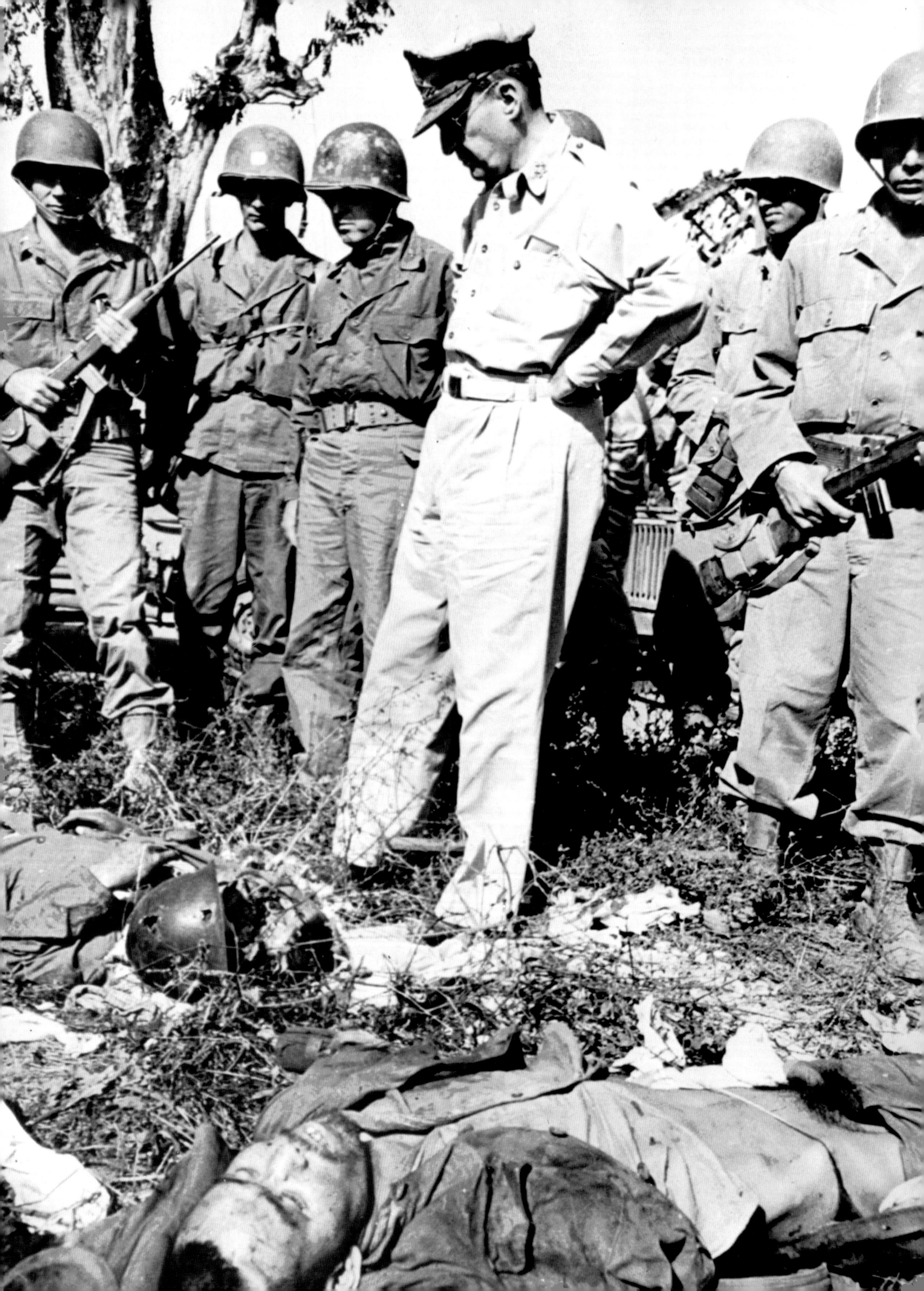

INTRODUCTION

They have been called the "Greatest Generation" and their experiences have been recorded many times over in document, story, movie and song. While American "G.I.s," "Leathernecks," "Bluejackets," "Flyboys" and all those who supported them have left a lasting impression of World War II, one must not forget that it was a global conflict and people around the world, from more than 34 million in the Red Army to the 246 members of the Guam Insular Guard, were sent and sacrificed by their nations in the name of conquest, stability or peace.

Their particular rationales for serving were as varied as their dialects, be it duty, honor or compulsion. And while politics will be discussed here, this work is not a political work and does not intend to apply judgment to reasons for service or actions taken. War is a persistent form of societal conflict resolution and military forces are the instruments of the disagreeing parties. History is the best teacher of human behavior and so the study of the human condition in its most stressful state – war – is a valuable study indeed. This work seeks to understand war by learning from those who waged it.

There is another reason why this series of books is needed now. There is a necessary rush of organizational efforts to record the stories of veterans. As new generations take their place on the planet, benefiting from but not having experienced this world war, their direct connection to the participants and eyewitnesses of World War II will be lost. The effort to use technology to preserve these stories is noble, but the need to communicate these stories in a concise and interesting format that explains them remains. *War Stories: World War II Firsthand* hopes to advance that idea and this first volume is an important step in that process.

Eyewitness accounts are funny things. As police and others who deal with these things on a regular basis will say, two people can witness the exact same event and retell what happened differently. Time can also erode the interpretation of conditions and deeds but the most significant events of a person's life remain more vivid over time than days of dull routine. Combat thus remains a most memorable part of veterans' long-term thoughts. Some veterans have repressed these memories; have resisted many years of talking about the war. Some never will. But many more have opened up, realizing that if their impressions of the war are not given soon, they many never be recorded and preserved.

In his foreword, Edwin C. Bearss, a World War II Marine and renowned expert in many aspects of American history, explains how the war – from its fragmented beginning to its global conclusion – impacted his life and the lives of people he knew. A great number of the more than 200 veterans interviewed for this project – so far – have similar memories of the war from its earliest development. They have also expressed opinions on how war service set their lives in motion afterwards. These post-war decisions have had lasting influences on what the world is today. Therefore *War Stories: World War II Firsthand*, with the great assistance of many others worldwide who are interested in preserving the stories of World War II veterans, will continue on this mission to collect and tell stories that collectively give an idea of what the war was like for those who survived it, and how their experiences changed them and the legacy of the war that survives and will continue into the future.

Gen. Douglas MacArthur examines Japanese soldiers killed just hours before he toured this Bataan battleground during the retaking of the Philippines by American forces in 1944-45.

Jay Wertz
Phillips Ranch, California
September 12, 2010

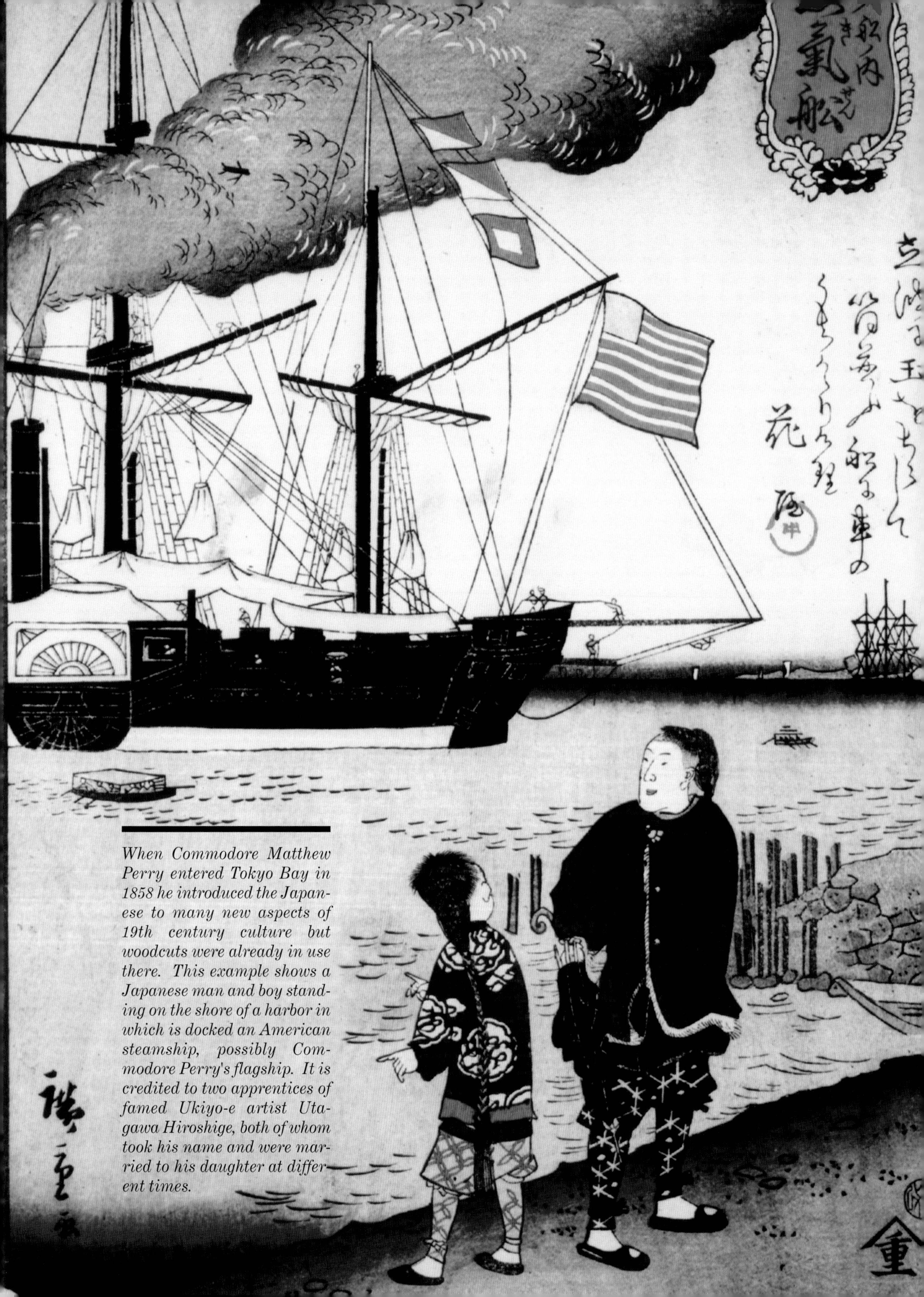

When Commodore Matthew Perry entered Tokyo Bay in 1858 he introduced the Japanese to many new aspects of 19th century culture but woodcuts were already in use there. This example shows a Japanese man and boy standing on the shore of a harbor in which is docked an American steamship, possibly Commodore Perry's flagship. It is credited to two apprentices of famed Ukiyo-e artist Utagawa Hiroshige, both of whom took his name and were married to his daughter at different times.

CHAPTER I

Prelude to War

Japan Emerges and Builds an Empire

One must reach back in history more than one hundred and fifty years to find the roots of the fundamental differences that brought the United States and the Empire of Japan to the brink of war in 1941. Reach back to U. S. Navy Commodore Matthew Perry's visit to Tokyo Bay in 1853 that opened the island nation to the rest of the world. Perhaps one has to go back even further, for centuries, to Japan's feudal tradition of warlords and Samurai spirit. Not wishing to succumb to the domination that 19th century Western colonial powers wielded over their neighbor to the southwest – China – Japan, led by Emperor Mutsuhito (who overthrew Shogun rule in 1868 and reestablished the power of the monarchy) decided to embrace the technology and ideas of the West in order to compete in world trade and prosperity. That thrust to bring Japan to an equal footing with the world's major powers, the Meiji Revolution, included the establishment of a strong naval tradition. A powerful navy not only would protect Japan against the aggression of colonial powers, it would be the vital component of any imperial design to project the island nation's power and influence beyond the country's borders.

It was not long, less than fifty years, before Japan shaped that naval tradition into an impressive armada – the Imperial Japanese Navy (IJN) – backed by the national will to use it to promote Japan's imperial ambitions. Looking around, the Japanese saw the vulnerability of strategically located Korea and, after fighting China there in 1894-95, annexed the peninsula in 1910. They saw the potential menace of an eastward expanding Tsarist Russia, and a victorious war against her in Manchuria in 1904-05 opened with a surprise Japanese naval attack on Port Arthur and ended with Admiral Togo's stunning victory over the Russian fleet at Tsushima Straits. They saw China, wracked by internal dissension and humiliated by colonial control, picked apart like Peking duck at a feast and dreamed of an Asia controlled by the power of the Rising Sun. Even though the Perry expedition had loosed some naval gunpowder in Tokyo Bay to announce its presence when it forcibly opened the "closed" country to Western trade, Japan considered the nation on the other side of the Pacific Ocean a friend at that time. Later events would conspire to strain relations with the United States to the breaking point.

Although Japan nominally sided with Great Britain and the European allies against Germany in World War I, her par-

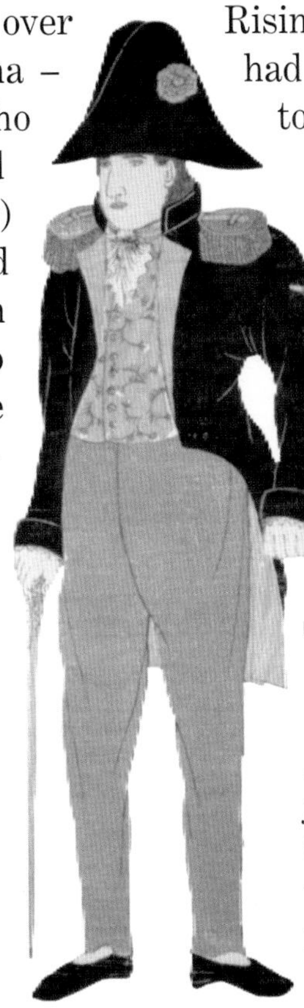

Another of the Japanese woodcuts shows a full-length portrait of Commodore Matthew Perry in uniform. Ukiyo-e "pictures of the floating world" were an emerging art during the Edo (the city which became Tokyo) period which lasted until 1868 and were printed for popular consumption on hōnsho paper.

ticipation in the fighting was minimal. Japan's rewards for siding with the war's victors, however, were significant. The island nation was allowed by treaty to retain the German colonies in China that she had seized during the war and to take possession of Germany's Pacific island territories lying north of the equator. These Mandates, as the prized possessions were called, whetted the appetite of Japanese expansionists to obtain more Asian territory. Yet, an interesting development took shape in Japan during the 1920s: democratic forces eroded the power of the military, and the representative body, the Diet, began to institute progressive reforms. Japan even joined the League of Nations and agreed to various non-aggression treaties.

In Japan, military tradition runs deep and is based on a spiritual, as well as a class, foundation. Afterlife rewards await those who sacrifice their earthbound bodies in combat for the Emperor, a convincing offer to mass thinking (it remains a powerful motivating force wielded by radical fundamentalist leaders today). Military service was not only an honor in pre-World War II Japan, it was mandatory for all men – with two years active duty and eighteen years reserve service. The militarists, forced underground, began to work class as well as nationalist issues to undermine the Diet. And perhaps unwittingly, the United States government adopted policies that put it directly in the sights of the Japanese militarists.

Commodore Matthew Calbraith Perry is pictured in a Matthew Brady studio photograph made between 1854 and 1858. Perry, the younger brother of War of 1812 hero Oliver Hazard Perry, first planted the U. S. flag in Key West, was a leading proponent of steam-powered warships and fought in the Mexican-American War. He studiously prepared for the mission to open Japan to foreign trade. His mission, beginning in 1853, followed several modest unsuccessful attempts to do so and was the basis for the Stephen Sondheim musical Pacific Overtures.

In 1921-22 agreement among world leaders to prevent a naval arms race in the wake of World War I led the United States along with Great Britain and Japan to a pact signed in Washington, D. C. which put strict limitations on war fleet expansions. The treaty specified a 5:5:3 ratio – the U. S. and Great Britain would be allowed to build five new capital ships each to every three built by Japan. This naval agreement favoring the U. S. and Britain at Japan's expense, combined with the American-sponsored "Open Door" trading policy in China, was perceived by the Japanese as a severe threat to their nation's burgeoning Far East influence. To make matters worse, the U. S. Congress, in a growing isolationist climate, completely eliminated Japanese immigration while retaining a quota system permitting immigration from European nations. The militarists sold this policy to the Japanese masses as racist and, along with the 5:5:3 rule of the Washington Naval Treaty, as an affront to national pride.

By the beginning of the 1930s the Imperial Japanese Army (IJA), through a reactionary army general staff, was regaining control of the government by eliminating liberal officials, sometimes violently. The idea of creating an expanded Asian sphere of influence was beginning to take shape. Japan took a bold step, although it began with the actions of a subordinate officer. A fabricated incident in September 1931 led to the Kwantung Army invading Manchuria from Korea and setting up a puppet government in the re-

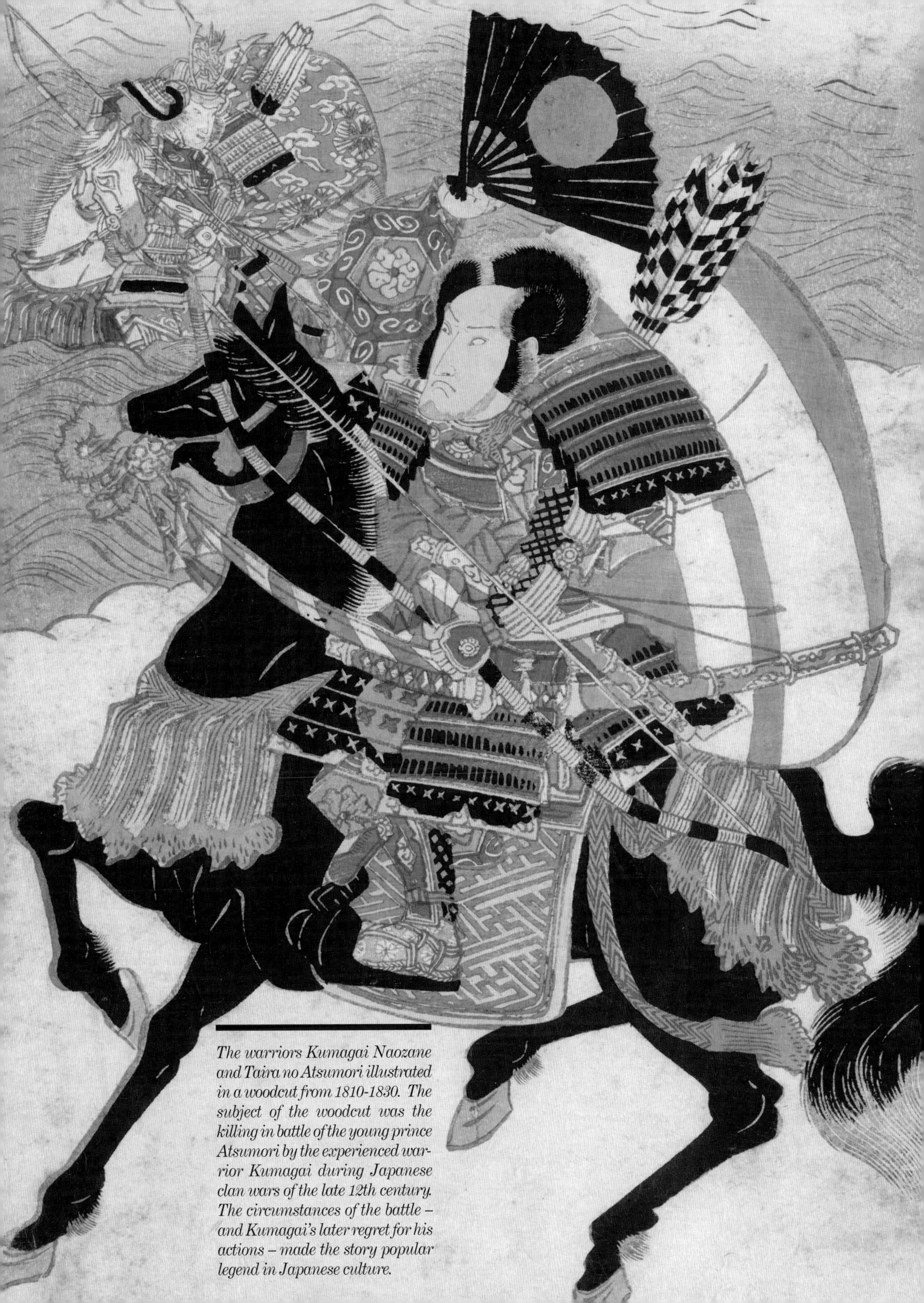

The warriors Kumagai Naozane and Taira no Atsumori illustrated in a woodcut from 1810-1830. The subject of the woodcut was the killing in battle of the young prince Atsumori by the experienced warrior Kumagai during Japanese clan wars of the late 12th century. The circumstances of the battle – and Kumagai's later regret for his actions – made the story popular legend in Japanese culture.

gion (renamed Manchukuo). Japan's aggression sparked an international outcry and prompted vocal opposition by the United States. A League of Nations' investigation and subsequent condemnation of the move led to Japan's walking out of the League in 1933. The die was cast as Japan's Army and Navy, responding to new (as of 1926) Emperor Hirohito's Showa Restoration ("enlightened peace"), began to reverse the democratic policies of the previous decade. If Japan's announced expansionist policy to create a New Order in East Asia did not sound like peace to Westerners, it made perfect sense to the Japanese. Their idea of peace was the repose of a region dominated by a superior, chosen race. And as with all of history's examples of such thinking, war was bound to follow.

Unlike much of the rest of the world during the Great Depression, Japan remained at near normal industrial capacity in the 1930s, although the Japanese population suffered economic deprivations. In 1936 Tokyo ignored the restrictions of the Washington Naval Treaty and went on a ship building tear. At the same time that the navy was

USS Panay, *(PG-45), is pictured here underway on August 30, 1928 off Woosung, China. One of a small fleet of American river gunboats sent to defend U. S. citizens and interests in China, the December 12, 1937 attack by Japanese naval aircraft on the clearly marked* Panay, *and attempts to kill the sinking ship's survivors, was met with diplomatic outcry, but no war declaration by the United States on Japan. Thus the attack failed to achieve the intended result of the Japanese militarists who planned it.*

Japanese soldiers pose in Manchuria in this photograph, possibly from 1939. The well-armed and supplied Japanese Imperial Army was faced with occupation duties in Manchukuo, a strong potential Soviet foe and stubborn resistance from Chinese Communists and Nationalists in its bid to control East Asia. When the army bogged down in its efforts the perception of the Imperial Navy as the leading military force rose.

expanding, the Japanese army was moving beyond the Manchukuo borders, testing resistance in central China and Mongolia (nominally independent, but in reality a protectorate of the USSR), where an alert Soviet response soundly defeated the probe. These offensives served the Japanese military as proving grounds, testing tactical deployments, including air combat, and gave battlefield training to promising officers such as the radical militarist General Hideki Tojo.

In July 1937, using as an excuse an incident at the Marco Polo Bridge near Beijing during which Japanese and Chinese forces exchanged gunfire, Japan provoked an all out war with China. Although Western nations would not be drawn into a war with Japan until 1941, historians generally date the beginning of World War II in Asia as the July 7, 1937 Marco Polo Bridge Incident. The China war would become Japan's longest military adventure, eventually merging with the larger effort of World War II in the Asia-Pacific Theater, and would last until Japan's final surrender to the Allies in September 1945. Over time the China war consumed

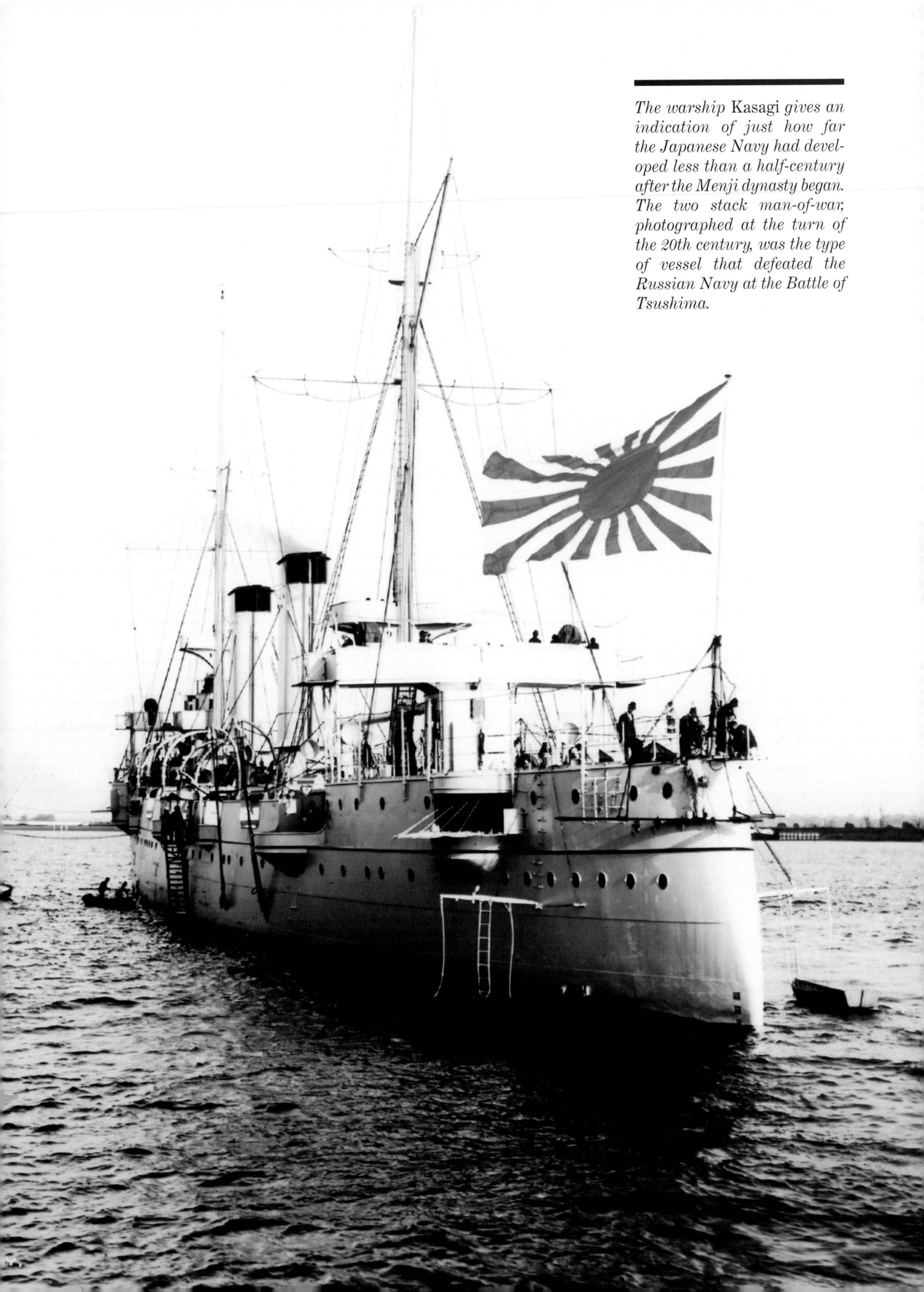

The warship Kasagi *gives an indication of just how far the Japanese Navy had developed less than a half-century after the Menji dynasty began. The two stack man-of-war, photographed at the turn of the 20th century, was the type of vessel that defeated the Russian Navy at the Battle of Tsushima.*

vast amounts of Japanese resources – men and materiel – and the bitter struggle would witness some of warfare's worst atrocities; yet, in the early part of its invasion of China, the Japanese military achieved stunning successes. Beijing, Shanghai and the Chinese capital, Nanking, fell within months of the war's beginning in 1937, and Japanese armies numbering hundreds of thousands of troops achieved phenomenal success against huge but outclassed Chinese armies. China, however, with seemingly inexhaustible manpower reserves, refused to surrender. Japanese commanders could not win a quick victory – they settled in for a long war.

The administration of U. S. President Franklin D. Roosevelt, though mired in the immense domestic issues of the Great Depression, was increasingly forced to deal with this new Japanese aggression in Asia. One incident focused this attention like a distress flare. On December 12, 1937 USS *Panay*, an American gunboat, was sunk by a Japanese air attack on the Yangtze River in central China while transporting and escorting Americans evacuating Nanking in the face of the Japanese attack and capture of the capital of Chiang Kai-shek's Nationalist China. Other attacks on Americans and their interests in China occurred as well. Alarmed about the growing menace of Nazism

USS Astoria *(CA-34), a heavy cruiser, is shown underway near Hawaii in early 1942. Three years earlier, the warship had a special mission – to return the ashes of former Japanese ambassador Hiroshi Saito home. The mission was designed by the U. S. State Department as counterpoint to rising tensions between the two nations. During the voyage to Yokohama the ceremonial urn stood in the unoccupied admiral's cabin guarded around the clock by U. S. Marines wearing dress blues including Cpl. Bill Persky. He fondly remembers many places the ship visited on the return trip, but one had future implications. "We began circling the island of Truk and these photographers with their long photographic lenses were up on the bridge taking pictures of Truk. We at that time learned the Japanese had fortified the island, and they had fortified it very well."*

and Fascism in Europe, the Roosevelt administration gave Japanese issues subordinate attention, applying diplomatic and trade pressure but with only limited results. To make matters worse, Japan joined Germany and Italy as an Axis Power. In 1937 the Japanese completed the Anti-Comintern Pact with Germany which three years later was expanded into the Tripartite Agreement (Axis Pact) with Germany and Italy. This broadened the threat posed by the Rising Sun.

Petroleum became the growing crisis issue in Asia. Japan needed it and the United States, Europe and their trading partners had it. Prior to a July 1941 complete embargo on American oil, Japan procured 80% of its petroleum supply from the United States. A prevailing sentiment in Washington was that if the United States did not sell it to Japan, Tokyo would seize it from European colonies such as the Dutch East Indies. The U. S. continued diplomatic pressure and measured embargoes of war-waging goods. The September 1, 1939 German invasion of Poland began World War II in Europe which further complicated the possibility of a negotiated settlement to a Japanese stand down or pull back in Asia. Not only could Japan help its Axis partners by threatening Allied interests in Asia, it could justify aggression against them under this pretext. In late June

1940, the French capitulated to the Nazi blitzkrieg and the puppet Vichy government set up in unoccupied France allowed Japan a free pass into its Indochina colony. The political and strategic situation was playing into Japanese hands and only the United States seemed to be a potential foil to their goals.

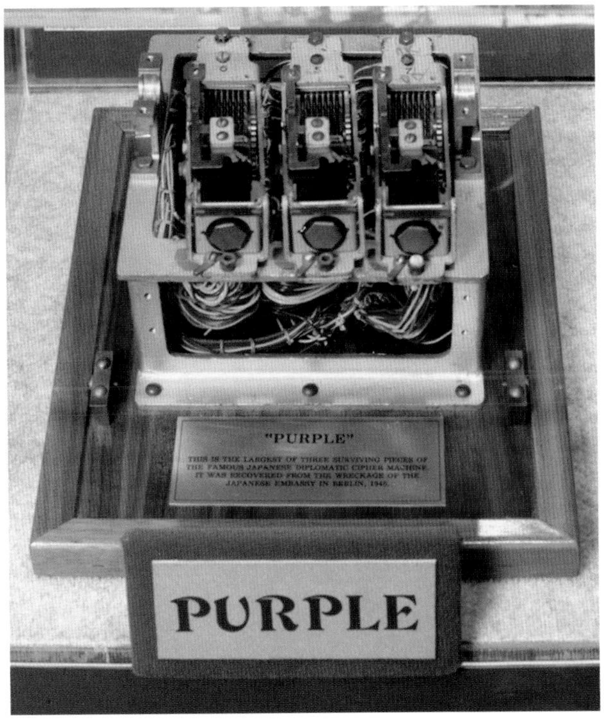
"PURPLE"
PURPLE

The Japanese code machine for encoding and decoding top secret diplomatic correspondence. Like many other encryption devices of the time, it depended on a series of electrically wired rotors that would generate alternative letters for an encrypted message. The encoding and decoding of messages depended on a changing "key" of starting indicators to set up the machine. American cryptologists working in the military's Signal Intelligence Service (SIS) branch quickly broke Purple and other Japanese codes in pre-war efforts dubbed "Magic" and built Purple machines. None of the eight machines the Allies had in late 1941 were in Hawaii.

Pacific Naval Power

One other development signaled the move towards war against the United States. It was no secret that the strategic importance of the U. S. Navy bases and associated build-up of a military presence in Hawaii would make an inviting target in the event of war. Indeed, from the turn of the century American policy of expansion in the Pacific, which gained for the U. S. in war the Philippines and other Spanish possessions, and in purchase and annexation the islands of Wake and Hawaii, had resulted in overseas forward basing of naval forces as a de facto benefit. On Oahu, with the excellent natural basin of Pearl Harbor, the U. S. military presence rapidly escalated, taking over agriculture as the island's primary industry. When the renamed U. S. Pacific Fleet was transferred from the American west coast to Pearl Harbor in mid-1940 the implications were clear – the U. S. would have its largest fleet 2400 miles closer to the most powerful and dangerous maritime nation in the Pacific.

To say it was no secret that Pearl Harbor was open to surprise attack is an absolute truth. The idea was discussed in numerous quarters for decades and had even been included in an aircraft carrier battle exercise in February 1932 planned by Admiral Harry E. Yarnell (a mock surprise aerial attack on Oahu's army air installations). The answer, then, to the troubling question of how the Japanese managed to pull off a devastating surprise aerial attack on Oahu in December of 1941 is a complex maze of decisions, suppositions, circumstance and luck. And it started with one man.

Admiral Isoroku Yamamoto enjoyed great prestige in his role as Commander-in-Chief of the Combined Fleet of the Imperial Navy, in many respects the most powerful force afloat at the time. Seeing war with the United States as inevitable, Yamamoto began to formulate his plan for a surprise air attack on the U. S. fleet at Pearl Harbor in the spring of 1940 and made a formal presentation to the Naval General Staff in January 1941. Yamamoto was a firm believer in the emergence of air power as the new decisive force in naval warfare and he was instrumental in guiding the IJN in creating a powerful air arm. But his plan met with stiff resistance among the traditionalist "battleship admirals" of the Naval General Staff and only Yamamoto's personal commitment, even to the point of threatening to resign, kept the idea alive.

Yamamoto's strategic logic for the Pearl Harbor attack was sound. Only with a quick and decisive strike at America's largest sea force could Japan hope for success. He had no faith in the politicians being able to keep the United States at bay while Japan moved south to seize the resource-rich Pacific regions nor did he believe in the success of a long war with America. However, if Japan could force the U. S. into an early armistice that would cause her to abandon the defense of China and the colonies of the European allies, then Japan could exploit and control East Asia as she saw fit. Since the U. S. was a nation where there was still much rhetoric and dissension against becoming involved in another foreign war – and in America the collective voice of the people counted – Yamamoto's strategy had merit. Though he knew American resolve and industrial might would ultimately win a long war with Japan, even Yamamoto failed to predict the rapid commitment of that resolve by the American people.

Yamamoto did a thorough study of all elements of the proposed attack and called on able associates to plan different aspects in detail. He studied the success of the recent (November 11, 1940) British surprise

COMBINED JAPANESE FLEET JULY, 1941

Commanded by
Admiral Isoroku Yamamoto

FIRST FLEET
(Battle Force)
based at Hiroshima Bay
3 Battleships
1 Heavy Cruiser
2 Light Cruisers
27 Destroyers, auxiliaries

SECOND FLEET
(Scouting Force)
bases at Hainan
3 Heavy Cruiser
2 Light Cruisers
28 Destroyers, auxiliaries

THIRD FLEET
(Blockading and Transport Force) based at Formosa
1 Light Cruiser
12 Destroyers
6 Submarines
46 Transports
auxiliaries and gunboats

FORTH FLEET
based at Truk
4 Light Cruiser
8 Destroyers
16 Submarines
41 Transports
auxiliaries and gunboats

FIFTH FLEET
based at Maizuru
and Ominato
2 Light Cruisers and
a few destroyers

SIXTH FLEET
(Submarine Fleet)
based at Kwajalein
40 "I" Type submarines
and auxiliaries

CARRIER FLEET
(Kido Butai) based at Kure
6 Aircraft Carriers,
4 Light Aircraft Carriers
16 Destroyers

raid on the Italian fleet at Taranto, in Italy's boot, by Fairey Swordfish torpedo bomber bi-planes from HMS *Illustrious*. For tactical air planning he turned to experienced aviator Commander Minoru Genda. Other close confidants aided as well until the idea was fully realized in a detailed plan. The hard work paid off – Yamamoto's Pearl Harbor attack plan was accepted by the Naval General Staff. Since strict secrecy was paramount to the operation's success, knowledge about Yamamoto's "Hawaii Operation" was divulged only in limited and metered form. Perhaps inevitably, however, some information on the planned attack did leak out, although from an unlikely source. The first word of it to reach the ears of a United States official was in January 1941 when the Peruvian minister in Tokyo reported the idea of an attack on Pearl Harbor being planned by the Japanese to a U. S. embassy staffer. The staffer in turn told the ambassador to Japan, James Grew. The senior American official, who was a Goliath in managing the complex issues in the capital of a belligerent nation, dutifully reported the matter to Washington where it was mulled over but discarded in military circles. The first early warning sign of the fateful attack was lost.

A Well Planned Gamble

The Imperial Japanese Navy continued preparation and training for the attack in earnest in the months leading up to December 1941. One of the major obstacles that might sink the operation – but not U. S. ships – was ingeniously overcome in the course of this work. Air launched torpedoes of the era were designed to submerge about 100 feet below the water's surface then proceed upwards to their targets. But shallow Pearl Harbor (with a mean depth of only 45 feet) would result in a standard air launched torpedo harmlessly burying itself in the anchorage's mud bottom. Applying knowledge learned from the British torpedo attack at Taranto, the Japanese adapted their advanced 24-inch "tin fish" with wooden fins that kept the torpedo's descent shallow to permit an effective attack with deadly results. This and other ideas forged by Genda and his associates were rehearsed in numerous sea trials before the attack.

Another key component of the attack's preparation was espionage. The various codes used to send messages during these tense times, including the Japanese diplomatic "Purple" code which was broken early on with "Magic" and machines developed to mimic and read this code, were subject to monitoring and scrutiny by both sides. Intercepted communication between capitals was added to military coded messages not yet deciphered and information gained from reconnaissance and espionage to provide decision makers with valuable information about the enemy. Various messages were intercepted and passed on to civilian and military leaders, but on the American side, at least, they were not always correctly evaluated. One source of po-

UNITED STATES NAVY IN THE PACIFIC: MAY, 1941

Commanded by Admiral Harold R. "Dolly" Stark United States Chief of Naval Operations

U.S. PACIFIC FLEET
based at Pearl Harbor
9 Battleships,
3 Aircraft Carriers
12 Heavy Cruisers
9 Light Cruisers
67 Destroyers
27 Submarines
auxiliaries and patrol boats

U.S. ASIATIC FLEET
based at Cavite, Philippines
1 Heavy Cruiser
2 Light Cruisers
13 Destroyers
28 Submarines
auxiliaries and patrol boats

BRITISH COMMONWEALTH AND THE NETHERLANDS NAVIES
also maintain warships in East Asian waters
1 Battleship
1 Battle Cruiser
1 Aircraft Carrier
4 Heavy Cruisers
16 Light Cruisers
13 Destroyers
15 Submarines

tential espionage activity that the Americans should have capitalized on was so obvious it seems incredible that it was overlooked – the Japanese consulate in Honolulu. The consulate staff had access to important ship movements from, among other sources, the local newspaper that routinely publicly announced the comings and goings of vessels. When more sophisticated spying was needed, the Japanese were easily able to bring in a specialist, Takeo Yoshikawa, who brazenly plotted the exact locations of U. S. warships at Pearl Harbor to aid Yamamoto's attack. Yoshikawa's espionage, some of it carried out in broad daylight, was never detected by American authorities. Maps and other information about Pearl Harbor found later in Japanese documents attest to the success of these efforts. Among the ultimately useful information reported by the consulate was the invariable pattern of U. S. warships – most were anchored in port every Sunday.

As tensions rose in the Pacific, American military leaders tried to look ahead to plan for any potential trouble caused by a Japanese advance into resource-rich Southeast Asia. To this end, starting in 1938 and continuing through the spring of 1941, conferences were held with America's regional allies: Britain, Australia and the Netherlands (representing the interests of that country's colony, the Dutch East Indies). American naval representatives to the talks were dismayed that the British were not prepared to offer fleet protection to Singapore, a colonial outpost Great Britain considered vital.

Pacific Theater of Operation December 1941

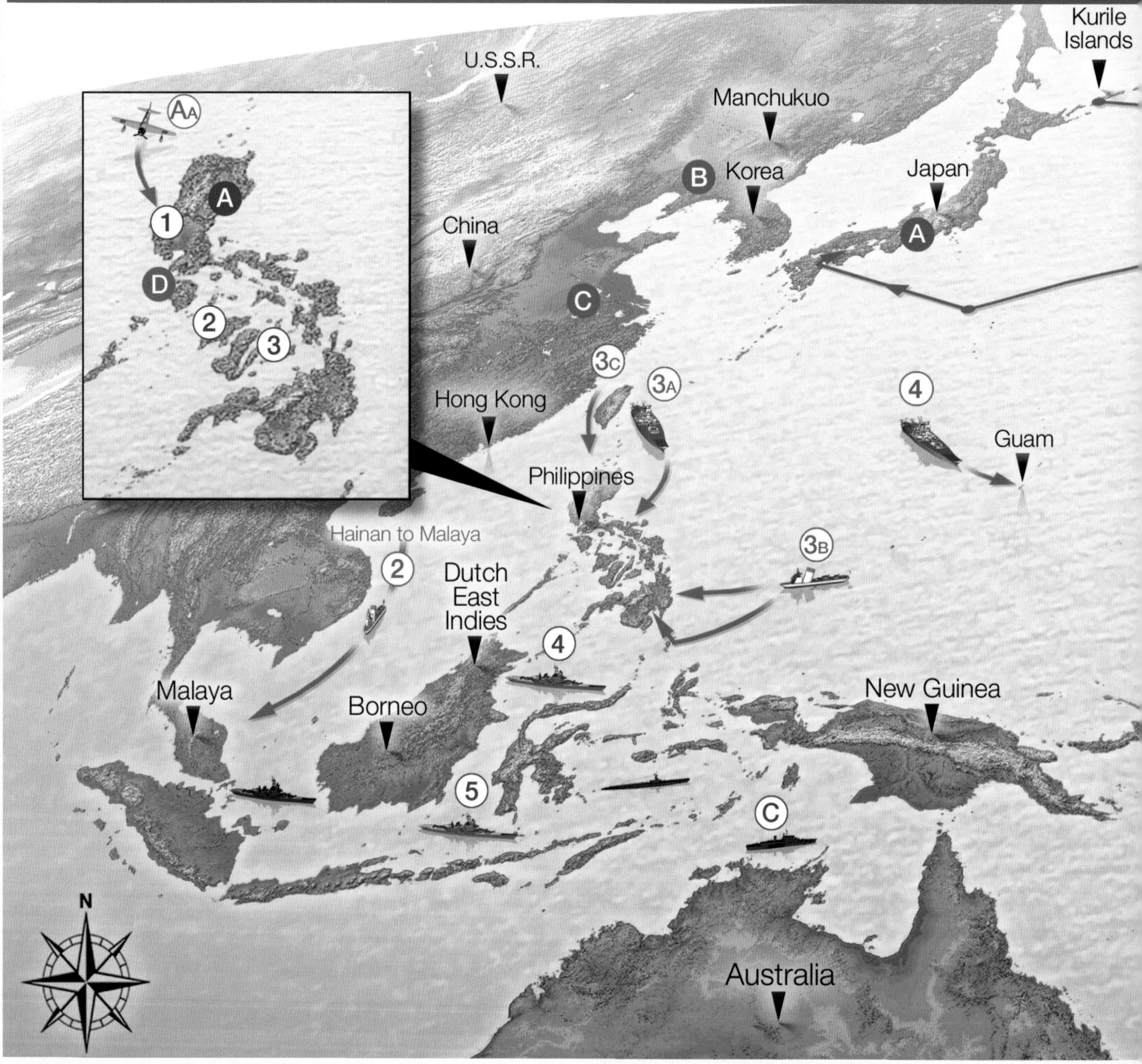

Kurile Islands
U.S.S.R.
Manchukuo
Korea
B
Japan
A
China
C
3C
3A
4
Hong Kong
Guam
Philippines
Hainan to Malaya
2
3B
Dutch East Indies
4
Malaya
Borneo
New Guinea
5
C
Australia
N
AA
1
A
D
2
3

The political character of lands in and adjacent to the Pacific Ocean was formed by discovery, conquest and treaty over a four-hundred year period. In 1941 the Japanese sought to change that character rapidly. Starting with the First Air Fleet (Kido Butai) that left the Kurile Islands in November as the Pearl Harbor Task Force, the Japanese military executed simultaneous advances throughout the Pacific and Southeast Asia on a specific timetable.

The advance to Pearl Harbor was the strategic blow that Admiral Yamamoto and the Japanese high command hoped would keep the powerful American navy scattered and debilitated. That way they could keep the understrength outposts and military forces of the British Commonwealth, her European ally, the Netherlands, and the United States isolated and defeat them in detail. That is how the first six months of the war unfolded as Japan scored victory after victory in the Philippines, Malaysia, Singapore, Borneo and elsewhere. The Japanese not only seized areas with raw materials they coveted while effecting their dream of a united Asia under Japanese rule, they worked hard to create a buffer zone anchored on Pacific islands and other occupied areas to keep their enemies at bay. Over the course of the war, the Japanese wound see these areas of conquest slip from their grasp through a determined effort by the U. S. and her allies.

United States and Allied Forces
Blue Numbers in White Circles

1. Elements of the United States Asiatic Fleet, Adm. Thomas C. Hart, commander

Destroyer Division 59; Asiatic Fleet Submarines; Patrol Wing 10; 4th Marine Regiment; auxiliary ships in Subic and Manila Bay bases

2. USS *Houston*, Heavy cruiser at Iloilo

3. USS *Boise*, Light cruiser at Cebu

4. USS *Marblehead*, Light cruiser; Destroyer Division 58 and Destroyer Squadron 29 at Tarakan, Borneo

5. Destroyer Division 57 at Balikpapan, Borneo

8. Task Force 8; Carrier USS *Enterprise*, Heavy cruisers USS *Northampton*, USS *Indianapolis*, USS *Baltimore*,: nine destroyers of Desron 6; Vice Adm. William F. Halsey, Jr., commander, with Vice Adm. Wilson Brown and Rear Adm. Raymond A. Spruance

11. USS *Minneapolis*, Heavy cruiser and escorts, Rear Adm. Frank Jack Fletcher, commander

12. Task Force 12; Carrier USS *Lexington*, Cruisers USS *Astoria*, *Portland*, *Chicago* and destroyers, Rear Adm. J. H. Newton, commander

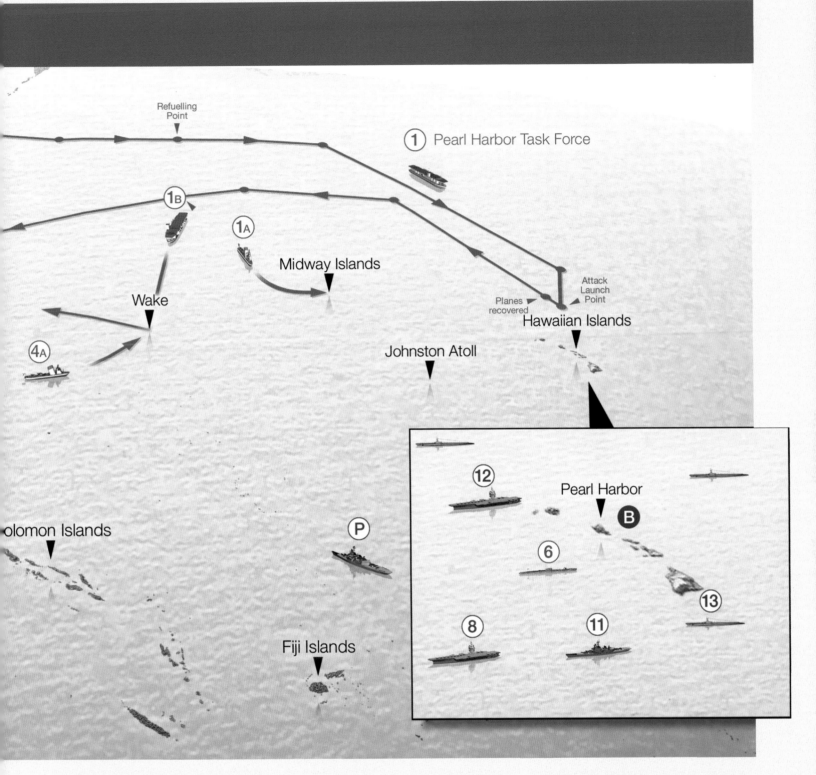

Refuelling Point

① Pearl Harbor Task Force

①B

①A

Midway Islands

Wake

④A

Attack Launch Point

Planes recovered

Hawaiian Islands

Johnston Atoll

Solomon Islands

℗

⑫ Pearl Harbor Ⓑ

⑥

⑬

⑧ ⑪

Fiji Islands

---

13. Submarines USS *Thresher*, USS *Plunger*, USS *Pollack*, USS *Pampano*, with Destroyer USS *Litchfield* off Oahu; Submarines USS *Triton* and USS *Tambor* off Wake Island, USS *Trout* off Midway Island

C. Royal Australian Navy and Royal Netherlands Navy (Cruisers, Destroyers, Submarines)

P. USS *Pensacola*, Heavy cruiser escorting Manila-bound convoy; USS *Louisville*, Heavy cruiser escorting U. S. Army transports slightly to the west

White Letters in Blue Circles

A. United States Army Forces Far East, Lt. Gen. Douglas MacArthur, commander

B. U. S. Army Hawaiian Department, Lt. Gen. Walter Short, commander

Japanese Imperial Navy and Army Forces
Red Numbers in White Circles

1. Pearl Harbor Striking Force, Vice Adm. C. Nagumo, commander

1a. Midway Neutralization Unit of Pearl Harbor Striking Force

1b. Carriers *Soryu*, *Hiryu* and supporting ships to Wake Island

2. Second Fleet (Distant Cover Force) based at Hainan

3a. Third Fleet based at Formosa; Third Fleet Lamon Bay/Legaspi Invasion Force

3b. Third Fleet Southern Invasion Force

3c. Third Fleet Lingayen Invasion Force

4. Fourth Fleet based at Truk; Guam Invasion Force led by Heavy cruiser *Aoba*

4a. Fourth Fleet Wake Island Invasion Force led by Light cruiser *Yubari*

6. Advance Expeditionary Force from Submarine Fleet based at Kwajalein

Red Letters in White Circles

Aa. Supporting Naval Air Forces based on Formosa

White Letters in Red Circles

A. Imperial Army Home Force

B. Imperial Army Manchukuo Force

C. Imperial Army China Force

D. Imperial Army Philippines Invasion Force, Lt. Gen. M. Homma, commander

The allies agreed to the strategic importance of the colonial city-state at the end of the Malay peninsula, but none other than the U. S. were ready to step forward and offer naval support. After the war began in Europe and once the United States added combat ships to active duty in the Atlantic, the British at last agreed to provide warships to protect Singapore and to convoy troops and supplies to their eastern colonies, while Australia and the Dutch kept their small fleets for local protection (from, among other foes, German commerce raiders). The findings of this group, the American-Dutch-British Commonwealth (ADB) War Plan for the Far East, included a recommendation to their respective governments that an attack on one by Japan would initiate a state of war against the aggressor by all.

Meanwhile, the on-scene commanders at Oahu, Pacific Fleet commander (CinCPAC) Admiral Husband E. Kimmel and U. S. Army commander of the Hawaii District, Lt. Gen. Walter C. Short, were taking on the task of protecting the fleet and guarding military shore installations with vigor. There were concerns on the island and in Washington that despite the fortress-like appearance of Oahu, the military presence was inadequate both for defensive considerations and fleet operations. Among the defensive concerns were inadequate anti-aircraft installations, a shortage of radar and a shortage of U. S. Army Air Corps pursuit planes. Navy fears were somewhat assuaged by the protection offered by torpedo nets and the knowledge that the narrow channel into Pearl Harbor restricted passage of most ships to one at a time. Although the two commanders got along well personally, Kimmel and Short had different viewpoints about the responsibility of protecting the fleet in port. Both men and their staffs, however, bemoaned the siphoning off of military supplies to the Atlantic Theater for convoy protection and

the Lend-Lease programs that prioritized new aircraft, for example, to go to Great Britain.

Another element which contributed to Japan's ability to accomplish a surprise attack at Pearl Harbor was the suppositions made by U. S. commanders about what might be Japan's next Pacific offensive and how it might be manifested. On a strategic level, the U. S. Joint Chiefs of Staff and many others foresaw a move by Japan into Southeast Asia; at Singapore and Malaysia (then Malaya), directly at the Dutch East Indies (the best source of raw materials) or, of greater concern to the U. S., at the Philippines and/or Guam. Lacking any code breaking success with the IJA or IJN encrypted messages, the intelligence available to the U. S. was strictly empirical, based on Japanese military movements. The Japanese were moving troops and ships to the Southwest Pacific and building up bases in places like Indochina and the Mandates (Caroline, Marianas and Marshall Islands). Such movements tended to support the Southeast Asia offensive theory. The possibility of a long range strike on Pearl Harbor was dismissed with little discussion because U. S. officials doubted the Japanese had the logistical capacity – or the nerve – for such an undertaking. They did not consider the huge gamble that Yamamoto was willing to take.

Suppositions made on the island of Oahu also seemed to be directed away from a carrier-based air strike. Locally, Short and others directed much of their attention and efforts toward the possibility of sabotage that might be instigated by Hawaii's large, indeed majority, Japan-born or native born Japanese population. To this end, base perimeters were secured and local informants employed; but this effort was not enough to prevent Japan's imported spy, Yoshikawa, from gaining valuable intelligence during his stint as a consular employee. On the Navy side, defensive measures were aimed at the possibility of submarine attack as well as sabotage, more than an air strike. These attitudes contributed to the lack of attention paid to the early warning signs of the attack.

Politics and Diplomacy

The final road that would lead to either peace or war began in the Oval Office of the White House. With no reversal forthcoming of Japanese aggression against China or an end to its occupation of Indochina, the United States' measured steps and diplomacy taken up until that time could only be viewed as making America an accomplice to Japan's imperial actions. On July 26, 1941, Roosevelt ordered a full embargo of oil and a freezing of Japanese assets in the U. S., where much of the island nation's oil-buying cash was deposited. The next months were a period of futile diplomacy while each side pushed forward preparations for war. The prime minister of Japan since 1940, Prince Fumimaro Konoye, however, kept negotiations going, even appointing a new and internationally respected ambassador to the United States, former admiral Kichisaburo Nomura. But time for negotiations was running out.

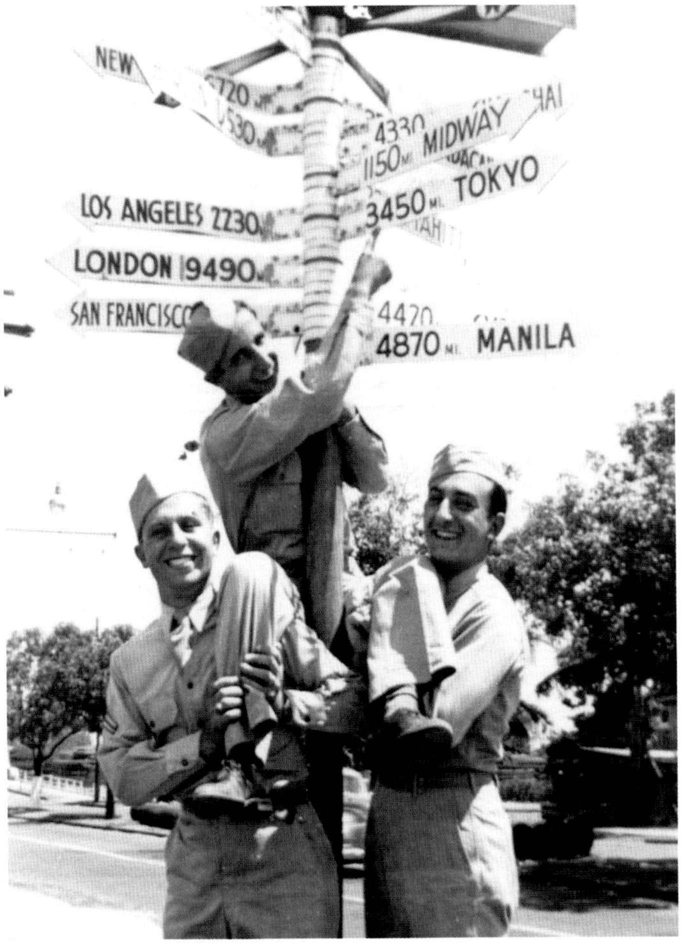
NEW
MIDWAY
LOS ANGELES 2230
3450 MI TOKYO
LONDON 9490
4870 MI MANILA

These American GIs pose at the "Cross Roads of the Pacific" sign at Honolulu's Kau Kau restaurant. Most U. S. military personnel enjoyed their pre-war duties on Oahu and enjoyed many of the activities offered in the cosmopolitan capital of Hawaii.

In the decades since the end of World War II there have been Revisionist theories promoted by historians who don't agree with the generally accepted history. They allege Roosevelt and his confidants were well aware of the Japanese plan to surprise Pearl Harbor. These theorists claim Roosevelt allowed the attack to proceed in order to justify entry into the European war to a population wary of such an entanglement. The overwhelming evidence of much study, however, defeats this Revisionist theory. Not only for all the reasons already presented here did Washington remain unaware of the plan, but opinion polls taken in 1939-1941 showed that Roosevelt had succeeded in turning U. S. public opinion away from its previous staunch isolationist attitudes – the American people were willing to go to war to stop the unchecked aggression of Japan, Germany and Italy.

Konoye, Nomura and other moderates in the government still hoped for an acquiescence to the Japanese "Hakko Ichiu" (under one roof) plan for Asia, but that was not going to happen. The IJA, having mishandled the China war, would not accept the shame of a pull back there – and the U. S. would not proceed in further negotiations with Japan without it. The army had a strong advocate for their views in Japan's belligerent War Minister, that former staff officer in the Mongolia expedition, Hideki Tojo. Among the most radical of hard-liners, Tojo refused to negotiate anything that would cause the army to give up territory. With the conclusion in April 1941 of a non-aggression pact with the Soviet Union (and after their Axis partner Germany had invaded the USSR in June 1941) there was little left to do but complete the planned move south. Finally Konoye felt he could do no more to affect a compromise and resigned. Tojo assumed the mantle of Prime Minister as well.

On November 26, after the Japanese high command gave its final approval of the operation, the Pearl Harbor Strike Force, also known as the First Air Fleet (Kido Butai), left Hitokappu Bay on Etorofu in the remote northern Japan Kurile Islands. The ships had gathered there after arriving en echelon from naval bases to the south. Under the command of Vice Admiral Chuichi Nagumo, the force consisted of six carriers including the most recently built, *Shokaku* and *Zuikaku*. Rounding out the force were two battleships, two cruisers, three "I" class (combat) submarines, nine destroyers and a train of eight tanker and supply ships.

The Pearl Harbor Task Force's mission was one element of the comprehensive plan approved at the Supreme War Council on September 6, 1941 for the Greater East Asia War. The other elements – those for which the Allies had observed Japanese movements – included subjugation of the Philippines, Guam, British Malaya, Borneo, Sumatra, Java, and other islands of the Dutch East Indies. The Japanese attack on Malaya included an invasion of Thailand, for which the government there had already been infiltrated and prepared. In addition, an island defense perimeter would be extended to the east on the island chains already under Japanese control and augmented by invading Wake and the Marshall Islands; extending west to the Burma and India perimeter, and south to the Bismarck and New Guinea archipelago.

Taking a route through the Northern Pacific, Nagumo's ships maintained radio silence, broken only by incoming messages received by the two battleships in the rear of the dual column task force. On December 2, while underway along the northern route, the highly disciplined sailors and airmen of the task force received announcement of their final destination and it was met with joy by those whose minds had been consistently shaped to view the United States as a monstrous single foe, not a nation of freedom loving people.

Though the seas were at times rough, the journey east and then southeast was accomplished without major incident. The weather, often foggy and stormy, helped to further cloak the task force as it steamed toward Hawaii. The mid-ocean refueling operations were successful. Though orders were out to immediately destroy any Allied ships encountered, none were. Neutrals were to be boarded; yet only one, a Russian freighter headed toward Siberia, was sighted and passed the force without being stopped. Why a normal sighting report was never filed by that vessel remains a mystery (some historians do not acknowledge that this incident occurred).

The clandestine operation remained just that until the task force arrived 200 miles north of Oahu in the early morning hours of December 7. At the same time, a fourteen-part diplomatic message, to be delivered by the Japanese ambassador and special envoy Saburo Kuruso to the State Department in Washington thirty minutes prior to the attack, was being transmitted in sections from Tokyo. The message was being intercepted and broken down by Magic cryptographers in the U. S. capital, but the last and most important part was lagging behind. A lightning strike was about to be unleashed that even the Blitzkrieg of the Third Reich could not match.

Japan's World Debut: The 1904-05 Russo-Japanese War

Japan virtually leaped onto the world stage with its stunning, unexpected victory over Tsarist Russia in the 1904-05 war, immediately establishing the island empire as a force to be reckoned with and a major Pacific power. The war was the clash of two imperial powers – established Russia and upstart Japan – both seeking to extend their influence into Manchuria, Asia's Pacific coast and the Korean peninsula. The phenomenal success won against the forces of a major European power by Japan's modernized Army and newly-created Navy – less than a half-century removed from the era of feudal princes warring with swords, spears and bows and arrows – validated the country's efforts to industrialize begun in 1868 and started Japanese militarists on the fateful road toward more imperial adventures.

Thirty-seven years before Japan launched its "Day of Infamy" Pearl Harbor preemptive strike that began its war with the United States on December 7, 1941, it initiated the Russo-Japanese War on February 8, 1904 with a surprise naval attack on the Russian Far East Fleet lying at its Port Arthur base on Manchuria's Liaodong Peninsula. Three hours after Admiral Togo's torpedo boats opened the Port Arthur attack, the Russian government received Japan's formal declaration of war. A stunned Tsar Nicholas II took eight days to send back Russia's declaration of war on Japan. The Japanese triumphed on land and sea during the war's 16-months of combat, notably massive land battles at the Yalu River, the siege of Port Arthur and Mukden, and Togo's brilliant naval victory at Tsushima. Naval observers closely studied Togo's triumph; yet it was the war's land battles that should have drawn the attention of European military officers who, within a decade, would face eerily similar conditions on the battlefields of World War I – deeply-entrenched defenders wielding machine guns and protected by barbed wire facing massed infantry attacks; combat dominated by the devastating power of indirect artillery fire (cannon positioned well behind the front lines linked by telephone to forward observers to deliver deadly accurate fire); and the overwhelming importance of modern logistics to secure battlefield victory by maintaining an uninterrupted flow of bullets, shells and men into the maelstrom of combat. The Russo-Japanese War was the 20th century's introduction to all the horrors of modern, industrialized warfare, a brutal, gory preview of the 1914-18 war.

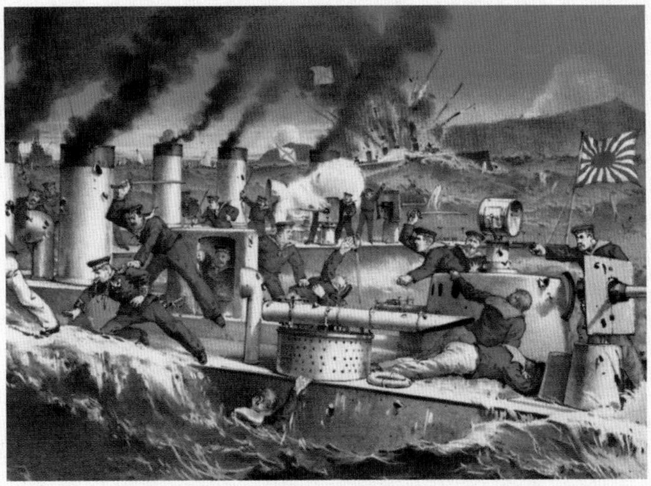

This April 1904 lithograph shows sailors from the Japanese torpedo boat Sazanami *boarding a Russian torpedo boat off Port Arthur.*

The Japanese Army, nearly always the attacker in the war's combat, suffered twice as many battlefield deaths as did its Russian opponent (about 60,000 Japanese killed versus 30,000 Russians). Yet, despite the disparity in casualties, Japan triumphed through superior leadership, more effective tactics (on land and sea) and, perhaps most telling, the superb discipline and élan of Japanese soldiers – "human bullets" one young Japanese officer called them – who fearlessly kept advancing despite massive losses from storms of machine gun bullets and exploding shells. Japan's debut on the world stage in 1904-05 was not only a preview of World War I – and Pearl Harbor – it introduced Western military observers to one of the toughest and most formidable warriors in history, the Japanese soldier.

Honolulu Star-Bulletin 1-

ning Bulletin, Est. 1882, No. 11287
waiian Star, Vol. XLVIII No. 15359

HONOLULU, TERRITORY OF HAWAII, U. S. A., SUNDAY, DECEMBER 7, 1941

WAR!

(Associated Press by Tra

SAN FRANCISCO
ident Roosevelt
morning that Japa
attacked Manila a

OAHU BOMBED B JAPANESE PLA

SIX KNOWN DEAD, 21 INJURED, AT EMERGENC

Attack Made On Island's Defense Areas

By UNITED PRESS

WASHINGTON, Dec. 7. –Text of a White ouse announcement detai ling the attack on e Hawaiian islands is:

"The Japanese attacked Pearl Harbor from e air and all naval and military activities on e island of Oahu, principal American base in e Hawaiian islands."

Oahu was attacked at 7:55 this morning by panese planes.

The Rising Sun, emblem of Japan, was seen plane wing tips.

Wave after wave of bombers streamed rough the clouded morning sky from the uthwest and flung their missiles on a city sting in peaceful Sabbath calm.

According to an unconfirmed report re-ived at the governor's office, the Japanese

CIVILIANS ORDERED OFF STREETS

The army has ordered that all civilians stay off the streets and highways and not use telephones.

Evidence that the Japanese attack has registered some hits was shown by three billowing pillars of smoke in the Pearl Harbor and Hickam field area.

All navy personnel and civilian defense workers, with the exception of women, have been ordered to duty at Pearl Harbor.

The Pearl Harbor highway was immediately a mass of racing cars.

A trickling stream of injured people began pouring into the city emergency hospital a few minutes after the bombardment started.

Thousands of telephone calls almost swamped the Mutual Telephone Co., which put extra operators on duty.

At The Star-Bulletin office the phone calls deluged the single operator and it was impossible for this newspaper, for sometime, to handle the flood of calls. Here also an emergency operator was called.

HOUR OF ATTACK–7:55 A. M.

An official army report from department headquarters, made public shortly before 11,

ANTIAIRCRAFT GUNS IN ACTION

First indication of the raid came shodtly before 8 this morning when antiaircraft guns around Pearl Habor began sending up a thunderous barrage.

At the same time a vast cloud of black smoke arose from the naval base and also from Hickam field where flames could be seen.

BOMB NEAR GOVERNOR'S MANSION

Shortly before 9:30 a bomb fell near Washington Place, the residence of the governor. Governor Poindexter and Secretary Charles M. Hite were there.

It was reported that the bomb killed an unidentified Chinese man across the street in front of the Schuman Carriage Co. where windows were broken.

C. E. Daniels, a welder, found a fragment of shell or bomb at South and Queen Sts. which he brought into the City Hall. This fragrent weighed about a pound.

At 10:05 a. m. today Governor Poindexter telephoned to The Star-Bulletin announcing he has declared a state of emergency for the entire territory.

He announced that Edouard L. Doty, executive secretary of t he maior disaster council,

Hu Ci

Hundr
who hur
Punchbo
began to
before th
roma of
defense.
Far of
the whi
dotted
smoke.
Rolling
base wer
ugly blac
burst of
black sou
Out fro
mouth of
destroyers
smoke pou

Sch Clos

All scho
lic and pri
until furt
Doty, terri
defense, an
day. This
in the ter

CHAPTER 2

Attack on Pearl Harbor

Prelude to the Attack

As war raged across Europe, North Africa and China, America was in the process of whipping its "sleeping giant" of a military into fighting shape. The political and economic climate after World War I had tied the hands of U. S. military planners for nearly two decades in maintaining and developing weapons, bases, armies and strategies. Long-delayed but finally expanded readiness efforts, such as the 1941 Louisiana maneuvers — elaborate war games involving thousands of U. S. Army soldiers centered in that state — helped prevent the nation from being completely flat-footed going into war. Of all the expansion and improvement of standing bases around the globe, none received more attention than Oahu. With the transfer of the Pacific Fleet's home port to Pearl Harbor and upgrades to the army's presence on the island as well, an upsurge in personnel needed in Hawaii followed.

They came from all over the United States where the Great Depression was still severely limiting opportunities for those from the country, the cities and small towns. Although the military draft started in September 1940, all naval personnel serving on Oahu on December 7, 1941 were volunteers.

"I graduated from high school in Wapello, Iowa in 1937 and I tried to get a job," says Woodrow Derby. "There were no jobs, nothing to do and on December 7th, 1938 I joined the navy. After I completed the training there I was assigned to the USS *Nevada* which was in Bremerton, Washington. Now why would I go to the *Nevada*? Our company commander that I was being trained by said, when we graduated, 'now I just want to let you know I was on the USS *Nevada* and it was a good ship. It's in Bremerton undergoing training now.' Fifty of us out of that company went to join the *Nevada*."

James Baund tells the story of how

The headlines in this Honolulu Star-Bulletin *December 7, 1941 Extra does not come close to the final human cost of the Japanese attack on Oahu, but it demonstrates they did what newspapers do – publish the news people need to know as quickly as possible.*

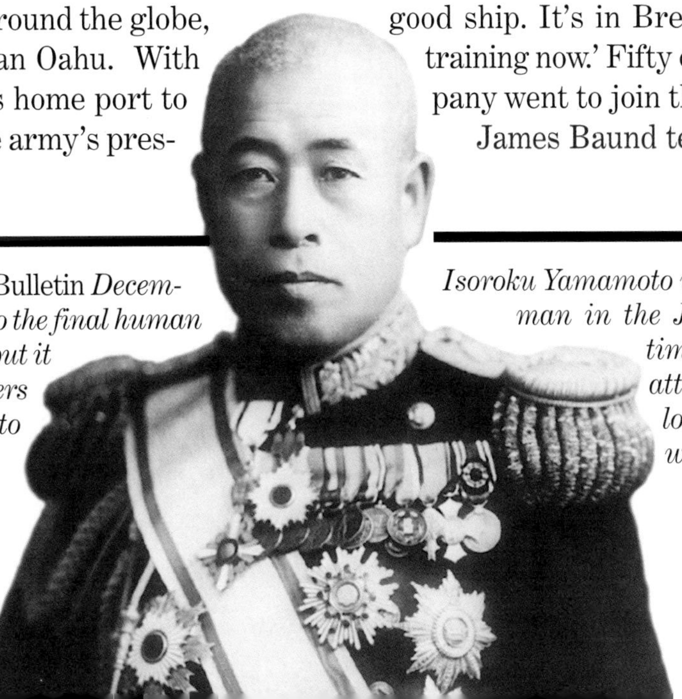

Isoroku Yamamoto was the most powerful man in the Japanese navy at the time of the Pearl Harbor attack. His prestige allowed him to sway those who doubted the plan.

he left the family compound near Big Creek in the bayou country of northern Mississippi, joined the service and ended up in Pearl Harbor as a crewman on USS *Oklahoma*.

"Some older boys were sitting in front of this little barber shop and they were discussing what they were going to do. That was hard times and there wasn't any jobs there. So I decided I was either going into the navy or the Marines. Soon as I turned 18, I caught a truck out of Big Creek. I went in a Marine recruitment office first and they was out for lunch. So I went next door, there was the navy and the chief was sitting at the desk. Once he got a hold of me he wasn't going to let loose. I joined the navy August 7, 1940.

"I was sworn in at New Orleans and got on a train. I went through Texas and recruit training was in San Diego. I caught the destroyer from San Diego up to Long Beach and the *Oklahoma* was there. There were about 39 new recruits going aboard and I guess I was lucky. When the XO [executive officer] — [Cmdr. Jesse] Kenworthy was his name — the XO and department head came by and looked at me and he asked the navigator, Commander Cullens, 'Aren't you a man short in navigation?' He said, 'Yes sir.' And a lot of guys were trying to get into navigation but he asked how would I like to go into navigation. I really didn't know what it was all about; navigation to me was following the old mule up and down the road, you know? And I said 'Yes, sir.' He said we'll check your records out and we will let you know. I was assigned to what they called the N division which was the quartermasters and that was the

This October 1941 photograph of a portion of Pearl Harbor shows just how developed Oahu's premiere harbor had become as it took on the role of the Pacific Fleet's home. This view looking north focuses on the submarine base and a portion of the supply depot. The U-shaped building in the center housed fleet headquarters.

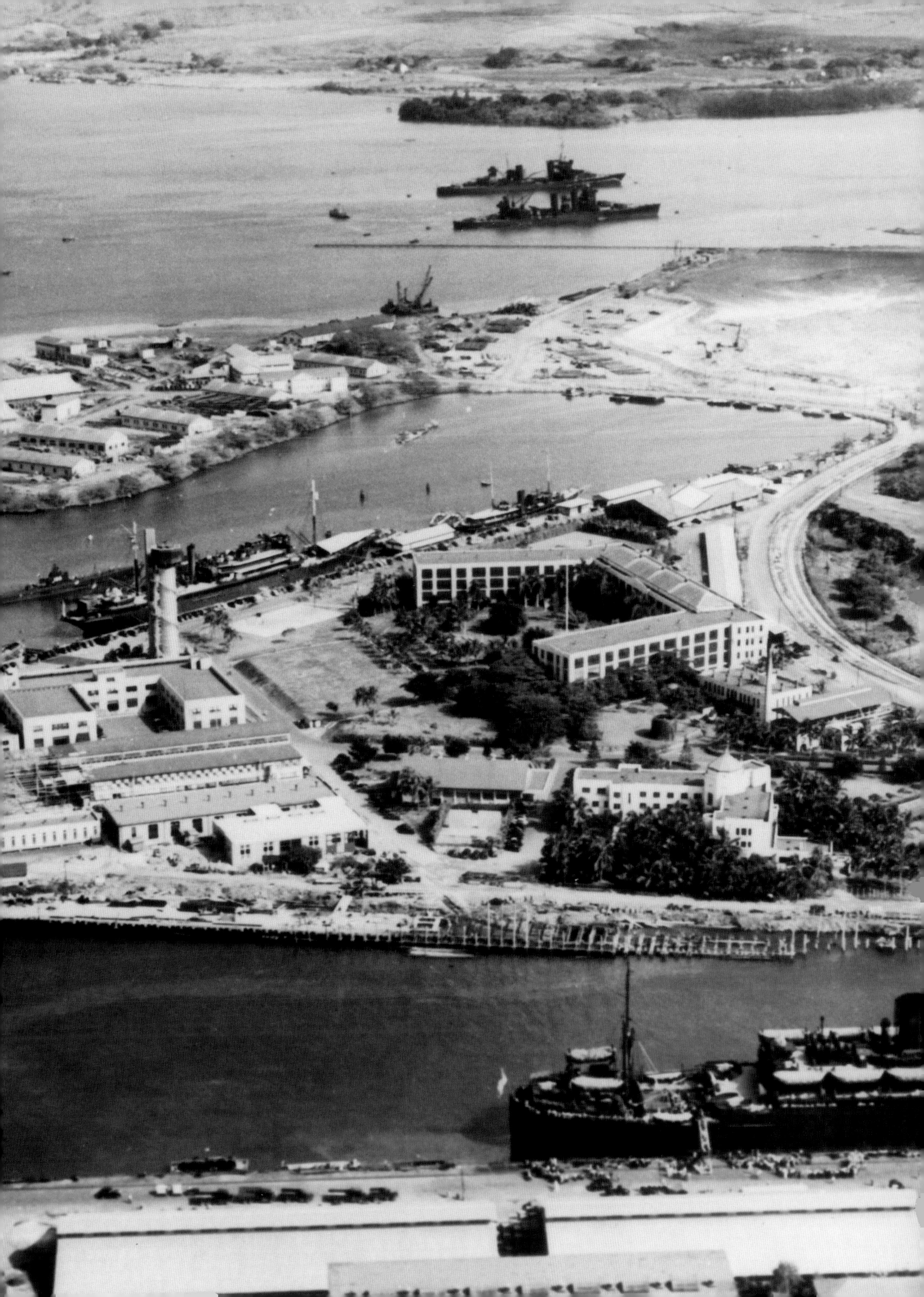

navigation department and I was lucky at that."

Don Lester from Flatwoods, Kentucky was looking for an opportunity in life and eventually also joined the crew of USS *Oklahoma*.

"I was raised in the Great Depression and that led me to the service. First thing I had in mind there was an ad in a magazine for the forest rangers, and that sounded pretty good to me because I would be involved in the outside, in the woods and stuff. I couldn't figure out a way to get to Denver. So I'm going up to the main post office to check in, see what they can do. I walk up to the post office and here's this A-frame sitting in front of the post office and it had a Hawaiian girl on it, beautiful gal. And it said 'Join the Navy, See the

USS Oklahoma *in a photograph from 1917 showing experimental camouflage paint. In 1929 the ship was modernized and the ship's smokestack, seaplane cranes and two tall tripod masts were a visible part of this modernization.*

world.' I forgot about the forest ranger stuff and went up to an old chief up there, he had his arms full of gold hash marks, and he starts talking to me about it. I was just a little kid and I was nervous and he asked how far I went to school and I told him about five miles. He thought I was a wise guy but he realized I was serious. He said 'I'll reword this.' I thought we got off to a bad start but it got straightened out and he enlisted me in the Navy the day of my birthday in May, 1940. I was 18 years old. After training at Great Lakes, Illinois I went to the battleship USS *Oklahoma* and she was in dry dock in Bremerton, Washington."

This scenario was repeated many times as economic despair combined with the potential for ad-

venture to peak interest in joining the peacetime armed forces. But peace was becoming a fragile commodity in the U. S. as the world situation was crumbling and leading America ever closer toward war. In the meantime, training was the order of the day for those men, boys really, recently enlisted. The navy was much further along than the army in preparing for war. Even with adherence to the Washington Naval Treaty, the U. S. Navy had many ships at sea and Roosevelt was interested in a strong navy, even pressing for new ship construction in 1937 that would greatly impact the wartime fleet. Oklahoman Ray Richmond was one of thousands of young men to go through basic training and to be assigned to a warship in 1940.

These navy gunners on USS Ward *are positioned by the number three gun in full combat dress. The World War I vintage four-stack destroyer would play an important part in the events of December 7, 1941.*

"I got to San Diego and went into boot camp. After the boot camp I had to await orders to go to the ship. My company was one of the top companies and so they had a movie company come there for the exercise and the name of the movie was *Navy Blues*. I was [film star] Ann Sheridan's escort through the buildings at the time. We had six weeks of good filming there. She was very good. She's from Dallas so we had good rapport. Then my orders came in and I went to Pearl [Harbor] for my ship. As I walked up the gang plank I was very happy, very excited. When I got to the topside landing, I got my gear and started for my casemate and I was whistling, something you don't do in the navy. I was so happy! When I was putting my gear in my locker, right behind me was a bosun's mate and he said,

'Sailor,' and I turned around and said 'Yes, sir.' He asked me what did I think I was doing and I said, putting my gear away. He said, 'There's only two people in the navy that whistle, that's a bosun's mate and a damned fool. Don't give yourself away.'

"I started striking [training] for gunner's mate and I was on a broadside 5-inch 51 [naval cannon with a five-inch diameter bore]. It was good duty. When we was on maneuvers out at sea my ship got the Navy E for gunnery for the best. So when we come back in, the Japanese had hit the ship so I didn't get the ten dollars [premium pay] that they would allow for the E."

While the Japanese navy's Pearl Harbor Task Force (Kido Butai) was steaming its way across the North Pacific in the last week of November and first week of December 1941, the U. S. military establishment on Oahu was operating in an essentially routine manner. Since the army's Hawaiian District was, in principle, the islands' major defensive force, the attitude among the naval brass was that the role of the fleet was offensive action. Battle groups would take short cruises outside the harbor for gunnery practice or training but these missions would usually only last about five days and most ships returned to port for the weekends. Training for offensive operations was the main aim of Admiral Kimmel's plans as many new recruits and ships in need of crews were arriving at the fleet. Fuel oil supply was also a fleet concern and any prolonged patrolling could have hindered the fleet's ability to execute war plan "Rainbow 5" which specified a U. S. long range strike toward the Japanese mandates. With few exceptions, the routines of the Pacific Fleet did not include defensive measures beyond protection against sabotage. The major exceptions were the PBY Catalina seaplane patrol squadrons at Ford Island and Kaneohe Naval Air Stations. Under the command of Admiral Charles Bloch, the seaplanes made surveillance flights to the south and west.

Surveillance patterns took these planes out about 75 miles south of Oahu — the explanation given for not patrolling the northern area was that there were no Japanese bases to the north. This was an example of the interconnected reasons why the attack on Pearl Harbor came as such a surprise, evidence of the Americans' profound misunderstanding of Japan's actual capabilities and true intentions. In Kimmel's honest appraisal delivered during the Congressional hearing in the wake of the attack, he admitted the staff was concerned about submarine attacks on Pearl Harbor, not air attacks. This was the general opinion of U. S. Naval commanders at the time, including those who would go on to prove their formidable strategic and tactical abilities during the war (such as pugnacious Admiral William F. "Bull" Halsey).

Even the potential for submarine attacks on the fleet lying at anchor in Pearl Harbor was not given the utmost vigilance, and this attitude emanated from Washington. Some of the steps recommended, including torpedo nets around the battleships, were not implemented for various reasons. Hawaiian area navy and army commanders were also dealing with a lack of material support, particularly anti-aircraft guns, fuel oil, interceptor aircraft and aircraft ammunition. Both Kimmel and General Short did take seriously warnings from their respective department and staff heads in Washington concerning the increased likelihood that Japan would move to expand its reach by military force before the end of the year; but most among the military and civilian leadership in the U. S. (and the British Commonwealth) expected that aggression to be directed at the Philippines and Southeast Asia. They were only partially correct.

Routine also influenced the army plan for Hawaii and protection of the fleet at Oahu. Air operations were geared toward training and ferrying equipment to other areas. The use of Army Air Corps planes as interceptors to defend against an air attack was a distant third in priority — even drilling for this function had never been put to the test. The planes mostly sat on airfield runways packed closely together in their anti-sabotage formations. Most of their ammunition was safely locked away.

Kimmel took one step that would prove fortuitous to the American cause – reinforcing the U. S. island outposts west of Hawaii. He decided to strengthen the small Marine garrisons at distant Wake, Midway, Johnston and Palmyra Islands with men and planes. As a result, the two Pacific Fleet carriers based at Pearl Harbor (a third, USS *Saratoga* was still thousands of miles away in Washington's Puget Sound for repairs) were dispatched on missions in early December (and therefore not in port on December 7). Two task forces were formed to deliver aircraft for land based operations from the islands' airfields; one, Task Force Eight, included USS *Lexington*. The other formed around USS *Enterprise*, under Admiral Halsey, the stern but brilliant Pacific Fleet air chief. Halsey kept his Task Force Twelve steaming toward Wake Island under combat readiness condition having been advised by Kimmel of the deteriorating diplomatic condition in Washington.

Bert Stolier was a U. S. Marine attached to the task force. He had enlisted in his home city of New Orleans on February 7, 1940 and was assigned to a ship.

"I was aboard the USS *Northampton* with Captain Smith as its captain and I was his orderly at that time. When I was not an orderly for the captain I was in charge of four 5-inch guns. We let off the six Grumman fighters that Midway got. On the way back to Pearl Harbor one of the ships came alongside of us and one of the ropes got caught in our propeller so we had to lie to until the *Enterprise* and destroyer went way south to Pearl Harbor. That's why the Japs didn't get them."

The errors and omissions by the American military and civilian leaders who had the capability to anticipate and the responsibility to react to the surprise attack at Pearl Harbor can more easily be summed up than cited individually. The idea of an air attack lessened after August 1941 in the minds of U. S. military planners — just as Japanese preparation for the attack was increasing – chiefly because the Americans wrongly concluded that the Japanese were incapable of conducting simultaneous operations in Southeast Asia and against the Pacific Fleet in Hawaii (whether at sea or in port). And while American leaders seemed certain that the Japanese would never be so foolhardy as to attack the United States and thereby create a powerful, united and galvanized foe, these same U. S. leaders had allowed the Pacific Fleet to be woefully unprepared to offer much resistance to Japan's imminent Pacific aggression.

Island Paradise

Daily life in the Hawaiian Islands for American service men and women on the eve of the attack was not unlike the many previous months of accelerated build-up that had preceded that early December weekend of liberty (for most personnel). Since the 1893 takeover of Hawaii by the United States, the influx of U. S. mainlanders to Hawaii was joined by another group coming to the islands. These were Japanese itinerant workers imported to work the large agricultural holdings of American businesses. In fact, by 1941 immigrant and native-born Japanese made up the largest racial group in the islands. This was a major reason why sabotage — and even an uprising to aid an invading army — by a Japanese "fifth column" was such a dramatic concern prior to the surprise attack. Though they mostly kept to themselves and caused few problems, Hawaii's Japanese population had been monitored by the military since the first part of the century.

The measures taken to guard against sabotage varied from command to command. Some of the steps taken included parking planes wingtip to wingtip away from hangars and buildings to facilitate guarding against land-based intruders, and locking away all but the "ready" ammunition. Although this likely would have protected the planes from saboteurs, it made them sitting ducks during an air attack. Stuart Hedley, a New York native who first served in the Civilian Conservation Corps and joined the navy in August 1940, observed the impact of anti-sabotage measures while a seaman aboard USS *West Virginia*.

"I didn't learn this until March, 1942 when I read the Roberts report and I found out the day the Japanese departed the Kurile Islands, on November 26th, 1941, word came from the White House to General Short and Admiral Kimmel, 'prepare for sabotage.' Well, when they looked that up in Bluejacket's Manual [it said] 'bring in everything you've got and keep a close watch on it.' Therefore on Thursday [December 4] we are ordered into port and as we were coming into port the *Tennessee* was with us and the *California*. USS *Maryland* was already in port, the *Oklahoma* was tied next to her. The *Arizona* was already in, the *Nevada* was already in and the *Pennsylvania* was in dry dock. The *Utah* [then a target ship] was tied up over on the other side of the island."

Some sailors headed to Hawaii as new recruits; others who had served for years reached Pearl Harbor for the first time as the Pacific Fleet changed its base permanently in 1940 and other military units increased their presence in the islands. Some of these men were wide-eyed upon introduction to the balmy tropic location with its lush green topography and dramatic rocky volcanic peaks. Hedley remembers *West Virginia's* cruise to Hawaii and his impressions upon arriving there.

"A lot of us recruits were looking forward to going through the Panama Canal but I learned that within five minutes orders can change. When we got our orders on January 3rd [1941], they said you're going to Hawaii. A lot of the guys who had been on the ship had been out there and they didn't like it — they called it "the rock" — but this is a new adventure for me. We were a little over 6 ½ days crossing from Long Beach to Hawaii and I saw that beautiful mountain, Diamondhead. We got out there and we pulled into Pearl and we tied up to the quay there and it was just beautiful, the palm trees, the weather, everything."

Beyond the ever changing confines of the bases, growing by leaps and bounds to accommodate the buildup, new arrivals had pleasant choices facing them. From the sailor-friendly Hotel Street with its bars and showgirls, to Waikiki Beach, there were plenty of opportunities for diversion on the typical weekend liberties afforded enlisted men and officers. Shoulder-board wearing officers could stay out overnight. Single swabbies had to be back on board their ships by 2400 hours, as James Baund understood.

"The married group did get overnight liberty, but we had to be back no later than midnight regardless. You had to be back at the landing to catch a boat to go to the ship. I went to the YMCA — I had a locker there and I spent a lot of time at Waikiki Beach when I could because I loved to go swimming. My routine was normally I'd go over there to wash at the YMCA and I'd get something to eat on the beach. On Sundays I'd go to this civilian church there by the YMCA. That way I could go right out of church and go to the beach. I went by [the Marine] canteen and I'd have one or two of

Commandant of Hawaii's 14th Naval District Rear Adm. Harry E. Yarnell poses with officials of Pan American Airways on April 17, 1935. One of the airline's famous "Pan American Clipper" flying boats built by Sikorsky looms large behind the group.

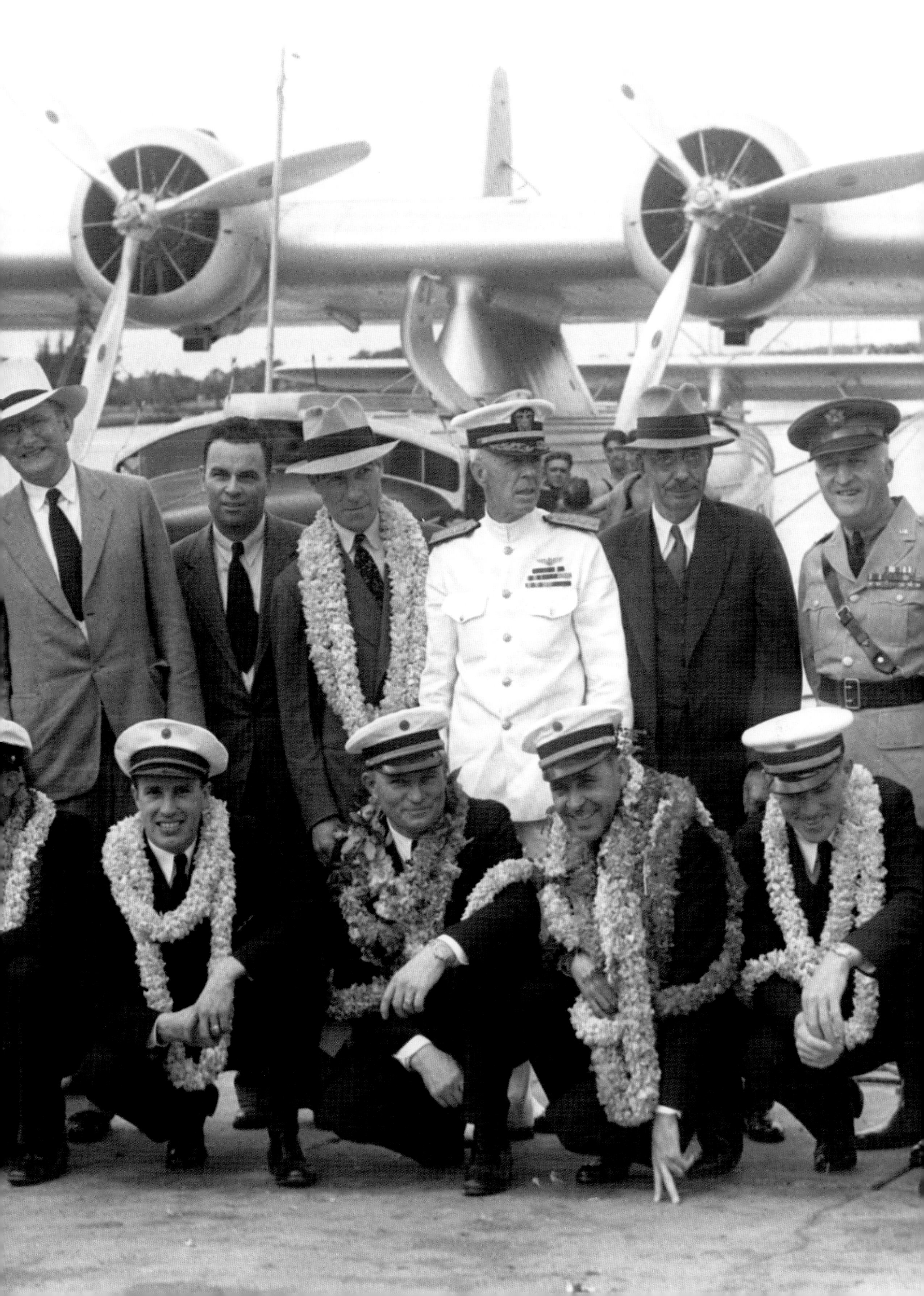

As USS Honolulu *(CL-48) pulls into Pearl Harbor in 1939 Hawaiian women perform the traditional hula dance to the delight of officers and sailors hugging the rail.*

their good cold draught beers and something to eat and then I'd go back to the ship. That was my routine, I was behaving myself really."

Joseph Kawka came from a very large family near Albany, New York. After basic training in Rhode Island, he was part of a large group sent to Pearl Harbor in 1941. By December, he was assigned to duty on USS *Cassin*.

"I was a signalman at the time and I kept going up, [Signalman] 2nd Class and all the way up like that. Then I got in the flag [commander's staff on a designated ship, in this case a destroyer squadron commander]. The captain I worked for had four destroyers under command, and being the signalman, I had good duty. I read all the flags and that's what I did.

"I didn't have any duty [while *Cassin* was undergoing repairs] so I never stood any watches. When we was in dry dock the officer I worked for he said take your liberty, so I went downtown, Pearl Harbor, and I'd spend a lot of my time down there. That's where all the girls were. Oh, we went to a lot of parties. We got the bus or the streetcar took it all the way downtown and went to all the bars they had down there. We saw movies downtown and then we used to go swimming down there at the hotel that's on the beach there. We spent a lot of time there because they had a lot of things going on there."

Baund remembers Waikiki beach at a time when Honolulu was still in its infancy as a tourist destination for mainlanders.

"Waikiki Beach was open there — you had plenty of room; you could go surfing, swimming and they even had inner tubes you could check out. The natives there wasn't the friendliest people in the world to us sailors and I noticed that. There were a lot of civilians, but we had a lot of service people from all the ships we put in there. [In December 1941] we had put eight battleships in there all at the same time. We never did that all at the same time, it was kind of funny all the battleships were in and that never happened that they got them all in there at one time and that's a no-no. You generally have a division [several ships] out."

These experiences were enjoyed by many in the islands up through the first Saturday in December, 1941. That night, in addition to other activities on shore, there was a "Battle of the Bands" concert among Pearl Harbor ships' bands, won by the band from USS *California*. Stuart Hedley remembers what he was doing on December 6.

"Saturday I was on liberty and my girlfriend and her mother, we went out to lunch and I went out to

Waikiki and that evening we went roller-skating, Juanita and myself. About 11:30 Saturday night Juanita's mother brought us back to the pier and I caught the boat. As I was riding the liberty boat back to the ship there were about five submarines departing the harbor. When I got on board I asked Ensign Lombard where are all those submarines going? He said they're sailing under sealed orders, that's all we know. Juanita and I had talked it over and her mother was in agreement that Sunday we would go on a picnic on the north end of the island."

Hiryu, built in 1937, was one of the six carriers of the First Air Fleet (Kido Butai) used in the Pearl Harbor attack. It is seen here during trials on April 28, 1939.

Missed Opportunities

The quiet of Pearl Harbor after midnight was only slightly disturbed by maintenance operations and the normal routine of minesweepers and destroyers departing for or returning from patrol. The serenity of the night belied the fact that 27 Japanese "I" Type submarines of the Advance Expeditionary Force had reached their designated rendezvous positions off the harbor to provide reconnaissance and communicate with the carriers of the First Air Fleet as well as to torpedo any ships attempting to escape the harbor. An additional mission was launching five two-man submarines (single screw, ninety-feet long with two torpedoes) to infiltrate the harbor. Unlike most of the Japanese aircraft pilots the two-man midget submarine crews did not expect to survive their missions. After torpedoing whatever ships they could find in the harbor these volunteers expected to go down with their crafts. Nearly all did.

The first of these midget subs was sighted about 0345 hours by an officer on the sweeper USS *Condor* who related the discovery to USS *Ward*, a World War I-vintage four-stack destroyer. *Ward* could not locate and destroy this sub but with the help of a PBY patrol plane located and sunk another with depth charges three hours later. But the light duty schedules at command posts meant that the report did not reach Kimmel in a timely manner. Even had it arrived at once, however, the report of engaging a submarine likely would only have reinforced Kimmel's belief that enemy submarines – not enemy aircraft – were the real threat to the Pacific Fleet at Pearl Harbor.

The final missed opportunity to discover the attack and alert U. S. forces came from one of six mobile SCR-270 radar stations of the Air Warning Service in Hawaii. The Opana location near the northern tip of Oahu was considered a training site and was only manned from 0400 to 0700 local time. This was the case on Sunday, December 7, as Pvt. Joseph Lockard, an experienced operator, was training Pvt. George Elliot. At 0645 Lockard picked up one of two spotter planes launched by the Japanese ahead of the main attack. It was reported but dismissed. Later he noticed tracks on the radar device's oscilloscope screen indicative of a large formation of aircraft. With experienced operators in short supply in Hawaii, it was fortunate that Lockard happened to be on duty to notice the unusual activity.

The radar installations under the Signal Corps and the Air Corps intercept operations center at Fort Shafter (where air targets were plotted on a large interactive map using wooden models) were at the time new and struggling to coordinate their activities. The intercept operations center was on skeleton crew that Sunday morning and the small staff was leaving in anticipation of the end of the Air Warning Service shift at 0700 when Lt. Kermit Tyler, senior officer on duty, took the call placed by Elliot on behalf of Lockard. Tyler was a pilot who was learning the center's operation as part of a plan to make the pilots savvy on pursuit strategy. Knowing (but not able to reveal to the Opana operators) that a squadron of six Boeing B-17 Flying Fortress bombers was due in any minute on a stop to their destination in the Philippines, Tyler dismissed the finding by telling Elliot, "Don't worry about it." Perhaps if Lockard had communicated his seasoned estimate of the blips size being fifty planes or more, Tyler would have treated the call with greater concern.

In one of those ironic coincidences that make war the most fascinating and studied of all human endeavors, the radar blips of unusual size and composition that confounded the Opana Point operators were not the six B-17s headed for Oahu that Tyler knew were scheduled inbound from the north. They were, rather, the first group of Japanese planes in Captain Mitsuo Fuchida's first attack wave. The Japanese bombers flew in on a south by southwesterly course that was a mere one degree from the expected course of the Army Air Corps planes.

By 0600 the first wave of 183 Japanese bombers and fighters were launching from the carriers at the designated launching point a little over 200 miles due north of Oahu. Fuchida's forty-nine Nakajima B5N-1 bombers in the first group were slow moving, 1,115 hp level flyers that began service in the Manchukuo War. However, they carried armor-piercing bombs that would prove devastating soon enough. The second four sections included forty B5N-2 models that were substantially the same as the B5N-1s except they were adapted to carry one 1760-lb. Type 95 torpedo. Following them were 51 Type 99 dive bombers and 43 Type 0 fighters. The United States adopted children's names to designate these planes: the B5Ns were designated as "Kates" whether carrying torpedoes or bombs; the dive bombers were "Vals;" and the fast Mitsubishi fighters were "Zekes" (although "Zero" is the name most often used for them).

The Quietest Time

Of several code phrases used in official Japanese communication during the Hawaii Operation, the most famous is "Tora, Tora, Tora" ("Tiger, Tiger, Tiger"), the sig-

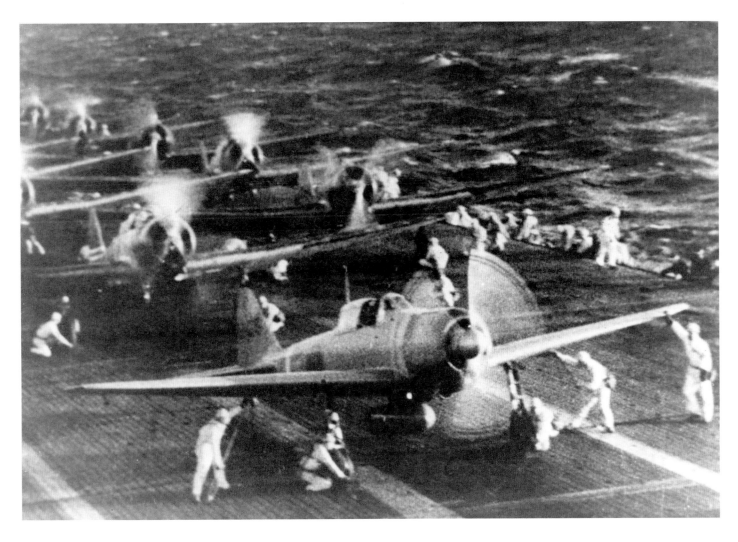

Mitsubishi A6M2 "Zeros" (code name "Zeke") and Nakajima B5N2 bombers (code name "Kate") warm up on the flight deck of Shokaku *early on the morning of Sunday December 7, 1941.*

nal made by Fuchida to the Japanese Navy that U. S. ships were in Pearl Harbor and unprepared for the air strike. The objective sighted, all Japan's plans would come to fruition with the commencement of bombing.

On December 7, one military official in Washington, D. C., Colonel Rufus S. Bratton, a military intelligence officer in charge of the Far East Section, had been piecing together the meaning of the complete decoded Japanese diplomatic message Tokyo had sent to its embassy and intercepted by the Americans. Bratton understood Japanese and had attended Japan's Imperial War College a decade earlier. He particularly studied one de-

coded fact – an unusual instruction for Japanese embassy diplomats to deliver the message to the U. S. State Department at a definite time, 1300 hours. One of Bratton's counterparts in the Navy Department, Lieutenant Commander Alwin D. Kramer, focused on the hour as well. He began to calculate the clock time at strategic places around the globe. It dawned on him that the hour translated into 0730 Sunday Honolulu time, which was as he put it "probably the quietest time of the week aboard ship at Pearl Harbor."

Indeed, it was a quiet time for most of the military personnel on Oahu. Only one ship, the destroyer USS *Helm*, was underway in the harbor. As the first of the faster Val dive bombers appeared, circling over Pearl at 0730 awaiting the slower Kate torpedo bombers, a few sailors took note but assumed the craft to be friendly. At 0755 the first Kates screamed in from the west and began to drop down to unload their deadly cargo. A bomb struck the seaplane ramp on the south end of Ford Island, followed by another explosion – a torpedo which struck the light cruiser USS *Raleigh*. Klaxons sounded "General Quarters" on one after another of the 94 ships scattered about the harbor. At 0758 the tower on Ford Island on the order of Rear Adm. N. L. Bellinger broadcast this message to the nation. "Air Raid — Pearl Harbor — This is no drill." The recollections of those who were on the ships and the military installations of Oahu and survived the attack provide vivid details of what happened in those first violent minutes.

USS *Pennsylvania*, in dry dock, was the flagship of Kimmel's fleet. Leland Lester from Colfax, Iowa, had joined the crew of *Pennsylvania* nearly a year earlier in Bremerton, Washington. On the morning of December 7, he was performing his normal duties.

"During the latter part of 1941 my job at the time of Pearl Harbor was a mess cook. I had just fed my 25 men and had gathered up all my dishes, silverware and whatnot and took it across the ship from the port side to the starboard through the bakeshop passage. I put it all in the dumbwaiter on the starboard side and just as I was coming back and was about halfway across the bake shop and a terrible explosion happened which almost blew me off my feet. It wasn't until just recently that I realized that it wasn't an explosion on the island, it was right on our own ship. I whirled around and ran over to the starboard side and I just looked up, there was a Japanese Zero flying over. He was so

low I could've tossed a hand grenade up and hit him. My gun happened to be just about 20 feet from me over and up a bulkhead. I climbed that thing [steel bulkhead ladder] and went over the chain fence, took the canvas off the gun, got on the gun and trained it out to the outer position. Then I run over to the other side of the gun and trained it up into the firing position, and I did this all before they sounded the alarm. So I was already on the gun when they sounded General Quarters."

Just forward of *Pennsylvania* in dry dock were two destroyers also in for repairs, USS *Cassin* and USS *Downes*. From his vantage point on the *Cassin*, Joe Kawka also saw the low flying Japanese aircraft.

"I was up on the bridge and then we had planes come by and one guy [Japanese pilot] waved to me. The captain said, you know when you're in dry dock you don't have ammunition so the only ammunition on this ship is potatoes. So I took a bucket of potatoes up on the bridge and then some guy came by in a Japanese plane and he waved to me so I hit him with two potatoes. We had one of our destroyers over where they had a floating dry dock, he got hit too. When they hit him, when they hit that ship they killed everyone on it. It was the *Shaw* and then I saw the *Arizona* get hit, it was the second ship."

Don Lester, on the *Oklahoma*, recognized the potential danger quickly developing on the battleship.

"Admiral [J. O.] Richardson had a run in with the big shots in Washington so he was relieved of his command and Admiral Kimmel took over the

An Aichi D3A Type 99 dive bomber (code name "Val") is photographed banking over Pearl Harbor. The wing bombs have not yet been released.

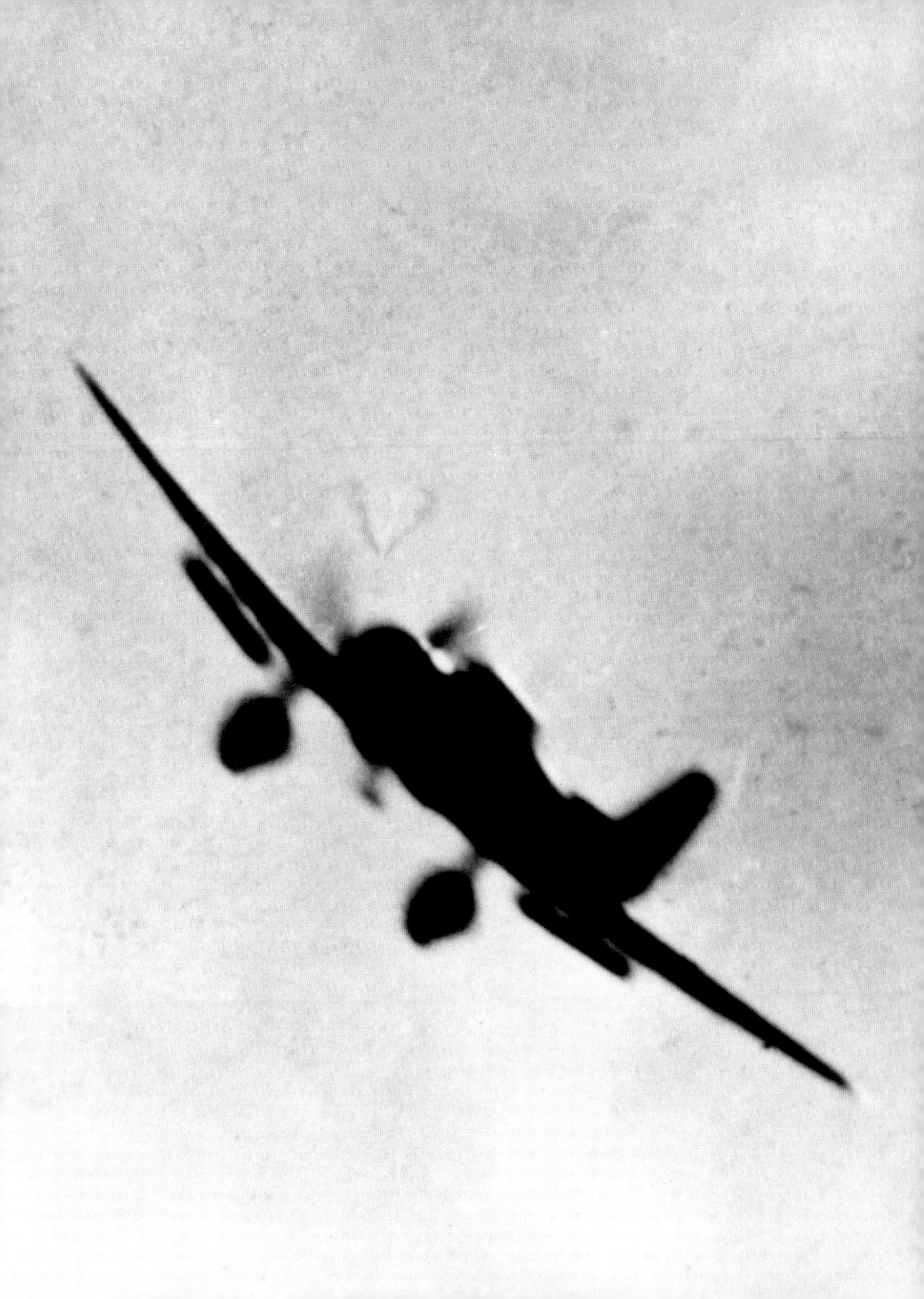

United States Navy ships in Pearl Harbor at 0755, December 7, 1941

1. Destroyers *Tucker, Conyngham, Reid, Case, Selfridge* (left); Tender *Whitney* (right)
2. Destroyer *Blue*
3. Light cruiser *Phoenix*
4. Destroyers *Aylwin, Farragut, Dale, Monaghan*
5. Destroyers *Patterson, Ralph Talbot, Henley*
6. Destroyers *Worden, Hull, Dewey, Phelps, Macdough* (left); Tender *Dobbin* (right)
7. Hospital ship *Solace*; Destroyers *Allen, Chew*
8. Light minelayer *Ramsey* (left); Destroyer-minesweepers *Gamble, Montgomery* (right)
9. Destroyer-minesweepers *Trever, Breese, Zane, Perry,* Wasmuth (left); Repair vessel *Medusa* (right)
10. Seaplane tender *Curtiss*
11. Light cruiser *Raleigh* (left); Light cruiser *Detroit* (right)
12. Target ship (former Battleship) *Utah* (left); Seaplane tender *Tangier* (right)
13. Battleship *Nevada*
14. Battleship *Arizona* (inboard – toward Ford Island); Repair vessel *Vestal* (outboard)
15. Battleship *Tennessee* (inboard); Battleship *West Virginia* (outboard)
16. Battleship *Maryland* (inboard); Battleship *Oklahoma* (outboard)
17. Oiler *Neosho*
18. Battleship *California*
19. Seaplane tender *Avocet*
20. Destroyer *Shaw*
21. Destroyers *Downes* (left); *Cassin* (right)
22. Battleship *Pennsylvania*
23. Submarine *Cachalot* (above *Pennsylvania*); Minelayer *Oglala* (outboard of Dock 1010); Light Cruiser *Helena* (inboard)
24. Destroyers *Jarvis, Mugford* (inside); Auxiliary vessel *Aragonne*, Gunboat *Sacramento*, Seaplane tender *Swan* (left to right)
25. Oiler *Ramapo*, Heavy cruiser *New Orleans*, Heavy cruiser *San Francisco*, Light cruiser *Honolulu*, Light cruiser *St. Louis* (left to right)
26. Repair vessel *Rigel*, Destroyer *Cummings*, Light-minelayers *Preble, Tracy*; Destroyer-minesweeper *Grebe*, Destroyer *Schley*, Light-minelayers *Pruitt, Sicard* (left to right)
27. Destroyer *Bagley*
28. Submarine tender *Pelias*
29. Submarines *Narwhal, Dolphin, Tautog*; some accounts also place Submarine *Gudgeon* here

PEARL HARBOR

Pearl City
Middle Loch
East Loch
Ford Island
Waipio Peninsula
Hospital Point
Harbor Entrance
N
2
2
2
2
3
3
3
3
3
3
8
9
10
11
12
19
20
32

30. Seaplane tenders *Thornton, Hulbert*
31. Auxiliary vessel *Sumner* (top); Auxiliary vessel *Castor* (bottom)
32. Minesweepers *Bobolink, Vireo, Turkey, Rail* and *Tern*

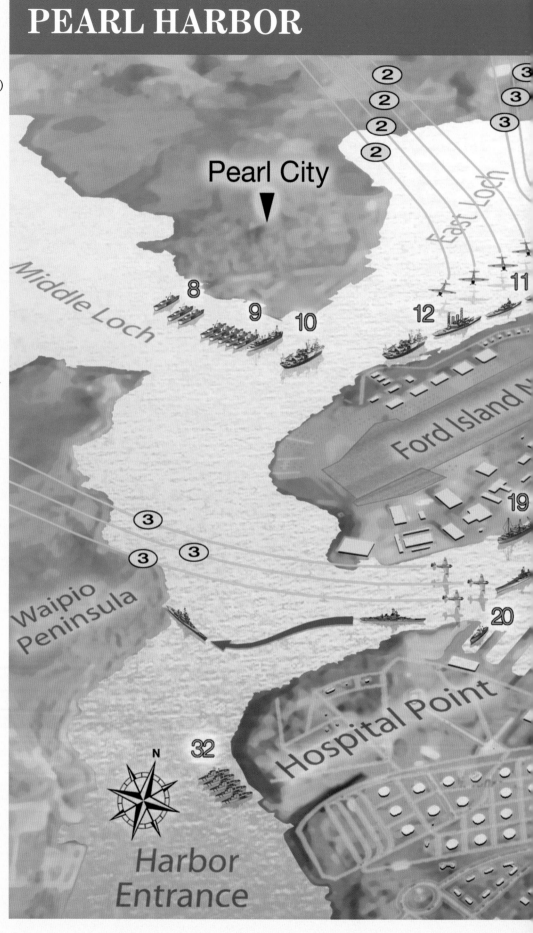

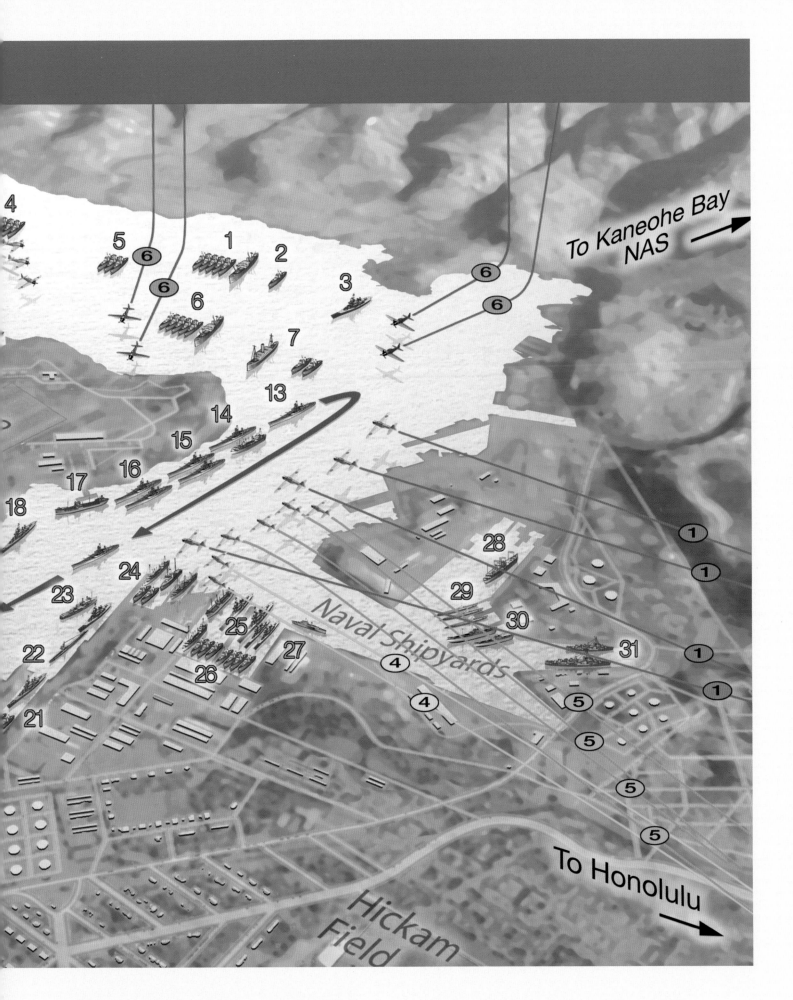

Japanese Carrier Planes in the Attack

1. Fifteen "Kate" high-level bombers from *Akagi*

2. "Kate" torpedo-bombers from *Soryu*

3. "Kate" torpedo-bombers from Hiryu

4. First wave "Kate" torpedo-bombers from *Akagi* and *Kaga*

5. Second wave "Kate" torpedo-bombers from *Soryu* and *Hiryu*

6. "Val" dive bombers from *Akagi*

To Kaneohe Bay NAS

Naval Shipyards

To Honolulu

Hickam Field

command. For some reason he had all the ships in Pearl Harbor. He came in on Friday and struck over ammunition below decks on Saturday and took the firing pins out of the guns. We opened up the ship for inspection; all the manhole covers were open and so forth, and the Japanese hit Sunday morning. I was on the third deck that morning of the attack and it was a shock to all of us, we couldn't figure out why they was having a drill on Sunday morning like that in port, until we realized it was the real thing."

The torpedo bombers which came in from the southeast over Hickam Field and Merry Point were flying at 40 to 100 feet above water level and then pulling up quickly after unleashing their single "fish." The first torpedoes struck *Oklahoma* and *West Virginia* almost simultaneously. Stu Hedley recalls the first tense moments on *West Virginia*.

"I was up at 5:00 o'clock on December 7th and I showered and shaved and I had my civilian clothes all pressed out and everything, and I polished my white shoe-skates and oiled the wheels. I looked for my dress shoes and they were gone. I asked one of the fellows in the compartment if he by chance had seen my shoes, dress shoes. He said, 'Oh yeah Pete Hartley wore them last night.' I said, 'Where in the world is he?' 'He's asleep down in the after-steering.' That was five decks below so I went prancing down there and I got to the after-steering and there's Pete Hartley drunk as a skunk and sound asleep. I took my shoes off of him and as I was walking out, Cherry, a 3rd class quartermaster, said 'Stu how about having a cup of coffee?' I said sure and we started talking about what we were going to do tonight. We were drinking the coffee and batting the breeze and all of a sudden we hear 'away fire and rescue party.'

"That meant I was to get up to my quarters, grab my hat, fall in, and wait for orders. I ran up on topside. Hicks, one of the 1st class bosuns' mates,

hit me right in the seat of my pants and said, 'Get to your battle station on the double this is the real thing.' I wondered what in the world is he talking about but I ran out on topside and planes were diving all over the place. I saw our pilot, Lt. White, under a gun tub — it was a 20 mm gun — and he was underneath that so I dove under there with him and here he is shooting with his .45 at the planes going by and I'm wondering what in the world kind of war is this. I didn't ask any questions and he said, 'Son, where's your battle station?' I pointed up to turret three and he said get up there as fast as you can. I ran out from under the tub and of course across the quarter deck and up the ladder and as I was going up the ladder to go in the turret here comes a Japanese plane down along our port side and I could see the pilot, the co-pilot and they're laughing like everything. Their machine guns were spitting out their .50 caliber bullets. We got inside the turret; Croslin and I were the only two that manned the right gun, the left gun was fully manned, or at least partially manned. When we got in we could hear the machine gun bullets hitting our turret and we also felt the thud of the torpedo. We took nine torpedoes but during that

TOP – A view from a Japanese plane looking toward "Battleship Row" at Pearl Harbor approximately 0800 on Dec. 7, 1941. USS Nevada *is in the foreground. Beyond* Nevada, West Virginia *and* Oklahoma *have already been torpedoed as evidenced by the wakes fanning from their port sides. USS* Arizona *had not yet been torpedoed when this photograph was taken but splashes from torpedo drops and running tracks are visible at the center and left. In the background grey smoke emanates from the cruiser USS* Helena, *hit at the 1010 dock and in the far distance, white smoke rises from attacks at Hickam Field. BOTTOM – USS* West Virginia *is a ball of flames after torpedoes slammed into her port side from Japanese "Kate" bombers flying low. USS* Tennessee *sits behind* West Virginia *and received more damage from her sister ship's debris then from attacking Japanese planes.*

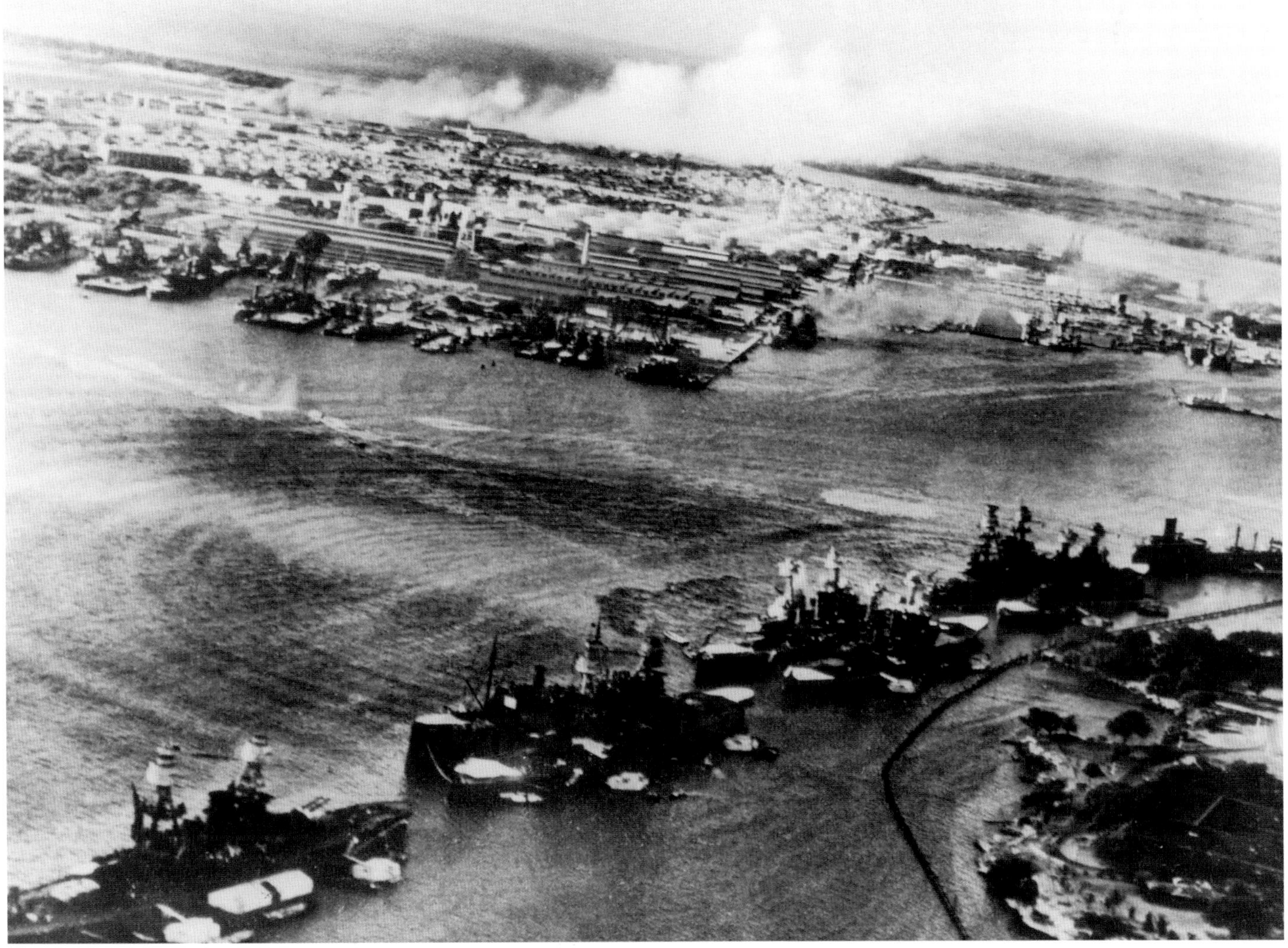

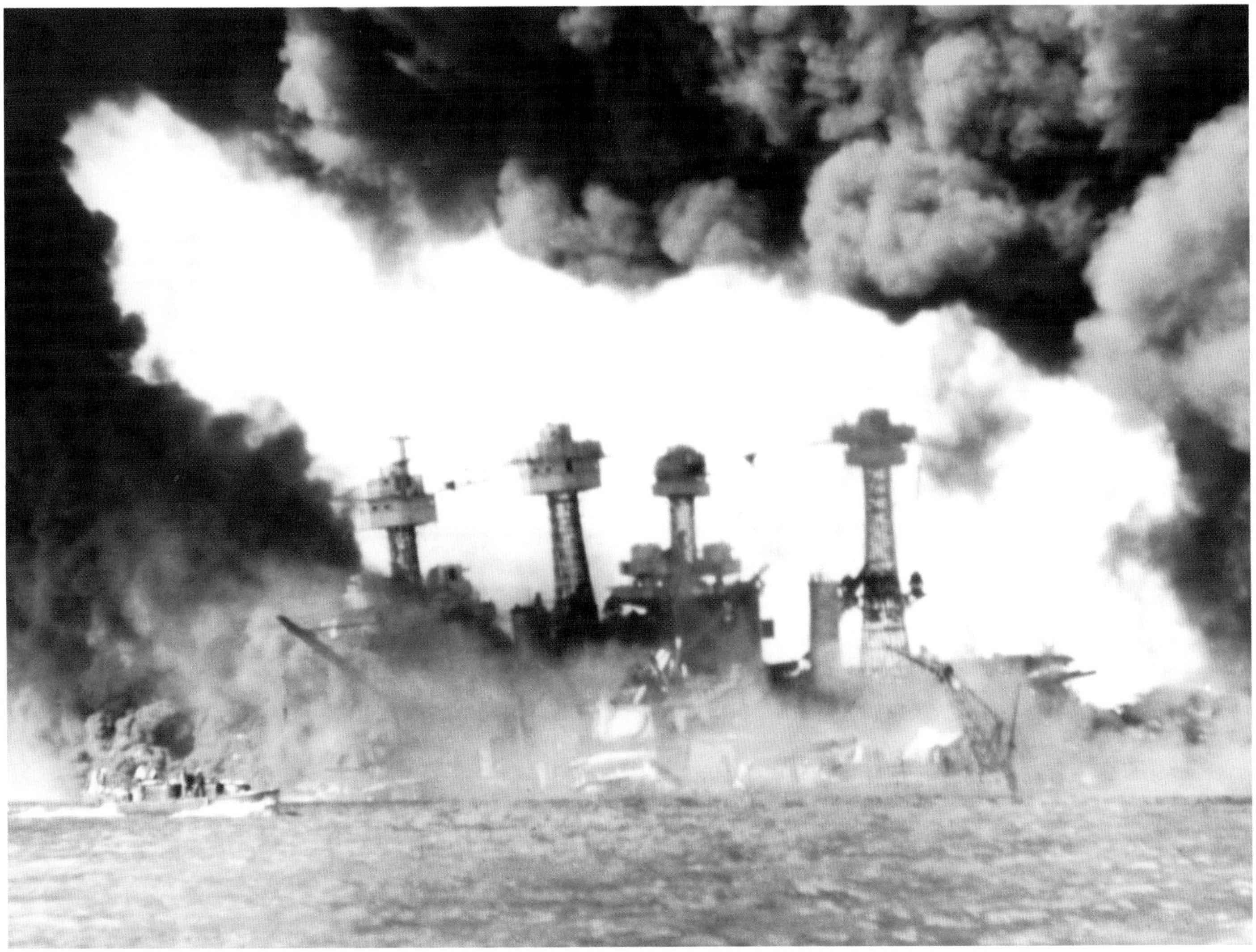

period I think I felt the explosion of two of them."

USS *Oklahoma* was hit very early by three torpedoes. Because the watertight compartments were open on the battleship, she took on water rapidly and the command was given to abandon ship. Don Lester describes what he did when the order was sounded.

"I moved from the middle of the carpenter shop over to the only hatch that was available going out and went out to the main deck. A man who used to live very close to me; I got to the hatch to go out and he was standing there. I told him I had to go to the boat deck, my battle station was an anti-aircraft 5 inch/.25 gun. He told me just to stand fast. Of course he was a 2nd class petty officer and had a .45 strapped on so I had only one choice, that was to stand fast. A seaman 1st class had his foot up in the hatch and wouldn't let anybody out. He said we'll leave when we get the order to abandon ship. The ship starting rolling pretty fast; the ship took nine torpedoes and that number six hit pretty close to the stern where we were at. The carpenter shop was on the starboard side, well it run completely across the ship and I was on the starboard side and the hatch was about ten foot off the center line to the starboard. A few minutes after I talked to the guy on the sound power phones, all phones went dead, and we were to abandon ship. He took off and I went in right behind him up this ladder, I'll explain this a little bit.

"They had this steel ladder welded to the side which is the bulkhead or the hull, when we got the word abandon ship that ladder was [horizontal] just like you'd have taken it off and laid it on the floor. By the time we got to the main deck water was shipping in the hatch which means she was ten feet past center line over. She was rolling over fast and the only thought that came into my mind at this time was to get as far away from her as I could because I wanted to make sure I wasn't caught in the structure of the ship. The one thing I didn't realize, I was concerned about the structure more than I was the suction of the ship because she was going fast. It took about 10 or 12 minutes for her to roll completely over. I hit the water and started swimming and I got caught in the down draft of the ship when she went on over and that was the craziest feeling you could ever get a hold of. I couldn't swim out of it as hard as I tried, it was pulling me straight down and my hair was straight up in the air, I could feel it pulling and I went down to the point where I felt like mud on the bottom and it was about 35 feet of water there. I went into this mud up to my knees and a completely different temperature of the water. As soon as the ship hit the bottom she had a blow back, just the same as the down, and came back up. This guy I mentioned earlier that was in charge — we both had the same story almost word for word — he was right in front of me and we both went down the same way. I come back up all my hair was just reversed it was down in my face now and I said I'm coming up and I shot out of the water around my waist, very fortunate because there was a lot of debris, stuff in the water from the ships. The first thing I noticed was my chest was very sore and my lungs were emptied out I guess and I was having trouble. But there was a group of guys in this one area close to me and I found out they was hanging onto the pontoons, we had seaplanes on the *Oklahoma* and they broke loose and was in the water upside down and they was hanging onto the pontoons."

Ray Richmond also recalls his struggle to get off *Oklahoma* once the "Abandon Ship" order was given.

"I was taking a shower and one of four torpedoes hit us. It felt like somebody just pushed the ship up in the air and for a minute it shuddered and sat down on the water. When the ship went up I went

up; I was fussing around in the shower and I thought maybe the navy was having a sand bag [practice bombing run] on the *Utah*. We took all the superstructures off her, and put a wooden deck on that thing and they were dropping 50 pound bags on there. I thought they must be getting heavier sand bags and all of a sudden, abandon ship! It was already turning over to the port side and all the lights went out. I'm two decks below so I come along

In this photograph from Ford Island shortly after the first wave attack, the torpedoed USS California *is listing to port in the center. Billows of smoke rise up from USS* Arizona *in the background. On the other side of Ford Island, on board USS* Utah, *a battleship stripped of its guns and used as a target ship, was Seaman 2nd Class Bob Ruffato. "We were hit by two torpedoes. After they dropped their bombs, the airplanes would circle Ford Island, machine gunning everybody in the water and still aboard ship 'til they ran out of ammunition. To get away from the machine guns, we went underneath the forecastle, where the yeoman's office was and we hid in there. When the furniture started sliding across the deck, we knew we had to get off that ship 'cause she was goin' over."*

by the galley and held on to the rail by the galley. The deck had water and oil on it and we couldn't hardly stand up. We were leaning on anything we could get so if you didn't know the ship you were in trouble. As I was walking along the deck I came to a ladder way to go up topside and you couldn't use the ladderway because the bottom wasn't secured and it was flopping around. By the time I got to the ladderway the ship was already laying on its side, my wall where I tried to get in turned out to be the deck.

"I was trying to get in my casemate and Commander Kenworthy was topside and reaching down to pull us up to the casemate. After I got up to the casemate I walked outside and the ship was laying on its side. So I had to jump out flat level to get to the bottom and so my tail bone hit the rail and broke my back and fractured my hip, but I didn't know it at the time. I was about 100 feet from the fantail and I scooted off to the water, the oil was on fire in the water. I hit the water and went under and I had to agitate the water on the surface on account of the oil. I pushed bodies, pieces of bodies in there it was so many. I swam over to the *Maryland* and started to get up on the ladder, everybody was using me as a stepladder, stepping on me. I was at the point where I said I can't go on so I said well this is it. At that time somebody grabbed me by the hair and the head and pulled me up to a toehold, and that man had pulled me up was my friend, Fogel. From this day on we have never seen where he went, it was just like a ghost."

Like a calm sea suddenly agitated by a sudden squall, the attack rippled through Battleship Row. Inboard from *West Virginia* another great battleship, USS *Tennessee*, was moored next to Ford Island. Baltimore native Ed Wise joined the navy in 1940 and was assigned to *Tennessee* after basic training.

"On the morning of December 7, 1941, we had reveille at 5:30 a.m. We did our usual morning chores, sweeping and scrubbing down the decks. Then we went to chow. After chow I sat down in a corner to read the Sunday paper. The weekend

In one of the most dramatic and deadly scenes of the attack the foremast and turret Number Two of USS Arizona *burn after a torpedo had exploded in the forward magazine of BB-39.*

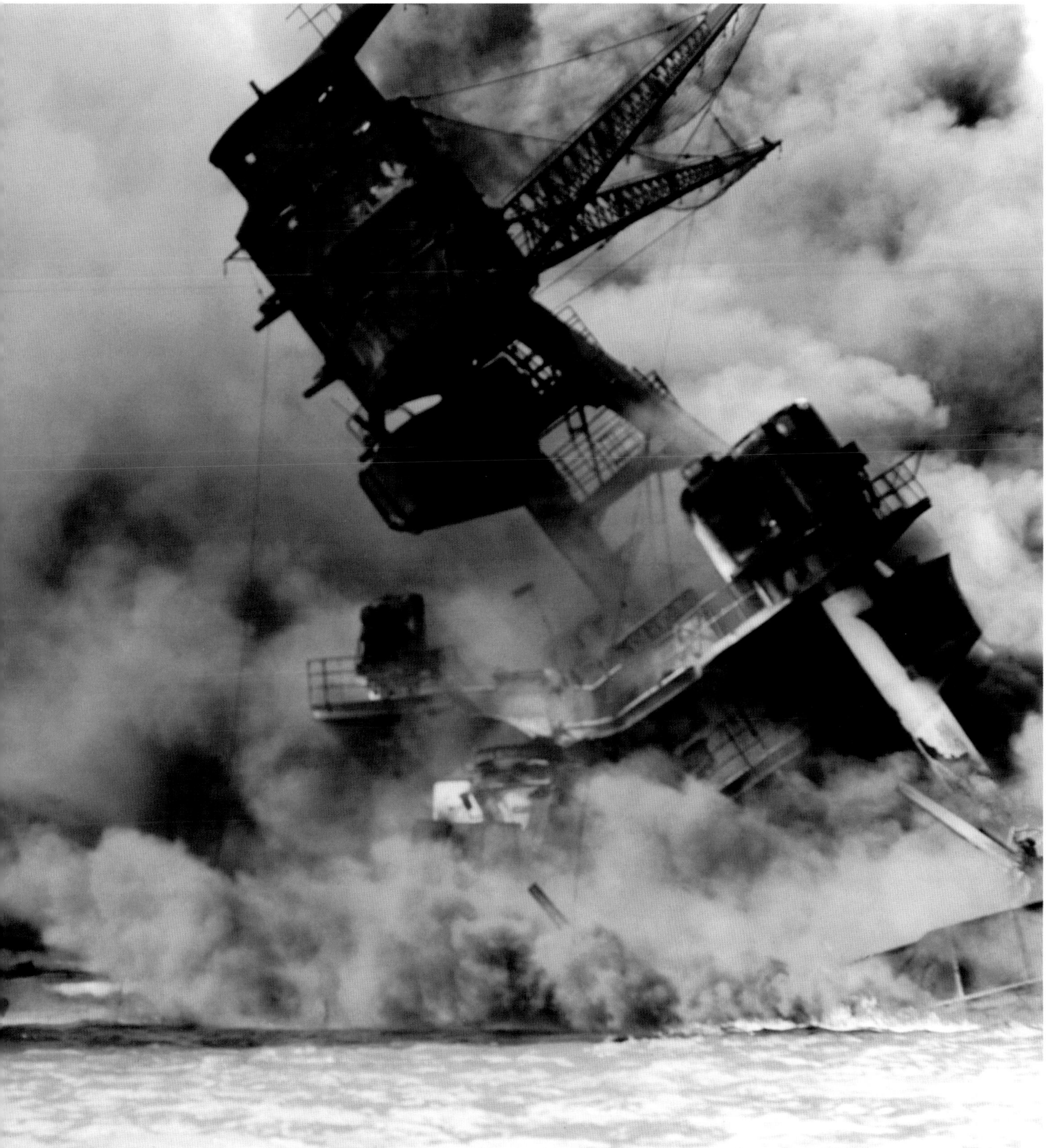

was usually holiday routine. A day of relaxing. About five minutes before 8:00 a.m., the general quarters alarm was sounded. The voice over the PA system kept saying, 'Man your battle stations. This is no drill. Man your battle stations.' As we were trained to do, we immediately ran to our battle station. My battle station was in turret four with three 14-inch cannons. My station was as a gun pointer in the center gun. That is elevating the gun up and down. I started to run out on the deck which was the shortest and fastest way to get there. I stop suddenly at the hatch, look up, and saw a big red circle on the wings of the plane strafing our quarterdeck and bullets bouncing everywhere. Then I took another route, manned my station and reported to the gun booth that I was manned and ready. I could hear all kinds of explosions on the outside; still not knowing what really was going on."

Tied up outboard of *Tennessee*, *West Virginia*, like *Oklahoma*, was taking a heavy beating. As Stu Hedley and his gunmate Croslin scrambled to their battle stations in turret three they soon discovered that, as bad as things were for them, another battleship was about to fare much worse.

"We knew we couldn't fire those 16-inch guns on Pearl, so consequently I was at my station, the pointer, he [Croslin] was at his station, the trainer and we have this 16 inch gun between us. It has an elevating screw that separates both of us but separating the right gun from the left gun is about 4 inches of solid steel. It's a partition and right down by my feet is a hatch which has 4 dogs [handles], and it's locked down tight. Croslin says, 'Stu, let's see what is going on.' So we took the sight cap off our periscope and bam! there went the *Arizona*. I told Croslin that must have gone right down the stack. We later found out it didn't go right down the stack, it went down the starboard side of the forecastle deck and into number

one handling room and exploded. I estimated about 32 bodies went flying through the air and little did I ever know that I was going to meet one of those bodies in the 8th Pearl Harbor Organization here in San Diego.

"Jack McCarran, who was aboard the *Arizona* and was getting ready to go on liberty, was a 2nd class gunner's mate and he had charge of all the 5 inch guns on the starboard side. He was preparing to go over on the beach for Shore Patrol so he was in his whites and everything and when the explosion took place he was thrown from the starboard side all the way across to the burning oil. Sixty-two percent of his body was burned and he didn't think he was going to live. He had just been married and his wife was back in Long Beach [California] and they were 3,000 miles separated and she doesn't know what's going on. He didn't want her to even know he was alive. They took him to the *Solace* and from there he went to the naval hospital in Brooklyn [New York] and I think he was there 4 or 5 months and he was starting to heal. Right after that explosion on the *Arizona*, we heard a dynamic explosion on our turret. They dropped it from a high level bomber and the armor-piercing shell hit the wing of our SO-2 scout observation plane, which is the gas tank — they were always gassed up and ready to go. That exploded and the SO-2 just burnt to a crisp, but on the catapult was also the Admiral's plane, which is known as the Kingfish. It blew that off of the catapult, split the catapult in half and then penetrated the 5 inches of steel and came down inside the turret and even though the shell did not explode it hit the recoil cylinder which is on the top of the gun.

"Being in my position as a gun pointer my feet would normally be out on a platform and I would bend over and crank in the dials so that the arrows would be pointing at one another, that's when I would be giving the order to fire. Croslin's is the same way but our feet were back up underneath us. When the explosion took place in the left gun the real explosion came from when the shell hit the recoil cylinder. The recoil cylinder is filled with glycerin so that when you fire that 16-inch gun you want it to come back to ready load not to oscillate. Well it split that casing and the glycerin flash fired killing 12 men in that left gun and it blew the hatch right off the four dogs right past my legs underneath the elevating screw and across Croslin's legs and hit against the barbet. It simultaneously picked both of us up and threw us back eight feet where the elevating screw came out of the deck. We picked ourselves up off the deck and said let's get out of here, though we didn't say it that nice. I had the JA [sound powered] phones on and I ran up the primer deck. I got to the primer deck level and I still had those crazy phones on and I reached the end of the cord. I grabbed it and snapped the cord and threw it down in the pit, and I never gave it a thought. When we got out on topside and were standing there Ensign Sears was screaming at us and we heard a weak voice from the bridge and it was our commanding officer [Captain Mervyn S. Bennion]. We did not know that he was mortally wounded, but the last words he uttered [were], 'abandon ship.'

"The commanding officer's battle station is the conning tower which is 16 inches solid steel all the way around. If he had stayed in there he probably would have survived. He [Captain Bennion] came out of the conning tower walked around to the starboard side of the flying deck and an armor-piercing shell hit the corner of turret two on the *Tennessee* and the shrapnel flew up and tore his stomach completely out. [Cook 3rd Class Doris] Dorie Miller who was his orderly was going to try to get him down to sick bay because he didn't realize how badly wounded he was."

USS *Nevada* was moored by herself north of *Arizona*. Woodrow Derby recounts how he spent the first few moments of the attack on *Nevada*.

"On December 7th 1941, I was sitting in my bunk reading the morning paper and I was going to go ashore. About five minutes of eight they said general quarters, all hands man your battle stations. We all said, 'What the hell's going on here?' Training on a Sunday morning that doesn't seem right, but up we went. So I went forward crossed over went down two more decks and I was in the broadside 5-inch gun powder magazine. We were there and I heard this thumping, a couple of bombs hit topside and all of a sudden just forward of us there was a tremendous explosion and a torpedo exploded in two compartments forward of where I was between turret one and turret two. Fortunately there was no 14-inch [gun] powder in those magazines because it was all unloaded the previous week working every day getting that powder up into a big barge that was still alongside the ship. If they had hit that barge and blown it up that would have wiped [out] the harbor completely, but they didn't know about it. In the magazine I was in about fifteen minutes after that torpedo hit water started coming in; it had split the welds in the bulkhead and water was coming in within 15 or 20 minutes. I had water up to my waist and we had to get out of there and up to the third deck."

Other than USS *Pennsylvania*, the battleships were all moored to large concrete quays southeast of Ford Island. Five of the battleships were moored in pairs and the inboard ships, *Maryland* and *Tennessee*, escaped the lethal damage of the torpedoes. USS *Arizona* was also moored inboard — inboard of the repair ship USS *Vestal*. At the very beginning of the attack, a torpedo passed forward of *Vestal* and struck the exposed forward part of *Arizona* under turret one.

"It all happened so fast," remembers USS *Arizona* survivor Lou Conter. "You have to remember, Pearl Harbor is two hours of a four-year war. It was burning all around us." He was ordered to keep calm whoever was injured or burned. "We grabbed them, laid them down on deck. The ship

was settling in the muck. We picked up bodies and body parts and people for a couple hours."

Ed Wise saw the explosions on *Arizona* from his vantage point in turret four of *Tennessee*, the closest to the doomed battleship.

"I looked through my [sighting] telescope and could see a big explosion from the USS *Arizona*. She took a direct [hit] bomb that went through her deck near

Navy personnel observe the attack's destruction on Ford Island where 1st Class Petty Officer Herb Franck was an Aviation Machinist Mate. "I was finishing breakfast and we heard boom, boom. As a matter of fact, the first bomb of the attack was dropped on Hangar Six on Ford Island. Then we heard the unfamiliar roar of the strafing Zeroes and we ran out to see what was happening. At the time the only lethal weapon that I had was my breakfast roll which I threw at one of the Zeroes going by. And I saw another Zero with the blips coming out of the wings so I dove behind a clump of palm trees, which was overlooking the California." *Sixty-five years later Franck observed the director of the Pacific Air Museum dig a 7.6 mm slug out of one of those trees and joke, "This must have had your name on it, Herb."*

turret one [actually turret two; a torpedo hit below turret one] at the bow and exploded in her magazine. All I could see was smoke and debris coming down on our ship, starting small fires, which were put out quickly. The ship shook violently and seemed to jump partly out of the water, then settling down. I could hear other explosions from the *West Virginia* on our port side. We stayed on station getting ready for a defense if needed."

Within ten minutes of the first bomb's drop, anti-aircraft fire was blazing from most of the ships in harbor. Bud Taylor, from Texas, was on *Pennsylvania.*

"On December 7th, when the attack come I had just bought me the paper, the *Honolulu Times* I think it was, and I lay down by a casemate and I was fixing to read it when the first bomb hit. I looked out this gun cut for this 5-inch which was sticking out broadside at Ford Island and I seen that airplane with a red circle on it — I said, 'Oh, my, that's it right there.' Of course we went to our battle stations. My battle station was on a .50 caliber on the

USS Cassin *(left) and USS* Downes *are seen during salvage operations a few months after a bomb hit in dry dock Number One and collapsed them toward one another. The bomb was meant for USS* Pennsylvania, *which was outboard of the two destroyers. In this photograph USS* Raleigh *(CL-7), also undergoing repairs for damage in the attack, occupies the space where* Pennsylvania *was on December 7.*

forward, starboard side and it was just right above the bridge of the battleship.

"We had targets, they were coming in from every which way; this way, that way, they just flied in a swarm; they's just like a hive of bees coming through there. You just picked out the one you thought you could get, and I got a bullet, I got it off that plane and I got it at home. It come in off our port bow and it seemed like his wing wasn't far at all when he made his circle across our bow like that. He hit right even with us and of course we picked him up, when it come to our part we picked him right up. I see this Japanese right now sorta raised up in that rear seat back there and had this machine gun, tat-a-tat that was right here, say, and of course my head is exposed — the shield wouldn't have stopped it anyway probably. After the battle was over we was cleaning up this trash we had on the deck, and I found this bullet. It was smashed and had hit the superstructure right above my head and then fell down on the deck. I could see it put a dent in the ship. I still have it."

Ray Richmond and Don Lester were among many who survived the attack on *Oklahoma* by getting off the ship. Many in the crew were trapped by the sudden capsizing of the battleship. But thirty-two sailors survived the ordeal including James Baund.

"We were out a couple of weeks before the 7th for training, firing guns. We came in late on Friday the 5th and we had admiral's material inspection on Monday so we had to start cleaning up. They asked me if I would clean up the steering department, so that's where I was on Dec. 7th. I was just ready to start cleaning; all I had on was my underwear ['skivvies' in navy slang]. Down there cleaning you know, it's hot, nobody showed up that far down on the ship. I was cleaning up and next thing I heard they passed the word, Jap planes attacking Ford Island. I'm willing to say no drill because that instant — Rommel was his name — run by the speaker 1-MC there and pass the word and he went on to turret number 4. He was a forward division officer and he was in charge of turret #4 but he used a 4-letter word. I looked at the other guys — there's seven of us down there and I looked at them — I'd never heard a word like that used on the 1-MC — you don't do that. So immediately we tried to go to a normal general quarters down there and set up, but everything began to happen. We got hit by three rapid torpedoes and it really shook the ship, it seemed like the ship raised up and then started to settle back down but then it started turning to port. The lights went out and no emergency battle lanterns came on. We got one light down there and that was a 1st Class electrician's mate and he was the only guy we had and he had a flashlight.

"Well anyway when the lights went out and the ship started turning to port and all this stuff began to break loose, we had spare parts and of course we had some jocks down there too, wrestlers, and we had barbells but that wasn't secured, the other stuff was. It began to break as the ship turned to port. I put my hand on the bunk head locker there way on the port side and I was going to run to the starboard side near these four wheels and I put my hand up there and my thumb got caught between the bunk and the locker. I had to really stretch that before I could get it out, it took two men to put those lockers up and I moved it with my left hand. You can imagine what a guy can do when he has to, and that still, you can see it right there, I never realized it was broken 'til later. The ship kept turning over and it turned over to 151 degrees and the mast stuck in the mud. I think that harbor channel was beneath sea level, 40 feet beneath sea level. Our draft at that time was about 32 feet because we had loaded up. But anyway after it turned over and settled in the mud water started coming in. These big old mushroom vents that they had up on the 01 level at the top of the ship, nobody took those down so the vent system, when it turned over, water came in that system.

"We took everything we could there and when the water started coming in we tried to stop it in one length of that tubing and it'd break out some place else. We took turns beating on the bulkhead, we had 2 wrenches, and of course this water coming in — it was as much oil as it was water — coming in the compartment. You could hear the guard workmen working and probably the ship's repair from the ship were working. You could hear them come to and then go so far in a space they couldn't quite get to it on account maybe there's oil in that void,

that space. So they had to stop and go back and try another way. So we were down there between 32 and 36 hours, closer to 36 hours I guess taking turns beating [to make noise]. By the time the guys got there you could hear each other breathing. It had filled up about to my waist and air pressure held it, just like getting under an old tub or something and that's all the air you have what's under there until it disappears. So the fate of us and breathing that you could hear each other breathe. One of the guys, maybe it was the electrician's mate, said, 'Hey, let's don't talk save your breath and air here', so we did. About 20 men from shop 11 was credited with cutting us out the day after the attack. In fact there were a total of 32 men

A B-17 bomber, one of those that arrived from California during the attack, burned in half after being strafed near Hangar # 5 at Hickam Air Field.

cut out of the ship after it turned over and all and the 32 got cut out, they received citations, the navy gave them citations. We were next to the last group to get out — there were two guys who got out of the ship after my group back there. I was probably about the 29th one of the 32 cut out of the ship."

Of the battleships, only *Nevada* was able to get up steam and get underway during the attack. Woodrow Derby describes *Nevada*'s trip down the southwest rim of Ford Island and the state of the battleships she passed.

"Shortly after that the ship got underway and

started down the channel. I don't know where we were going to go, but we were going to move out. We were under the stern of the *Arizona* when we got underway and passed the *Arizona*. We had to cover — up on deck they had to cover the ammunition with their bodies because the heat coming from the *Arizona* was so hot they were afraid they'd blow up. The next one was the *West Virginia* in a sinking condition. It settled straight down and the *Tennessee* was inboard of it but it was not damaged, not much anyway. Next was the *Oklahoma*, hit with 9 torpedoes and rolled over on the side. Now think of this, if you're in this room you can see but if all the lights go off and you're down deep in the ship and it rolls over like this and the ladders all fall off — you don't know where the hell you're going. How are you going to get out? The next one was the *California*, right forward of the *Oklahoma*. She was hit with two torpedoes and a large bomb went in and killed 85 or 90 people and she settled. It took her two days before she got down to the bottom. The *Nevada* was the first one to be raised and we went into dry dock, partially repaired and we went back to Bremerton and they rebuilt it."

As *Nevada* steamed down the channel, dive bombers originally headed for *Pennsylvania* turned on the ship underway. Derby describes this action.

"As we got started down the channel the second wave of Japanese planes came over and we were hit with five, six or seven more bombs. The ship was then in a sinking condition. It nosed up on the beach at Hospital Point but the tide was coming in and it swung the ship out into the harbor, in the channel. Two tugs took us and pushed us to the far side of the channel and it settled down on a coral reef. I always say coral reef because that sounds better than mud bank. We didn't know what was going to happen then; we lost 50 sailors who were killed and six or seven Marines were killed and we had over 100 crew members who

were seriously injured. Our 5-inch guns were 5-inch 25-caliber guns. They were operated with 'swing by hand' to move around and during drills the previous time a plane would come over towing a target behind it and they would shoot at it and they would say 'slow down, we can't keep up with you' so that was another thing that wouldn't work. We sent up powder to the broadside guns. They were 5-inch shells that weighed about 85 – 90 pounds. There was no [time] fuse on them so they had to hit something to explode [impact fuse]. We sent that up and they started shooting at the Japanese planes coming in but there's no way they're going to hit those planes. The shells went over and landed in Honolulu and there were 68 civilians killed and they were probably our shells. They always said it was the Japanese bombs, but it was our shells that were going over and some of the other ships also. I think we knocked down two planes and that was about it."

Of the 94 ships tied up in Pearl Harbor that fateful Sunday morning, only eight were battleships. One, *Utah*, was a decommissioned battleship converted to a target ship. While the well-planned Japanese attack focused on the battle wagons, nearly every other ship was targeted by horizontal bombers, dive bombers and strafing by all of Fuchida's aircraft. The ships on the northwest edge of Ford Island took some unintended fire because these berths were normally occupied by aircraft carriers, a fact no doubt passed on by Japan's Honolulu spies. Ships such as the destroyer USS *Shaw*, minelayer USS *Oglala* and light cruiser USS *Helena* were destroyed or severely damaged, probably due to their proximity to the exposed 1010 dock and *Pennsylvania* in dry dock. Destroyers USS *Downes* and the previously mentioned *Cassin* were demolished by Japanese pilots trying to get at *Pennsylvania*.

In its meticulous planning to destroy the fighting capability of the U. S. Pacific Fleet, the Ris-

ing Sun Empire's military seemed to discount the support facilities of the fleet's principal base. Headquarters buildings, communications centers, petroleum tank farms and even the sub base received no direct bombing and only collateral strafing damage. Tucked back in the easternmost berth of the base sat USS *Caster*. The unassuming supply ship had a deadly cargo that, according to one crew member, could have radically changed the attack that Sunday morning.

John Morrill from Rochester, New York was part of a group of recruits from that city who joined the Navy in 1940. *Caster* was Morrill's first active duty ship.

The first targets hit were Ford Island and Kaneohe Bay seaplane bases which were primary targets so "the navy couldn't put up planes to locate the Japanese carriers," says Gordon Jones. Jones is seen here with his back to the camera by the wing of a Catalina seaplane at Kaneohe Bay while the opposite side of the wing burns.

"We pulled in late on Friday the 5th and tied up. There was not much doing on Saturday; they did get a rail car on the dock side for off-loading it. We barely got started on Saturday off-loading when it was time for us to take our leave. I didn't go ashore, I stayed aboard and I was off watch Sunday morning. I got up and went up to the galley and shot the breeze for a half hour or so and then I decided to go down and start writing my Christmas cards. I just sat on my bunk and was about to write my first when a petty officer came through the compartment screaming, 'The Japs are here, the Japs are here, man your battle stations!' I just dropped everything and jumped up and went up to head for my battle station, which was down in the ammunition locker

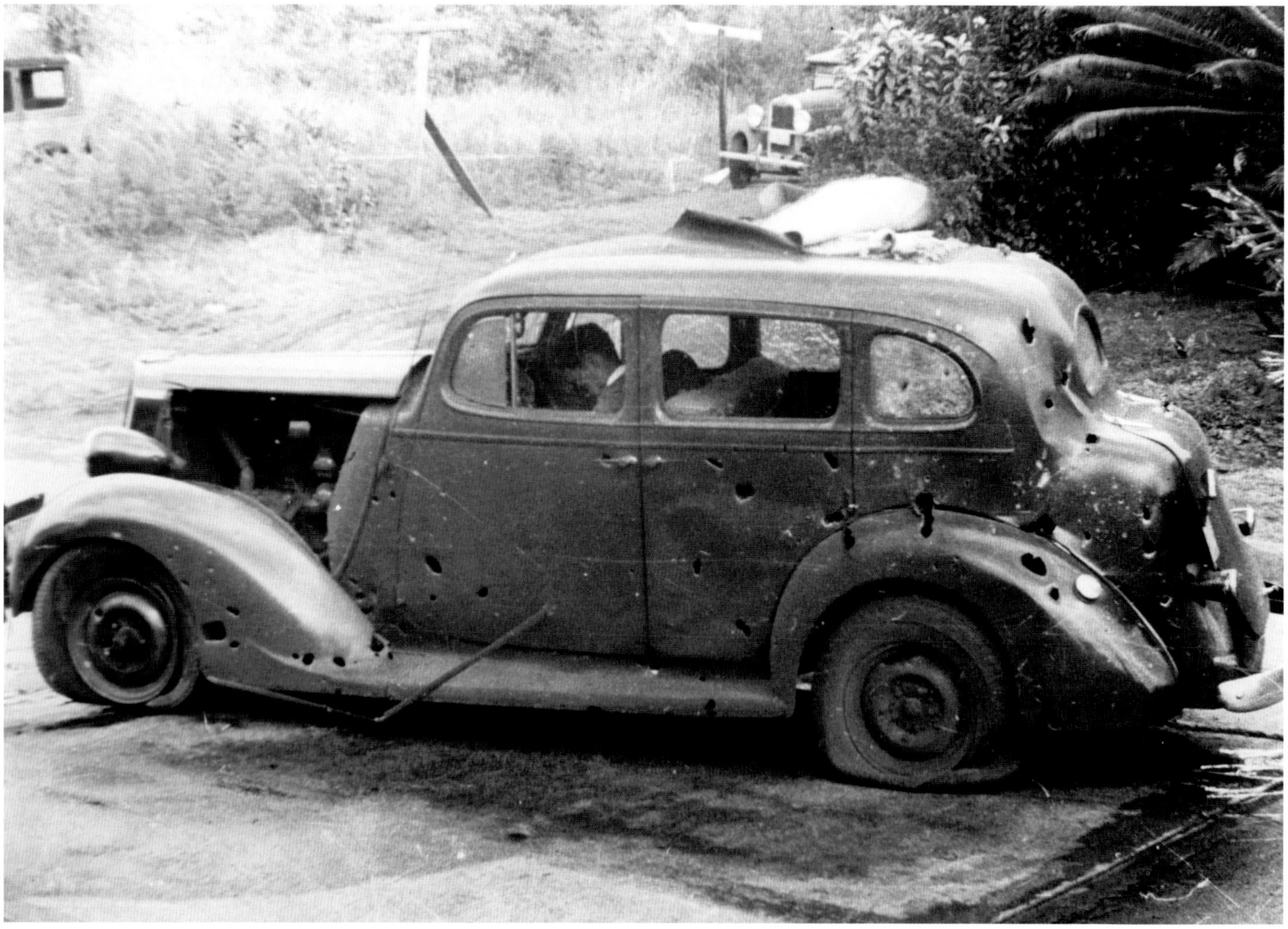

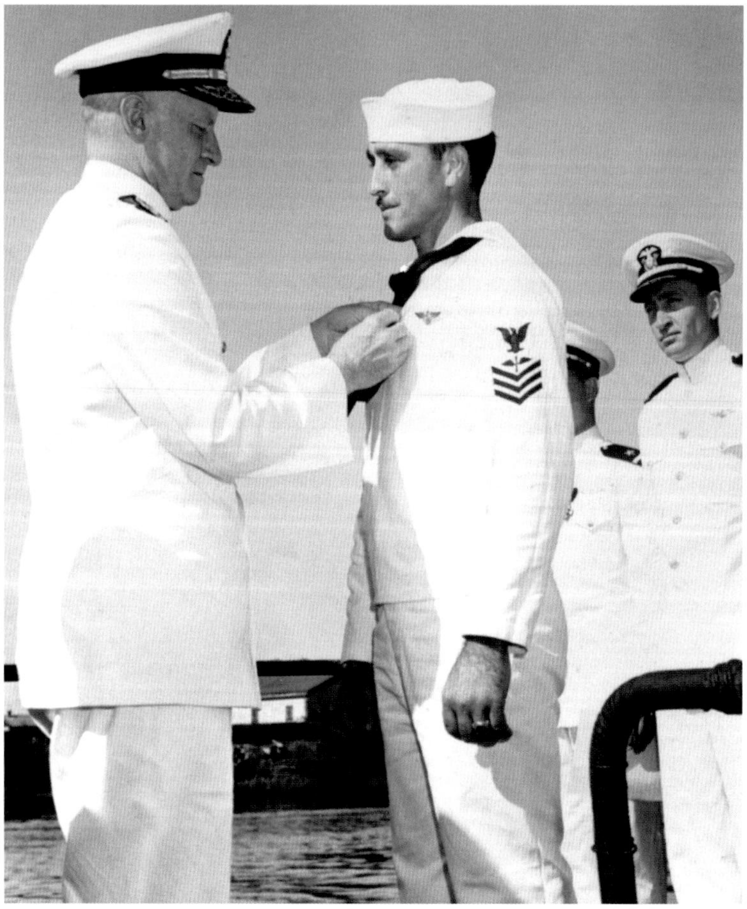

TOP – Not all of December 7th casualties were in the U. S. military. This car carrying four civilian navy yard workers heading to Pearl Harbor was struck by shrapnel from a Japanese bomb, killing three and mortally wounding the fourth occupant eight miles from the base. Large ordnance fired by U. S. Navy ships during the melee also landed indiscriminately in Honolulu even though precautions were taken. Art Kowalski was aboard Pennsylvania*. "We couldn't use a five inch, because the local citizens would be blasted away. So they dispersed all the people from all secondary guns — go back to your station. My second station would be damage control, or aid and assistance. And we couldn't do anything at that place, so they shipped us over to the forecastle to start cleaning up the debris. Don't throw it over the side because you got oil down there. And that was it." BOTTOM – Admiral Chester Nimitz, as one of his first duties after assuming the CinCPAC command, decorates some of the many individuals who acted heroically on December 7. These naval airmen receive medals in this photograph aboard the submarine USS* Grayling *(SS-209).*

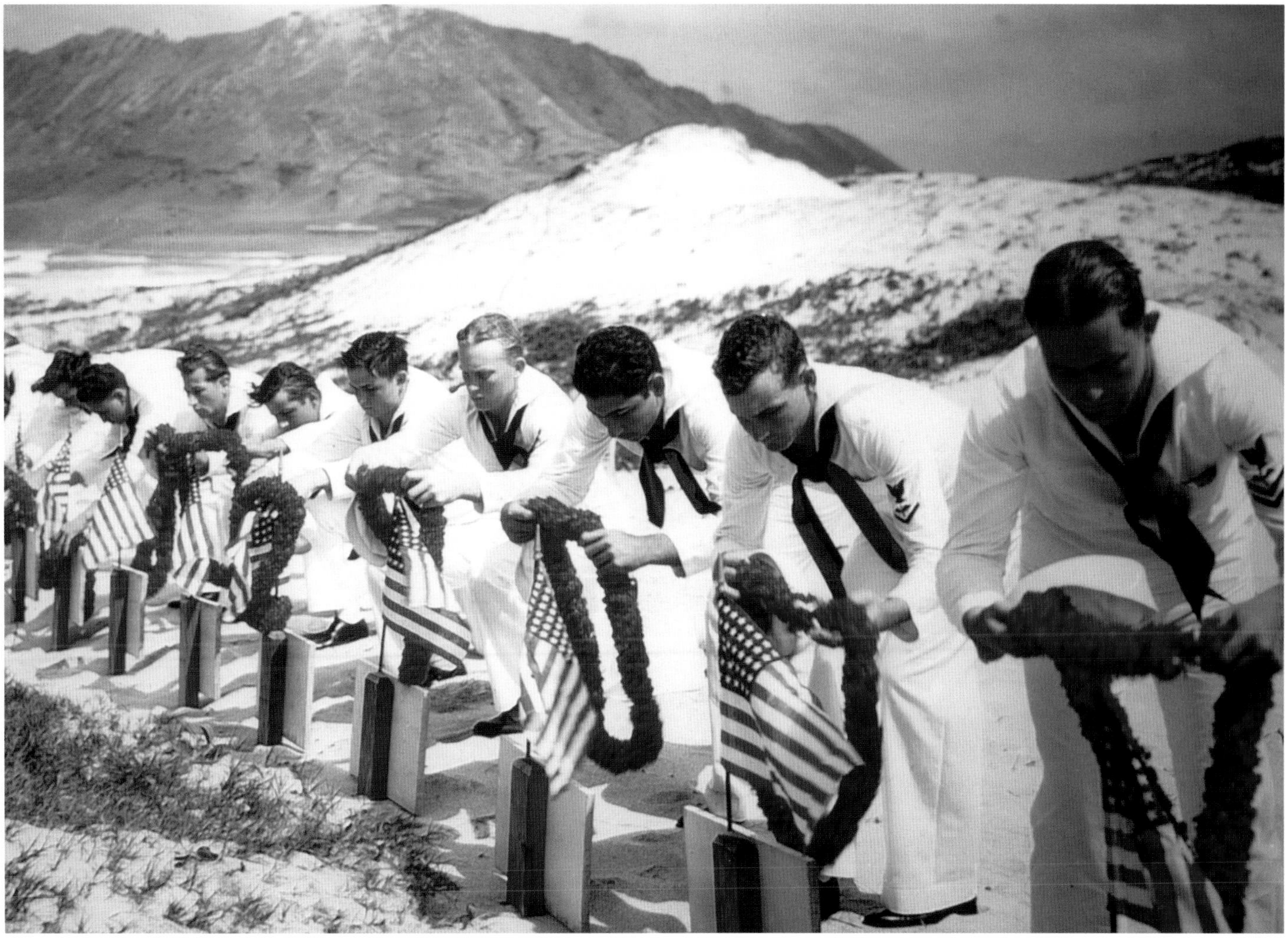

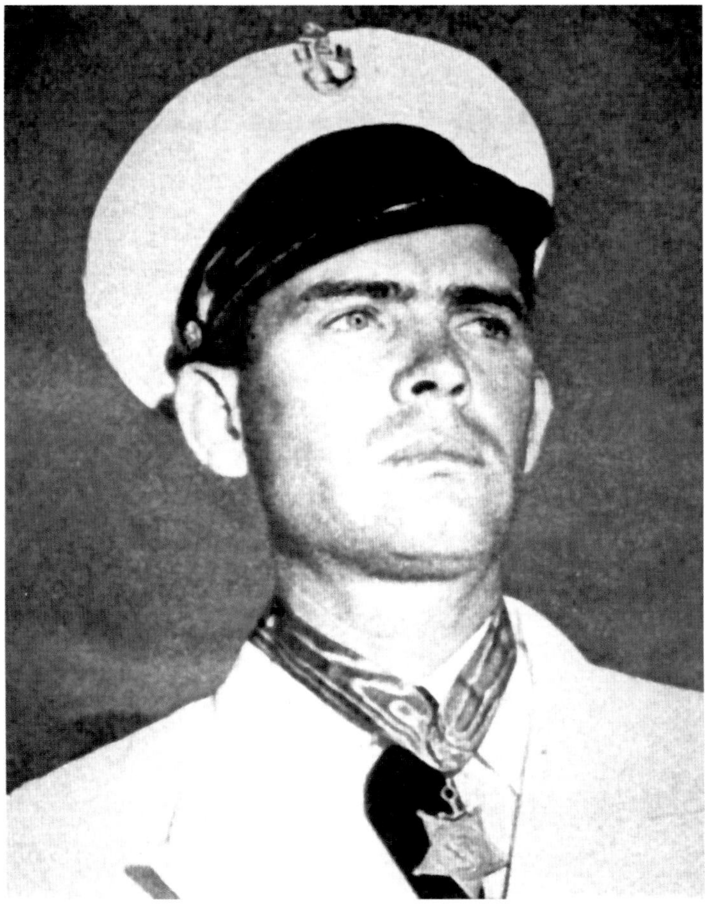

TOP – At Kaneohe Bay on Memorial Day, 1942, a ceremony in the Hawaiian tradition honors men killed in action on Dec. 7, 1941. BOTTOM – CPO John William Finn was aviation ordnance chief for VP-14 at Kaneohe Bay in December 1941 and received a Medal of Honor for manning a machine gun in the hanger area. Despite receiving five wounds from attacking Japanese planes, he refused to leave his post.

sending ammo up to the guns. As I was racing across the starboard side of the ship [topside] I happened to look over my shoulder and here was a Japanese plane on his approach with his torpedo coming out there and about that time his machine guns started chattering. I didn't think much about it that day but I think today he must have been shooting at me.

"I had the earphones on so I could hear what ammunition they wanted and all I could hear was screaming by the gun captain training the gun here and training the gun there and I wondered what was going on up there because he seemed to be unsettled. They were coming from all over and he had to train the gun wherever he saw a plane coming. Where we were — they hit us and the oil fire up there would have wiped out the submarine base. During the attack they said we had to get them [*Caster*] out of there because we had all that ammo on there. When you're loading ammo or carrying ammo or oil you put up a red flag for a dangerous situation — so everybody approaching you knows to be careful. A lieutenant going to his battle station said, 'Somebody get that flag down,' and I know that fellow who did it. The Japanese had precise information about what we were doing and I can't understand today how come they didn't take [advantage of our dangerous situation]. Well, supposedly we were probably going to be in the third grade [wave]. The first grade was to take the air force so they couldn't get up and the second grade was to get the battleships and the fighting force and the third would be mop-up. I think that's what we were and fortunately the Japanese admiral in command of the whole works cancelled that third grade. I guess that saved me really."

Bravery and casualties crossed all pay grades at Pearl Harbor. Stu Hedley, a *West Virginia* survivor, talks about one of the many decorated heroes of that day.

"When he [Captain Bennion] died right there on the bridge old Dorie Miller was furious and he grabbed a machine gun and started shooting at planes as they went by. Dorie Miller stood about 6 feet 3 inches and weighed about 298 pounds, but I'm ashamed to say this, at this time the Blacks and Hispanics could not serve as bosun's mates [or] storekeepers at those rates [ranks]. They were mess attendants, were cooks and orderlies, that was it. The very act that Dorie Miller performed, in my estimation, rightfully deserved the Medal of Honor for his bravery and for what he did. However when they had them all lined up on the deck of the *Enterprise*, there were 12 Medals of Honor awarded [to White sailors] and he received the Navy Cross."

Aboard *Akagi* and the other Japanese carriers, preparations for the second air strike began as the first group flew off. The largest contingent of the second wave was the dive bombers, a group of 78 planes. By 0900 hours the second wave appeared over Pearl Harbor. Bud Taylor aboard *Pennsylvania* describes the second wave.

"Well, the second wave wasn't so bad. They had these high altitude bombers when they came over and dropped them bombs, and they got battleship row where all these battleships was lined up. We was over in this dry dock where we wasn't supposed to be. Flagship, the *Pennsylvania* was a flagship, you know. So they really went to work on these battleships on Ford Island. They were dive bombers. They come right in, just about the time that [they] come by me I was shooting at this guy and I don't know he might have been the guy who hit either the *Shaw* [actually USS *Downes*] or I forgot the name [USS *Cassin*]. He either hit the side of one of them, or right in between because it turned both of them like this and burned up both of them. Without a doubt, the *Shaw* [*Downes*] was down. They put one in construc-

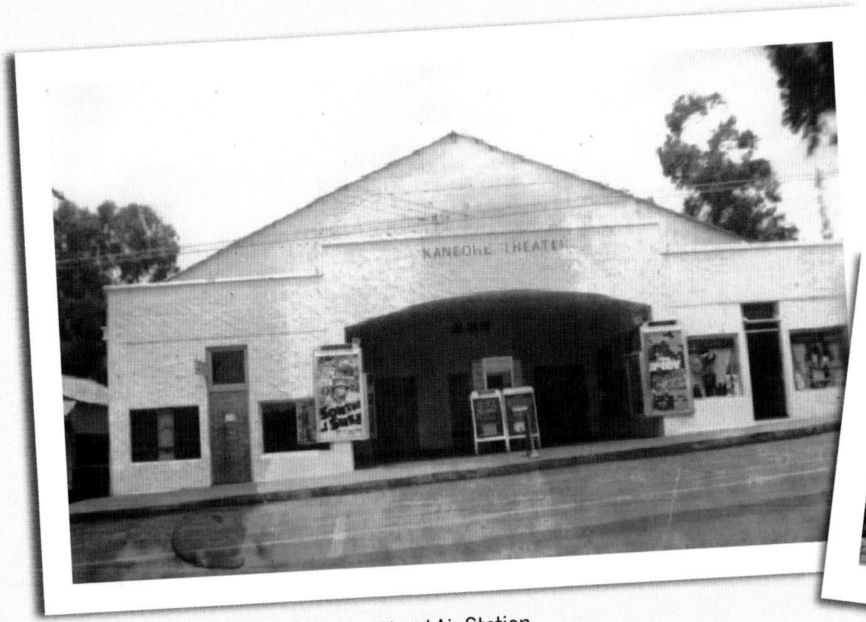
KANEOHE THEATER

The movie theater at Kaneohe Bay Naval Air Station.

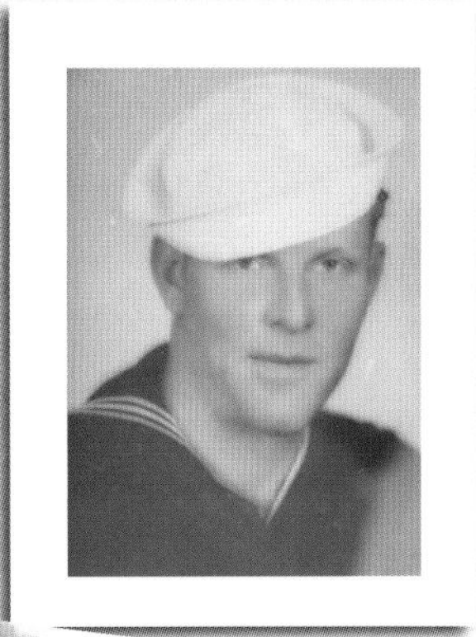

Don Lester as a young sailor in a hand-tinted photograph.

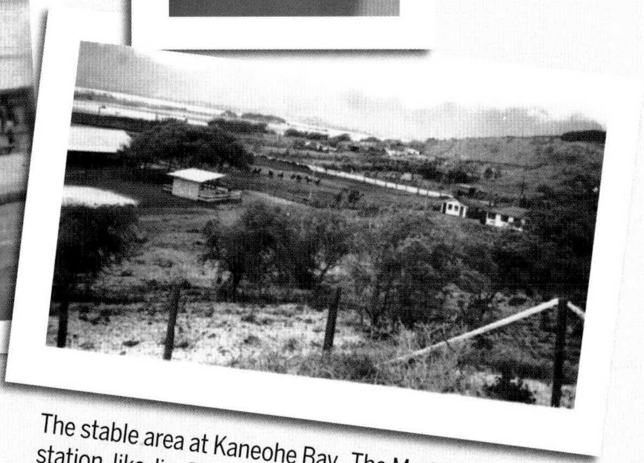

The stable area at Kaneohe Bay. The Marines at the station, like Jim Evans, were formed into mounted squads to patrol the expansive base.

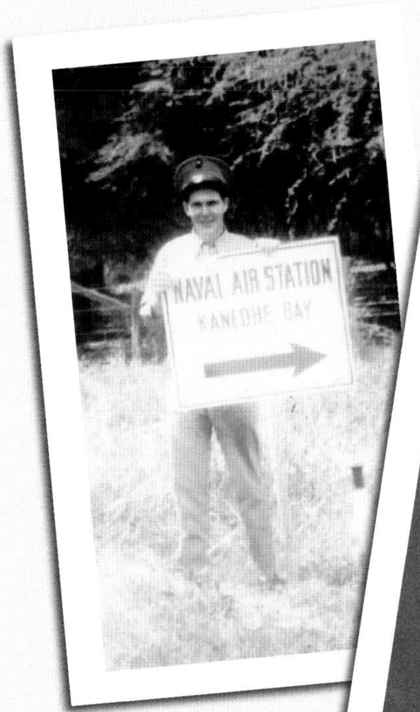
NAVAL AIR STATION
KANEOHE BAY

Cpl. Jim Evans in a pre-war photograph.

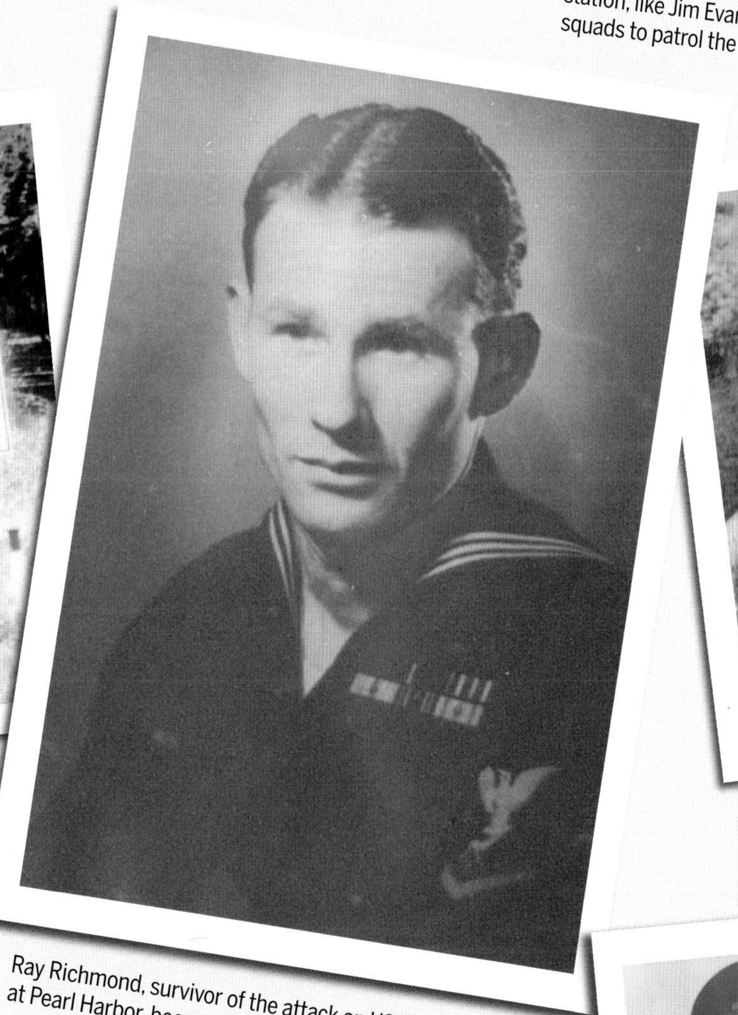

Ray Richmond, survivor of the attack on USS *Oklahoma* at Pearl Harbor, became a graphic artist for the navy after recovering from his Pearl Harbor wounds.

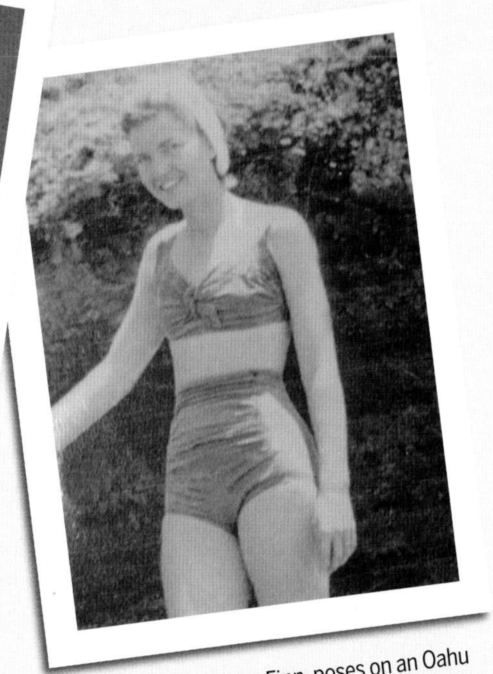

Alice Finn, wife of John Finn, poses on an Oahu Beach during Finn's tour of duty at Kaneohe Bay.

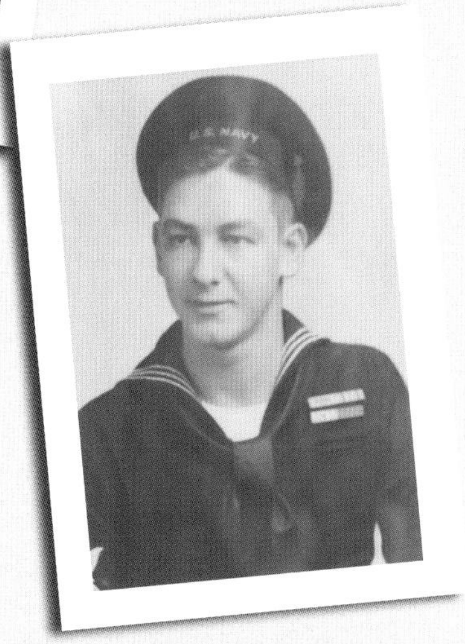

Joseph Kawka in a hand-tinted wartime photograph. Like many sailors whose ships were damaged or destroyed at Pearl Harbor he was quickly reassigned after the attack.

"In December of 1940 I went out to Kaneohe for TAD, temporary additional duty. They were just building the place, sending the Marines from all over for the guard duty and stuff and then they made the TAD permanent. There were about 90 of us out there. It was really good duty. A long time in the distant past it would have been a vacation [spot] for the rich people, I guess. It was a beautiful duty station, the paradise of the Pacific, until December 7th. After that it was pretty bad." —Jim Evans

tion [*Cassin*], fixed it and put it back in service, but the other [*Downes*] was just all burned up so they just salvaged it and then threw it away."

John Morrill mentioned an important fact that is often overlooked in the sensational attacks on the battleships at Pearl Harbor — the Japanese strike's early concentration on destroying U. S. air assets. A portion of the attacking force in the first wave headed for Oahu's navy, Marine and Army Air Corps bases. Among the first targeted were the navy's PBY *Catalina* scouting seaplanes. With the scouts out of action, the ability of the American forces to track the Japanese planes back to their carriers would be eliminated. Knocking out the fighters — a task made simpler for the Japanese by the fact that the U. S. planes were parked closely together in the open, out on the airfields' tarmacs — prevented the attackers from being challenged in the air. The first strike on U. S. airfields, by accident or design, was at Ford Island Naval Air Station (NAS). Soon, other Japanese squadrons separated north of Oahu to bomb and strafe the Army's Wheeler and Hickam Fields, the Marine Corps Air Station at Ewa and the Navy's PBY base at Kaneohe. John Finn, a fifteen-year Navy veteran, was an ordnance chief at the Kaneohe Bay NAS when the attack came. He was driving

TOP: President Franklin D. Roosevelt addresses a joint session of the U. S. Congress on December 8 and asks for a declaration of war in response to Japan's surprise attack on Pearl Harbor and their war declaration on the United States. Only one representative, Jeanette Rankin of Montana, a strict pacifist, kept the vote from being unanimous. RIGHT: The first draft of President Franklin D. Roosevelt's war declaration speech delivered on December 8 with FDR's hand-written revisions. The speech was full of strong oratory which began with, "Yesterday, December 7, 1941– a date which will live in infamy…," a phrase that became a brilliant and lasting battle cry for a nation so wronged.

some groceries back to his house only to find the base under attack.

"When I left my place, the speed limit on the base was 20 miles an hour and it was very strictly enforced. Of course, I was going along in high gear, about 25 mph. And about that time, an airplane came from the stern of me, behind me. I heard it coming. And when he got right along side of me, I was driving along and I looked out the side window and he was right in my field of view. But he just put a wing down, one wing down a little bit. I looked at the underside of that wing and there was that Japanese old rising sun [laugh] and I said, 'Buddy, this is the real McCoy. This is the damn Japs.' I broke every speed limit that they ever had on that base. I got right down there to Search Point. The road made a hard right turn — sand over here — right down there was the docks — deep sand in that there. I turned around that corner. And I remember that I picked up a sailor right after I left my parking area. This is before I knew it the Japs were there. So he was in the rear seat and I said 'What squadron, bud?' And he says, 'Right here.'

"I skidded to a halt, he jumped out and he slammed the door and I took off, about a half a mile straight down this road. The last hangar on the left was my squadron hangar, VP14. There

DRAFT No. 1 December 7, 1941.

PROPOSED MESSAGE TO THE CONGRESS

Yesterday, December 7, 1941 — a date which will live in ~~world history~~ infamy — the United States of America was ~~simultaneously~~ suddenly and deliberately attacked by naval and air forces of the Empire of Japan ~~without warning~~.

The United States was at peace with that nation and, at the solicitation of Japan, was ~~continuing the~~ still in conversations with its Government and its Emperor looking toward the maintenance of peace in the Pacific. Indeed, one hour after Japanese air squadrons had commenced bombing in ~~Hawaii and the Philippines~~ Oahu, the Japanese Ambassador to the United States and his colleague delivered to the Secretary of State a formal reply to a ~~former~~ recent American message ~~from the Secretary~~. While this reply ~~contained a statement~~ stated that it seemed useless to continue the existing diplomatic negotiations ~~must be considered at an end, but~~ it contained no threat ~~and no~~ or hint of ~~an~~ war or armed attack.

It will be recorded that the distance ~~of Manila, and especially~~ of Hawaii from Japan makes it obvious that the ~~se~~ attack ~~were~~ was deliberately planned many days or even weeks ago. During the intervening time the Japanese Government has deliberately sought to deceive the United States by false statements and expressions of hope for continued peace.

was plenty of parking there. I just shot right into that place, threw on my brake, shut off my engine and everything, jumped out of my car and started to run. [laugh] I could hear machine gun fire. My armory was right in the far corner of the hangar. Then I heard machine guns going off quite loud."

Gordon Jones, from Wildwood, New Jersey, had recently joined the navy and was also in VP-14 squadron at Kaneohe Bay. He and his brother, another sailor, had just arrived in Hawaii at the beginning of December. Jones was expecting a visit from an army buddy that Sunday morning who was coming over from Schofield Barracks.

"We were awakened earlier by the sound of a machine gun, rat-ta-tat-tat and kiddingly we said it must be the Army doing a wake-up call. We looked down toward the hangars which was some distance from the barracks and there was smoke coming up. I had my clean white uniform on and was ready to go meet my friend, and a bunch of us ran down toward the hangars where the planes were parked outside. We had thirty-six planes and there were three of them flying that day. In fact one of them was actually hit by one of the Japanese aircraft going back to his carrier. The rest of them were fighters and they had used incendiary bullets, according to the ordnance people. We had never seen any incendiary bullets with chemical in it.

"Our aircraft were twin-engine PBY's and no one had ever seen what they [incendiary bullets] did to them, the wing panels were fabric with heavy lacquer and they immediately caught fire. The gasoline leaked out of the planes and we tried to put it out with different methods. I got by the firehouse and fighters were firing with machine guns to get into the firehouse and the fire engine was gone. We learned later that it was machine-gunned which killed the guys on the

fire engine, so they wouldn't put out the fires. The Japanese were very good about that stuff, they had it planned right down to the instant. One of our officers called the naval station on Ford Island. He said send some planes over here, we're being attacked and the reply was 'go to hell we're being attacked ourselves.' So we were actually attacked about four minutes before Pearl. They wanted to get our seaplanes so they couldn't scout and find [the Japanese] fleet and they did a marvelous job of that. While that was going on we had one plane, a spare, and we tried to launch it but it was machine-gunned and it was leaking."

The casualties for the day for the American military forces were 2,402 killed (or died later of wounds) and 1,247 wounded. Sixty-eight civilians were killed and 35 wounded in and around the bases and by bombs that fell in Honolulu and elsewhere, including shells fired by American ships. The most casualties occurred on USS *Arizona* which incinerated and sunk quickly after the magazine explosion. The number of dead or missing, 1177, included Rear Adm. Isaac C. Kidd and Capt. Franklin Van Valkenburgh, *Arizona*'s skipper. Forty-four officers and enlisted men of the ship's complement were wounded. Citations for bravery were plentiful: African American seaman Doris (Dorie) Miller, as mentioned, received the Navy Cross; John William Finn was awarded the Medal of Honor, as were others. Many commanders reported afterward that their crews and officers acted professionally, efficiently and without panic during the surprise attack.

The Day After

The attack on Pearl Harbor was not a diversion in the Japanese war plan as some accounts have suggested. It was an integral part of the strategy designed by Admiral Ya-

California Here I Come

The attack on Pearl Harbor threw the United States into panic and confusion. On America's west coast, the alarm was particularly acute. The closest any Japanese force got to the U. S. mainland were the "I" class submarines submerged off the coast of Oregon and California on December 7; but the idea of an invasion via the cliffs and beaches of California and the sounds and inlets of Oregon and Washington was a genuine concern. Searchlights and machine guns were set up in major cities. On the great military compound of Angel Island in San Francisco Bay and other bases, army and navy personnel were put on alert. Military units up and down the coast prepared as best they could, while civilian officials dealt with a brewing panic in the civilian population.

Bill Persky was a Marine assigned to Camp Elliot north of San Diego. He remembers, "We had a radio in our barracks and we had it on all day every day. Pretty soon all the music stopped and the announcer started coming on, 'Pearl Harbor has been bombed, Pearl Harbor has been bombed,' and the action really started. This was about noon and they got everybody on the post together and assigned duties, and I was assigned to take a .50-caliber machine crew to the beach in La Jolla. We got ammunition and sand bags and trucks and hauled the .50-caliber machine guns and spent the night there and the next day and another night. Pretty soon they decided maybe the Japanese weren't going to land here so they called it

A mainland army unit prepares its gun for an impending attack. But the Japanese never came.

off and we never did fire a shot."

Lloyd Kingston was also at Camp Elliot. He recalls the order to his tank training company after the Japanese bombed Pearl Harbor, "On December 7th they had us running up and down that sunny afternoon, running up and down the coast highway [in our tanks], you know, expecting the Japanese to attack the west coast, but they didn't."

Glenn Boeck, who on December 7 was in the command bunker at Fort Shafter manning a radio-telegraph, was in artillery training at Camp Callen, La Jolla, California six months earlier. The recruits were firing 8-inch French artillery pieces on what is now Torrey Pines Golf Course. Boeck wonders if America would have been ready for an invasion. "If the Japanese had decided to invade California those artillery pieces would have been obsolete," recalls Boeck.

mamoto and accepted by Japanese officials up to and including the Emperor. In timing it was the lynchpin of the Greater East Asia War. The first bomb dropped by one of Fuchida's planes signaled the start of offensives in Malaysia, the Philippines, Wake Island and elsewhere, which due to their location west of the International Date Line began on December 8 [December 7, Honolulu time].

As seconds stretched to minutes and then to hours after 0753 hours on December 7, nearly every American and many others around the world remember where they were when they heard the news. Secretary of State Cordell Hull received the fourteen-part Japanese diplomatic message late from Kichisaburo Nomura and Saburo Kuruso at the state department – Hull already knew that Japanese bombs had fallen on Pearl Harbor. By 0900 Honolulu time President Roosevelt gathered with his secretaries of War, Navy and State at the White House to listen to Admiral Claude Bloch (CO of the 14th Naval District which included Pearl Harbor) describe the situation over the phone. Winston Churchill was dining in his London residence, Chequers, with his daughter, Mary, and American diplomats when an aide brought in a portable radio for the prime minister to learn of the attack from BBC news. Later that evening, Churchill received a transatlantic call from Roosevelt. "We are all in the same boat now," Roosevelt told the embattled British Prime Minister.

Shock, despair and sadness shrouded the United States throughout the day. But by the next morning, those who had foreseen the possibility of attack joined those still in shocked disbelief to manifest a burning desire for revenge against the "sneak attack's" perpetrators and to demand America's rapid war mobilization. As military and political leaders tallied the casualties, assessed the damage and sifted through the information coming from Pacific bases and out-

posts, President Roosevelt galvanized the country for war with his address to the U. S. Congress and the American people, calling December 7, 1941 "a date which will live in infamy." Young men across the nation took immediate action – they jammed recruiting stations.

At Pearl Harbor, the wounded were treated, the dead were identified when possible and, as related by many of the survivors, sailors were reassigned to crew ships readying for action. Thanks to immediate and aggressive patrolling, no ships were damaged or sunk by the Japanese submarines and midget subs in the Advance Expeditionary Force, which quietly withdrew in groups of 20 for Kwajalein except for nine subs that were directed to join the two already prowling along the U. S. West Coast.

While the U. S. Pacific Fleet planned for offensive action with its serviceable ships, personnel in other military units were attending to their jobs. The thankless task of assessing damage to ships, aircraft and facilities had begun. In time, salvage operations would begin; but first welders and rescuers concentrated on the desperate work of cutting through the thickly armored hull of the overturned *Oklahoma* to reach the trapped sailors still alive after the attack. Inevitably, reputations would also be salvaged or sunk based on perceived blame for the lack of preparedness at Pearl Harbor and Oahu. Though the investigation would last for years, Admiral Kimmel and General Short were sacked within weeks. They were the most visible members of an American military leadership that had grossly underestimated the capabilities of their new foe.

Mess attendant Doris (Dorie) Miller received the Navy Cross for his actions aboard USS West Virginia on Dec. 7. Many say he should have received the Medal of Honor but was denied the nation's highest military honor because of his race.

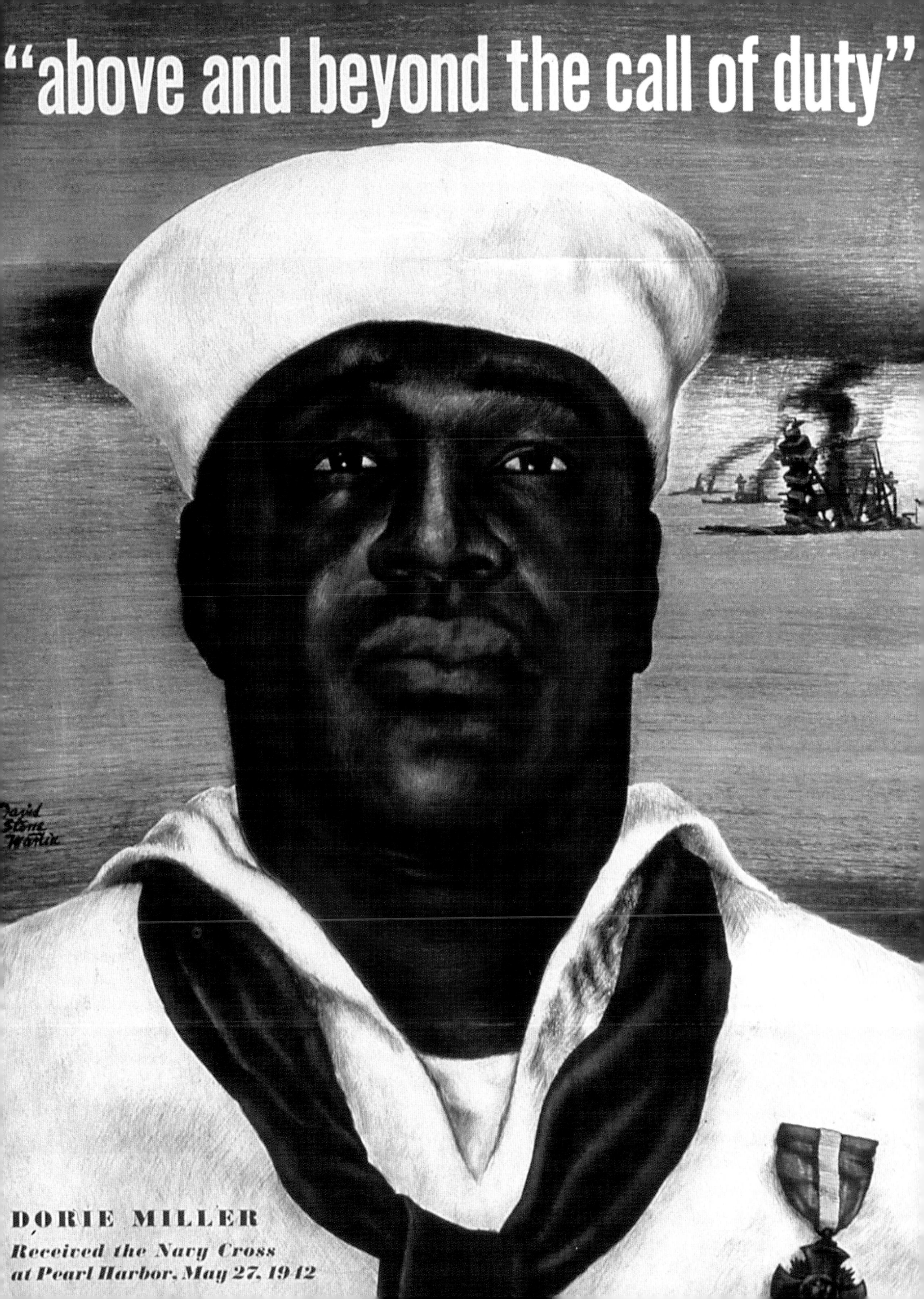
"above and beyond the call of duty"
David Stone Martin
DORIE MILLER
Received the Navy Cross
at Pearl Harbor, May 27, 1942

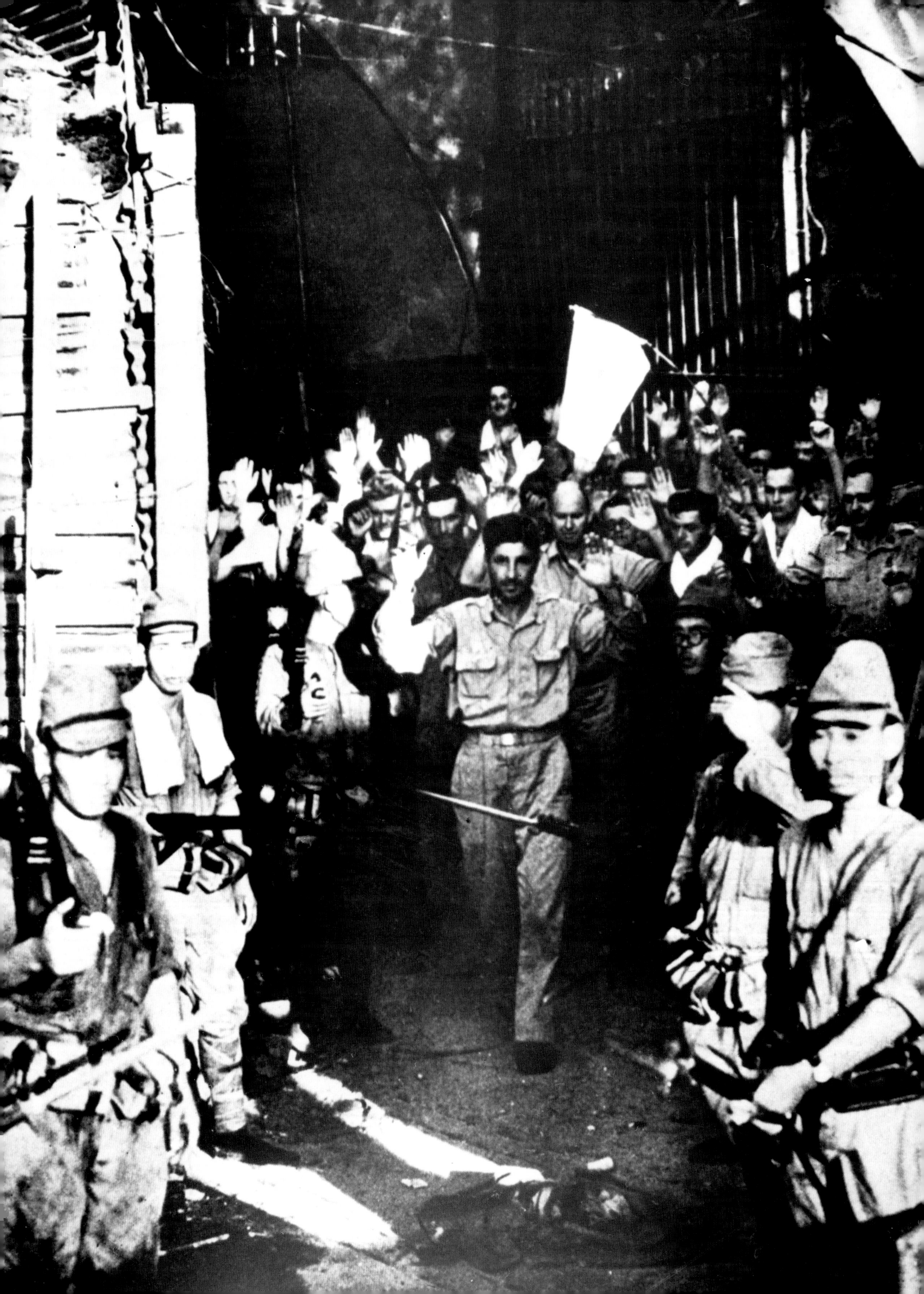

CHAPTER 3

Japanese Expansion after Pearl Harbor

Campaign for the Philippines

The United States began her military presence in the Philippines on May 1, 1898 and continued occupation of the islands after the December 1898 treaty signed in Paris to end America's brief War with Spain. The Filipino resistance under Emilio Aguinaldo, allied with the Americans against Spain, was sorely disappointed when the United States delayed Philippines independence. Yet the opportunity for a strategic military presence in the Far East, based in the nearly 7100 island archipelago (primarily on the largest island, Luzon) was too good to pass up. The Filipinos then turned their highly effective guerilla tactics on the Americans for a few years and eventually would use them on the Japanese. Though the U. S. set up a Commonwealth with independence scheduled for 1945, Japanese aggression interrupted that plan. Meanwhile, the American military created an elaborate defense scheme to protect the ward nation. Of prime strategic interest were four islands that guarded the mouth of Manila Bay, the largest being Corregidor, a rocky volcanic island comprising an area of two square miles. The name had its origin in the Spanish word for passage check and the island was used as a port of entry station for many years.

The American military figure most associated with the Philippines is General Douglas MacArthur. He and his father, American Civil War hero General Arthur MacArthur, both served there. Upon retirement

American and Filipino prisoners crowd the entrance to Malinta Tunnel on Corregidor during their surrender to victorious Japanese troops on May 6, 1942.

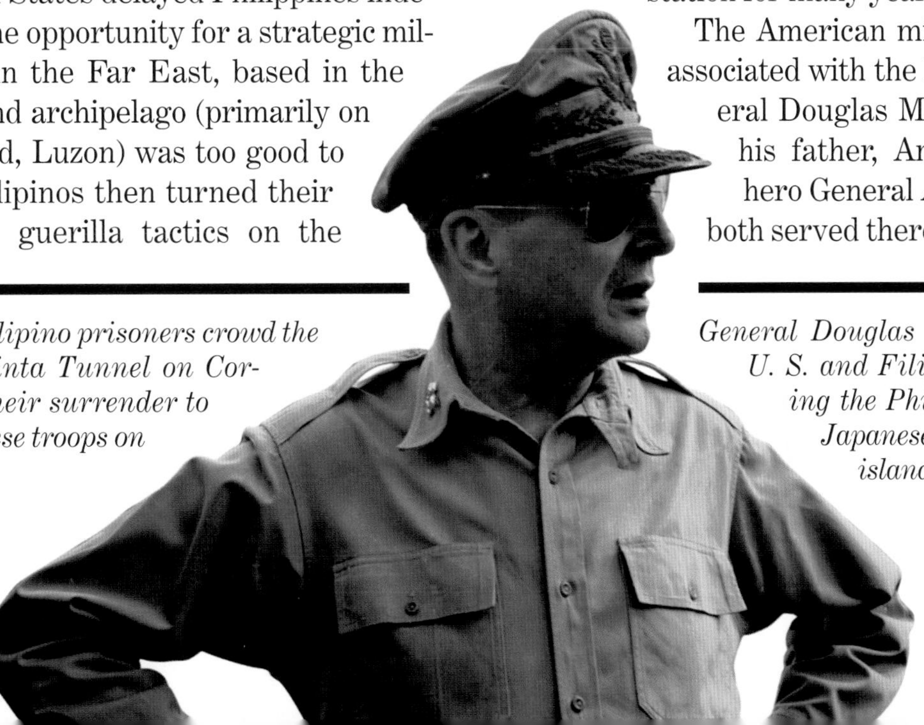

General Douglas MacArthur led the U. S. and Filipino troops defending the Philippines against the Japanese invasion and led the islands' liberation in 1945.

from the U. S. Army as Chief of Staff in 1937 Douglas was appointed Field Marshal in the Philippine Army, but continued to coordinate the efforts of the American military presence in the islands with Washington. In July 1941 he was recalled to active duty in the U. S. Army and promoted to the rank of lieutenant general. In light of the Japanese occupation of Indochina that month the islands were effectively surrounded and a war plan was drawn up in which the Philippine Army was folded into the American forces. A defense plan, War Plan Rainbow (WPL-46), which also included the Asiatic Fleet under Vice Adm. Thomas C. Hart, called for the army making a slow retreat to the Bataan Peninsula where, with the support of the navy and Corregidor chain

USS Houston *(CA-30) was the largest and best armed ship in the U. S. Asiatic Fleet when she was photographed in Manila Bay in the year before the war. Along with most of the navy's best assets in the Philippines, the flagship of TF-5 was sent to the Dutch East Indies by Admiral Hart when war came to the islands in December 1941.*

of defenses, Manila Bay could be held until American reinforcements arrived. MacArthur and the U. S. War Department in Washington began to have a more favorable opinion of the situation when lend-lease B-17 bombers in Europe were seen as being effective in combat against the Nazis in Europe – Washington agreed to send B-17s to MacArthur.

That's not to say the Philippines, and especially Luzon and the capital, Manila, were not ready for war. Indeed, Corregidor, with its batteries of 12-inch disappearing rifles (large coast artillery cannon), anti-aircraft emplacements, and support facilities; the other three islands of the chain (Caballo, El Fraile and Carabuo) and locations around the bay

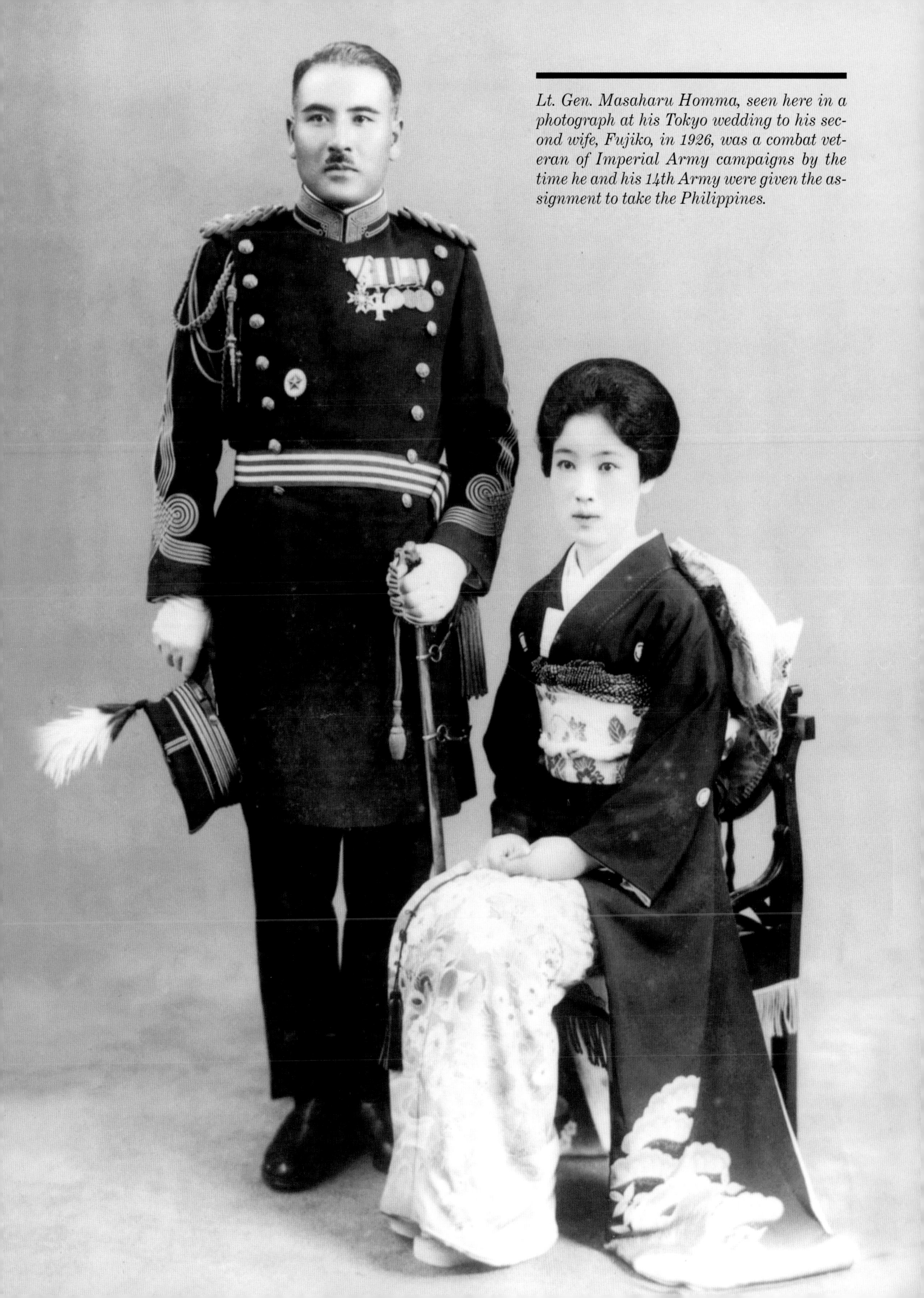

Lt. Gen. Masaharu Homma, seen here in a photograph at his Tokyo wedding to his second wife, Fujiko, in 1926, was a combat veteran of Imperial Army campaigns by the time he and his 14th Army were given the assignment to take the Philippines.

with similar coastal artillery pieces, were well prepared and staffed. The problem was these defensive preparations were designed for earlier in the century, when capital ships dominated the seas. And though the islands at the mouth of Manila Bay kept Japanese ships from entering that body of water, they did little to deter an invasion in a war in which air domination was a major strategy.

Naturally, there were U. S. military command hospitals and medical facilities on Luzon on the eve of war. Ann Bernatitus was an operating room supervisory nurse in the navy since 1936. She asked for an assignment in the Philippines and arrived in July 1940. She talks about the uniqueness of life in the islands before the war clouds gathered.

"I had no idea what the Philippines looked like; I hadn't read up on it or anything. Of course somebody met us at the dock to take us to Canacao. All I can remember is the smell of copra which seemed to be everywhere, the nipa huts, the kids running around naked, the houses on stilts, the carabao [water buffalo]. But life was very good out there too. We went to work at 8 o'clock. You went to lunch and then didn't have to go back on duty because only one nurse had to go back to supervise. We had golf, bicycling, swimming. You could go to the markets if you wanted to. For $5 a month you took your shoes, put them outside the door, and the house boys would take them downstairs, polish them up, and when we got back they would be sitting by your door It was the same with the women who did your laundry. On your way to work you dropped it off in the washroom and when you returned there it was all pressed for you."

Kelly Davis joined the army at a recruiting station in Salt Lake City. He wanted to get into the Army Air Corps and found himself in the Philippines within weeks of joining. He went from knowing nothing about the country to immersing himself in the culture.

"I joined the army in June 1939 and I was in the Philippines before the end of July. I found it to be an adventurous place, and I was glad I got it. I learned to converse with the natives. I learned a little bit of their language which was Tagalog and the other major language was Spanish. At that time the Philippines was a commonwealth, so we were the protectorate of that set of islands. I bought a Japanese bicycle and I peddled every weekend that I had a chance to go out in the boondocks; I just enjoyed learning about the Philippines.

"I was working with the Morse code, repairing and installing radio equipment in various planes of the 3rd Pursuit Squadron, which were Boeing P-26As. Every time they had a bomber flight that was going to other islands I would manage to get on as the communications man, so I could manage the Morse code there and get a ride at the same time. I was getting a lot of rides.

"I'd been playing tennis since high school and that was my pastime. I also got my amateur radio license in the Philippine code and they allowed me to use my initials, KSD, so when my squadron wanted to talk to their friends back in the states, that's all there was to it. I remember one of the officers in our squadron, I don't know what his title was but he was our security man, and he came to me. He said, 'Kelly, every time you go out and bar hop — there was an area outside the gates with Filipinos and businesses and bars — every time you leave the base I want you to be alert, anybody who questions soldiers and are asking about different things around here because we figure there might be spies every Saturday.' I didn't see or hear anything but at any rate we finally got sent up to Clark Field which was the bomber base."

The Philippine Islands had no place in Japan's Greater East Asia Co-Prosperity Sphere. The

country lacked the raw material caches of other objectives in the area and the population – with 400 years of Western influence – would not fit in with Japan's paternalistic totalitarianism. But as a strategic objective, both to deny a base for U. S. resistance to Japan's plan and

One of the 12" disappearing rifles that made Corregidor an imposing fortress against sea attack is manned in its battery, with another 12-inch cannon in the background. The disappearing aspect of the guns was their ability to be raised and lowered from behind thick concrete barbettes by recoil and steam action. They were, however, fully exposed to air bombardment, though their crews could take cover from air strikes when not manning the guns.

Realizing the need for reinforcements, the U. S. was beefing up the manpower and air strength of the Philippines. But the schedule to bring the army to projected strength was early spring 1942. In mid-1941, B-17 Flying Fortress bombers were arriving in the islands

as a base for Japanese military operations, it was vital, sitting on the route between Japan and the rich resources of the south. Manila Harbor was one of the best natural harbors in the Pacific. So Japan dedicated its Third Fleet under Vice Admiral I. Takahashi to take the island in 45- 50 days. It was an optimistic schedule to oppose a foe with the resources and determination of the United States. That's why it was important to the Japanese war machine to strike quickly and at a time when their strength in the region was greater.

at the three principal air bases – Clark in central Luzon and Nielson and Nichols on the outskirts of Manila, but they were overwhelming the support and training mechanisms. New units were arriving, including armor. Lester Tenney, of Chicago, volunteered for the army, joining a reserve group at Maywood, Illinois that he describes as "a great bunch of guys." The unit mobilized on November 25th, 1940. "We went to Fort Knox, Kentucky and I ended up going to radio operator's school," says Tenney. "I became a radio operator and then tank

commander. All of a sudden we were marked to go overseas in late September of '41. We got new tanks [M-16s] and they put them aboard flatcars and brought us to San Francisco. We boarded a ship and the next thing we knew we had landed in Manila on September 25th of 1941. And the war started Dec 7th, so we were there only a short period of time before all hell broke loose."

Robert Garcia was an army medic who had been in the Philippines for a few months. He describes the routine of life on base before the attack.

"The first few weeks it was kinda like not that bad because everybody was running around trying to get organized. They put us up there in a

Clark Field was a principal base of the U. S. Far East Air Force in the Philippines and was located at Fort Stotsenburg in central Luzon, about 50 miles northwest of Manila. By the time that Japan began the Pacific war, B-17 bombers and P-40 fighters had joined older aircraft stationed at Clark.

bunch of barracks, not like the ones they've got now, these were just big tents. Our officers were pretty young and they were just trying to get things going and organized because somewhere down the line they knew what was coming.

"When we landed we went to Clark Field, a big air base and we were anti-aircraft. We did have some big heavy artillery guns, but the guns we had mostly were anti-aircraft. I was still a medic, and every day we would practice and we would practice every night. Battery B was a company that tracked planes coming in and the big guys would track with 3-inch heavy guns. There was maybe 2 or 3 medics assigned to every battery and we just hanged around there and practiced what was going to be and that was

The headquarters of the 26th Field Artillery, Philippine Scouts, at Fort Stotsenburg is a peaceful place in a pre-war photograph. As the home of Clark Field and army units vital to the defense of Luzon, Fort Stotsenburg was one of the initial targets attacked by Japanese planes on December 8, 1941.

it. We were having a ball — we'd never been out of the country and we were young and everything but there was Captain Riley, Major Long and you could tell what they was talking about. I kinda thought them officers knew."

The navy, with bases at Cavite on Manila Bay, Mariveles on Bataan and Olongapo on Subic Bay north of the Bataan peninsula, had to manage with the roster of ships current to the Asiatic Fleet at that time. The sole exception was USS *Boise*, a light cruiser from the Pacific Fleet that had escorted army troops to the islands. Admiral Hart was humorously accused in navy circles of "shang-hai-ing" the vessel for his fleet. The important inland waters, Manila and Subic bays, were mined in mid-summer 1941. According to WPL-46, when

hostilities were perceived to be imminent, Hart was to begin moving his larger surface vessels — cruisers and destroyers — south to the Dutch East Indies in preparation for cooperating with the British and Dutch units. The Washington brass felt the smaller gunboats (augmented by those withdrawn from China) along with twenty-nine submarines of the Asiatic Fleet could harass the Japanese invasion armada. On November 20, the ships began the move south. An air patrol scheme was set up hastily. The B-17 bombers of MacArthur's Army Air Forces Far East, with greater speed and altitude ceilings, formed the basis of patrols to the north, while the navy's PBY patrol seaplanes scouted the Indochina coast to the west.

Captain A. H. Rooks, commander of heavy cruiser USS *Houston*, flagship of the Asiatic

Fleet's Task Force 5, never doubted the ability of the Japanese to mount a campaign on several fronts at one time as most others did. Perhaps that is why the information received on December 6 that a large Japanese flotilla was sailing from Camranh Bay, Indochina toward Malaysia was not a source of immediate alarm for U. S. forces in the Philippines and the Pacific. Air patrols yielded no indication that an attack on the Philippines was imminent. The Japanese Second Fleet, headed toward Malaysia, was covering the Philippine invasion from a distance, and the Third Fleet's move in the direction of Luzon was undetected. The flight plans for the air operations which began the attack did nothing to reveal the naval invasion force's approach. Although the Japanese air strikes began as a surprise, the American command had some warning.

At 0300 hours on December 8 (Manila time – it was still December 7 in Hawaii) the U. S. Asiatic Fleet duty officer delivered news of the attack on Pearl Harbor, which was then underway, to Admiral Hart. This gave the American command in the Philippines a few precious hours to blunt the Japanese air attack which would begin at dawn. The weather also helped by delaying some Japanese air strikes. Army aircraft from Clark Field were scrambled in response to the Pearl Harbor report and the planes got airborne quickly – but nothing in the way of enemy planes was spotted. Though a naval attack was made against a seaplane tender in Mindanao, and Japanese army heavy bombers were attacking Baguio and an airfield in the northern part of Luzon (actions not immediately reported to American commanders), the large waves of enemy naval bombers and Zero fighters were still on the way from Formosa. The American planes returned to base for lunch and refueling. As at Pearl Harbor, the defects in an untested early warning system came to light. The only radar station which spotted the incoming Japanese planes in time, at Aparri on the north-

ern Luzon coast, failed to relay the message. As a result, at 1245 hours American aircraft were attacked on the ground at Clark Field and the Manila air bases. Les Tenney remembers those first hectic hours of the attack.

"They brought our tanks early in the morning, about 5:30 in the morning, around to Clark Field. Fort Stotsenburg and Clark Field were together. So they took our tanks from Ft. Stotsenburg to our station and they had us surround the field expecting paratroopers. Of course at 12:30 that day when the Japanese came down we were right there as the bombs began to fall, and then the Japanese Zeros started to strafe and it was all hell. Airplanes went up in smoke, the buildings were all destroyed, the tents were all destroyed. I mean everything at Ft. Stotsenburg was destroyed at the same time. Two hours later when the Japanese bombers left and the Zeros left, we started to count up our dead. That was the first day of the war."

Robert Garcia also remembers that day:

"We were having lunch when the first Japanese fighter came in. And then they started coming. They had done this at Pearl Harbor in the morning but it was one day different there in the time. We were hit about 12 o'clock, noon, and all hell broke loose. Some guy heard it on the radio, 'Hey, the Japanese bombed Pearl Harbor this morning. There are still a bunch of guys down there and battle wagons and stuff like that.' But then the guy disappeared.

"I looked around and couldn't see nothing and then we got talking that maybe American planes were coming in. Then all of a sudden I seen maybe from 25,000 – 30,000 feet that the bombs started coming down. Our airplanes, our hangars, everything bombed and fire all over it. Maybe about ¼ mile we were [from the runway]. I think it was

about as far as you could get from the base, where the airplanes were and the hangars were. We didn't have any foxholes, we never thought — we didn't dig one. The bombs are dropping and here come the fighter planes flying three or four hundred feet up in the air, strafing everything they could find, a bunch of them.

Far East Air Force P-35 fighters sit in a pile of destruction a Nichols Field near Manila. This air base was a secondary target after Clark Field. Confusion and command problems caused most of Clark's planes to be on the ground during the first aerial attack, but fighters from Del Carmen, a nearby base, shot down three Japanese planes over Clark Field.

"They were right there, right there you looked up and you could see them right there. Round and round, and round on their way until they destroyed most of our fighter planes, P-40s and our B-10Bs and all of our aerial bombers and they left our runways full of nothing but holes. When they were gone the captain started hollering, 'Medic, medic, medic! Hey go down there and see what you can do for them.' And you go down there and there's nothing you could do, he's dead. I went

down there and there was two or three of them badly wounded, and there was this one fella, a real young boy from Dallas and he said, 'Robert help me, help me. I'm burning up. It's my stomach.' He had a hole about that big [as big as a fist]. I put my hand in to see if I could find the shrapnel, I guess I did find the shrapnel but there was nothing I could do. He could talk so I tried to find an ambulance and the guys who were driving the ambulances were all over. We had four, five, maybe six ambulances but they were busy. He finally got to the big hospital in Manila then later I learned this boy died about 2 – 3 days later."

Seventeen B-17 bombers and half the pursuit planes were destroyed or severely damaged immediately. Air strikes continued on December 10 at Clark, Nielsen and Nichols fields and on navy patrol planes, unprotected in the air and strafed at their moorings, so they could not warn of future attacks. Eventually the planes that survived were flown south. By Christmas there were only 33 usable pursuit planes among the air squadrons based on Luzon. Without air protection and anti-aircraft guns capable of reaching the high-level bombers, the navy yard facilities at Cavite were destroyed by the Japanese. Losses included one submarine and other naval craft, along with military targets throughout Luzon. Dorothy Still Danner was a nurse at the Canacao naval hospital at the navy yard. She recalled:

"I and the other nurses were awakened in the middle of the night and told that Pearl Harbor had been hit. We were sent to the hospital as soon as we got dressed. Since the hospital was right in the target zone, we sent all the ambulatory patients back to duty and the rest to Manila. Arrangements were made to admit the patients to what had been a dependents' ward at the Sternberg army hospital.

"On Wednesday the 10th, the navy yard was bombed. It was wiped out. This raid lasted about an hour. After the raid, we rushed to the hospital, and patients were all over the place. There were Filipino women, children, and men and our own people from the navy yard. It was really a shocking scene. The power to the hospital was knocked out. It was a pretty hectic afternoon. Triage was impossible. You just tried to find out which were the worst ones to go to surgery and so on.

"Sternberg hospital too was quickly swamped. The only place that was available was Estado Mayor, an old army base; we used the barracks as a temporary hospital. In the meantime, they de-

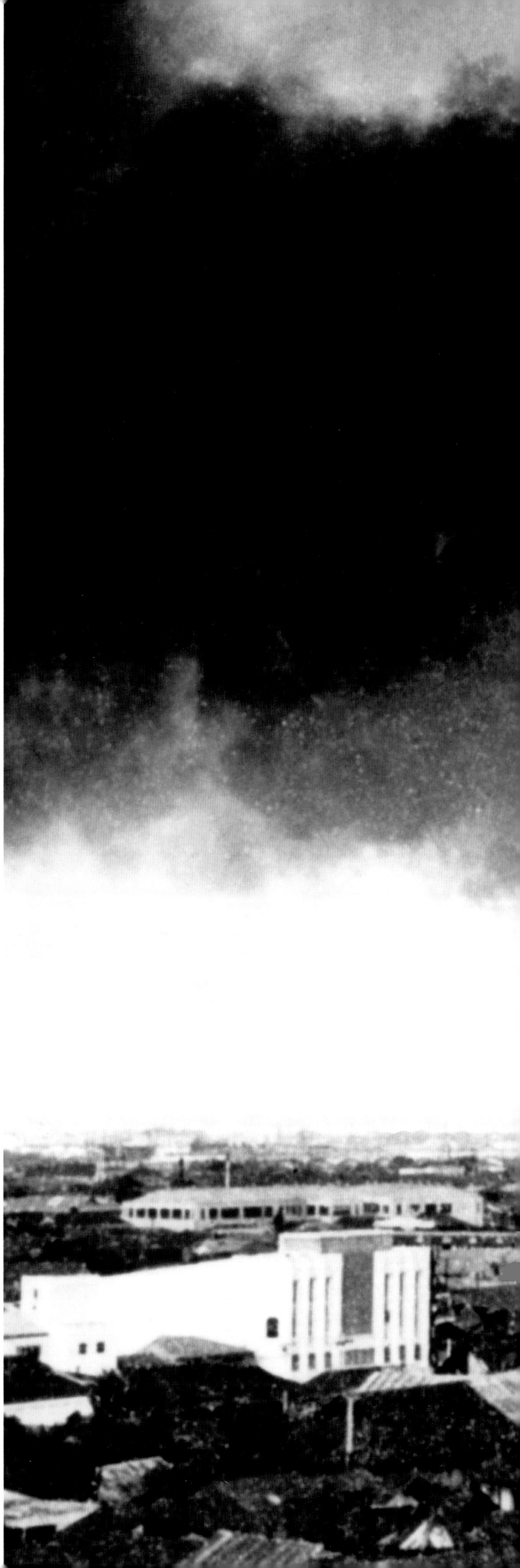

Smoke rises from Manila during Japanese bombing attacks on the city in December 1941.

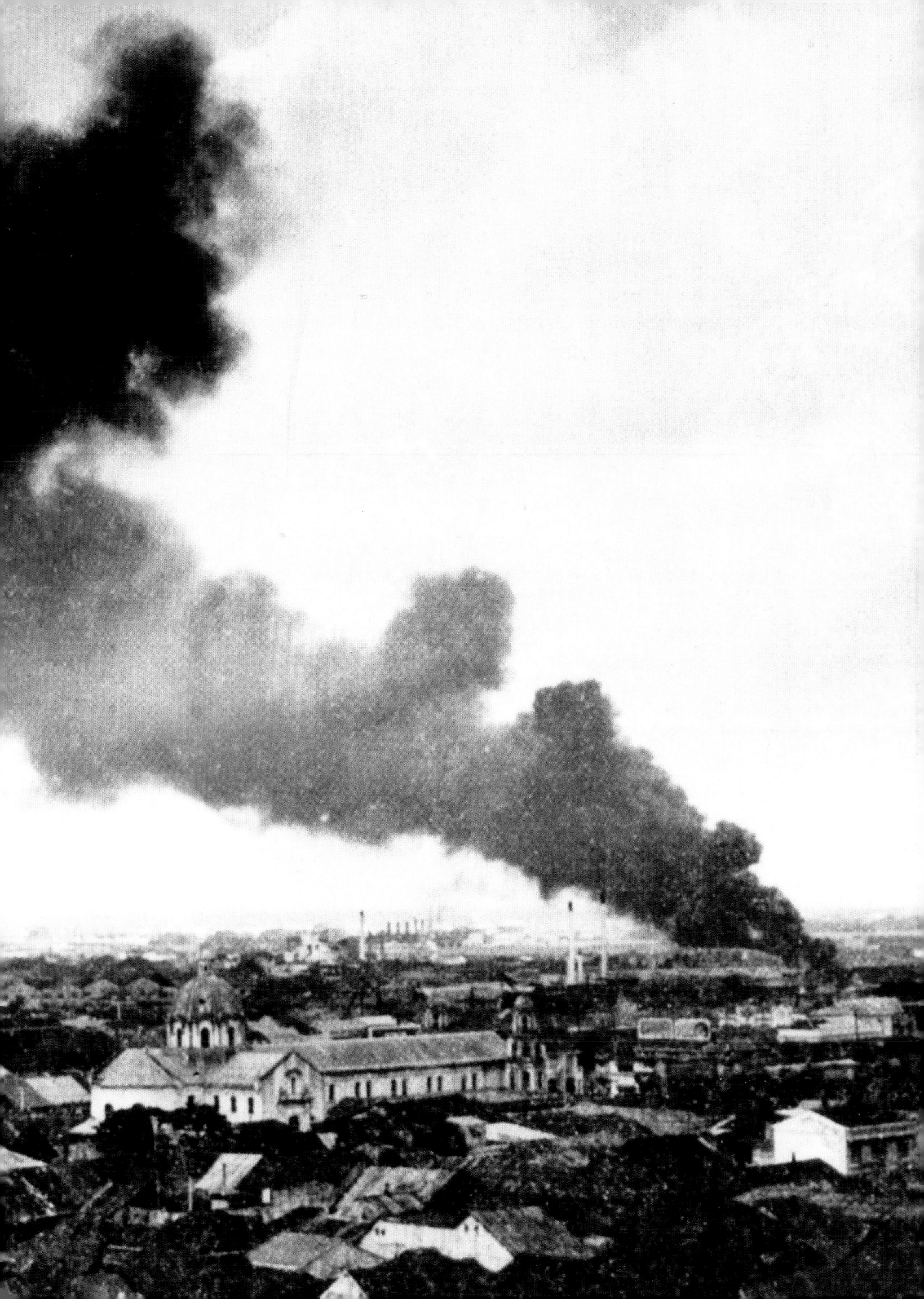

cided to set up joint surgical teams [with Army and Navy Medical Corps] throughout the city. I was with the group assigned to the Jai Alai Club. Our purpose was to care for anyone that was hit — civilian or military — that would come into these emergency centers. We set up a little receiving station near the front of the building, but didn't get any patients."

Amphibious Operations on Luzon

Even as the air strikes continued, the invasion by a well-prepared Japanese amphibious force began. On December 10, after the Japanese had captured a few small islands to the extreme north, they landed on the mainland near Aparri. The small contingent of soldiers facing this landing, a company of the 12th Infantry Regiment, was aided by high seas and some air support from serviceable B-17s and P-40s. The persistent attacks by these brave aviators harassed Japanese warships and frustrated the subsequent landings in northern Luzon through December 17, and also made trouble for the landing of the opposite pincer of the Japanese plan to squeeze Manila. The landing at Legaspi in the extreme south on Luzon on December 12 gained a foothold and the San Bernardino Strait was mined, but B17s succeeded in damaging Japanese ships and planes during the assault. On the other hand, the American submarines, worrisome to the Imperial Navy, did no damage during this critical period of time. With the relocation of the last fourteen B-17 Flying Fortresses to Australia after the 17th, it would be up to the subs, gunboats and land forces to hold the islands.

The main attack came in the form of seventy-six transports of infantry, armor and supplies at Lingayen Gulf, 120 miles up the west coast of Luzon from Manila. Once again heavy seas hampered the operation. A few daring American pi-

lots disrupted the execution of the landing and harassed warships of the Japanese Third Fleet that were supporting the landing operations. Hart ordered the submarine command to the area and before they located the convoy, on December 21, most of the Japanese ships were too near shore to become targets of underwater attack. However, a few transports and support ships were sunk or damaged, giving the Navy subs their first kills of the campaign. Although these subs, American planes (when they were uncontested in the air), the fire of coastal batteries and the weather mangled the Japanese invasion at Lingayen, the force of numbers was just too great – by Christmas, the Japanese had landed Lt. Gen. Masaharu Homma's 14th Army in a position giving it a straight shot for Manila . Les Tenney was there.

"The first [U. S.] tank battle of World War II was on Dec. 21st in the Philippines up at the Agno [River]. Our tanks [Company C, 192nd Tank Battalion] went in and we needed tanks in the Philippines like tits on a boar – ridiculous. But MacArthur wanted tanks, he had to have tanks and there was no reason for them – they were pretty useless. We were able to operate only down a road one tank behind the other; the only tank that could fire at the enemy was the front tank. It was stupid, it really was. We lost our first tank that first day and the rest of us turned around and started our withdrawal back into Bataan which we were ordered to do.

"The Japanese came in on Dec. 21st and we were already up there. We were there trying to meet them but our G-2 [intelligence officer] told us there was only small arms and ammunition, foot soldiers. What we found was 55,000 troops, anti-tank guns, flame-throwers, cannon, everything. Our G-2, they didn't know what was going on so that's how we started up in the Lingayen Gulf, where they landed and then we started the withdrawal. We were up there with the cavalry scouts, the 26th Cavalry of the Filipino Scouts. A great fighting group of men, they were all fighters and all heroes, they were fighting on horseback when we were in our tanks. They came back and then our infantry came back; we stayed there until they started. And then we ended up with what they called piggy-back, they would move forward then we'd move in, we would move forward and we protected their flank until we moved back day after day until we were back into Bataan."

One member of the 26th Cavalry was platoon leader Felipe A. Fernandez. He describes his participation in defending the Agno River line.

"On the 25th of December 1941 my machine gun platoon and the remainder of Troop E under the command of 1st Lieutenant William P. Leisenring were positioned on the eastern bank of the Agno River leading to the town of Tayug. My orders were to deny the enemy from crossing the river and to hold my position at all cost until relieved. I positioned my guns about three yards from the bank allowing ten yards interval between guns. On my left were four heavy machine guns and their supporting men from the 91st [Philippine Army] Division and on my right was a rifle squad led by Cpl. Jeremias de la Cruz.

"Just as the sun began to set the Japanese advance snipers began firing their rifles. At first there were a few scattered shots then there were more and then a lot more that sounded afar off and because the rays of the [setting] sun were impeding our sights I ordered my men to hold their fire. There was a full moon that night. Suddenly a mortar round fell a few yards in front of me which luckily landed in the depth below. This awakened me from my day dreaming and as I scanned the river bed I saw many Japanese, like a multitude of giant hermit crabs, creeping towards our positions. I alerted my men and gave the orders to fire at will. The gunners saw what I

had seen and they expertly trained their fire at the creeping shadows. They fanned their fire right and left cutting down the advancing Japanese like a big scythe cutting a field of 'cogon' grass. The gunners tilted their guns to shoot down those who were attempting to scale the twenty foot-bank of the river.

"Suddenly all hell turned loose and the firing became so intense, like the celebration of a Chinese New Year, as the Japanese desperately made their utmost effort to dislodge us from our positions but my men held their own. Suddenly I noticed that some of my guns and others on my left were no longer firing. I jumped and ran to check what was happening and found that some guns had ruptured cartridges and others had just run out of ammunition. Having the only combination tool, I ran from gun to gun extracting the ruptured cartridge and ordered an ammunition carrier to replenish those that had run out. I ventured on my left to find that the gun positions had only two men left, the rest had withdrawn to the rear. I checked with the men manning the guns and found out that they had the same problems as my men. I told the men that they are now under my command and for them to hold their positions until further orders. I made the guns operational and had ammunitions brought to them.

"During all of this time Lieutenant Leisenring kept shouting at me to be careful and not to take unnecessary risk but I kept on doing what was to be done, sometimes unavoidably exposing myself to enemy fire. I lost track of the time but about two o'clock past midnight, there was silence. After a few minutes I ordered Pfc. Jesus Gonzales and Pfc. Alberto Lazo to check what was happening below. On their return they reported that there were countless dead Japanese together with dead animals which the Japanese used as shields when they attempted to break through our lines.

"Lieutenant Leisenring sent his orders to with-

draw so I ordered my guns to withdraw with my four riflemen covering the withdrawal. The lieutenant commended us for a job well done and recommended me for an award of a Silver Star medal."

An aide helps General Homma ashore during the Japanese landing at Lingayen Gulf on December 22.

By Christmas Eve, the 48th Division, the principal infantry of Homma's force, was advancing toward Manila. The American and Filipino forces facing them, the 11th and 21st Philippine Army Divisions, the 26th Cavalry Philippine Scouts and two battalions of tanks under Major General Jonathan Wainwright, could do little to slow down the advance. Many of the Filipino reservists evaporated as fighting began. As Les Tenney indi-

cated, the cavalry and scouts distinguished themselves in the earlier fighting and later in the campaign as well. Wainwright received permission from MacArthur's headquarters to set up a defensive line behind the Agno River. The 26th Cavalry fought a brave delaying action to achieve the withdrawal. Les Tenney recounts the withdrawal from northern Luzon.

"I really don't remember getting any supplies of any kind — we had some food that was delivered up there to us, it was about once every two or three days wherever we happened to be. They'd get a mess truck to us but that's about all.

I don't think we ate much during that first week. The second week after we were coming down we would go through Filipino villages and we would grab hold of some live chickens, swirl them around and kill them, skin them and eat them. We cooked chicken, did our own cooking and that's what we were doing. Until we ended up back on our forces which was on the Limay Road which was the Japanese final line; but up until that time we just came back, and I don't remember too much about getting fed. I don't think it was on many of our minds at that time."

Many miles to the south, the small Japanese landing party at Legaspi, which was just a feint, was joined by a much larger landing which surprised the Allies by landing at Lamon Bay seventy miles east of Manila on December 24. This force was virtually unopposed in its journey over central Luzon toward Manila as the scattered South Luzon Force was first bypassed, and then ordered back to the capital.

The rapid advance of the numerically superior Japanese army, the lack of U. S. naval support and virtually non-existent air force caused MacArthur to revert to the idea of withdrawing all ground forces to Bataan except those manning the defenses on Corregidor and the neighboring islands. A decades-old strategy, War Plan Orange (WPO-3), was put into effect on December 23 and all units not engaged in combat commandeered all manner of motorized transportation, including colorful Filipino buses and trucks, to move men and supplies to the peninsula. The objective of WPO-3 was to hold out with six months of supplies until a U. S. relief amphibious force could fight its way from Australia or across the Central Pacific from the Hawaiian Islands. In a precautionary move, Philippine president Manuel Quezon, U. S. government officials, MacArthur and his family and staff left Manila for Corregidor during the latter part of December 24.

The Battle of Bataan

Less than 48 hours later, the Agno line collapsed and Wainwright's North Luzon Force, joined by Major General George M. Parker's force from the south, began fighting delaying actions toward Bataan. On December 26 MacArthur declared Manila an open city to spare buildings and civilians the destruction of bombings and siege. The Japanese entered the city on January 2, 1942 and the Battle of Bataan began five days later. The combined force under Wainwright and Parker included I Corps, three divisions, holding the left and II Corps, four divisions, on the right; 30,000 men defended a line bisected by Mt. Natib — anchored on the west on the South China Sea and the east on Manila Bay. It was a solid defensive line, with support facilities extending down the peninsula to and through the port of Mariveles. For the next two weeks, Homma mounted unsuccessful assaults on the line, and the Japanese 20th Infantry Regiment made a pair of amphibious assaults on Bataan's west coast behind the lines. One of these was near Mariveles and was first opposed by a motley group of naval air and shipboard personnel under Commander Francis J. Bridget. With help of the 57th Philippine Scouts, these incursions were forced back to the sea. The Japanese soldiers who made it that far dug into caves on the South China Sea facing cliffs, but were then greeted by machine gun fire from U. S. Navy gunboats and launches from USS *Canopus* (reinforced by boiler plates to give them protection).

Throughout the Bataan campaign, *Canopus* (AS-9), a submarine tender, had an exceptional adventure. One of two tenders remaining in the Philippines after most of the American fleet sailed south, she first served the submarines off Manila, then moved to Mariveles harbor coincident with the withdrawal onto the Bataan peninsula. She was bombed constantly until her skipper camou-

BATAAN

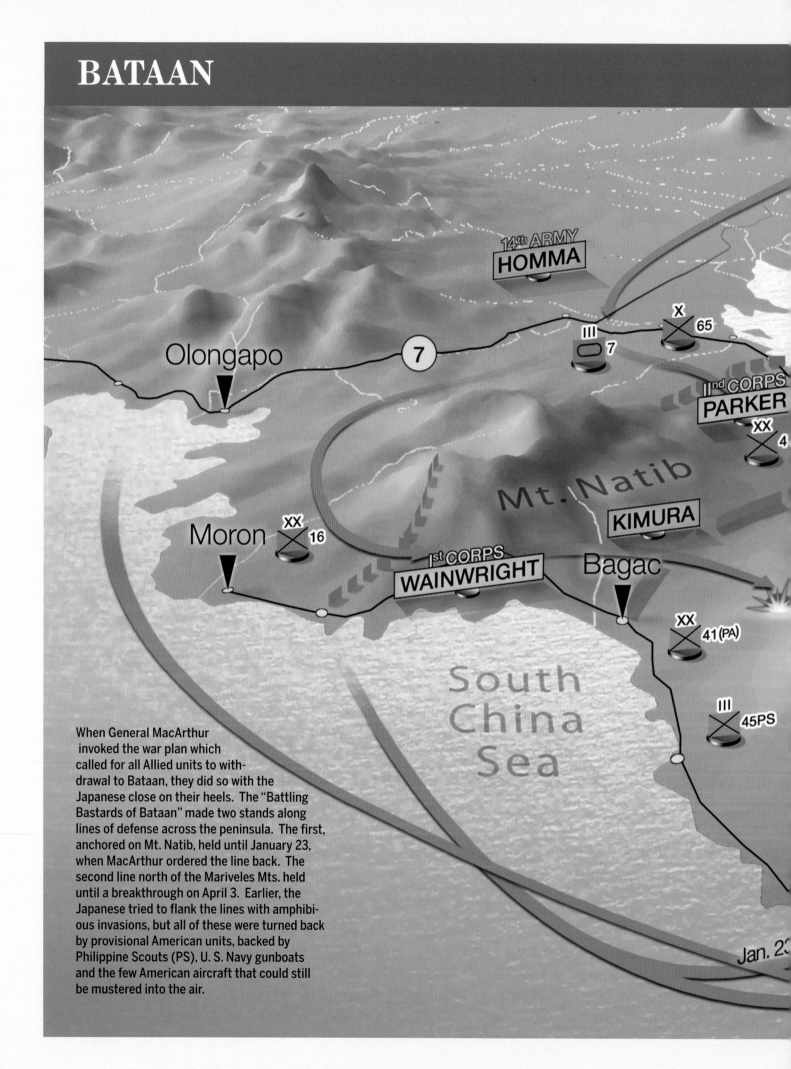

14th ARMY
HOMMA

Olongapo

7

III 7

X 65

IInd CORPS
PARKER

XX 4

Mt. Natib

KIMURA

Moron XX 16

1st CORPS
WAINWRIGHT

Bagac

XX 41 (PA)

South
China
Sea

III 45PS

Jan. 23

When General MacArthur invoked the war plan which called for all Allied units to withdrawal to Bataan, they did so with the Japanese close on their heels. The "Battling Bastards of Bataan" made two stands along lines of defense across the peninsula. The first, anchored on Mt. Natib, held until January 23, when MacArthur ordered the line back. The second line north of the Mariveles Mts. held until a breakthrough on April 3. Earlier, the Japanese tried to flank the lines with amphibious invasions, but all of these were turned back by provisional American units, backed by Philippine Scouts (PS), U. S. Navy gunboats and the few American aircraft that could still be mustered into the air.

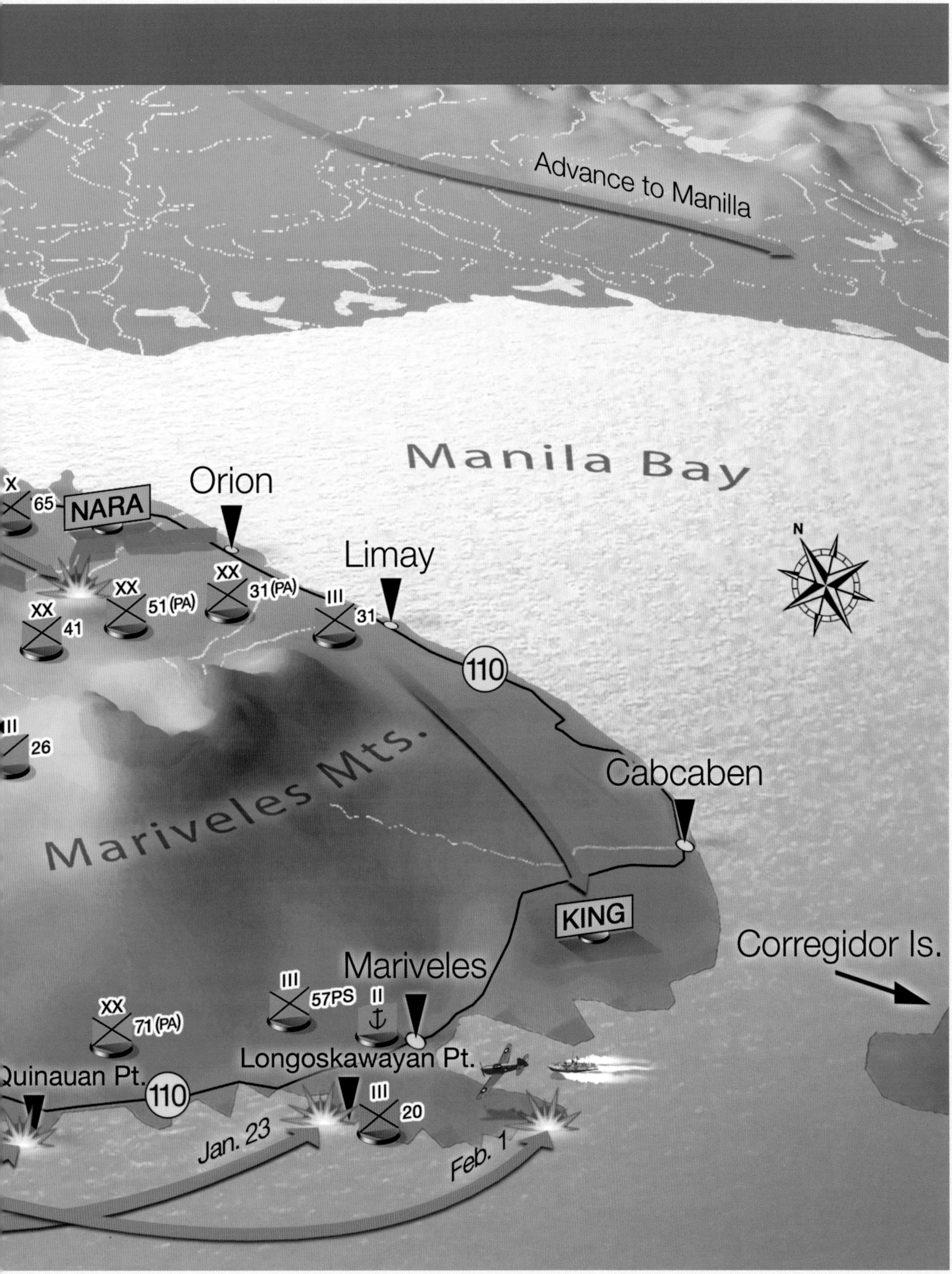
Advance to Manilla
Manila Bay
Orion
NARA
65
Limay
XX
51 (PA)
XX
31 (PA)
XX
41
III
31
110
26
Mariveles Mts.
Cabcaben
KING
Corregidor Is.
Mariveles
III
57PS
II
XX
71 (PA)
Longoskawayan Pt.
Quinauan Pt.
110
III
20
Jan. 23
Feb. 1
N

flaged her to look like a wrecked hulk. She continued to service all manner of boats and even performed repairs for land-based equipment, as well as provided the improvised attack craft, until Luzon was lost. Besides supplies, ammunition and manpower, the Bataan defense force needed appropriate medical facilities and hospitals were beefed up on the south peninsula. Officer-nurse Ann Bernatitus was among those to go.

"On December 22, Dr. Smith informed me about

TOP: Japanese Type 95 light tanks and a mule train roll along narrow Highway 3 a few miles north of Manila on January 3, 1942. The bridge in the foreground was repaired by Imperial Army engineers. RIGHT: Even as the Japanese advanced toward Bataan, Filipino and American units contested their drive in any way they could. Here Filipino soldiers prepare to sabotage a wooden railroad bridge.

7 p.m. that Manila was to be declared an open city and that surgical units were selected to go to Bataan on Christmas Eve. Our unit was included. On the 24th we left [Santa Scholastica, a temporary hospital in Manila] at 6 a.m. and were taken to Jai Lai, where the convoy was to form to go to Bataan. There were 24 Army nurses, 25 Filipino nurses and me, the one navy nurse. As we passed through the villages, the natives came out and cheered us giving us the 'V' for victory sign. Many times during the trip the bus would have to stop and we would dive

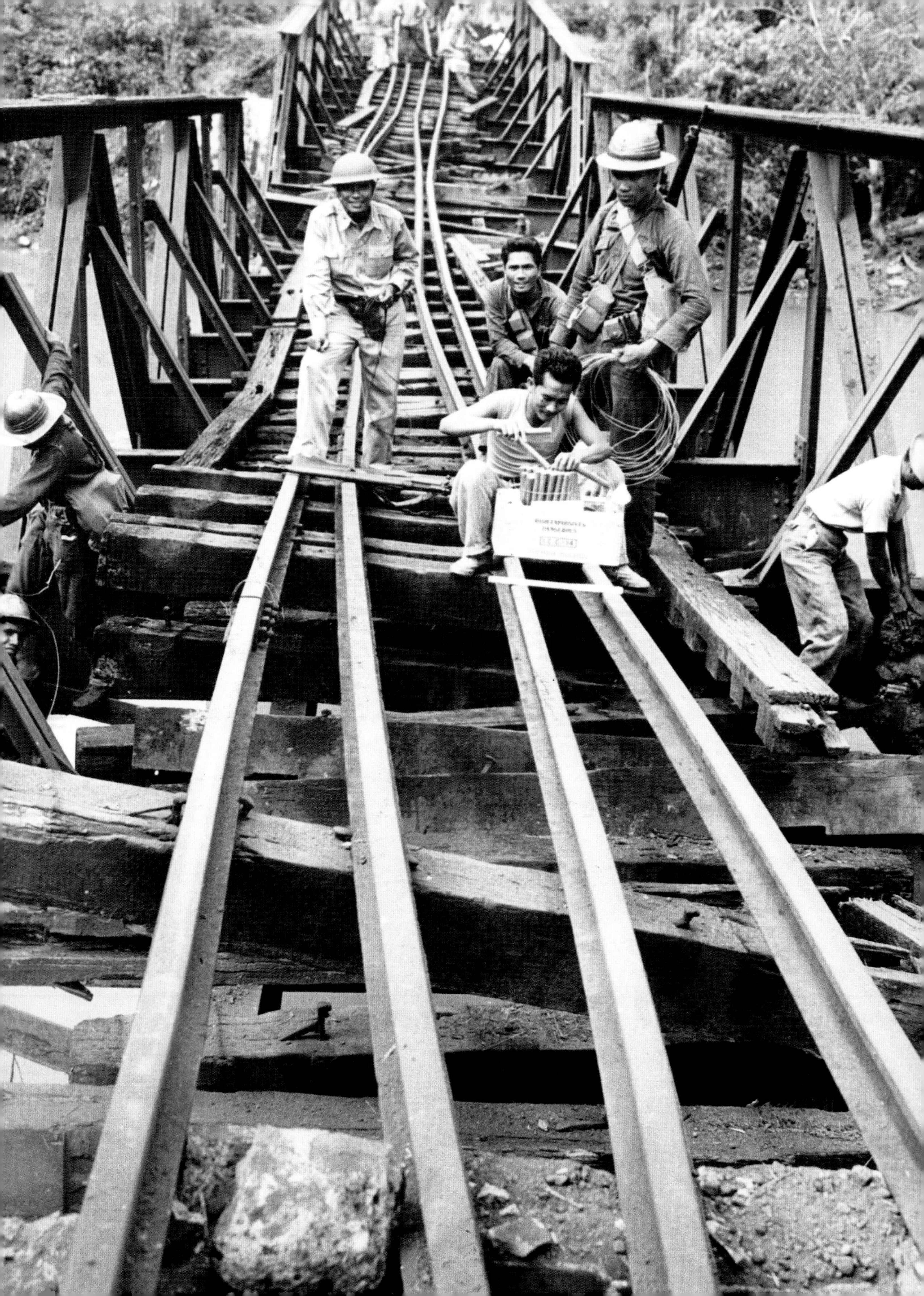

into gutters along the roadside because the Japanese planes were overhead. Late that afternoon we arrived at Camp Limay, Hospital Number One. There were 25 wooden, one-story buildings, 15 of them wards. A water pipe outside each ward provided water. The utility room for the bedpans and what have you was the back porch. The buildings were in a rectangle with the operating room building at the upper end with a generator and water towers alongside. At the further end was the building housing the nurses' quarters and the officers' mess hall. The remaining buildings were along each side. Behind the buildings on the left side of the beach was a warehouse in which were stored the equipment and supplies for the hospital. In the center of this area was grass and trees and foxholes dug everywhere.

"The operating room was a long narrow building with approximately seven or eight tables set up in the center. Along the window openings were the cabinets with supplies. There were shutters with a stick to keep them open. I'm a bit vague on how we sterilized the gauze and linen but it seems to me it was done in pressure cookers operated by kerosene. The instruments were sterilized by placing them in a foot tub filled with Lysol, then rinsed in alcohol. As the patients were brought in they were assigned to a table by Dr. Weinstein of the Army Medical Corps. The team assigned to that table took care of the patient regardless of what type of surgery was indicated. Casualties were heavy and the operating room was an extremely busy place."

Les Tenney recalls the time spent in the field on Bataan beginning in the first days of January, 1942.

"I would say we were attacked on a regular basis but most of the attacks started off with artillery and we were able to tell where the artillery was so we just kept on piggy-backing. We only came into contact with the Japanese troops during that period of time on two occasions. Once we got to our bivouac area on Bataan the first thing they did was set us up as a pillbox on the edge of the water, expecting the Japanese to come across from Manila and that's where we were for about four or five days until MacArthur realized it was a lost cause.

"From that point on during the next four months it was constantly moving into the pockets [advances into the American-Filipino defensive lines] that the Japanese would form. Our job with our tanks was as soon as they formed a pocket we came into that pocket to push them back up. That was our job for four months, constantly moving the Japanese up [north]. They would come down, we would go in, fight them and move them up, and then they'd come down again. That's what we did until the war ended for us."

Kelly Davis became separated from his air corps squadron during the pullback to Bataan. After setting up a communications station on the peninsula, he was assigned to an infantry unit at the front. He talks about his first days on the line.

"One day we were in foxholes in the dense jungle because we got indications that the Japanese were coming toward us so we formed a line with our guns and our foxholes across there. Now I remember I was sitting in my foxhole wondering what could happen and they started a barrage, the Japanese on us. They were actually sewing that entire area with shells. I remember hiding myself down in the foxhole with my helmet on my head. Mud was sticking on me and trees and twigs were hitting me on my head and my foxhole wasn't big enough for anything big to come in on me, but I thought the whole world was coming to an end.

"I think I got scared when I first went out on this patrol. At any rate when the barrage was over I thought in my head of the foxhole and all the sticks that were in there with me and I thought I'm the only living person. It was one mass of destruction, trees with broken branches, leaves, mud, it was terrible. I looked all around and thought I'm here all alone when all of a sudden here come up another head not too far away and another and I don't think they got a one of us; we were all down in our foxholes. Next thing we know we get a charge and the Japanese had been taught to charge with their bayonets and scream at the top of their voice, because they thought that would scare the enemy. I remember one coming in screaming and if any turned back at all the officer behind him would shoot him. I saw two Japanese soldiers shot by a sergeant or corporal whoever was in charge.

"The [American] sergeant from the infantry there, as with most of the infantrymen, told me to hit their legs, we don't want to kill them we want them to fall down and cry so just aim at their legs. So from then on nobody was aiming to kill them they wanted to wound them and get them down. He said if they had to climb over a couple of guys with shot-up legs, they'll slow down. All this happened in a matter of seconds. At any rate the charge was broken up, they backed off and here we were.

"A day later they put me on a patrol; they were trying to establish where the enemy was back in the jungle. We went out on patrol; I was in the lead of this patrol with men on either side of me and I spotted a Japanese soldier coming toward me down this jungle path less than 100 yards away. He saw me at about the same time I saw him; I just stood there, I didn't know what to do; he immediately had his bayonet and rifle and he took his bayonet, put it in charge position and started screaming. I'd never heard such screaming in my life and he was coming toward me. I couldn't pick out what he was doing, raising and shooting 30-40 yards. He and I thought this is it, it's either him or me, so I dropped him."

Robert Garcia continued his assignment as a medic on the front line on Bataan. One day during the standoff he himself was wounded.

"They were dropping light bombs and at the same time mortar shells and we could hear them coming and if you sit there and listen, you had an idea where they was gonna land, you know? We ran for the foxholes, everything being hit, the guns being hit, our truck was being hit and I felt something down my knee. I looked at my knee and man, it was full of blood and everything, it didn't hurt but I got hit. I could feel a little burn pain but it didn't bother me; you just keep on going."

Constant pressure by Homma's force wore down the II Corps and on January 23 MacArthur ordered the line back five miles. Ann Bernatitus' hospital was moved back also, to Little Baguio, where the facilities were more primitive. At this point the American and Filipino soldiers had their rations cut. It would not be the last time. The supplies hastily gathered on Bataan and Corregidor at the end of December were starting to run out. Although MacArthur was given permission by President Roosevelt to offer large rewards to inter-island haulers willing to run the blockade of Luzon set up by the Imperial Navy, few tried and none got through. Less food meant the soldiers were more apt to contract any of the numerous tropical diseases in the islands — malaria, beriberi, dysentery and others. But the Japanese were suffering from disease too.

The slow progress on Bataan was making the Tokyo leadership nervous, and though Homma was spared, his command was shaken up in an effort to speed up the campaign. A Japanese attack across the new front on January 26 was a failure, and Homma and his staff decided to extricate its units from the line and wait for reinforcements which he requested from Tokyo. A February 15 assault was recognized as a diver-

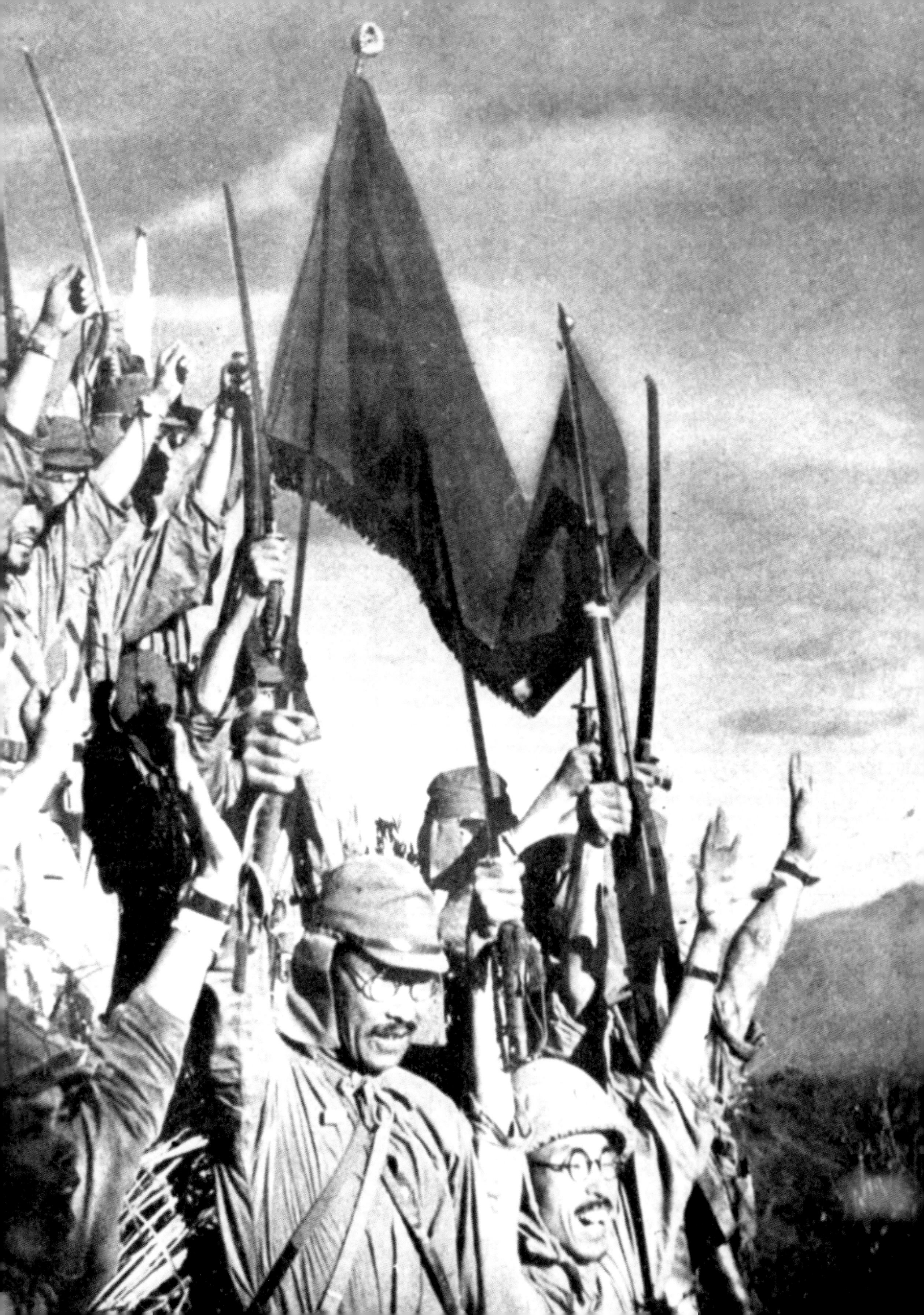

sion by the American leadership and the battle to pull back to a defensive position was also costly to Homma. By that time, his force had suffered 7,000 casualties and Tokyo's timetable had expired. Morale was high among Wainwright's officers and men. But time was running out on the "Battling Bastards of Bataan —No mama, no papa, no Uncle Sam" as they characterized themselves.

The Japanese Navy blockade and the air domination the aggressors enjoyed had a lock on Luzon. Despite the tactical situation that favored the defenders, any suggestions to go on the offensive were nixed. Officially, Washington had an announced "defeat Hitler first" policy; but in fact more supplies and equipment were shipped to the Pacific Theater in the early days of America's war. Yet these wouldn't save the Philippines. On March 10, MacArthur called Wainwright to Corregidor to personally deliver the news that President Roosevelt had ordered the commanding general to continue command of U. S. Army Forces Far East from Australia. Two days later, on March 12, MacArthur, his family and aides left Corregidor on four PT boats for a rendezvous with two B-17s at Mindanao's Del Monte airfield. President Quezon and other key government officials had already left the islands. Les Tenney recalls how the news of MacArthur's departure was received

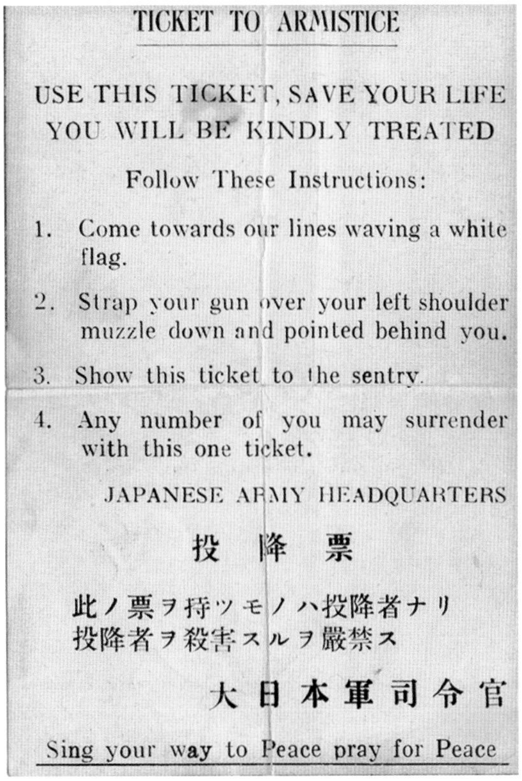
TICKET TO ARMISTICE

USE THIS TICKET, SAVE YOUR LIFE
YOU WILL BE KINDLY TREATED

Follow These Instructions:

1. Come towards our lines waving a white flag.
2. Strap your gun over your left shoulder muzzle down and pointed behind you.
3. Show this ticket to the sentry.
4. Any number of you may surrender with this one ticket.

JAPANESE ARMY HEADQUARTERS

投降票

此ノ票ヲ持ツモノハ投降者ナリ
投降者ヲ殺害スルヲ嚴禁ス

大日本軍司令官

Sing your way to Peace pray for Peace

TOP: In order to overcome their foe in the Philippines, the Japanese fought with paper as well as bullets. Leaflets such as this one in English and Japanese beckoned Luzon's defenders to give up and receive a warm welcome as POWs. Few bought into the propaganda and none had the pampered lives advertised once they were taken prisoner. LEFT: Elated by driving the Allied forces from Luzon and in a few months trapping them into a forced surrender on the Bataan peninsula, Japanese infantry soldiers let go a victory cheer.

among the Americans left behind.

"Well if you've read any of the poems, you know what the poems are, 'dugout Doug with a 155 strapped to his side and a howitzer strapped to his back,' and 'corrupt, courageous, Corregidor Mac.' First, MacArthur only came on [Bataan] once for about an hour, so he didn't know what in hell was going on, that's number one. Number two, at the end of January he thought the war was over and he took most of our supplies and he took them to Corregidor. Most of our food and ammunition is taken to Corregidor at the end of January; that was for the next three months. We'd have been living on one month's rations and eating monkeys, iguanas and snakes. So when MacArthur left it wasn't exactly a happy occasion — we sort of made some humor about it, and of course right after that the Japanese would drop the pamphlets saying MacArthur left us, so forth and so on."

A most unusual supply run was made by two U. S. Navy submarines that unloaded their torpedoes temporarily at Cebu and secretly brought 35 tons of supplies to Bataan. But this only amounted to one-half day's rations for the forces there. After MacArthur departed, U. S. Army Chief of Staff General George C. Marshall informed Wainwright that he was in command of all forces in the Philippines. Wainwright was promoted to the rank of lieutenant general and he moved his headquarters to Corregidor, leaving Major General Edward P. King to command the mainland force on Bataan. But it wasn't much of an army, with soldiers on 25% daily ration and three-quarters of the force suffering from diseases and ailments that rendered them effectively unfit for combat.

Homma received a new division in March — the 4th Infantry Division — replacements and more airplanes, based at Clark Field. The Japanese stepped up artillery and air bombardments beginning on March 26 in preparation for the next offensive. Nurse Ann Bernatitus, then a Lieutenant (j.g.) was very busy at the hospital in Little Baguio when the bombardment began.

"On March 30, the hospital was bombed, even though the warehouse on the beach had a big red cross. Outside the operating room was a bench. I almost killed myself trying to get under that bench. The alarm would sound and then you could hear the bombs coming down — a whistling sound. On April 7 the Japanese apologized. It had been a mistake. That hospital was right next door to the ammunition dump.

"Every operating table would be filled. They would come in from the field all dirty. You did what you could. There were lice; I kept my hair covered all the time. He [Dr. Smith] did a lot of leg amputations because we had a lot of gas gangrene out there. I remember one patient we were operating on, Dr. Smith didn't want to sew him back up. He had died. I remember telling him that I didn't want him to do that if anything happened to me. He said, 'I'll sew him up just to shut you up.' We were washing the dirty dressings that they used during an operation. We would wash them out and refold and sterilized them and use them again.

"I remember Dr. Fraley would go down to Mariveles scrounging for food. One time he came back with lemon powder. After that, everything

was lemon. After I got home I didn't want any lemon. He would go to the navy facility down at Mariveles and scrounge instruments and whatever. The [submarine tender] USS *Canopus* was there and the men aboard would make things we needed in the shops on the ship.

"On April 7, the following week, they bombed us again. It was terrible. They hit one of the wards. There were patients who were tied in traction. The nurses had to cut the ropes so they could fall to the deck [floor]. By that time, they [the Japanese] had stopped advancing for a while. Things were kind of quiet at the front lines. But we were getting a lot of patients with malaria, dysentery, all that. We ran out of beds. You'd go to bed at night and when you awoke the next morning you'd get out there and there would be all these two or three-decker bunks made of wood and patients in them. There wasn't much surgery going on, but the nurses taking care of the sick were very busy."

After more than a week of concentrated bombing Homma unleashed the new offensive on Good Friday, April 3. The 41st Division, Philippine Army, sick and worn out, could not hold the center where the two corps intersected in the hills above Mariveles. The Japanese continued to exploit this salient the next day and a rout was beginning. The nurses and some soldiers escaped to Corregidor but there was little to stop the Japanese front from pushing the Americans and Filipino defenders into the sea. A counterattack on April 6 by the exhausted soldiers failed and King knew the end was near. Without Wainwright's knowledge, King made contact with Japanese officers in the early morning hours of April 9, and an unconditional surrender was arranged for 76,000 troops, the largest surrender then and still involving U. S. military personnel. King wanted to make sure his men would be treated as prisoners of war (POWs) according to the provisions of the Geneva

As the campaign wore on through the early months of 1942 military personnel on Corregidor underwent psychological changes as a result of the long confinement in the underground tunnels of "the Rock." Here members of the Finance Office in Malinta Tunnel lateral Number 12 show signs of weariness and despair.

Convention. Colonel Motoo Nakayama, senior operations officer of Homma's 14th army who accepted the surrender, assured King, "We are not barbarians." Les Tenney was part of the surrender and has nothing but respect for General King and his decision, even though it led directly to the barbaric and aptly named Bataan Death March.

"He ended up being quite the leader. I don't know how many people know, MacArthur gave instructions on the 8th of April that under no circumstances was the command to surrender, if all else failed, charge. MacArthur gave instructions not to surrender, King violated those instructions given by his commander and so King, in my opinion, took the brunt off of Wainwright who was the principal commander. Wainwright said this is what MacArthur wants and King said I can't do that, it would be slaughtering my troops. So King turned out to be quite a reliable officer, well-respected and well looked up to by all the men on Bataan.

"It was in the morning of April 9th that we were told that King had told all troops through our tank — I was a radio operator and tank commander by that time — destroy all arms, destroy all equipment, surrender was taking place. That was about seven o'clock in the morning. We started to do what we were expected to do and there was a lot of talk, should they try to get to Corregidor, a fortified island, should we try to get to the hills and our commanding officer said that as long as we were fighting together we should surrender together, which we decided to do. We started to get rid of our small arms, ammunition and we started to get rid of our tanks by cutting the fuel lines and setting them on fire, firing shells into the loaders and then at about 9:30 the Japanese came along and started to bomb us. They started to strafe, now this was on April 9th, this was when we were told to surrender. But my God, that's when all hell broke loose, that's when we ran and just didn't know what would happen. We were sure that we were going to be slaughtered, but now that we surrendered they were just going to slaughter us. We found out later that the reason was because General Homma's representative [Colonel Nakayama] wanted King to surrender all the forces, and he had to convince Colonel Nakayama that he had no authority to do that, all he had authority for was Bataan. It took until noon to accept it.

"Up until noon the Japanese bombed and strafed us and we had nothing to fight back with, we had destroyed everything. It was a horrible feeling, just horrible and about noon the planes would come over, circle and go away. That's when we felt it was done. The fol-

Japanese soldiers of the 14th Army inspect an American M-16 tank destroyed in the central Luzon campaign.

lowing morning was when I came into contact with the first Japanese foot soldiers."

The fighting came to an end on Bataan even though for many American and Filipino defenders, the worst was yet to come. The Japanese command then turned their attention to the last remaining obstacle to their conquest on Luzon — Corregidor and its three small supporting islands.

Corregidor: Gibraltar of the East

Even though the large coast artillery weapons of Corregidor were designed and sited to duel the big guns of capital ships approaching Manila Bay – warfare of an earlier era — forcing the island into submission was going to be no easy task for the Japanese. Corregidor, with the three islands in its defensive chain, was often described pre-War as the Gibraltar of the East. Perhaps the Japanese were aware of the nom-de-guerre. "The Rock" as Corregidor was nicknamed, was generally divided into three areas, the names reflecting the levels' relative heights above surrounding Manila Bay: Topside (highest), Middleside and Bottomside (lowest). Interestingly, the most vulnerable point on the island was the central power plant, located just west of Malinta Tunnel. Light and ventilation for the tunnel, power for the big guns, am-

munition hoists and the electric railway were among the many facilities dependent on the current the plant produced.

From April 9 to May 6, when General Wainwright finally was compelled to surrender all American and Filipino troops in the islands, Corregidor received the full attention of Homma's army. The air bombardment that had begun when war came to the Philippines in December 1941 was stepped up. There was no Allied air force to challenge the bombers, few ships left and only the anti-aircraft guns of the islands at the mouth of Manila Harbor to offer any resistance. Added to the pounding from the air was the roar of additional artillery pieces placed on oc-

Imperial army soldiers mill around the parapet of one of Corregidor's large guns in May 1942 after the island's capture. This cannon rotated and recoiled on a metal superstructure built in the pit below the gun.

cupied Bataan and as far away as Cavite.

Angelo Borruano, Sr., from Louisiana, was with the 59th Coast Artillery and had already been on Corregidor about a year prior to Homma's efforts to capture the island. He talks about the Gibraltar of the East before it became a horrendous battleground.

"Corregidor was a regular war place. It had the longest barracks in the world [where he stayed]. Before the war started we'd go out into the field and drill for combat and we knew when war was going to break out. In fact I sent the last letter to my mother and told her when war was going to

CORREGIDOR

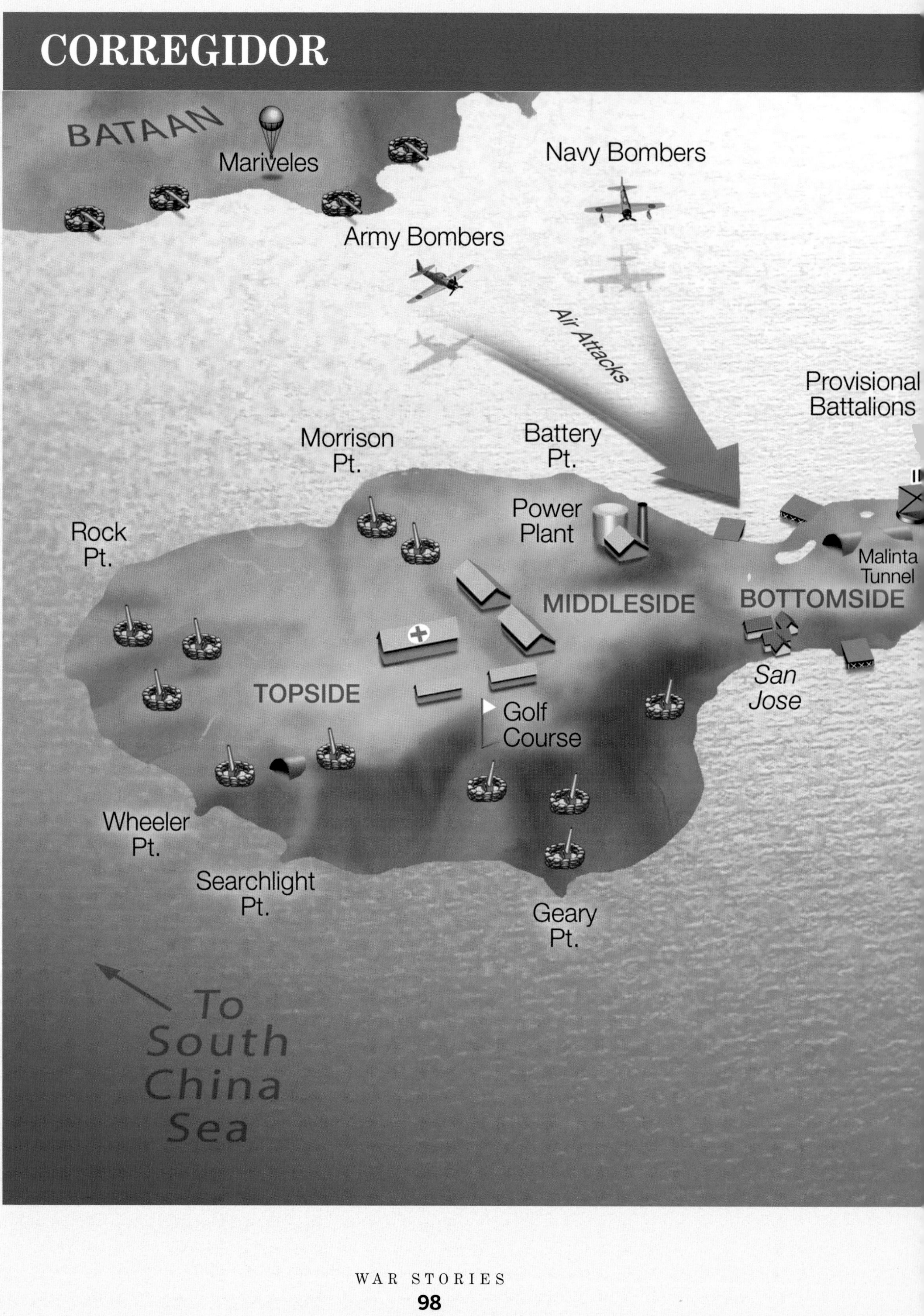

BATAAN
Mariveles
Navy Bombers
Army Bombers
Air Attacks
Provisional
Battalions
Morrison
Pt.
Battery
Pt.
Power
Plant
Rock
Pt.
Malinta
Tunnel
MIDDLESIDE
BOTTOMSIDE
TOPSIDE
Golf
Course
San
Jose
Wheeler
Pt.
Searchlight
Pt.
Geary
Pt.
To
South
China
Sea

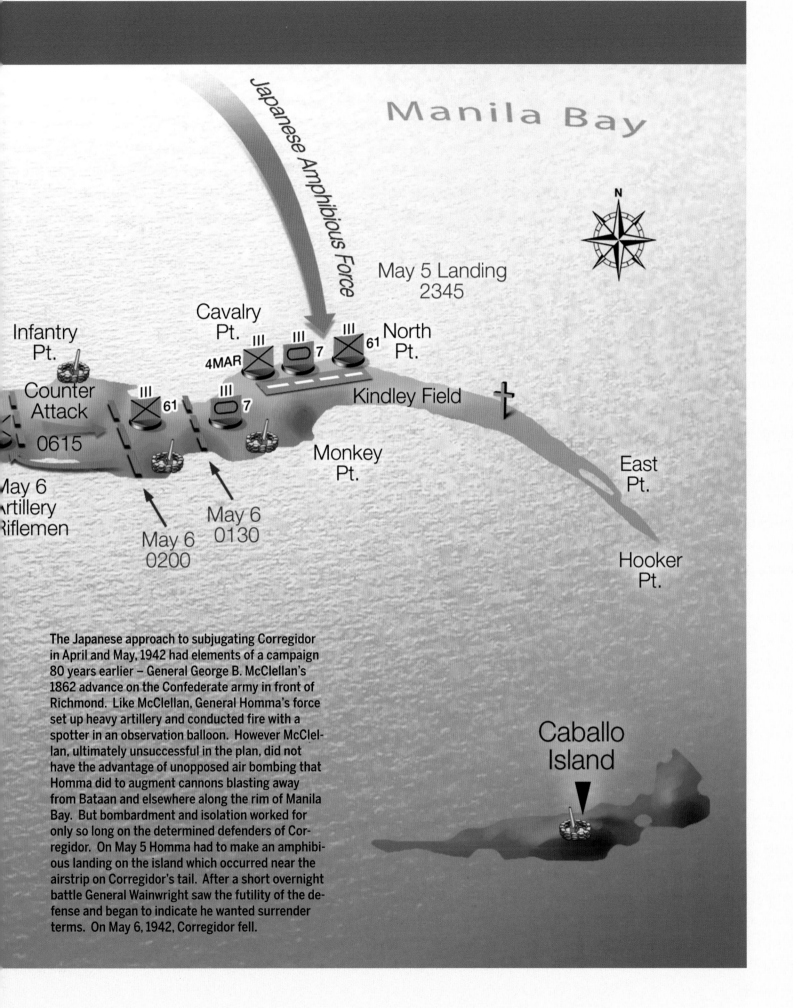

Manila Bay

Japanese Amphibious Force

May 5 Landing
2345

Cavalry
Pt.

Infantry
Pt.

4MAR · III · III · 7 · III · 61 North
Pt.

Counter
Attack

III · 61 · III · 7

Kindley Field

0615

Monkey
Pt.

East
Pt.

May 6
Artillery
Riflemen

May 6
0200

May 6
0130

Hooker
Pt.

Caballo
Island

The Japanese approach to subjugating Corregidor in April and May, 1942 had elements of a campaign 80 years earlier – General George B. McClellan's 1862 advance on the Confederate army in front of Richmond. Like McClellan, General Homma's force set up heavy artillery and conducted fire with a spotter in an observation balloon. However McClellan, ultimately unsuccessful in the plan, did not have the advantage of unopposed air bombing that Homma did to augment cannons blasting away from Bataan and elsewhere along the rim of Manila Bay. But bombardment and isolation worked for only so long on the determined defenders of Corregidor. On May 5 Homma had to make an amphibious landing on the island which occurred near the airstrip on Corregidor's tail. After a short overnight battle General Wainwright saw the futility of the defense and began to indicate he wanted surrender terms. On May 6, 1942, Corregidor fell.

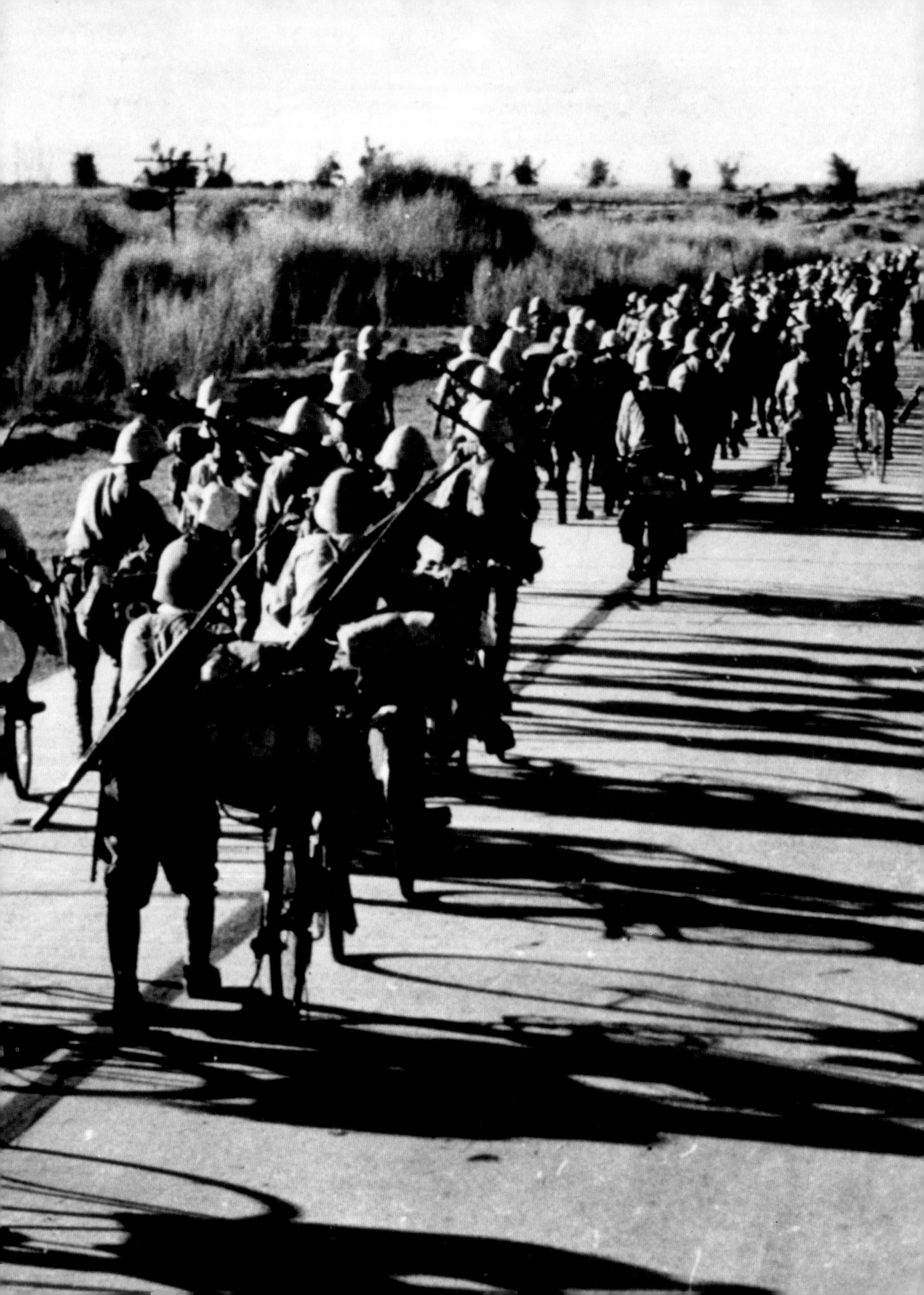

break out because we could see the ships of the Japanese coming in and out through the Philippines there. Before I went on the machine gun I was operating a sight that points guns out towards the sea. We were the only ones with guns that pointed out to sea that could fire on a baseline at the edge of the beaches.

"[On December 29, 1941] they [the Japanese] started bombing us, started bombing Corregidor with planes. They was firing from the ocean onto the beach with their ships, with their destroyers and all. We had quite a few men in the service over there with army, navy, Marines; all there from different organizations."

Borruano claims he got right down to business in his assignment to a machine gun set up on the golf course near the former Topside officers' quarters. "First time I shot I knocked a plane down, right on the golf course it fell."

Alfred McGrew was assigned to Battery H of the 60th Coast Artillery and shortly before the attack the men of the unit positioned their guns on Middleside, in the redoubt of a 6-inch seacoast battery. They had been on alert since late November.

"We knew they were coming, but we thought we could hold our own with them. Of course, we had some very good men in my battery, which consisted of about one hundred and twenty men. We began to be on twenty-four hour [shifts]. There was always something to do. After we were bombed on December 31st, which was a very severe bombing and lengthy, we were hard at work trying to fortify our battery, and put up camouflage and things like that. The first bombing, we lost our first man, a guy by the name of Arnold, who was dearly loved by all the guys. He jumped into a machine gun pit, and the Japs were coming in low with dive bombers, and they were dropping antipersonnel bombs and one of these went in. I was in my own pit, but I saw this gathering down below. From then on we lost [more]. We had [our] number one gun hit by shell fire, and we had shell fire coming from the southern part of Manila Bay, and coming across and hitting, and they hit our number one gun, killed two, or three, or four guys.

"The Japanese had good airplanes for the purpose, but they had a couple that we could reach, so we did hit quite a few aircraft. My position, fortunately, was located where the cliff dropped off on the south side of the island, and it was very difficult for them to hit. They did hit us, they drop-

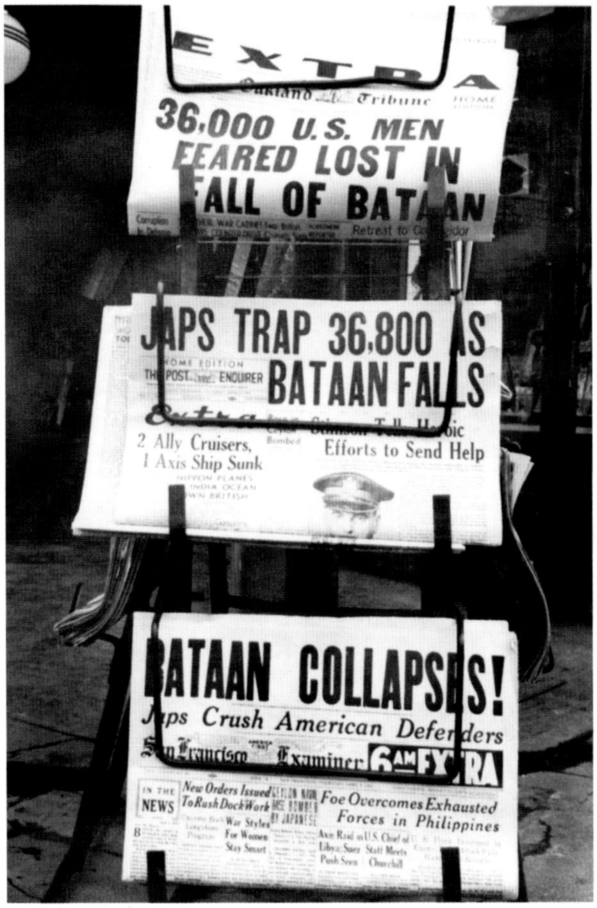
36,000 U.S. MEN
HOME EDITION
2 Ally Cruisers,
1 Axis Ship Sunk
Efforts to Send Help
Foe Overcomes Exhausted
Forces in Philippines

TOP: San Francisco Bay Area newspapers display the alarming news of Bataan's collapse on April 9, 1942. Seventy-seven years earlier and half a world away on the same date Robert E. Lee surrendered the Army of Northern Virginia at Appomattox Court House. According to reports, the irony did not escape General Edward King, a Southerner by birth. LEFT: Japanese bicycle infantry on January 3, 1942 advance on Manila along Highway 3 from twelve miles out.

ped bombs and shells, of course, but some of the batteries were just absolutely decimated. Like C-battery [which] was on the Bataan side of the island, and they were very vulnerable; there was nothing you could do. So, the big guns were hit very hard."

Herbert Hanneman was an Army clerk who was transferred from Manila to Corregidor when holding the capital city became untenable. He remembers a narrow escape on one of the many occasions of aerial bombardment.

"One day while I was there, they bombed the barracks we were working in. Dropped bombs there so everybody was running out. I remember running out of the building. One bomb, which did not explode — however it went through three floors, but never exploded — which probably saved our lives. And I was running out of there, and I could see planes coming that were doing some strafing. So I crawled into a culvert along a little road there. Couldn't quite get all the way in, so my head was sticking out and my head and face got covered with some of the stones that the strafers were hitting."

Homma's 5th Air Group, aided by the 11th Air Fleet, was responsible for the initial bombardment and by January 6 quite a bit of damage had been done to the exposed buildings and installations on Corregidor. A lull in the aerial attack marked the beginning of 1942 while Japanese efforts were focused on the mainland. Then on March 24 Homma, with the receipt of additional bombers, renewed the heavy pounding of Corregidor for the next week. The Americans had taken steps to protect themselves since the initial bombing forays of December, but the strong air and land shelling destroyed nearly everything above ground — buildings, vehicles, natural features.

The garrison began to endure some very nega-

tive effects of this action beyond the destruction of property and occasional loss of life when someone was caught unprotected. The psychological effects of the bombardment were beginning to change the mood of those who had already withstood much on The Rock. Refugees from Bataan, with no real command, wandered the island. Their weariness of fighting and desperation began to rub off on those who were stationed on Corregidor. Those gunners who stood by their cannon in dugouts adjacent to the big guns looked down on the "tunnel rats," those soldiers who wandered the underground shelters without official duties there. Angelo Borruano was one of those who stayed in the Topside area during the siege.

"I was out in the open, I never went in the tunnel. We got supplies but then it got to where we couldn't get any ammunition or nothing and we were surrounded. It took a whole month to take Corregidor. They thought they'd take it in a week's time but it took a month to take Corregidor."

The bombing from air and Japanese artillery emplacements increased daily. There were a total of 84 hours of air raids in the month of April and when these occurred, power was disrupted to Malinta Tunnel, making the already difficult conditions unbearable. The large artillery batteries at Bataan and Cavite were particularly effective in dropping shells into the protected gun emplacements. On April 24 a direct hit on Battery Crockett by a 240mm shell destroyed the two 12-inch seacoast guns there. The accuracy of the Japanese artillery was aided by a balloon observer on Bataan, called "Peeping Tom" by the Americans, as well as technology; sound and flash equipment that measured the accuracy of the fire.

Austin L. Andrews was a crewman aboard USS *Oahu*, one of the Yangtze River gunboats to arrive in Manila Bay on the eve of war. After the fall of

Bataan, *Oahu* took shelter at Corregidor. A lack of fuel restricted patrols to one gunboat on one patrol per day among *Oahu* and her two sister ships, USS *Luzon* and USS *Mindanao*. Andrews describes one day of the Corregidor bombardment and the fate of one of the largest seacoast batteries from his vantage point aboard USS *Oahu*.

"When Bataan fell, the Japanese moved 240-millimeter guns down Bataan. They had them lined up for about seventeen miles and used an observation balloon to direct their fire down onto Corregidor. That's how they were so accurate. This observation balloon was just out of range of our guns and we couldn't hit him. One day we were laying right off of Corregidor and planes hit the island. Artillery was firing and the whole island was burning. You couldn't even see the island through the smoke and the fire, and I said, 'Man, I don't see how in the hell anybody will be living over there.' But they did. They survived it. We were almost right off of Corregidor in the channel. The Japanese started firing on Battery Geary, and they would fire a dud from there, then they would fire a live round through, and they kept firing at that same spot until they broke through the wall, where the ammunition was located. Once it was penetrated, ninety-five-thousand pounds of black powder went up at one time. It blew them. There was four mortars inside and each one weighed more than a ton [actually ten tons]. I don't mind telling you they were bolted into concrete. It threw one of them clean out to the South China Sea. It threw another one out toward the golf course and another one they never found. I think about eighty or ninety men left the face of the earth at that time. That was the end of Battery Geary. We were still in the channel. We were tied up there, and when they bombed Corregidor and some of the bombs missed, they almost straddled us down below. That was just part of the war on Corregidor."

Alfred McGrew witnessed similar devastation.

"Of course, the Japanese, once they took Bataan, they could really hit us hard with 240-millimeter, about ten-inch shells. There was a battery, just above us, that had eight twelve-inch mortars, and it was struck with these 240s. It blew completely out; there were guns flying out all over the place."

The bombardment continued to soften up the Corregidor defenses and reduce The Rock to just that. The 260th air alarm on April 29, the Emperor's birthday, signaled a day of even more vicious bombardment. Wainwright and the garrison realized an assault landing was not far away. Despite MacArthur's vague pronouncement "I shall return" made to reassure the Philippines they would not be forgotten, the defenders felt they were to be sacrificed. Alfred McGrew remembers the commercial radio broadcasts they could receive from the states.

"The word that continually came over San Francisco radio was that, 'Help is on the way.' That was the common flag at that time. 'Help is on the way.' Spence [a friend] and I were saying things, 'Help is not on the way. There ain't no help.' We thought so early and we were planning what we were going to do when the termination came down, could we get off the island, etc, etc, you know. Of course, it was very precarious and difficult to try to get off the island. Three guys out of my battery tried it and they got shot all to pieces by the Marines, you know, just trying to get away in a small boat. No, we didn't have any hope. We really didn't. There wasn't anything to base any hope on."

Some would get off the island along with documents, gold and other things too valuable to leave. Priority was given to nurses, like Ann Bernatitus who had been sent from the hospital on Bataan to

Corregidor just before the mainland surrender.

"I don't know how I was picked. I remember the planes came in first to evacuate people. You were being treated to this terrific bombardment every single day and then one day they come to you and say 'By the way, we're taking you out of here.' Two PBYs came in first and they took some nurses on it [April 29]. How they picked them, I don't know. We were called to the mess hall and told we were going to be leaving that night [May 3]. They stressed that weight didn't matter as much as size. All I had was a duffel bag. I always said that I didn't want to go off there on an airplane. I would rather go by submarine. We were dreaming that that's exactly what was going to happen. They told us we would meet after dark in front of Wainwright's headquarters. But then the Japanese started shelling us so they canceled us. We were told to

General Wainwright, looking tired and gaunt from the ordeal on Bataan and Corregidor, sits opposite General Homma and other Japanese officers at the surrender table near a village on Bataan.

meet I think two or three hours later. Your name was called and you stepped out of the crowd because everybody was gathered around to see this.

"Wainwright shook your hand and wished you Godspeed and he said, 'Tell them how it is out here.' And then I got in a car and they took us out of the tunnel down to the dock. Everything was pitch-black, just some trees standing with no leaves, no nothing, charred. When we got down there we got on a boat that was even smaller than the one that took us to Corregidor. Then we shoved off. We had to go through our own minefields to get to the submarine. We learned later that it was taking us so long to get out there that the submarine wasn't sure Corregidor hadn't already fallen. Finally we saw this dark shape and we came alongside of it. You could hear the slapping of the water between the two objects. Then someone said 'Get your foot over the rail.' And then someone just pulled me, and then the first thing I knew I was going down the hatch. I got down there awfully fast."

In the first days of May the tempo of the bombardment increased again. Late on May 5 landing craft were detected by listening equipment and the much anticipated invasion of Corregidor began. The objective was a beach between Cavalry and Infantry Points, east of the eastern entrance to Malinta Tunnel; but the current carried Colonel Gempachi Sato's 61st Infantry to North Point a thousand yards farther away from the tunnel. There they were met by the last surviving artillery pieces in the area and two platoons of the 4th Marines, the unit that came from Shanghai. The opening phase of the operation turned disastrous for these soldiers of the Imperial Army 4th Division as they were cut to pieces.

With the 4th Marines joined by a provisional battalion made up of soldiers, sailors and some Marines, the defending force created a line across the neck of Corregidor about 1000 yards from Malinta Tunnel. At 0615 May 6 they mounted a counter-attack against the Japanese position on Battery Denver and created some havoc. General Homma was beginning to become concerned about the success of the landing but his artillery, armored units and the 61st Infantry Regiment were pushing ashore and eventually the defend-

Fulfilling the demands of his captors, Lt. Gen. Jonathan M. Wainwright broadcasts the surrender of Corregidor on May 6, 1942 from a Luzon radio station. The surrender effectively ended the fighting in the islands but also began a sustained guerilla resistance.

ers' left flank was turned.

General Wainwright decided that continued resistance would just sacrifice more men so in mid-morning he decided to surrender and broadcast a message declaring so. The Japanese failed to respond to the radio messages requesting a cease-fire. As a last measure to stop the bloodshed, Wainwright sent a party out with a white flag. Eventually it was arranged for Wainwright and the officers accompanying him to be taken to Bataan to meet Homma. At a rural house north of Cabcaben, Japanese press members were present for the meeting and the American contingent was photographed. Homma arrived in a Cadillac and the two sides met on the front porch.

Although he read and understood English, Homma had a translator survey the document brought by Wainwright. Homma was displeased that Wainwright was not prepared to surrender all forces in the Philippine Islands. Wainwright had turned over command of forces in the Visayas and Mindanao regions to Brigadier General William F. Sharp but from monitoring radio broadcasts, Homma knew Wainwright had command of all forces in the Philippines. His strategy to protect the forces outside of Luzon having failed, Wainwright backtracked but it was too late. Homma refused to accept the surrender. The theatrics finally ended when Wainwright and his party were returned to Corregidor and he was forced to sur-

render all the forces in the islands to Colonel Sato.

The Japanese by this time, midnight on May 6, were in full control of the island. Other forces in the Philippines would not all be surrendered until June 9 and Homma was recalled to Tokyo and his status downgraded for failing to meet the timetable in the Philippines capture. Once the strategic island group was in Japanese hands, the more important work to the south could commence, but the resolve shown by the defenders on Luzon was indicative of the resolve of those united against Japanese expansion. Angelo Borruano tells what happened to him and others captured on Corregidor after the surrender was worked out.

American and Filipino prisoners sit during an assembly stop or break on their way to Camp O'Donnell near Cababatuan. Most prisoners would march nearly forty miles to their incarceration in the former U. S. Army base.

"We stayed on Corregidor for a while. They kept us at a location where they fixed all the trucks. They put us in that department as the prisoners of war and we stayed in there about a month before they took us off Corregidor."

Alfred McGrew recounts in detail some of his experience after the surrender. The first night they were herded into a tunnel.

"We had no comprehension of what they'd do. I sat there, trying to get a little sleep until the next morning. An officer came in and he said, 'The Japs are outside, and they want us out of here.' So

we filed on outside and they lined us up and took us to the Middleside parade ground and they made us spread all of our belongings out, and they took what they wanted, which was about everything.

American soldiers are crowded along a road in the early stages of the Bataan Death March. Some of the guards grin and prisoners put their hands in the air — probably they were ordered to do so — in this Japanese propaganda photograph.

were trying to protect our men. There, in the first part of it, it was pretty brutal. Then they marched us down to Bottomside and through the tunnel, and then there were dead bodies laying around on the other side, of Marines and army, and they were put there on purpose because none of them had reached that point that close. We were marched, by them, down to 92nd Garage, and that's where, finally, my buddy hollered at me. He was already down there since he was out there in the first place. And that's how I got together with Spence. From then on, we had all kinds of adventures, until we left the island.

"These were what they called 'shock troops' and they were old and grizzled monkeys. You know, they had hair dangling, loose hair down and they didn't act to me like they were even intelligent. They were just cannon fodder. That's what we used to call them. That's what they used to invade with. They were cruel, very cruel. So, you might get your head hammered with the butt of a rifle for nothing, just for standing there.

"They killed several American officers who

"We realized that we didn't have anything to eat. So he talked me into going up the hill nearby,

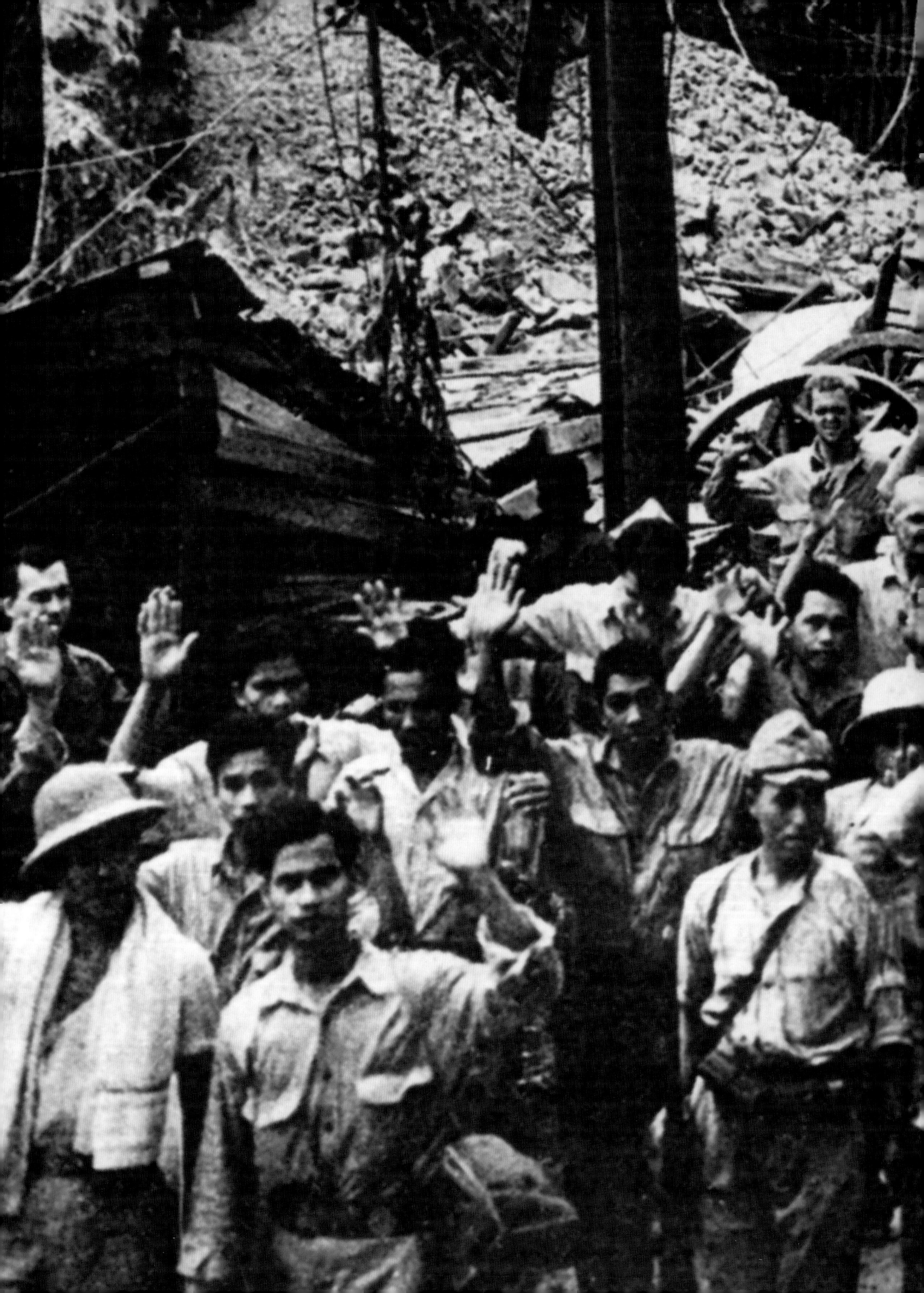

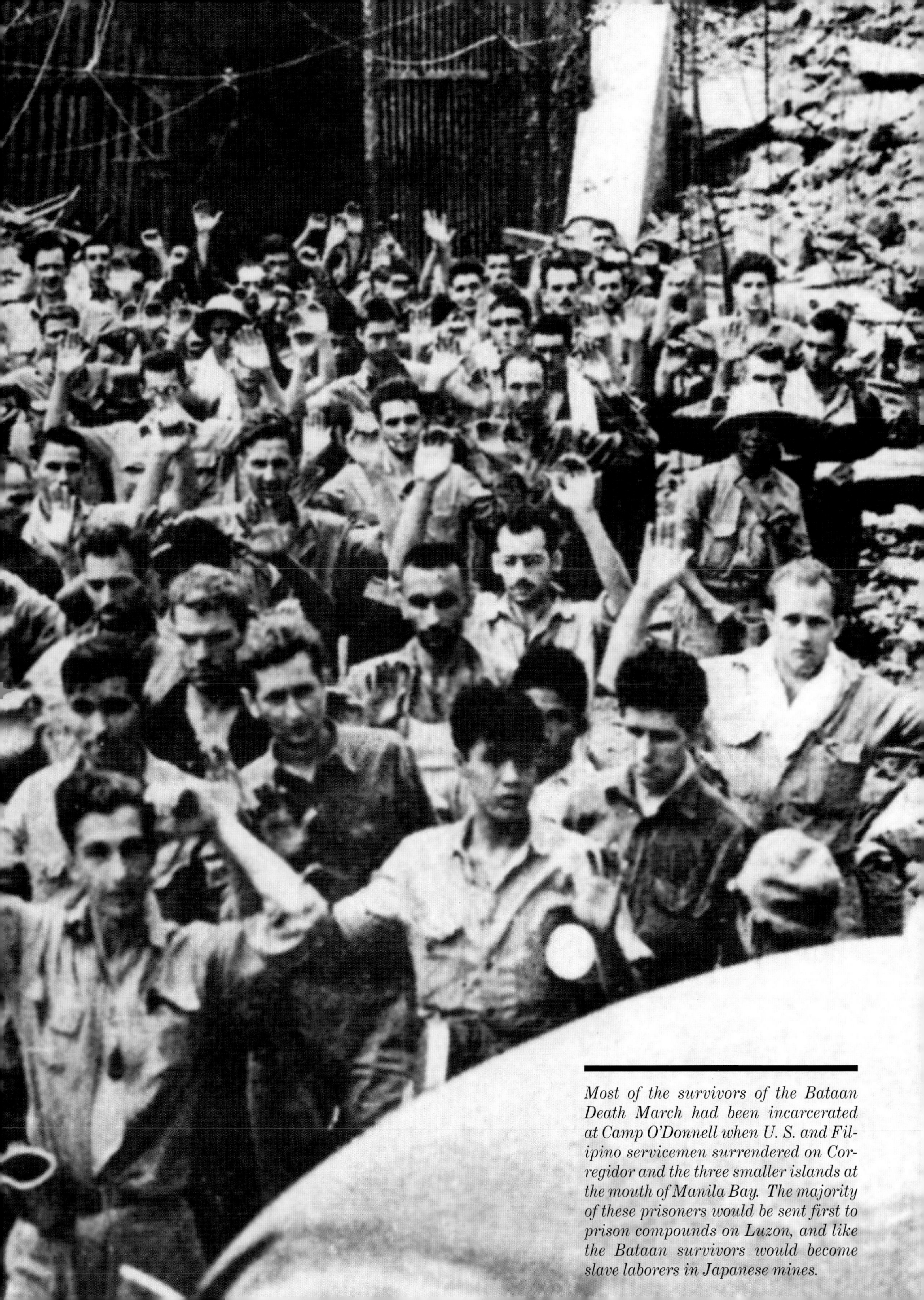

Most of the survivors of the Bataan Death March had been incarcerated at Camp O'Donnell when U. S. and Filipino servicemen surrendered on Corregidor and the three smaller islands at the mouth of Manila Bay. The majority of these prisoners would be sent first to prison compounds on Luzon, and like the Bataan survivors would become slave laborers in Japanese mines.

because there weren't any fences up yet and the Japs weren't paying any attention. So we went up to D battery, which was just up on the hill. We went up scrounging for food, and we did find some cans of stuff. We brought them back on a stretcher with some canvas stretched over it. We got stopped by a squad of Japanese and I told Spence, 'You know, put the thing down and salute.' They like saluting. So we saluted and bowed our head and stuff like that and they went on and left us be. We got down the hill, how, I'll never know, without getting interrupted. We got down to our little lean-to and we discovered that we had three number-ten cans, and they turned out to be all tomatoes, stewed tomatoes, and I hate tomatoes. To this day I can't eat tomatoes. So I traded, a navy guy in the next little cabal over there, I traded him a cup of tomatoes for biscuits. But we only had one little water source for all these twelve thousand people. So we found it, and there was an endless line twenty-four hours a day going through that."

Like the other troops on Luzon, the defenders of Corregidor and the other three channel islands would endure the longest terms in captivity of any U. S. soldiers in organized units — if they survived that long. Many did not.

The Bataan Death March

While the campaign to pound Corregidor into submission was going on, one of the greatest travesties of human conduct during warfare was taking place on Bataan. Ignoring all civilized rules of prisoner treatment at the time, the Japanese under Homma carried out what is known to history as the Bataan Death March. After the April 9, 1942 surrender of all forces on Bataan, American and Filipino military personnel were rounded up in groups. There was no particular organization of the prisoners as the march began at Mariveles and continued on roads north. The only thing known was the destination, Camp O'Donnell, a former U. S. base sixty-five miles northeast of Mariveles at San Fernando that was designated to be the holding compound for the American and Filipino POWs. Les Tenney was on the march and remembers when the enlisted men were separated from their officers.

"April 10th, that morning the Japanese came up there were no other comments from any of the officers, everything was one man for himself. You did everything the Japanese told you to do or you were beaten right then and there or killed. From that moment on that was the end of any instruction from or relationship with an officer.

"I was captured right near Mariveles where our tank battalion was, and I would say that, from what I remember, that we were probably the tenth group that was passing, I have no idea I'm just guessing. You'd see the marchers and then they'd stand you up and push you in line. Then all of a sudden the Japanese would stop it and the rest of the people would be told to sit down and this was just for your group. You could have your best friend go over here and you can't do anything."

Kelly Davis shares his experience at the beginning of the march when they were formed up at an airfield on the southern tip of Bataan.

"Our commander said, 'Now men we're going to lay our arms down. We're not going to approach that field with arms or they'll kill us on the spot. And don't try to take anything except your canteen and mess kit.' So we left anything extra and marched into the beach and there was a group of Japanese, soldiers and officers, standing right on the field. Every one of them had their guns out when we walked in. They made us assemble in a line and from there [the Japanese officers] turned the enlisted men on us and they shook each one of us down. Watches, rings, everything they could find, and then they'd butt [hit] you with a rifle or something. I think one man got killed by their shaking him down but that was all in the whole line-up. I had a bottle of iodine I used to take care of my hand, I had a wrapped up hand because I got in a firefight and cut it on some bamboo. I had this bottle of iodine in my shorts, I thought they'd never get that and they didn't. They'd taken about 50 or 70 men and they put them four across and I don't know how long it was, we marched up the road.

"The Japanese guards were — I think they'd been told that they didn't want survivors because periodically for almost no reason at all they'd take aim at a man and shoot him. Once in a while one of the people would try to run back into the jungle because they could see this was no orthodox way to finish the war and they got shot. The first day we were still working our way out from the very tip of Bataan. I remember we got on the side with a full view of Corregidor and all of a sudden we didn't hear the guns but we heard the shells. On Corregidor they had figured that we were Japanese troops and here are the shells going off. When I heard those things going over our heads, it sounded to me like a house flipping over and over and then blew up, maybe 100 yards behind us. No one was hit — we and the guards all laid down on the ground to hide. They fired a series of shots over and every one of them over-

Remember me? I was at Bataan

BUY WAR BONDS

Like the attack on Pearl Harbor, the Bataan Death March quickly became a rallying point for war efforts in the United States.

shot us. We were right on the beach which was our road at that time so we got settled back and started marching again. I don't know if any of the other groups had been fired at with Corregidor misunderstanding whether they were shooting at us or not, but there was no damage done from that.

"Well, we had no food and no water. We marched all that day and at night they let us lie down just in the middle of the road with the guards around us. If anybody moved they were shot, not if they tried to run or anything, if they just moved. So we laid there for maybe three or four hours and they started to march again. We marched all that next day and about noontime or afternoon, I had contracted malaria as had a lot of the men while I was on Bataan, so I had a few attacks of malaria since then. It starts out with the chills and turns into a fever and I started chilling. At that time I was in the tail end of the column of prisoners. I asked this one guy if he could see anything. I said I couldn't, I guess it was the fever. At any rate he said I could hold onto his pocket. So here I was, couldn't see, high fever, hanging on this man's pocket and I stumbled and fell. I started trying to get up and I heard this Japanese guard behind me, I didn't know what he said, 'kora,' whatever that means, and the next thing I knew as I'm halfway up he hits me with his bayonet right on the buttocks, I think it went straight to the bone because it really hurt. At any rate I man-

aged, with this man I'd been hanging onto his pocket grabbed my hand and I was back in the column."

Les Tenney talks about the march as it continued for him:

Not all of those who were on the Bataan Death March died of the march's deprivations along the way. In fact, more died once they reached Camp O'Donnell; of disease, maltreatment and denial of basic necessities during the march or when they reached the camp. The size and frequency of burial details at the camp such as this one attest to this.

that falling down meant death, period. If you didn't get up you were dead. The march you started in this way in a matter of minutes changed. We never knew, never knew from one day to the next, from one hour to the next who was going to be next to you.

"The man that I was next to when I started the march was somebody different 20 minutes later. The Japanese had come along and beat you in the behind and holler and make you walk faster. Two men would walk faster and four men would walk slower within a matter of five minutes you had different men next to you. Ten minutes later you had other people next to you. If somebody fell down they were dead, if you fell you died that's all there was to it. It didn't take long to understand

"Somebody says to me I know a friend of mine on the march and so forth. The one thing we never said to people on the march was, "Hi. I'm Les Tenney, who are you?' We didn't give a damn who the guy was there. My only goal was how to stay alive for another 10 minutes or 20 minutes, so we never knew who was next to us unless it was one of our buddies we knew from before but we never knew.

"Everyone on that march had some of the same experiences, the only difference could have been the timing of an experience. In my particular situation the group that I was involved with, about 400 men, we got no food or water for four days, the first four days we had nothing. We got water from the side of the road when we were able to dig into a water buffalo wallow and spread the water and drink some of the water. Luckily a couple of times we found an artesian well and if you went to get water from the artesian well you could be lucky and get some water or you could be unlucky and the Japanese comes over and shoots you. There was never a way of knowing what was going to happen at any one time. There was no way that we could say, do this, this will happen, impossible, we never knew, and that's the way it was for the first four days. During those first four days it was just every man for himself, we tried to help but there was nothing you could do. If a man fell down you could try to help him up, then the Japanese would come up and beat the hell out of you and make him get up. If he couldn't get up they'd kill him, it was a pretty miserable situation. You didn't have to be too smart to understand what was happening, and if you did certain things you were going to die. You'd try to convince your buddies it was better on your feet, stand up don't get down. If you fall down get up, let me help you up, but get up, start walking.

"It was not just getting up, getting up was one part of it you had to make your feet move so that they thought you were moving forward. On the fifth day we got a ration of rice, one bowl of rice. If the Filipinos were throwing you food, which they tried to do, and you catch a ball of rice, chicken and fish and you'd eat one or two bites of it and hand it to your buddy next to you, you didn't even know who he was, you never ate the whole thing — you'd hand it to somebody else and hope that the other guy would hand it to somebody else. If the Japan-ese saw a Filipino throwing food they would shoot him, it didn't matter what it was. Everything that was done during that period on the march was a period of not knowing what was going to happen the next minute, you had no way of knowing and that lasted until the march ended."

The men and women who defended the Philippines in the early months of the war between the United States and Japan felt like they were abandoned — expendable in the overall war effort that placed defeat of Nazi Germany first. Based on the Japanese strategy and the successful execution of it in December 1941, however, it would have been a risky proposition with many obstacles to reinforce the islands. The Japanese concentrated great resources toward the defeat of the American and Filipino forces and it would ultimately take years and much in the way of resources to retake the islands.

The shocking extent of the American loss in the Philippines ramped up a battle cry that started with Pearl Harbor. The story does not end here. The suffering continued for more than three years for many who survived the initial battles and bombardments. Dorothy Still Danner, along with many other nurses and civilians, became prisoners in Manila, confined to Santo Tomas or other designated heavily guarded areas. Lester Tenney, Angelo Borruano, and other brave men endured hardships beyond belief in Japanese POW camps and in slave labor operations in the Home Islands. The stories of their later captivity and final liberation will be told in a future work.

Subjugation of Guam and Wake Island

In their plan for domination of Southeast Asia and the Pacific, the Japanese placed high priority on establishing air bases, and denying the same to the United States and her allies. One of the areas that became strategic in this regard was Mindanao in the southern Philippines. In tandem with the invasion of Luzon, the Japanese Third Fleet landed a force in the southernmost large island in the Philippines in December which took over Mindanao with little resistance. The airfields established there were useful in the Japanese advance on Borneo in the Dutch East Indies, making dealing with the large Moro population on Mindanao a challenging but worthwhile occupation.

In order to slow down the anticipated American drive across the Pacific, the Japanese war plan included taking over two islands in the Central Pacific. Guam had long been a strategic position for the United States, and the last stopover on the way to Manila. A tiny spit of land called Wake Island was, like Midway to the east of it, a necessary position to hold for any mastery of the Pacific. Capturing these critical objectives was tasked to the Japanese Fourth Fleet, based at Truk in the Caroline Islands.

Guam was not well fortified when the Japanese invaded on December 10, 1941. In 1939 the U. S. Congress refused to authorize any strengthening of Guam's defenses and therefore its strategic importance as a link to the Philippines was negated. The island was destined to fall at the first sign of Japanese interest in invading it. That move came after two days of "softening up" by aerial bombardment. This was really unnecessary given the paltry size of Guam's defense force – three small patrol ships with a handful of navy and Marine personnel and the native Insular Guard.

Then Admiral Inouye sent in a landing party from his Fourth Fleet early on December 10. The U. S. Marines took up a defensive position at their base, but the first wave of the 5000 Japanese who landed that day, Special Naval Landing Force troops, were met by a small group of the native Insular Guard who put up a stiff but futile resistance. The governor of the island, after arranging a cease

fire and receiving promises of how civilians and military personnel would be treated, surrendered Guam. The promise of fair treatment was broken after one month when military and civilian prisoners were moved to Japan. Several U. S. Navy personnel escaped into the hills and bush assisted by the native Chamorro population. Naval radioman George R. Tweed survived until the eve of Guam's liberation in July-August 1944.

The situation on tiny Wake Island was different. Despite its size, just the top of a submerged volcano with a coral filled lagoon, Wake Island was seen as a logical stopover in a trans-Pacific air route. Initially developed in the mid-1930s by Pan American Airways for its China Clipper route, the U. S. military came later and despite the urging of Admiral Kimmel, help was too little and too late. However, twelve 3-inch anti-aircraft guns, fighter planes on a newly finished landing strip and four 5-inch seacoast guns did significant damage to the first wave of Japanese transports and their escorts. The December 11 landing never got near the shore and the Japanese lost two destroyers to the excellent artillery work of Major James P. S. Devereux and his Marines of the 1st Defense Battalion and Marine airmen of VMF 22. The Marines were supported by civilian construction workers on the island that took up arms to help.

A relief expedition was dispatched from Pearl Harbor with the centerpiece, USS *Saratoga*, the carrier that had just arrived from San Diego. *Saratoga* sortied Pearl Harbor with two other task forces, one built around USS *Enterprise* and the other built around USS *Lexington*. In com-

Although this war poster to stimulate production is a little misleading, American nurses who were still in the islands when the Philippines fell worked in captivity in hospitals in Manila or were incarcerated in Santo Tomas University with Filipino and foreign national civilians.

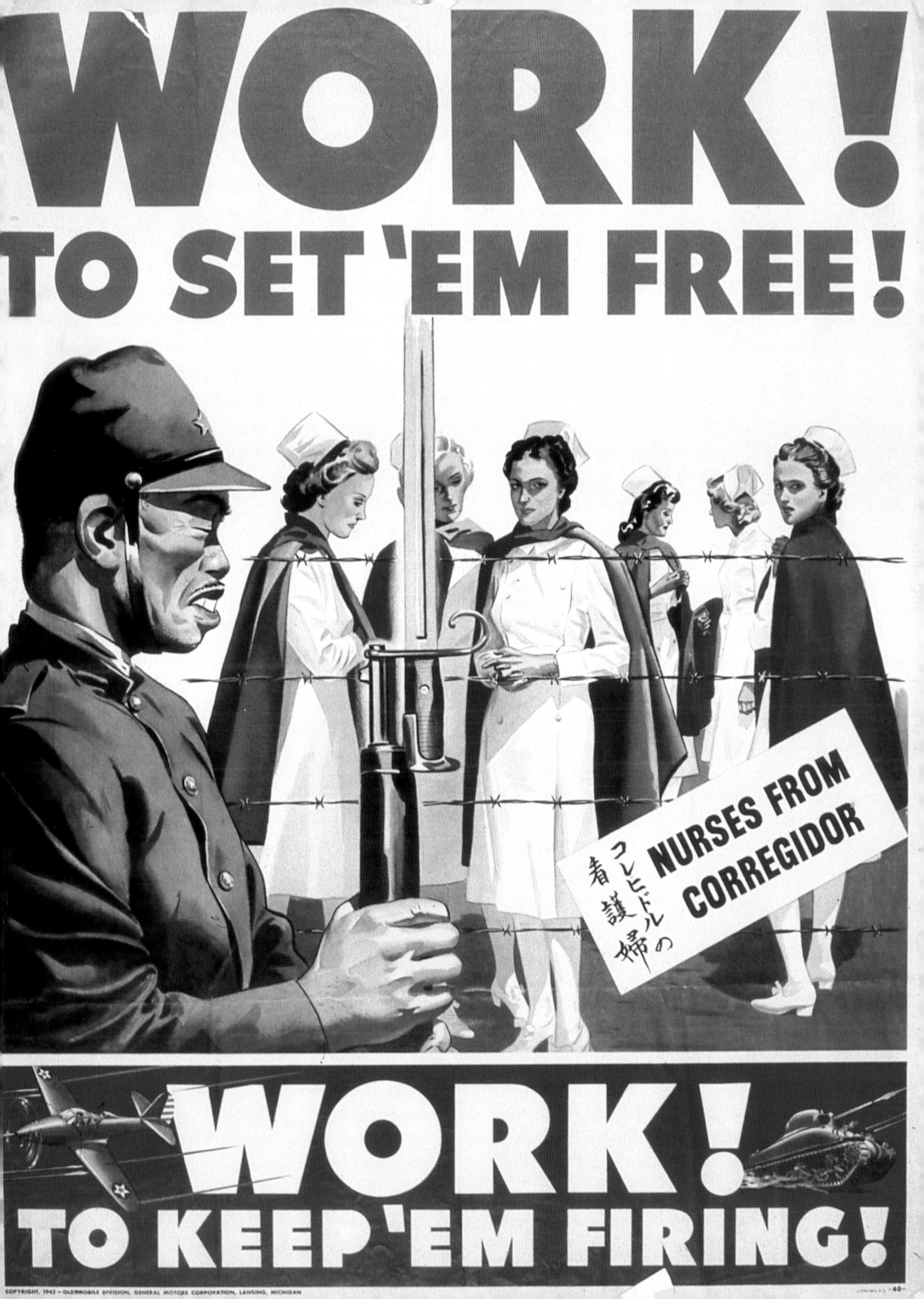
WORK!
TO SET 'EM FREE!
コレヒドルの
看護婦
NURSES FROM
CORREGIDOR
WORK!
TO KEEP 'EM FIRING!
COPYRIGHT, 1942 – OLDSMOBILE DIVISION, GENERAL MOTORS CORPORATION, LANSING, MICHIGAN
-40-

mand of the *Saratoga* task force was Rear Admiral Frank Jack Fletcher who approached the job with vigor, but proceeded cautiously. The entire operation, conceived by Kimmel, was late in getting underway and ran into bad luck. Kimmel was relieved by Vice Admiral William S. Pye on December 22 and Pye had no taste for going head to head with the Japanese Imperial Navy over Wake Island. He scrubbed the mission before any ship to ship combat might have not only saved Wake Island, it may have shown how ready the U. S. Pacific Fleet was to face down the Japanese navy. As a result, the brave garrison at Wake Island under Major Devereux was forced to surrender on December 23 and the last strategic piece of the Central Pacific puzzle fell into Tokyo's hands.

The Japanese augmented the triumphs of December at Wake Island, Guam and the Philippines

Wake Island was a strategic point on a short route between Hawaii and the Philippines but Congressional action before the war prevented the force there from mounting much of a resistance to Japanese invasion.

invasion (even though the latter turned into a long, drawn out affair), with a few other buffer occupations in the Gilbert Islands (Tarawa), and in the Bismarck Archipelago. But for the most part, their buffer to the east and southeast was complete. The Japanese military then turned its attention to completing the southwestern and southern buffer — a campaign started at the same time as that in the Philippines in Malaya, Hong Kong and Thailand — by extending their frontier toward Burma and the islands north of Australia. They also began to squeeze the last Allied military presence out of the southern resource area which they coveted so greatly. Japan's leaders were ready to wipe out America's last outposts and allies in the Far East, and believed that they had made the United States impotent in the region. In the latter they were sorely mistaken.

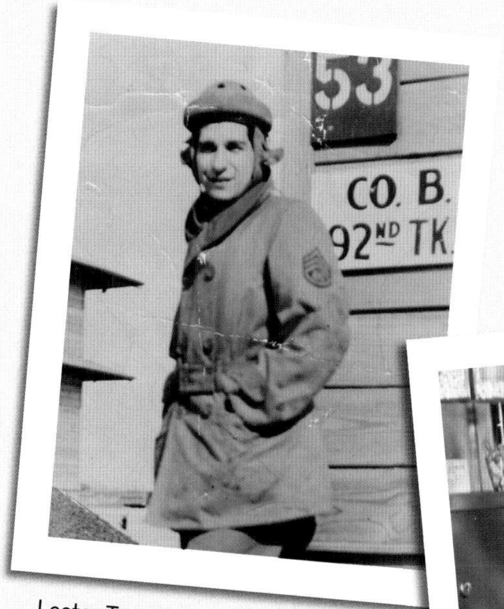
53
CO. B.
92ND TK.

Lester Tenney poses at Fort Knox during tank training in 1941.

Ann Bernatitus served with distinction as a surgical nurse, assisting in patching up those who were wounded in the Luzon and Bataan campaigns. She was one of the last people evacuated from Corregidor by submarine.

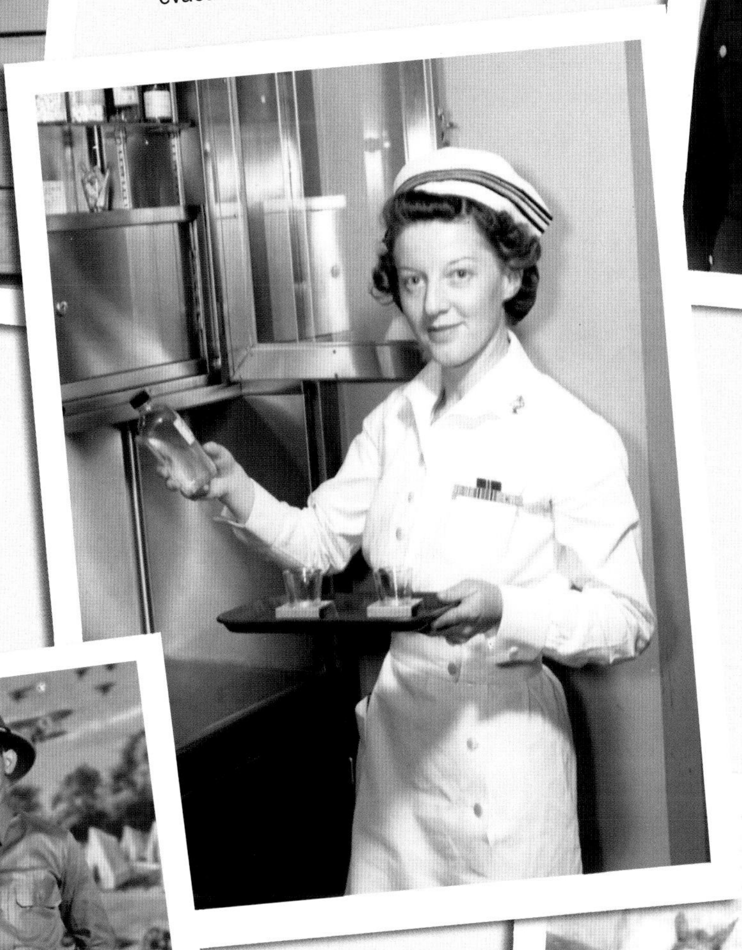

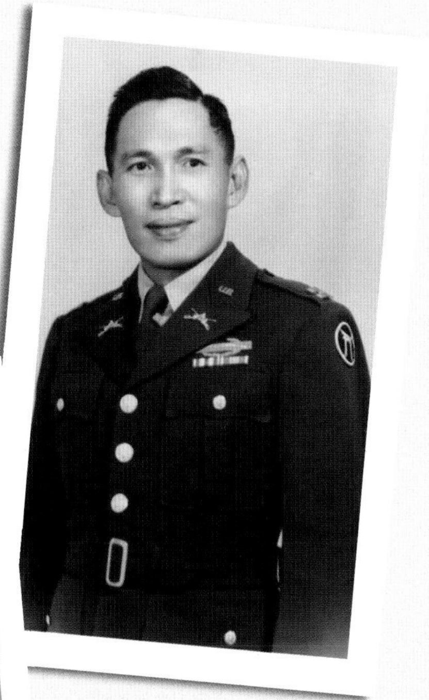

Felipe Fernandez stayed in the army for 30 years and retired as a sergeant major in 1967.

Angelo Borruano was a fearless young soldier when this photograph was taken on Corregidor as a 1941 Christmas present for his family back in Louisiana.

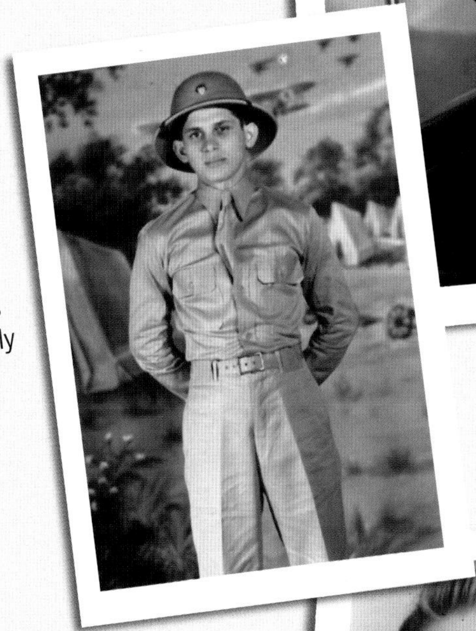

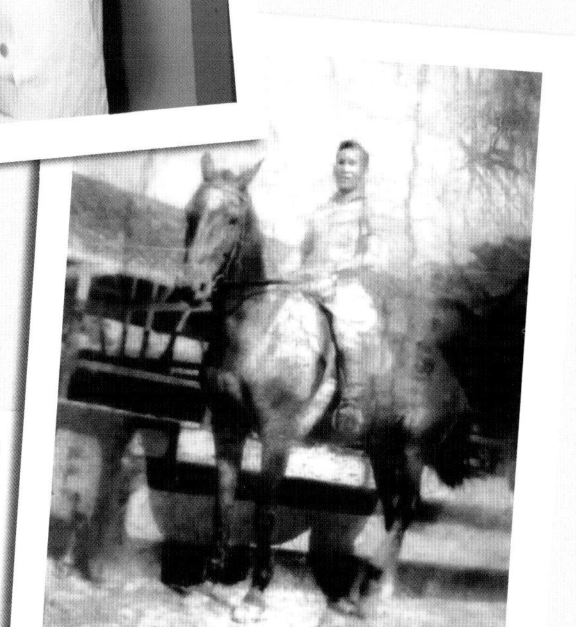

Like many cavalrymen, Felipe Fernandez developed a loving bond with his horse, Mike. Fernandez trained Mike in 1938 and the horse stayed with him until mounted units were disbanded on Bataan in 1942.

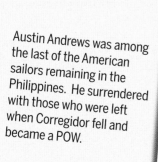

Austin Andrews was among the last of the American sailors remaining in the Philippines. He surrendered with those who were left when Corregidor fell and became a POW.

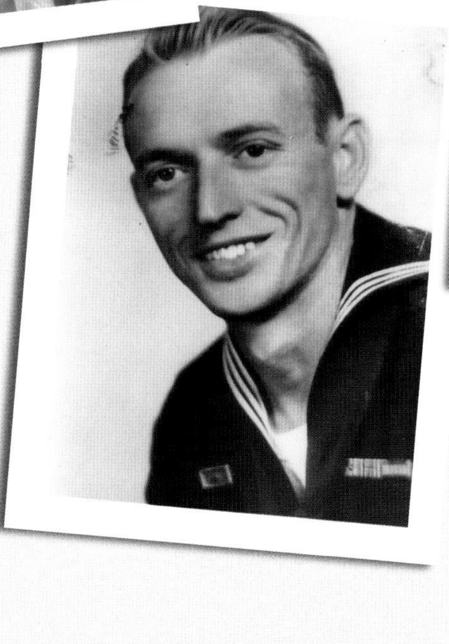

The Horse Cavalry of Luzon

December 7, 1941 was an important day for the 26th Cavalry Regiment, Philippine Scouts. The much anticipated polo game between members of the regiment and a team from the Manila Polo Club, who had international competitive status, was about to begin. There was much excitement in the air as four businessmen who formed the Manila team arrived with their families in sleek sedans at the home base of the 26th, Fort Stotsenburg in central Luzon. Four American cavalry officers made up the challenging team. The umpire was Major General Jonathan Wainwright, a former 26th Cavalry officer and current commander of the North Luzon Force. Troopers from the regiment whooped and cheered in the stands. The cavalrymen fell behind early, gave a spirited chase toward the end but ultimately lost the match. At a well attended party that night, Wainwright and others complimented the officers on their excellent play against stiff competitors.

As things turned out, the next day would prove to be even more important to the regiment. It was the beginning of the end for the Filipinos and their American protectors who occupied Luzon and the other islands of the Philippine archipelago. General Douglas MacArthur's United States Army Far East, the premiere American land force abroad, was in grave danger of slipping into oblivion after the surprise attack that began on Oahu rippled through the strongholds of the Anglo Allies in the Far East. Instead of the single day of fighting that Pearl Harbor endured to start the Pacific War, the horrendous ordeal in the Philippines lasted five months. For the Philippine Scouts — professional Filipino soldiers commanded by American officers — U. S. regulars, Filipino volunteers and the people of the islands, it was a terrible saga of defeat, humiliation and destruction that splashed across American newspapers daily. The 26th Cavalry — horse mounted soldiers and the elite unit of the army — would be in the thick of every major battle and engagement as the military tried to hold on until anticipated help from the U. S. arrived.

For most members of the 26th, war wasn't the farthest thing from their minds, but it wasn't in the forefront of their thoughts either. "Many of us weren't paying much attention to it because we were pretty busy," says Lieutenant Edwin P. Ramsey, one of the polo players. "Of course after the polo game we were out having a big party and we weren't worried about much of anything then." Ramsey was a rowdy teenager from Wichita, Kansas who struck a bargain with his mother, a widowed physician. He agreed to enter the Oklahoma Military Academy because he loved horses and wanted to be a cavalryman. He was recovering from a hangover on the morning of December 8, the result of an after party that went well into the dawn hours accompanied by alcohol and pretty Filipinas. "I went to the headquarters of the regiment and everybody was scurrying around. I said, 'What's going on?' 'We're at war, don't you know?' I said, 'No, I don't know anything about it.' So I had to run back to my quarters and grab a duffle bag for a war bag. I didn't even have one prepared."

Private Menandro Parazo awoke on December 8 to the sound of the post cannon. "We were told that when that cannon fires, we were at war or something. So when we heard it everybody jumped." Parazo joined the 26th in February,

1941 at a recruiting rally on his way home from college. He became a clerk in regimental headquarters. Like Ramsey, he was busy up to that time with his duties and paid little attention to war warnings. "During the time I was already with the 26th, there was no talk of war. There was no rumor about war except in the newspapers in the Philippines."

Corporal Felipe Fernandez was thinking of his upcoming wedding scheduled for December 22. Fernandez joined the army in 1936 and was accepted into the 26th where he became an excellent horseman and clerk for Troop E. "My fiancée and I went to visit her grandmother in Bacban and when we arrived Sunday night I stayed in their house and

Edwin Pierce Ramsey was a brash and confident young officer whose spirit kept him alive during the five years he was an American officer and guerilla fighter in the Philippines.

Luzon, the Japanese were pursuing a rigid methodical approach to taking the Philippines. First they struck at air resources and established landing fields for close support. They followed this with an all-out air, sea and land blitz to take the islands on a pre-set schedule — a necessary but inconvenient stepping stone toward their real objective, the Dutch East Indies with their plentiful natural resources.

Ramsey, a platoon commander in Troop G, was already on the road east to his deployment with horses and the troop's supplies loaded in trucks when the midday air attack came to Fort Stotsenburg. The bombers passed over the column without incident on their way to

I overslept. So when I went over there I was wondering why my horse and a few others were the only ones left in the stable. I saw my horse run to the door which he usually does when he sees me coming. I went over there and you know, a cavalryman talks to his horse, 'What's wrong, Mike?' And he just keep on nodding his head. 'I have to leave you here and I'm going to the barracks.' That's when I found out that the war broke out."

Where was the invasion? Rumors flying around that an airborne invasion was imminent gained credence. Unbeknownst to the forces on

Clark Field at the fort. "While we were at the headquarters," says Parazo, "somebody alerted us that they were hearing something unusual like roll of the thunder that was coming in nearer and nearer. So we went out and Colonel Pierce [Clinton A. Pierce, regimental commander] told me to count the airplanes which were already almost above us. And Captain Paul Jones, who was acting adjutant, said, 'How many did you count, Parazo?' I said about fifty. And I was still counting and they started dropping the bombs. We had to get away from the building and spread out

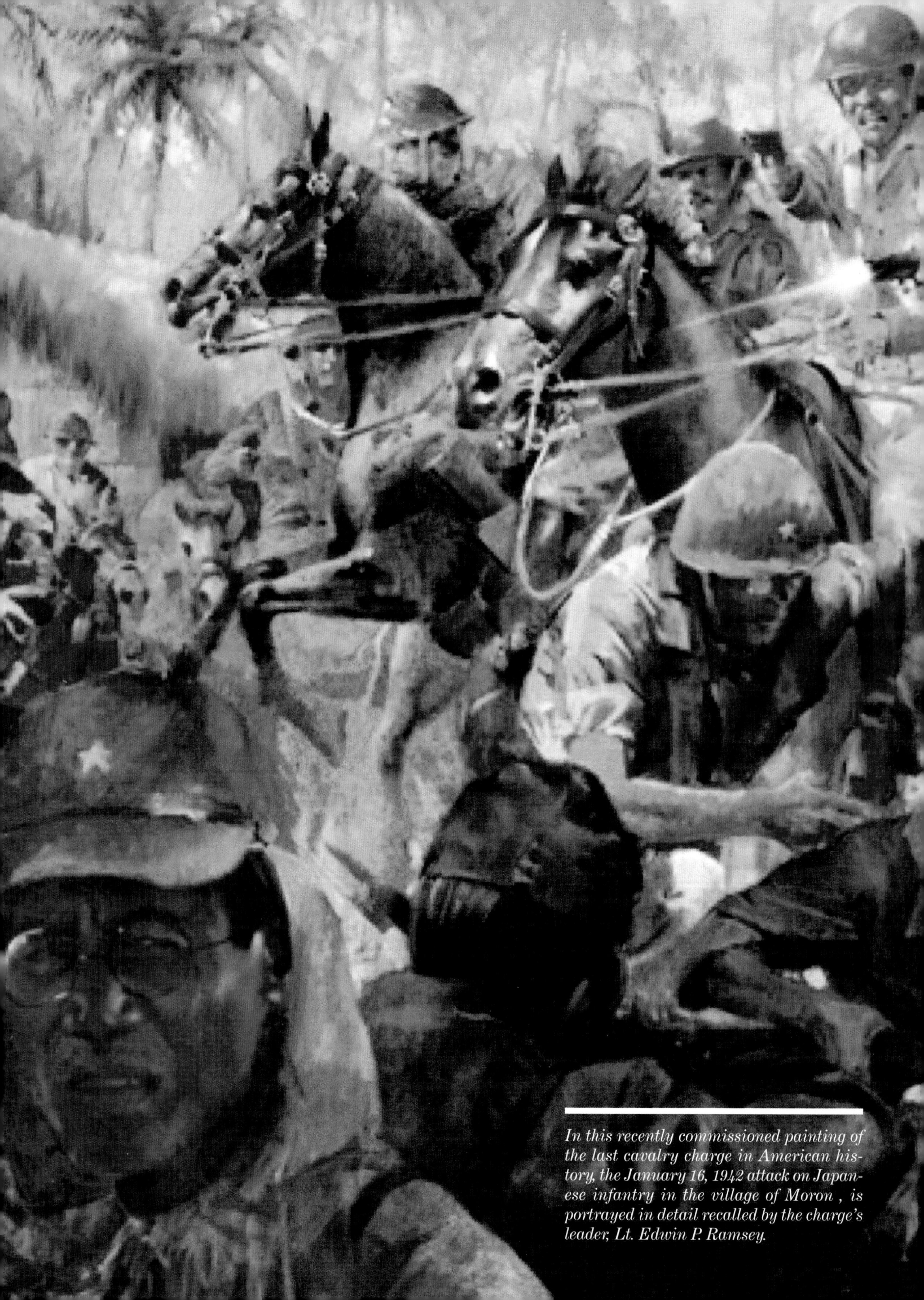

In this recently commissioned painting of the last cavalry charge in American history, the January 16, 1942 attack on Japanese infantry in the village of Moron , is portrayed in detail recalled by the charge's leader, Lt. Edwin P. Ramsey.

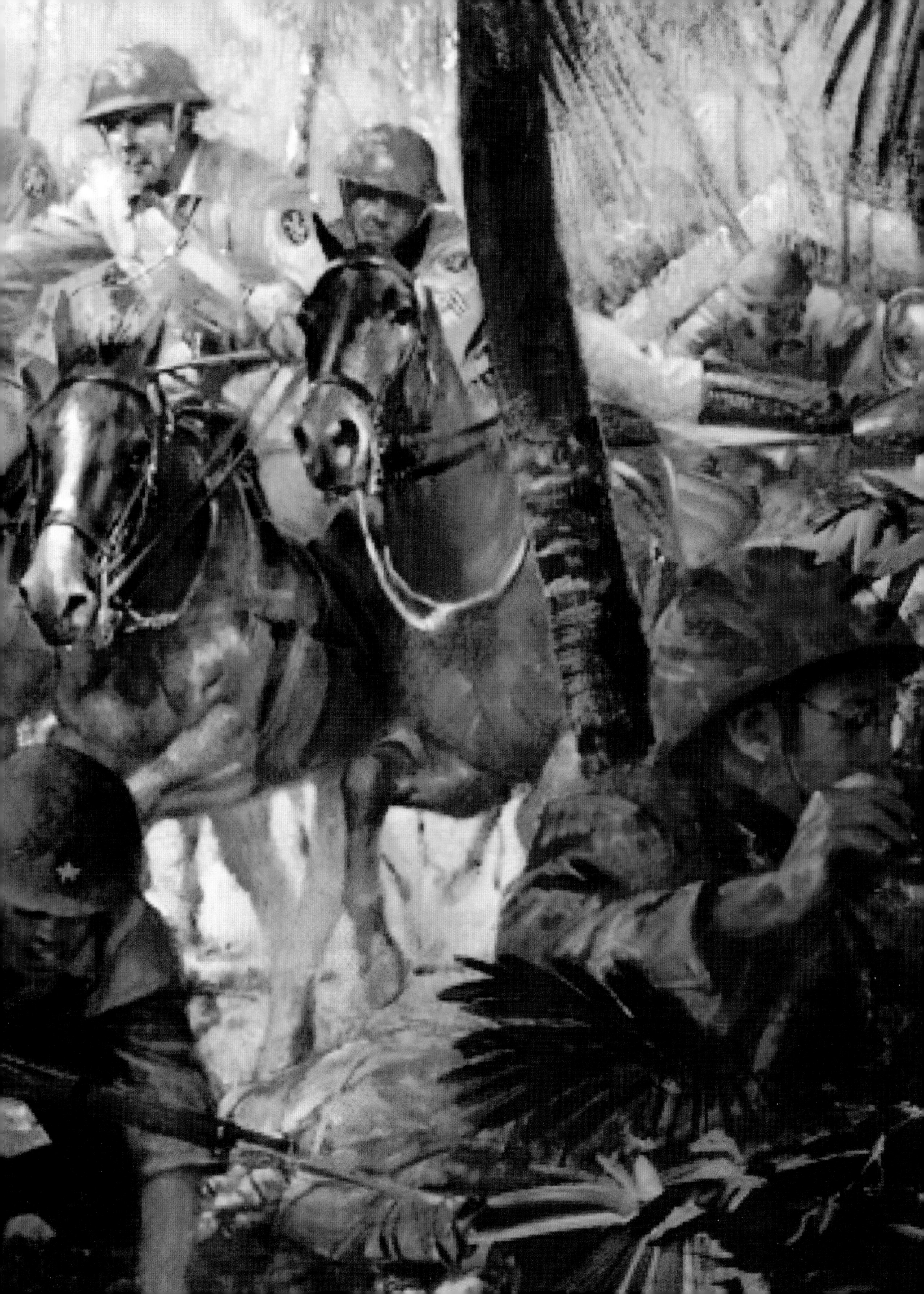

around the building under the acacia trees."

"Everybody started shooting the rifles," recounts Fernandez, "and I even saw my supply sergeant, Sergeant Barsillius, when he used up the rounds in his pistol he threw up his bolo knife. And he started shouting at the pilot, trying to tell him to come down 'you son of 'um bitch and fight like a man.' Oh, it was kind of funny at the time but you have to fire at them. I don't know, it was just a reaction. I found myself firing my pistol too."

At the beginning of World War II the cavalry branch of the United States Army was still a viable part of the fighting team. They got perhaps their best showing of the war in Luzon. The terrain was not conducive to mechanized warfare; thick steaming jungles, steep mountains, and roads that were principally dirt with a little gravel. As the two squadrons of the 26th regiment, six troops totaling 789 troopers and 54 officers, fanned out over northern Luzon they were the most mobile force in the army. They outpaced the other units on the island which included the 192nd and 194th tank battalions. "They [the tanks] had to move first," explains Parazo, "and then they had to stop. The cavalry moves on, we have to pass by them and they gave us the victory sign." Philippine army units packed civilian buses on the way to the front, the vehicles pressed into service voluntarily by their owners or under orders from American officers. The chief difficulty in getting to the front, after the main Japanese landing took place on December 22 at Lingayen Gulf, was not the logistical mess but the constant aerial bombing and strafing by the Japanese planes. "See they had complete control of the air from the very beginning," says Ramsey. "We had nothing. The first few days we had a half a dozen planes and then they were shot down."

While Ramsey and Troop G saw no action beyond bombing and strafing during their stint at Baler and Dingalen Bays on the east coast of Luzon fronting the Philippine Sea, the rest of the regiment was fully engaged to the west. Troop C was cut up and scattered after being dispatched to the resort city of Baguio in central Luzon to evacuate Americans and other civilians. Troops A, B, E and F formed advance defensive lines after the Lingayen Gulf landing. Corporal Fernandez recalls the first time his mounted platoon was ambushed by Japanese tanks. "Everybody is a good rider but I think I am one of the better ones. You know why? When we were first attacked and the first tank — the one that was moving to attack us from behind — discharged his gun most of the people were de-horsed, they fell down from their horses. But I was still on mine. That's the degree of horsemanship I had."

That event scattered the platoon. Fernandez gathered up stragglers — riflemen and machine gunners. He was given a temporary battlefield promotion to sergeant by troop commander Captain John Wheeler (who also asked Fernandez, as clerk, to process the paperwork when he had time), and led the platoon in a major engagement at Damortis, where he earned a Silver Star valor medal. Meanwhile, Parazo and the regimental headquarters unit often found themselves between the regiment and the enemy and had to fight their way to the rear. During a period after American tanks had withdrawn from Damortis and the headquarters was exposed, Parazo was ordered to report to the regimental commander.

"So I said, 'Private Parazo reporting.' Colonel Pierce said, 'Don't salute me while my stomach is on the ground. Parazo,' he said, 'go and look for my horse and my orderly.' I said, 'Yes, sir.' So I went to look for his horse and his orderly. Everybody said he was directly hit with the horse. So I went back to Colonel Pierce and I told him that I could not find the orderly or the horse because there was a bomb that dropped in the area where they were."

The series of defensive lines could only hold so long against the Japanese onslaught. Another invasion on the shore of Lamon Bay 50 miles southeast of Manila turned the situation grave and MacArthur invoked War Plan Rainbow (WPL-46), assembling all remaining forces on Bataan Peninsula. Troop G was recalled from the east. "We were put in lines of defense as we leapfrogged back," says Ramsey, "one following another and that's the way you go retrograde — you hold one position and then leapfrog another unit until you're in the final defense position.

"Finally, we withdrew into Bataan and were moved, the regiment, to Bagac which is on the west side. At that time the second squadron was sent forward to the area of Morong. And my platoon of Troop G was sent on reconnaissance beyond where Morong was. That was just a little village with a big old stone church there, Catholic church. And I reconnoitered with my platoon all the way to the edge of Subic Bay."

What Ramsey saw was the coral stone Lady of Pilar church, nearly 400 years old. It would become a landmark in the upcoming struggle for Morong. Upon their return, the mounted men of Troop G were called back to regimental headquarters north of Bagac, to be relieved by Troop E-F. Those two troops, having taken frightful casualties in the previous fighting, had been combined. Ramsey continues, "I was talking with the troop commander then of Troop E-F, Captain John Wheeler. He had no more American officers

Lt. Ramsey poses on his horse Bryn Awryn just before the war. The steeds for officers and troopers alike were raised on an army horse ranch in Oklahoma and shipped to the Philippines.

left. And I volunteered to stay back with him because I knew the area. We were well south of Morong and the headquarters of the 1st Regular Philippines Army Division was there. And General Wainwright was there chewing out General Fidel Segundo for having withdrawn from Morong because there was a river along Morong and that was a fairly good defense position. I can understand why they didn't want to stay there because there was no field of fire. It was a coconut plantation and on the other side of the river there was a lot of jungle. So Wainwright ordered Segundo to go back and take Morong.

"And as he turned around he saw me standing there. He said, 'Ramsey, isn't it?' 'Yes, sir.' The only reason he knew me is because of the polo game. He said, 'Take the advance guard.' And Wheeler said, 'General, he's been on reconnaissance for days and he just volunteered to stay behind....' 'Never mind! Ramsey, move out!' He [Wainwright] was a cavalryman and he had been a polo player years before."

On the morning of January 16, 1942 Ramsey took Wheeler's first platoon, twenty-seven men, and rode north. Other than the church, Morong was characterized by a group of raised nipa huts on a slice of land between the Batalan River and swamp extending beyond a coconut grove to the beach. Residents had already fled the village and the livestock was taken away by soldiers moving

Members of the 26th Cavalry Regiment, Philippine Scouts, withdraw from action late on December 23 near Pozorrubio south of Lingayen Gulf after doing their best to stall the large Japanese force heading for Manila.

through the area. The chief difficulty for the defenders of Bataan was the advance of Major General Naoki Kimura's detachment of General Homma's 14th Army. They threatened to flank the Americans and Filipinos fronting the South China Sea coast of Bataan.

"I was leading a platoon of Wheeler's that I'd never met before," says Ramsey. "That shows you how well trained these guys were. When we got near to the river, I turned left and branched out in three columns. When I got to the edge of the little village, they opened fire on us. I had a point [four troopers] out in front of me."

Firing erupted ahead and Ramsey saw the town square flush with Japanese soldiers. Others were crossing a small bridge from the north or wading through the river. It was then that Ramsey flashed on the idea of a mounted charge. Historically, the impact of charging steeds and whooping cavalrymen bearing down on unsuspecting foot soldiers had been effective. The scouts even practiced the tactic over and over again at Fort Stotsenburg. Instinctively he drew his pistol and dropped his arm. The platoon galloped ahead in a forage line.

"Wheeler and the rest of the troop were still well behind me. When I was fired upon we charged through the town, took the town, killed a few, wounded a few more and scattered what was left. And then the rest of the troop came in on foot. We got people along the river to prevent the main body of the other Japanese from going through the town."

Ramsey's dismounted skirmish line held the river crossers at bay. He dismounted and with other troopers began to flush out the Japanese hiding in the huts. Ramsey came upon one of the four point troopers, his face and uniform bloodied. The commander ordered him to the rear for medical attention but the man refused to budge until relieved from his post. By this time Wheeler brought the other two platoons up on foot and the firefight became general. At one point Ramsey saw an American hiding behind one of the buttresses of the church. He cursed the soldier for not joining the fight. The man turned out to be General Wainwright's Chief of Staff who had come for a look at the engagement. He would later recommend Ramsey for the Silver Star.

"We were able to hold them back there," says Ramsey. "and then the 1st [Philippine Army] infantry division relieved us. We were all shot up, beat up pretty badly, and we were withdrawn back to the rear areas."

Both Ramsey and Wheeler were wounded during the action. Wheeler, the more seriously hurt, was immediately evacuated to a hospital down the peninsula while Ramsey stayed at headquarters. "About three or four days later I began to turn yellow from infection from the wound. And so then I was shipped back there," says Ramsey. "I didn't even know when I got hit. In the middle of a battle, first you're so scared you don't know what you're doing. I think it was probably when we already went into the dismounted action 'cause the one that got me killed a horse standing next to me. I'll never forget that horse reared up and just went down like that. The soldier next to him was wounded. And I didn't even notice that until John came over and said, 'Look at you.' And his boot was covered with blood also."

Fernandez was assigned to headquarters on January 16 and recorded the engagement at Morong in the after action report. The passage of line under fire at Morong, from the cavalry to the infantry, was the only one on Bataan. The position was held until circumstances forced a withdrawal south. Even though the allies were inflicting heavy casualties on the enemy and shattering the Japanese schedule to take the Philippines, the de-

pravations were beginning to affect the "Battling Bastards of Bataan." In less than three months the Bataan defenders would surrender. Parazo was among those that did. Fernandez and some in the 26th escaped to Corregidor where they fought the invasion there until Wainwright surrendered the island. Ramsey and a fellow officer of the 26th escaped to the hills. Eventually, they made it off Bataan and found shelter among sympathetic villagers. Ramsey would go on to lead a large contingent in the Philippine resistance that frustrated the Japanese until the American army returned to Luzon in mid-January 1945.

The story of the January 16, 1942 action at Morong (sometimes spelled Moron) was first published in *Life* magazine on March 2, 1942. That account was related by Wheeler to a war correspondent from his hospital bed. He mentioned Ramsey's advance but not the charge specifically. Although it can't be measured how much the sacrifices made by the defenders of Luzon had on America's prosecution of the war against Japan, it certainly had to impact the dedication to defeat the Japanese. General MacArthur made good on his vow to return to the islands and the bitter struggle in the Philippines in 1944-45 closed a major chapter in the Japanese expansion begun three years earlier. Through it all, the service of the 26th Cavalry stands tall. As noted later by General Wainwright, "This devoted little band of horsemen, weakened by detachments and by heavy casualties–maintained the best traditions of the American Cavalry. I speak of this from the point of view of an eyewitness." It wasn't long after Ramsey led the U. S. Army's last horse cavalry charge that mounted cavalry ceased to exist in warfare and the use of horses in the army became strictly ceremonial. But that cavalry tradition has remained to inspire new units of the U. S. Army cavalry branch and the overall military heritage of the United States.

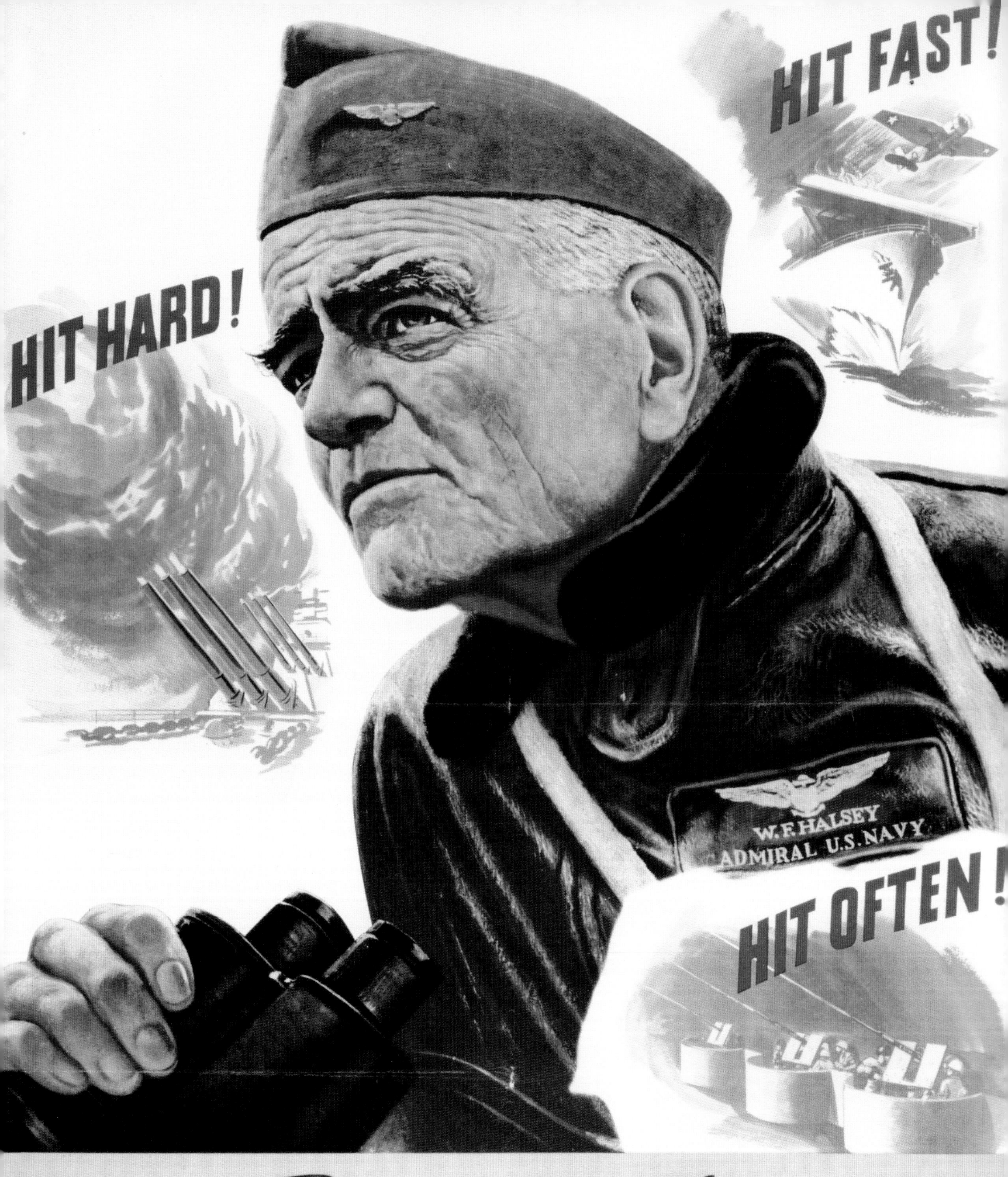
HIT FAST!
HIT HARD!
W. F. HALSEY
ADMIRAL U.S. NAVY
HIT OFTEN!

Produce for Your Navy

VICTORY BEGINS AT HOME!

CHAPTER 4

America Strikes Back

The Navy Takes the Lead

It seemed inconceivable, given the juggernaut that was the Japanese armed forces in December 1941 and early 1942, that the last Imperial strategic offensive would be staged in June 1942. In every other battle and campaign until the Pacific War ended three years and two months later the Japanese would be on the defensive. And while it is true that the vast majority of Japanese strategic objectives had been accomplished by mid-1942 – the conquest of the Dutch East Indies, Malay Peninsula and Philippines was complete; the U. S. Pacific Fleet was damaged and demoralized at Pearl Harbor; American, British Commonwealth and Dutch forces were pushed away and a menacing buffer of mainland and island bases protected the Greater East Asia Co-Prosperity Sphere – it is clear the Japanese were not finished in their efforts to dominate the land, air and sea in this vast region.

What happened to create such a rapid reversal in Japan's military fortunes was that the overpowering determination and resources of the Allied military were brought to bear on the aggressor by the governments and the citizens of those countries. America and its allies refused to acquiesce to Japan's view of the world order. Starting slowly, the efforts to regain territory and control would make headway on all fronts. Through interdisciplinary efforts, Japan's Achilles Heel would be exposed. When the Japanese lost the linchpin of their strategic plan - the carrier-based air superiority represented by the "Kido Butai" – with devastating losses at Coral Sea and Midway, the inability to build new ships and war material in step with their adversaries would expose the Rising Sun's basic weaknesses.

It was hard to forecast this sudden change of events in early 1942. The United States was in the process of losing the Philippines, Wake and Guam; Samoa, Fiji and even Alaska and the U. S. West Coast were threatened. Added to territorial losses was the loss of men, ships and planes at Pearl Harbor that had shaken American con-

This poster, "Victory Begins at Home!" featuring Admiral William F. "Bull" Halsey, was produced for the navy's Incentive Division by a New York contractor to encourage production for the navy.

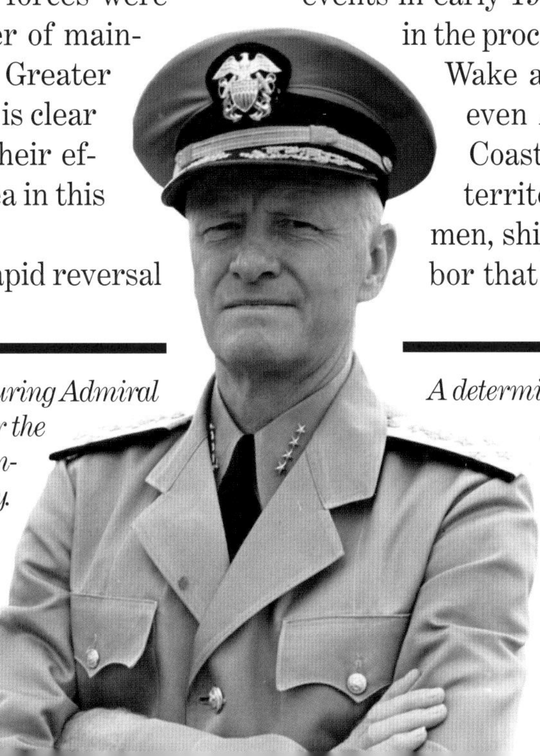

A determined Admiral Chester W. Nimitz faced a daunting task in 1942; lead America's effort to defeat the Japanese in the Pacific.

TOP: Vice Admiral Frank Jack Fletcher was a cautious surface ship commander who had early success at Coral Sea and Midway but later failed to grasp the urgency of his command responsibility. RIGHT: Marine pilot Capt. John F. Adams pauses on the wing of his single engine combat plane that is already fired up on Majuro Island.

fidence and moral. Logistics were in shambles. America's Far East allies were facing invasions everywhere and were looking to the U. S. for help. At a time when Washington's official military policy was "defeat Germany first," Army and Army Air Force leaders were hastily shifting scarce resources to and around the Pacific.

The U. S. Navy, however, was in better shape than other Allied service branches, especially in the Pacific. The fact that all the aircraft carriers and other key vessels were not in Pearl Harbor during the surprise attack made a huge difference

in the ability of the navy to recover. Naval construction plans already in progress would make a pointed difference in the months ahead. And while a change in leadership was inevitable in the Pacific – despite plenty of blame to go around, Admiral Kimmel and General Short would be relieved of command – in the navy the shakeup wasn't limited to that region. Though Admiral Harold Stark stayed on for a time as Chief of Naval Operations (CNO), the real power of the navy was soon vested in Admiral Ernest J. King, former chief of the Atlantic Fleet who became Commander-in-Chief, United States Fleet (Cominch) and in March also assumed the post of CNO. "Dolly" Stark was sent to Europe to command naval forces there.

To replace Kimmel, King and the Secretary of the Navy selected a soft-spoken rear admiral from Texas, Chester William Nimitz. The choice was one of important and lasting value as Nimitz had the ability to get the most out of subordinates and resources, the finesse to work well with colleagues, the patience to allow plans to develop and the ability to see the big picture. Advanced to the rank of admiral, Nimitz arrived at Pearl Harbor at Christmas and assumed his post on the last day of 1941. Though he had sought a post afloat during the coming war, Nimitz proved to be a key element of the success of the U. S. Navy in the Pacific and in the region since he commanded all operations in the vast Pacific Ocean Areas, (General MacArthur separately commanded the South West Pacific Area). With Nimitz's arrival at Oahu, morale in Hawaii's military establishment immediately soared.

Yet, it would take more than just new faces in the command structure to put the navy back on track. Admiral King, who had aviation experience including as captain of USS *Lexington* and commander of North Island NAS, wanted immediate offensive action in the form of raids to check Japanese advances. This was half of his blocking and raiding strategy. The other part

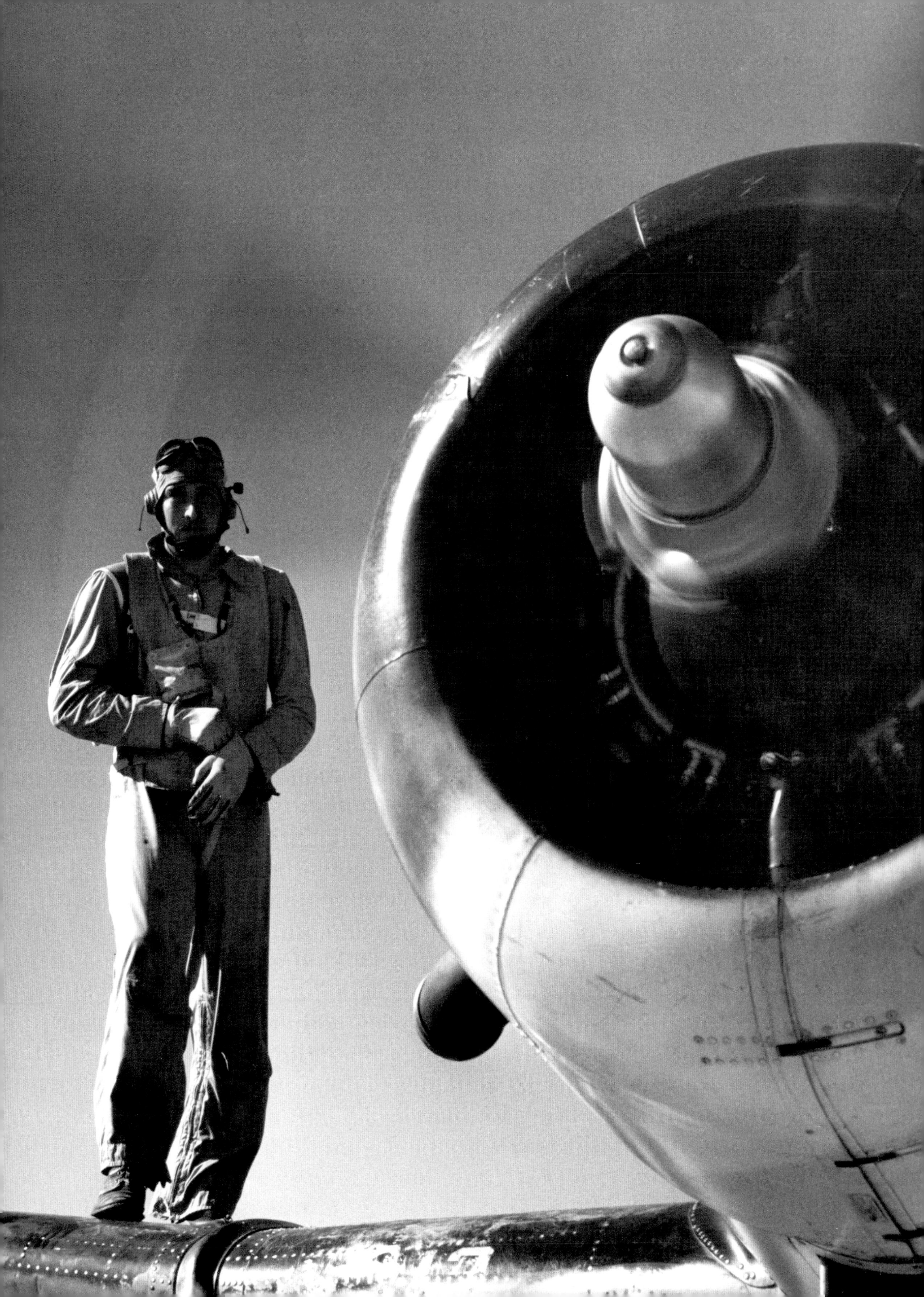

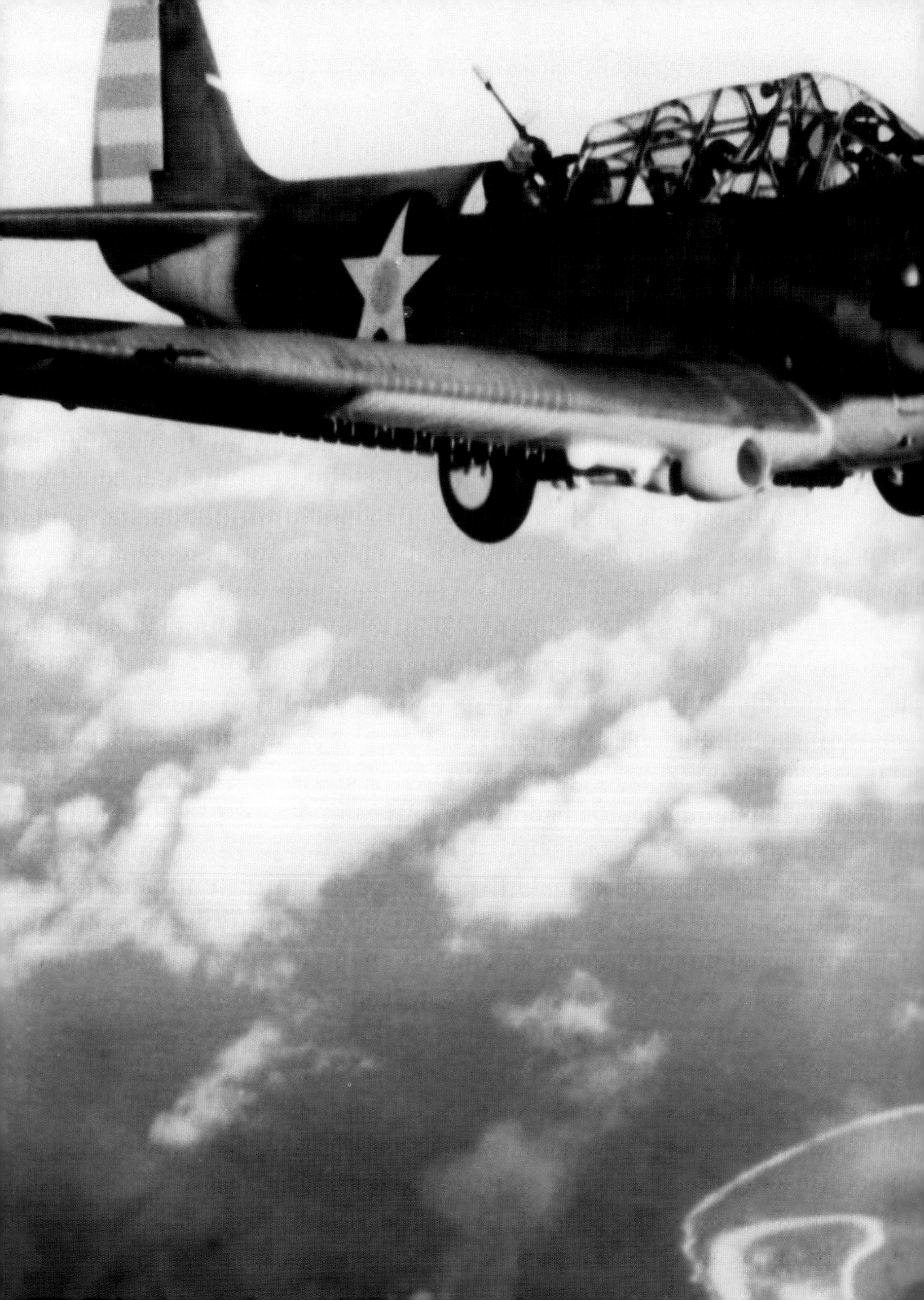

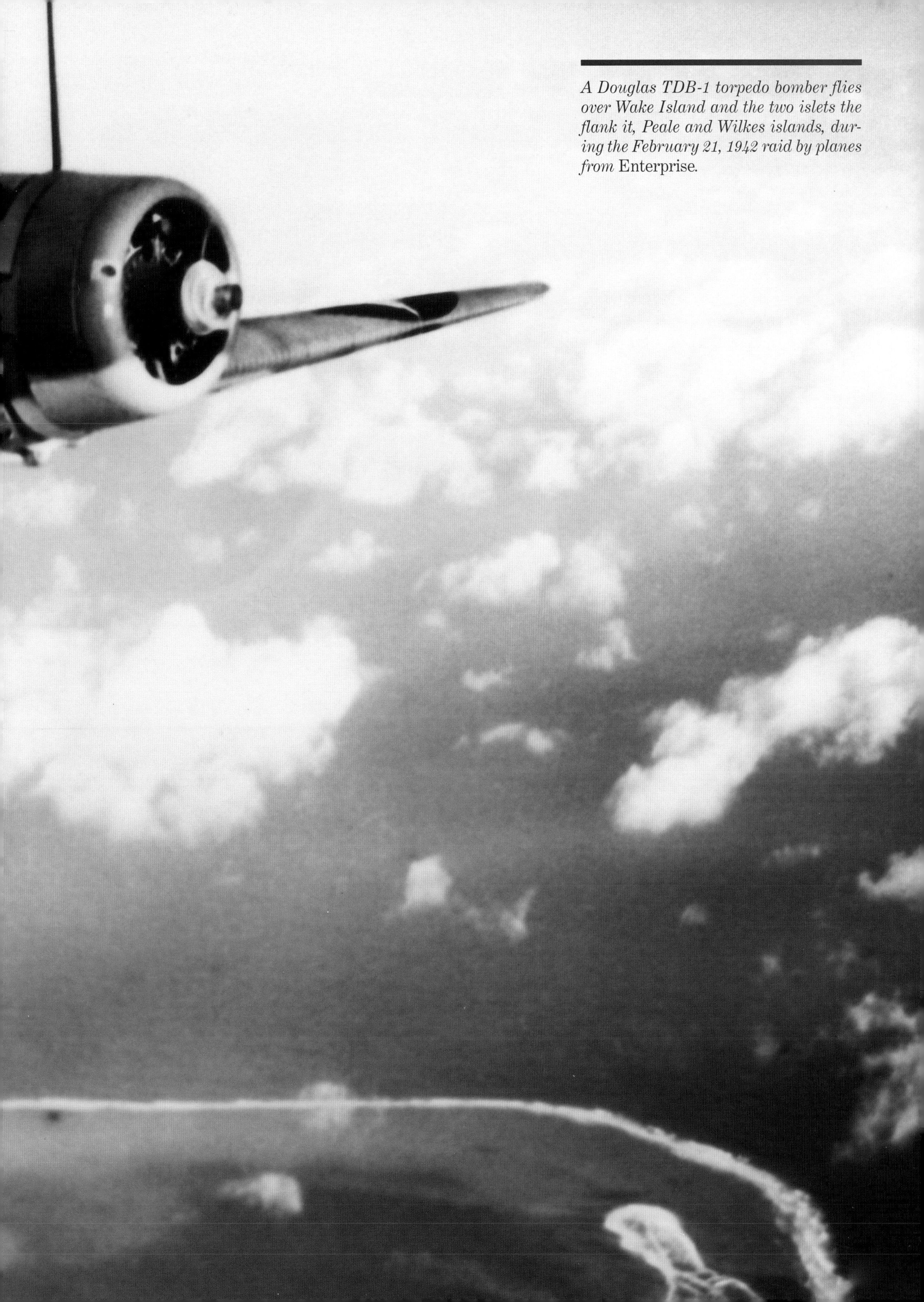

A Douglas TDB-1 torpedo bomber flies over Wake Island and the two islets the flank it, Peale and Wilkes islands, during the February 21, 1942 raid by planes from Enterprise.

was reinforcing outposts and patrolling waters on a southwesterly route from the Western Hemisphere to Australia to block any Japanese advance in that area. The Pacific Fleet gained another carrier, USS *Yorktown*, CV-5, and several other capital ships transiting the Panama Canal from the Atlantic. USS *Saratoga* arrived from the West Coast to join *Enterprise* and *Lexington*; but the first order of business for the carriers and their escorts was guarding convoys of American troops to garrison Samoa and other island possessions still in U. S. hands. Bill Roy joined the navy from his home in Florida after his part-time employer, a commercial photographer, convinced him it was the best service branch. After a stint in engineering aboard USS *Arkansas*, Roy went to the navy's photography school. He joined the crew of *Yorktown* at Norfolk Navy Yard as a Seaman 2nd Class Photographer's Mate when the carrier was reassigned to the Pacific.

"We got our airplanes aboard, got all the provisions on board and headed off through the Panama Canal. Coming out of the locks on the Pacific side at 7:00 o'clock in the morning, Japanese submarines were waiting for us. So they let loose a barrage of depth charges from the destroyers. We didn't have enough speed to launch airplanes, or do much of anything. Anyway, they bested the submarines of the Japanese, we went on up to San Diego and picked up [a convoy loaded with] Marines to take to Samoa to reinforce the island."

It would be up to the Pacific Fleet to conduct whatever operations were planned. The Asiatic Fleet, what remained of the surface contingent, was then scattered about the Dutch East Indies and Australian coast, still under the command of Admiral Hart, but now a fighting unit of the multi-national ABDA (American-British-Dutch-Australian) command in the Southwest Pacific. Another combined command, ANZA, also under an American admiral, was protecting eastern Australia and New Zealand waters. Allied submarines (mostly U. S. Navy and Royal Netherlands Navy), like their Japanese counterparts, were trolling the waters from the western hemisphere to the Indian Ocean, looking for opportunities.

Fast Carrier Strikes

Admiral King began to implement "fast carrier strikes" to raid strategic Japanese positions. Nimitz selected *Enterprise* task force under Admiral Halsey and *Lexington* task force under Vice Admiral Wilson Brown to begin these operations with quick strike air attacks that might alter Japanese plans as the U. S. military was gearing up for an enemy invasion of Samoa. But the first of these planned strikes, on Wake Island by Brown, was scrubbed when *Lexington*'s oiler was sunk by a Japanese I-class submarine. About the same time, *Saratoga* was also torpedoed by a Japanese submarine and left the fleet for extensive repairs and upgrades in Bremerton, Washington. Consequently, the first raid arranged by Nimitz was on Japanese bases in the Marshall and Gilbert islands utilizing Halsey's group and the *Yorktown*-led Task Force 17 under Rear Admiral Frank Jack Fletcher. Though not an overwhelming success, the February 1, 1942 attack on installations, transports and auxiliary ships on six Japanese controlled islands was the first by Pacific Fleet surface ships and carrier planes.

After this mission, *Yorktown* made its first visit to Oahu. Bill Roy remembers the scene as the big ship entered Pearl Harbor. "When we came into the harbor it was a very sobering sight. All of those magnificent battleships were burned and gutted and upside down and you could still smell death in the air. And also, the water was covered with oil that was still coming out of the battleships. Nobody was talking, just staring straight. And especially me because I'd served on a battle-

ship and I just couldn't believe the wicked damage that they'd suffered, and casualties. The way that they just sank these big battleships was intolerable."

A TDB-1 Devastator follows the signs of the landing signal officer on approach to Enterprise.

The Marshall-Gilbert raid did not slow down Japanese plans to continue on to the next objectives for establishing air bases, Rabaul on New Britain and Lae on the eastern finger of New Guinea. These locations could support air strikes to menace the Australian coast and the ANZAC command had great concern. *Lexington* left Pearl Harbor in early February and was assigned to Vice Admiral Herbert F. Leary's ANZAC naval force. *Yorktown* also departed for a later rendezvous with *Lexington*. Leary ordered an air attack on Rabaul with a task force led by Wilson Brown and *Lexington*, accompanied by American and Australian cruisers.

These ships approached New Britain from east of the Solomon Islands on February 21, but Japanese seaplanes on patrol discovered their approach. The combat air patrol (CAP) which *Lexington* put up to oppose the Japanese air attack that followed discovery battled air to air with the Japanese fliers for the first time in the war. The Navy flyers scored many hits – Lieutenant Commander Edward "Butch" O'Hare downed five enemy planes – with the loss of only one U. S. plane. The lack of surprise forced Brown to cancel the Rabaul raid. However the skill of the Navy fliers in this initial dogfight over *Lexington* impressed the ships' crews and commanders.

Though *Enterprise* finally carried out the planned attack on Wake Island and a combined task force led by *Yorktown* and *Lexington* returned to the New Britain area – this time to conduct a March 10 air raid on Lae and Salamaua in northeast New Guinea from the Coral Sea east of Port Moresby - the fast carrier strikes were causing only minor losses to the Japanese. They did, however, boost morale and help develop plans and combat training for the ship crews and air crews of the Pacific Fleet. Bill Roy recalls some high points of this mission.

"I flew some reconnaissance missions, both in the dive bomber and the torpedo plane. Also for the first time one of the large four-engine Japanese flying boats had been shadowing us, Task Force 17. Anyway, this Japanese four-engine seaplane had come in and out of the clouds, and 'Go get 'em' McCusky and his wingman went through the clouds and we saw this huge fireball coming out of the clouds. The seaplane was trying to escape in the clouds and suddenly within the view of the ship here it comes tumbling out and right into the water. Well, a big roar went up. When McCusky landed and his wingman, we had made up a great big cardboard gold set of wings. And they had a big ceremony on the flight deck when they landed. I took some pictures of it. Anyway, that was a real exciting time. That was the first victory and everybody's morale was boosted highly.

"The navy had not operated that much in the South Pacific. As a consequence they didn't have the charts to navigate by or any specifics on these different islands. One of the officers went into the library and found a geography book on New Guinea and found a map of [one of] the harbor[s]. And I copied that map and put it on semi-matte paper to put on your heading. So you could mark in grease pencil the targets and everything. And they bombed against that and bombed the Japs. Unfortunately our torpedoes malfunctioned – they were the old Mark 13 from World War I. They malfunctioned, or if they did go, they went under the ship because the transports had been unable to load the troops and the cargo. And they went under the ships, they were set too deep. And a couple of them did blow up some palm trees on the other side of the harbor, something like that. But the rest of them were duds. If they'd been good, and they bombed the hell out of the ships, and machine gunned and bombed the soldiers, it would have been awhile before the Japanese could recover."

Bombs Over Tokyo

Later information revealed that the March 10 Lae-Salamaua raid destroyed three Japanese ships. However one raid did much more. It was planned by Admiral King and his Washington staff as early as January 1942 and was among the best kept secrets of early war operations. A diversionary raid was planned for the most important Japanese target of all – Tokyo. Such a raid would send a grim message to Japanese militarists, raise American morale and serve as a retribution for the attack on Pearl Harbor. But no carrier planes then available had the range to conduct such an operation as the waters around the Japanese islands were patrolled diligently as far out as 500 miles. The Army's twin-engine B-25 Mitchell medium bombers could be launched from carriers at a safe distance but could not return to the flattops – they would have to fly on to China, landing at Chinese-held bases if possible or ditching on the mainland if necessary. After

TOP: Looking aft from the island of USS Hornet *(CV-8) to the rows of B-25s topside on the route to launch of the Halsey-Doolittle Raid. USS* Gwin *(DD-433) is approaching on the starboard side while USS* Nashville *(CL-43) guards the waters in the distance. BOTTOM: Lt. Col. James A. Doolittle is pictured here after he was promoted to two-star general and sent to Europe to command the 8th Air Force. He would soon receive a further promotion to lieutenant general.*

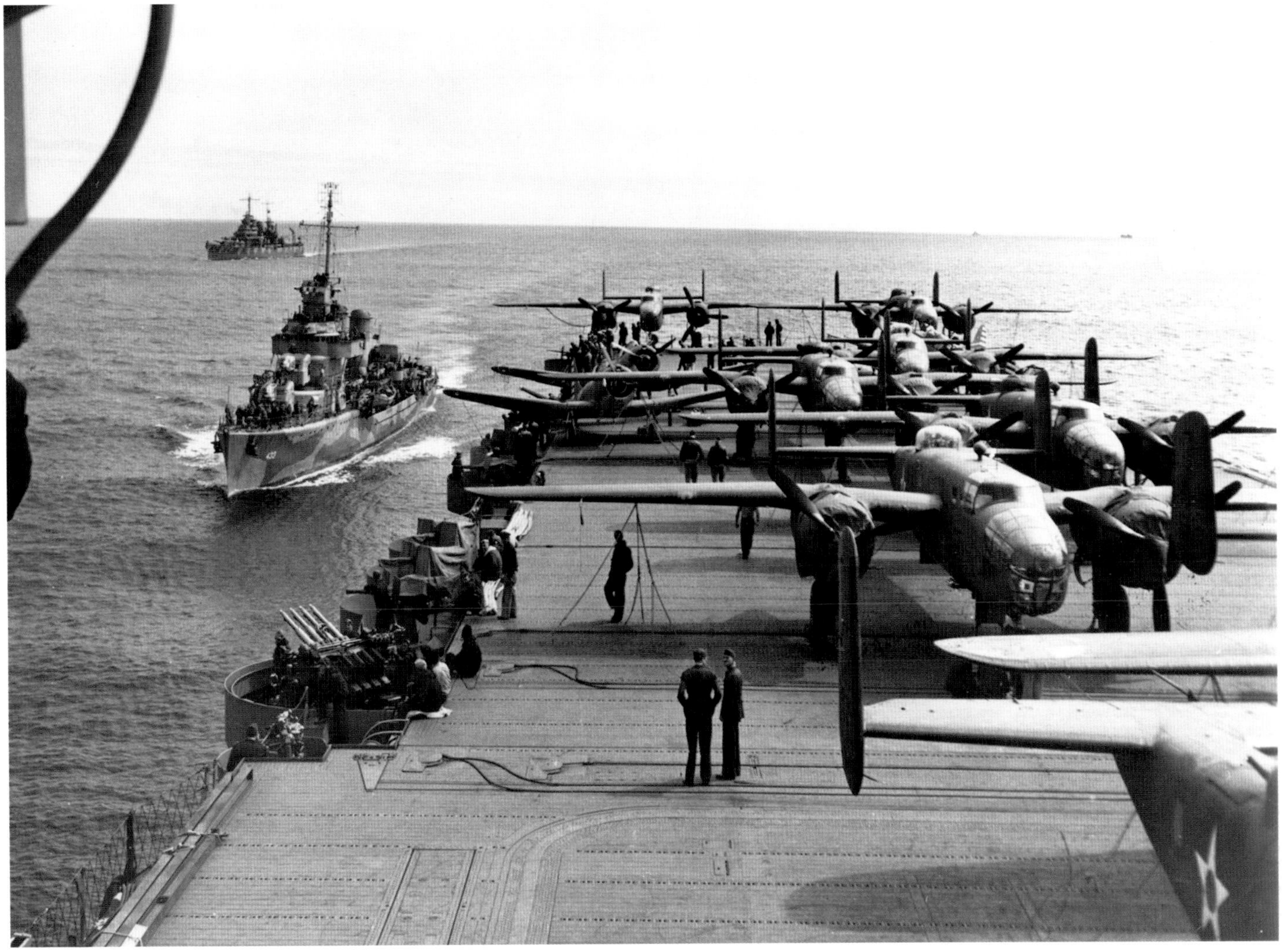

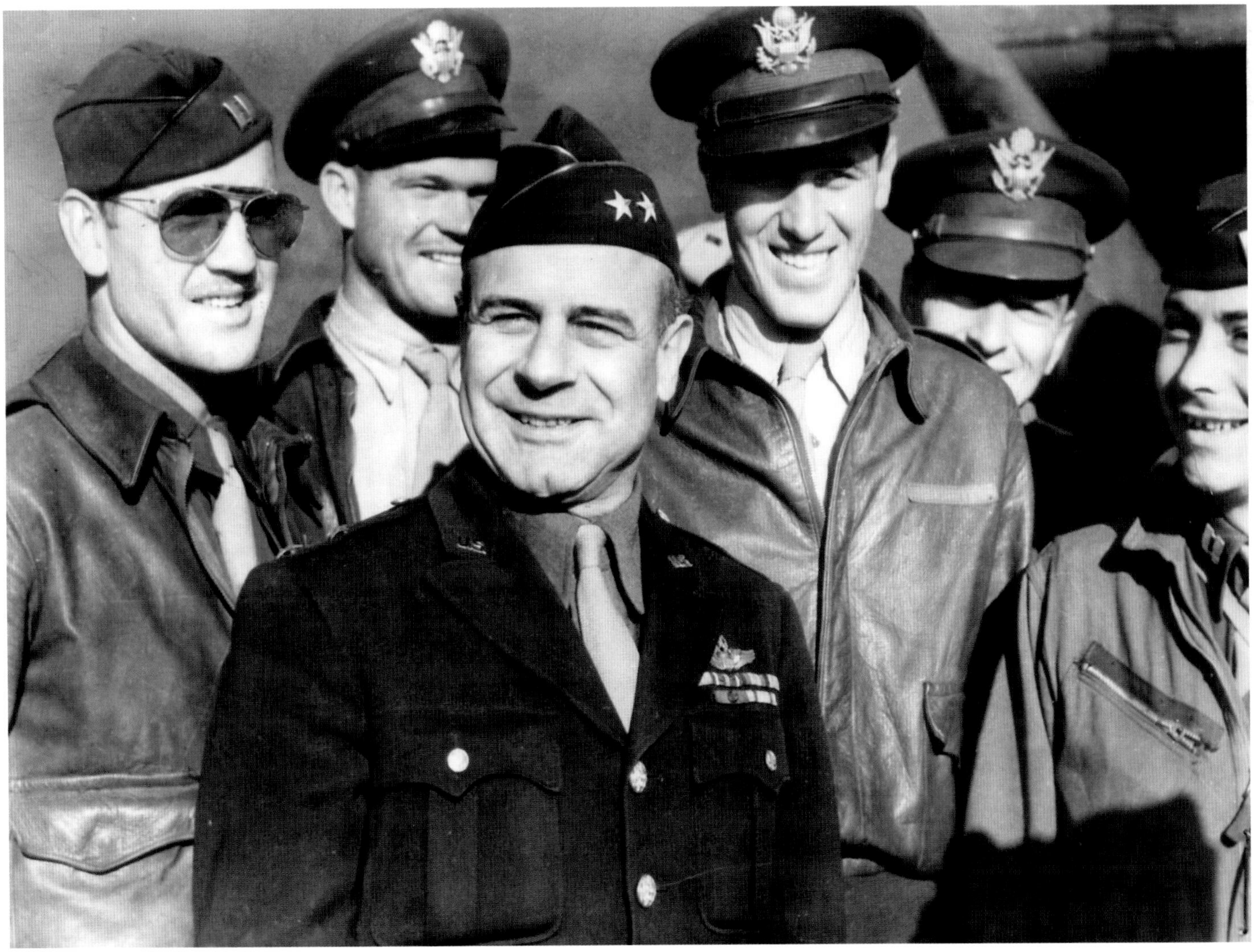

studying the problem, the navy called on the army and the Commanding General of the Army Air Forces, General Henry "Hap" Arnold, enthusiastically agreed to organize and equip the mission. Volunteer crews for sixteen B-25s were trained under Army Air Forces Lieutenant Colonel James A. Doolittle while the navy mapped out the composition and route of Task Force 16 under Vice Admiral Halsey.

After training on a simulated carrier airstrip at Eglin Field, Florida the Mitchell bombers, with special equipment for carrier take-off, were flown across country and loaded aboard USS *Hornet*, then docked at Alameda NAS in the San Francisco Bay area. *Hornet* left on April 2 with an escort and rendezvoused with *Enterprise*'s task force eleven days later in the North Pacific. After the ships were in open waters, the *Hornet* crew cheered vociferously when the air strike's targets were announced and all hands pitched in to assist and protect the deck-stowed army planes from the rigors of sea travel. *Hornet*'s own airmen played nearly non-stop poker games, betting to replace an army pilot or two in the cockpit; but the AAF officers cleaned them out.

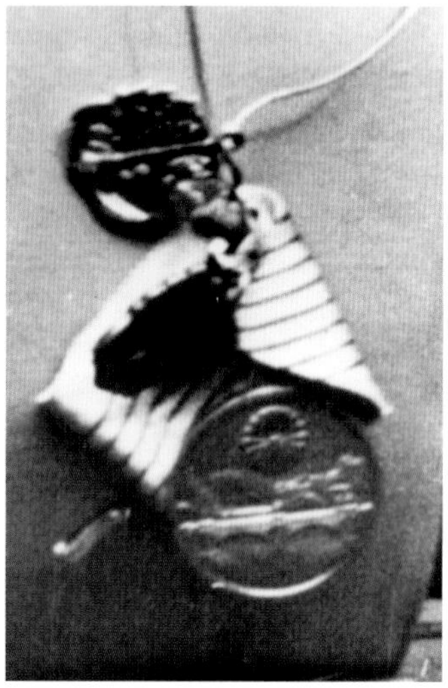

Bert Stolier was still in the Marine contingent aboard USS *Northampton*. The cruiser docked

RIGHT: On the deck of USS Hornet *"Jimmy" Doolittle wires a Japanese medal to a 500-pound bomb to "return" it to its originators in the Tokyo raid. (ABOVE) Detail of the Japanese medal.*

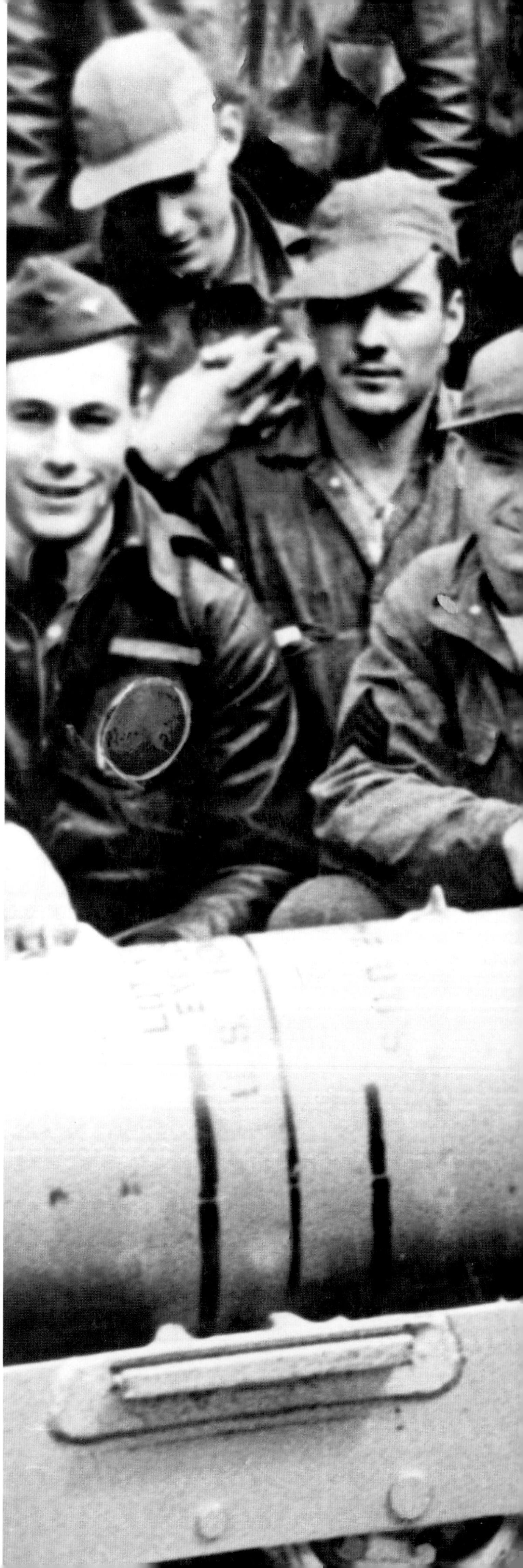

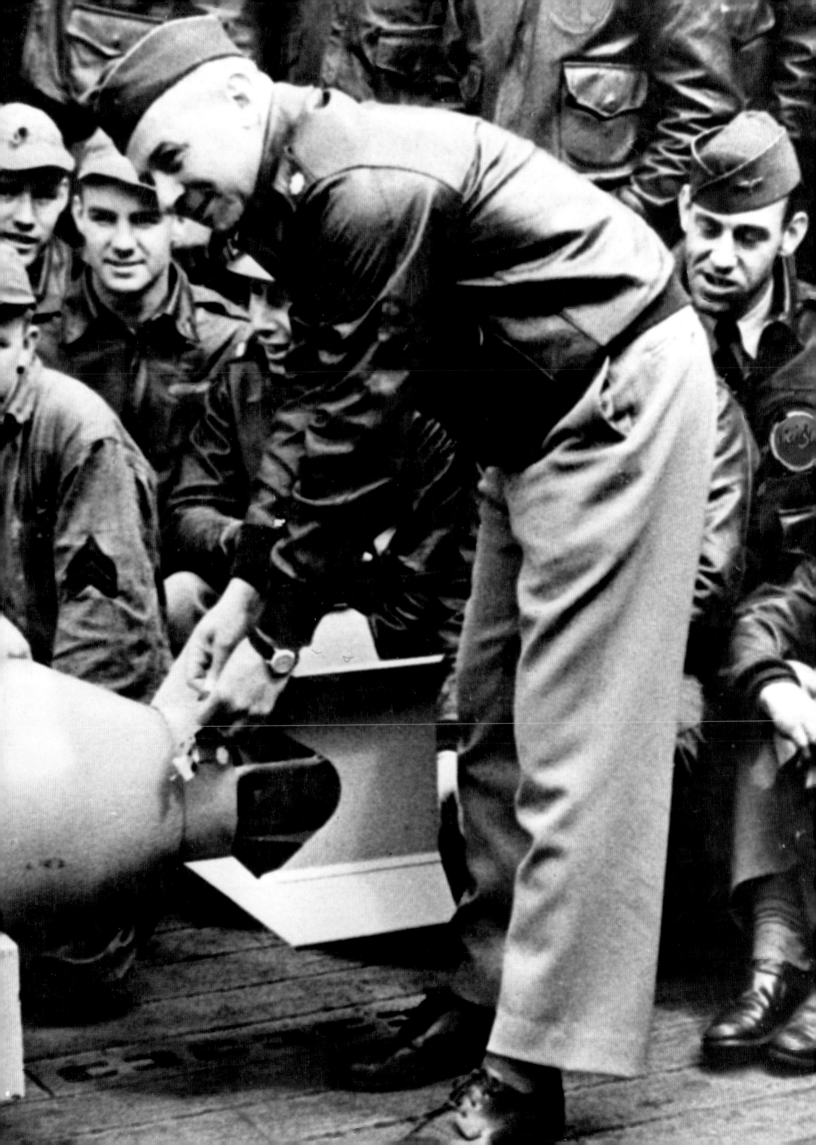

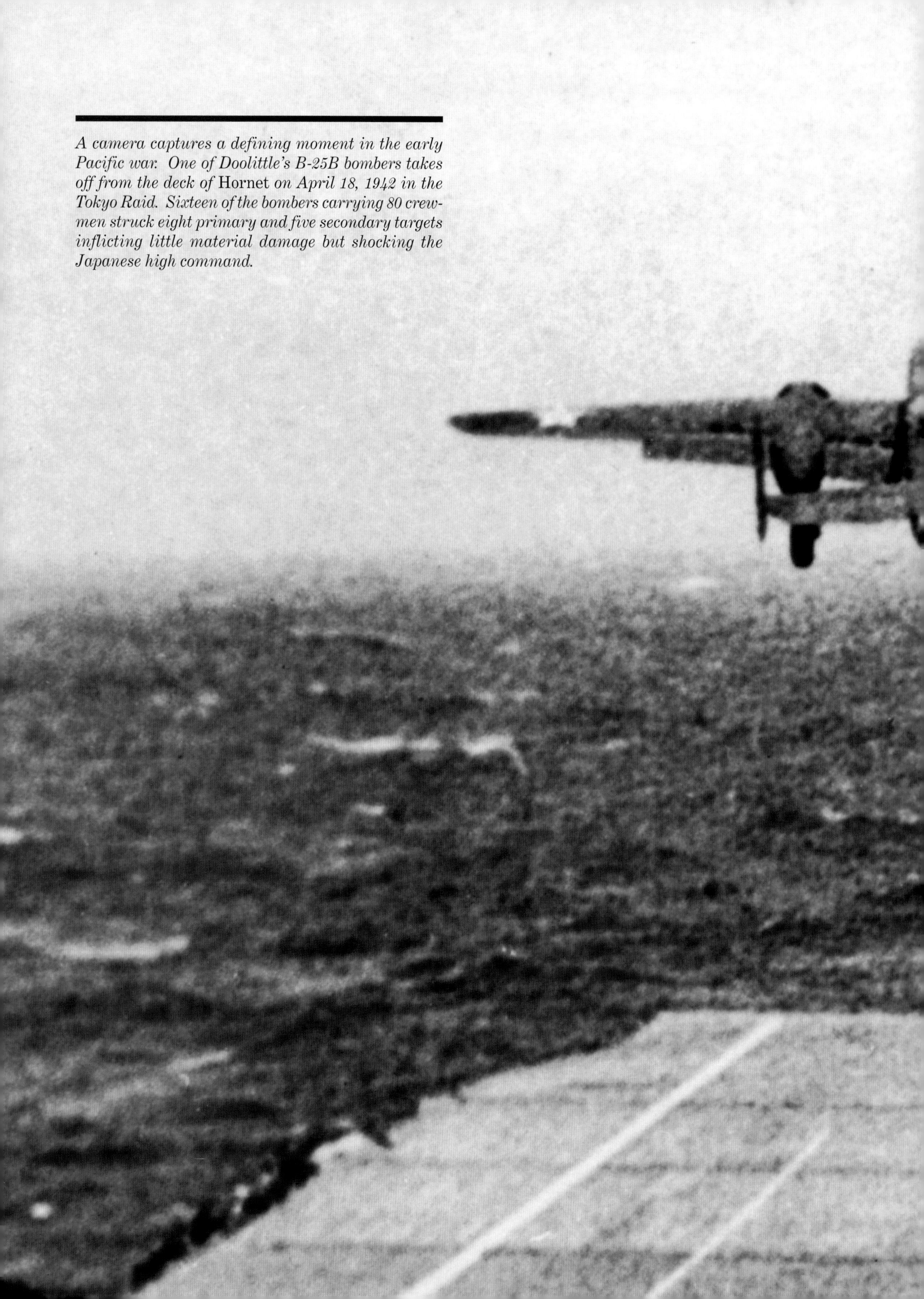

A camera captures a defining moment in the early Pacific war. One of Doolittle's B-25B bombers takes off from the deck of Hornet *on April 18, 1942 in the Tokyo Raid. Sixteen of the bombers carrying 80 crewmen struck eight primary and five secondary targets inflicting little material damage but shocking the Japanese high command.*

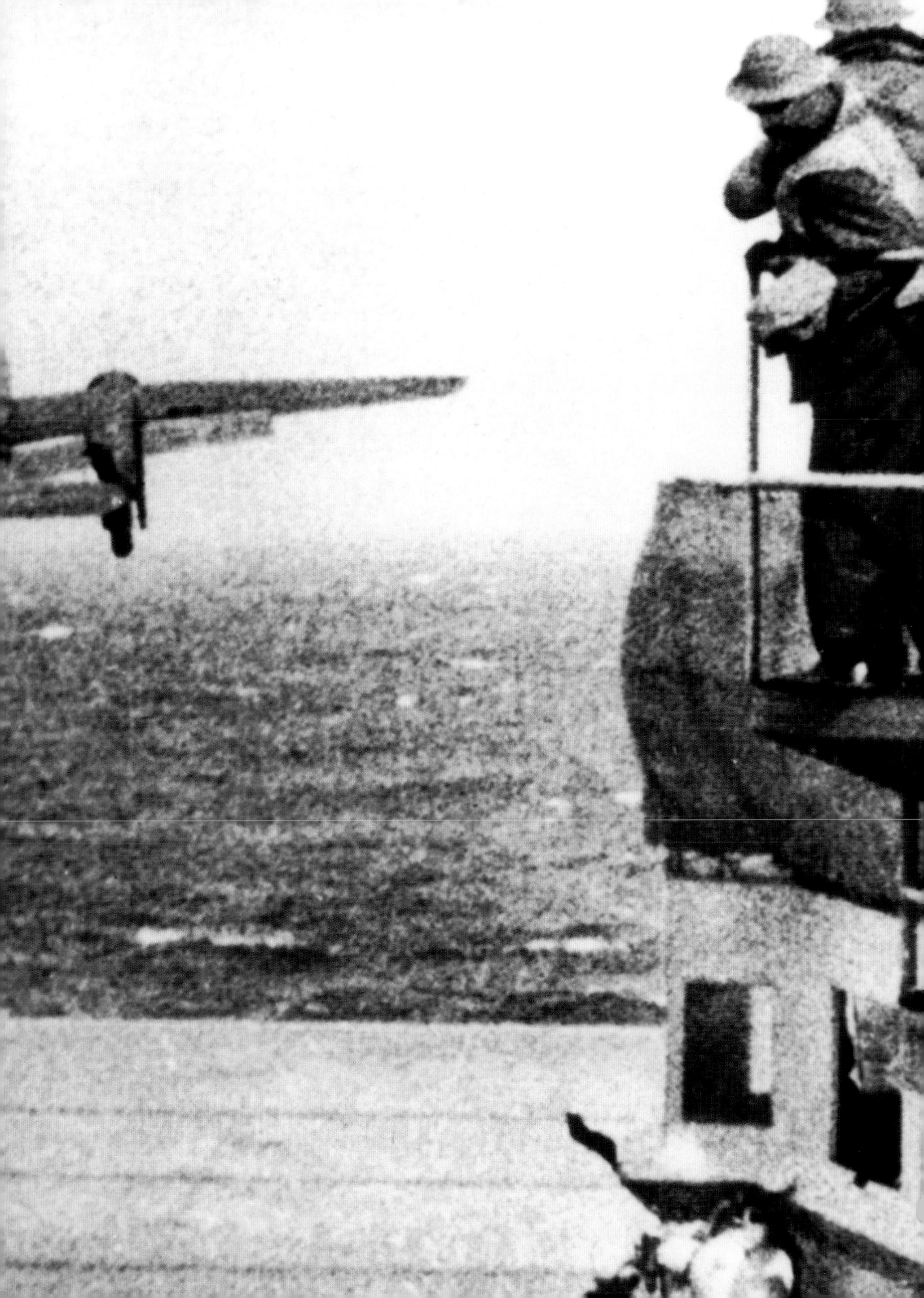

for repairs in San Francisco in early 1942 before returning to Task Force 16 and *Enterprise*.

Some of the pilots and crew from the Tokyo Raid pose with Chinese soldiers near where they came down after the Tokyo raid.

stroyer, and the *Northampton* and we proceeded to the raid on Tokyo."

"We had to go back to San Francisco to have some repairs done on the ship. One of them was to put on radar. While in San Francisco walking on the street, on Market Street, I saw some long johns in a window and I went in and purchased some. Unbelievable when I went back to the ship they said no more liberty, we're getting underway. Got underway next morning, we went west and then we went north and when we got off the coast of Sitka, Alaska it was very, very foggy but at noon time we sounded our horn and another ship sounded their horn and our ships continued to go due west, toward Japan. When the fog lifted there was the *Hornet* with the planes on it, and a de-

The rendezvous took place on April 13, and after refueling on April 17, the oilers and destroyers dropped back so the cruisers and carriers could pick up speed. The next day the planes prepared for an afternoon launch that would put them over their targets at night. The Nationalist Chinese under Generalissimo Chiang-Kai-shek were informed to expect the arrival of American bombers to aid them with no mention of the mission. The secrecy extended even to the details of the landing preparations in China which arrived after the task force was underway and could not be transmitted.

In the pre-dawn hours of April 18, while *Hornet* and the task force were still 700 miles out, a

Japanese patrol boat was picked up on radar. Evasive action was taken but other patrol boats also appeared, extending the Home Islands patrol well out from the 500-mile radius intelligence had determined. Having been spotted, with that information undoubtedly being reported to Tokyo, Halsey and company quickly had to change plans. The ships could not approach much closer without risking retaliation from land-based bombers. So with mission leader Doolittle in concurrence the launch was moved forward and plans were made for a daylight attack.

Carrying 1141 gallons of aviation fuel, four 500-pound bombs and a crew of five, the sixteen B-25s strained their way into air off the carrier deck between 0730 and 0824 hours. Before much time passed, Task Force 16 set a heading of 90 degrees and home. *Enterprise* put up a CAP and even though later the Japanese would put up air patrols, they were never discovered. Several enemy patrol boats were fired on and the crew of one was captured, confirming the discovery had indeed reached Tokyo. A story told by one of the captured crewmen was that when he reported from his lookout post the sight of two of their beautiful aircraft carriers, his captain examined the horizon through his binoculars and responded, "They're beautiful, but they're not ours." The skipper then went below and shot himself.

At noon, thirteen American bombers swooped in low over Tokyo to bomb factories and other military targets. The other three went to Kobe, Osaka and Nagoya to do the same. Ironically, a simulated air raid had just been concluded in Tokyo with Japanese aircraft flying over the capital, so when the American bombers came the people thought it was a continuation of the drill. Few knew the real thing had happened on April 18 as officials kept civilians away from bombed areas. A few non-military targets were bombed in error and Osaka was not hit, but the explosive and incendiary bombs generally struck their targets.

Air and ground flak did almost no damage to the B-25s – Japanese officials, expecting carrier planes, did not react to the intel immediately. They expected an attack to come the next day. Preparations were mishandled and execution of anti-aircraft operations was poor.

Critically low on fuel, the over-extended Mitchells made their way to China. One plane with fuel problems landed near Vladivostok, USSR, and the crew was interned thirteen months by the Soviets until they escaped what they originally thought were friendly forces. One ditched at sea and the crewmen were captured. The rest bailed out or crash landed near unlit Chinese air facilities. Nine of the eighty pilots and crewman died, including two lieutenants and a sergeant who were executed by the Japanese and one who died during imprisonment.

The Japanese could not figure out where the planes had come from. They did not reason that the B-25 attack could have originated at sea. President Roosevelt told a jubilant America that the flight originated in "Shangri-la," the mythical Tibetan paradise made popular by the James Hilton book and 1930s motion picture *Lost Horizon*. As a result, the shaken Japanese military was gravely concerned. The raid had endangered the emperor. Several squadrons of Japanese fighter planes, needed elsewhere, were committed to the Home Islands. Most importantly, their entire strategy changed as they had to rethink the limit of their protective barrier to the west and south. That new strategy would have immense implications as operation "MI" (Midway Island) became top priority.

Operation "MO" and the Coral Sea

The U. S. Navy got no credit at the time for the Tokyo raid. The military's insistence on keeping the details from the Japanese resulted in secrecy even after the fact. The pop-

BATTLE OF THE CORAL SEA

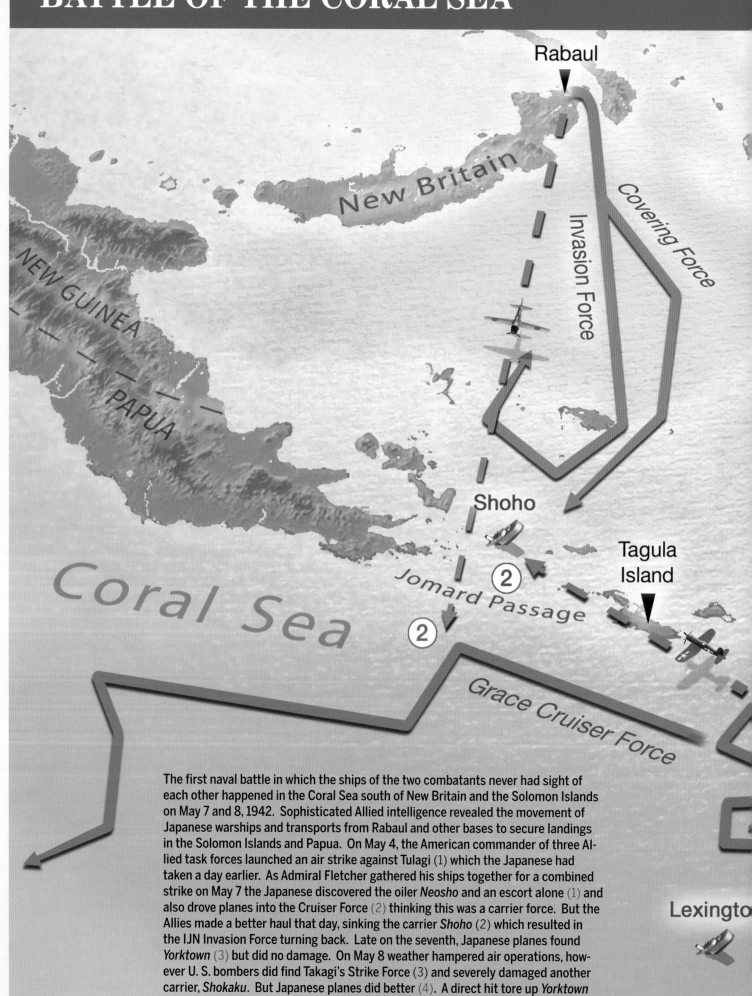

Rabaul

New Britain

Covering Force

Invasion Force

NEW GUINEA

PAPUA

Shoho

Tagula Island

Coral Sea

Jomard Passage

②

②

Grace Cruiser Force

Lexingto

The first naval battle in which the ships of the two combatants never had sight of each other happened in the Coral Sea south of New Britain and the Solomon Islands on May 7 and 8, 1942. Sophisticated Allied intelligence revealed the movement of Japanese warships and transports from Rabaul and other bases to secure landings in the Solomon Islands and Papua. On May 4, the American commander of three Allied task forces launched an air strike against Tulagi (1) which the Japanese had taken a day earlier. As Admiral Fletcher gathered his ships together for a combined strike on May 7 the Japanese discovered the oiler *Neosho* and an escort alone (1) and also drove planes into the Cruiser Force (2) thinking this was a carrier force. But the Allies made a better haul that day, sinking the carrier *Shoho* (2) which resulted in the IJN Invasion Force turning back. Late on the seventh, Japanese planes found *Yorktown* (3) but did no damage. On May 8 weather hampered air operations, however U. S. bombers did find Takagi's Strike Force (3) and severely damaged another carrier, *Shokaku*. But Japanese planes did better (4). A direct hit tore up *Yorktown* and damaged *Lexington* so heavily that the great carrier had to be sunk.

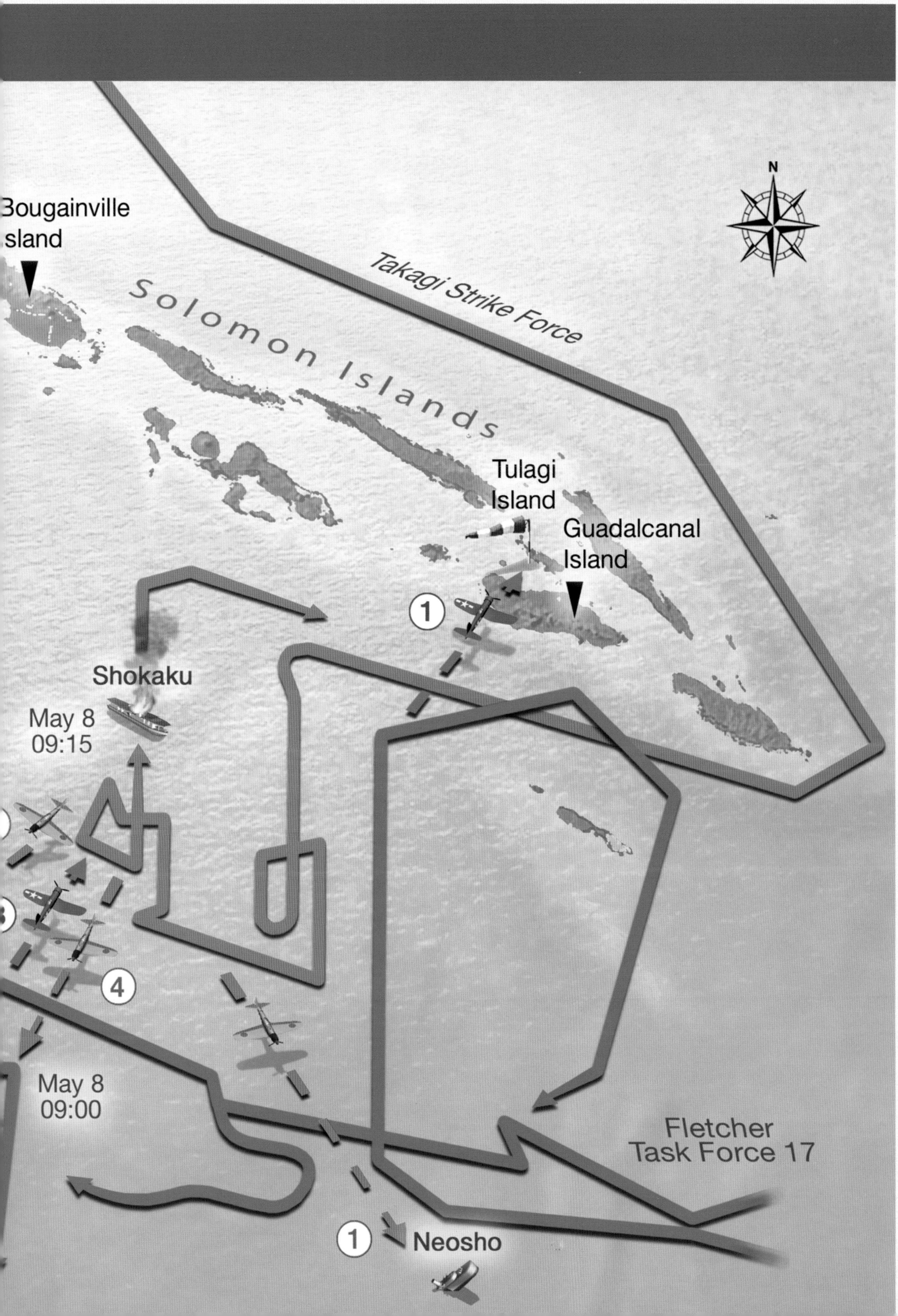

Bougainville
Island
Solomon Islands
Takagi Strike Force
Tulagi
Island
Guadalcanal
Island
1
Shokaku
May 8
09:15
4
May 8
09:00
Fletcher
Task Force 17
1
Neosho

ular name for the action was the "Doolittle Raid." Historians have stepped in to more correctly characterize it as the "Halsey-Doolittle Raid." But the navy wasn't finished with its new-found vitality in air operations. *Enterprise, Hornet* and their escorts entered Pearl Harbor on April 25, a week after the raid; but there was no time to celebrate their feat. Events in the Central and South Pacific were requiring the attention of the seamen and naval aviators of the Pacific Fleet.

The Japanese continued to look for ways to buffer their southern perimeter. The last big obstacle to security was the threat of Australia as a base of Allied operations. Post-war research reveals the Japanese rejected the idea of invading Australia as too large a commitment. After all, they wanted to get back to finishing the incorporation of China into the Greater East Asia Coprosperity Sphere. But they desperately wanted it to appear that Australia was an objective and did much to keep up the ruse. A devastating air raid on the Northern Territory port of Darwin in February 1942 gave credence to the idea.

Of immediate concern to the Japanese was Port Moresby on the southeast coast of Papua. An invasion was planned, dubbed operation "MO." The March raid on Lae by Brown's task force worried Admiral Yamamoto and hastened the risky offensive operation to command the Coral Sea area. By the time it occurred, Allied intelligence of Japanese movements was becoming very sophisticated. As the warning went out, two carrier forces were summoned to the area. *Lexington*'s Task Force 11 joined *Yorktown* TF-17 under Fletcher with Rear Admiral Aubrey Fitch as air officer. TF-17 was ordered to the Coral Sea along with the cruiser force of American and Australian vessels that had been accompanying the carriers, now designated Force 44 under Royal Navy Rear Admiral John G. Crace.

On the Japanese side, the sophisticated plan involved the Invasion Group, led by Rear Admiral Shigeyoshi Inoue, commander of the Rabaul base, with the Covering Group of one carrier, *Shoho*, and escorts and the Striking Force with two carriers under Rear Admiral Takeo Takagi to screen the Americans. An initial objective of the Japanese was also a foothold in the Solomon Islands to the east, and on May 3 part of the Invasion Group was sent to Tulagi to establish a seaplane base.

Learning this, Fletcher ordered oil-starved *Lexington* to refuel while on May 4 he headed *Yorktown* north and launched an air strike on Tulagi which destroyed some minor Japanese craft and told them the Americans had at least one carrier in the area. The plans went ahead and after the two American carriers rendezvoused on May 6, Fletcher was ready to strike. But bad weather limited the possibilities and when all was ready on the morning of May 7, Fletcher could only get information on Inoue's force. Crace's cruisers were sent to intercept the transports in Jomard Passage. After a few misidentifications and an ineffective B-17 night attack the previous day, *Shoho* was bombed and sunk by 93 carrier planes – Devastator torpedo bombers and Dauntless dive bombers – launched from the two American carriers. The Battle of the Coral Sea was on. "We bombed them and sank that carrier," says Bill Roy, "and that's where the famous words 'scratch one flattop' came from. That was a quote from the pilot."

A Japanese seaplane reported to Inoue the sighting of two American carriers and he launched a land-based attack from Rabaul on what turned out to be Crace's cruisers. The cruis-

TOP: The Japanese carrier Shoho, *seen here at Yokosuka naval base on December 20, 1941, was a type of aircraft carrier called "Sang-bong." This design was a platform built over a battleship hull. BOTTOM: IJN carrier* Shoho *is seen under attack by American planes in the Battle of the Coral Sea, May 7, 1942. This photograph was taken by a torpedo bomber from* Yorktown.

Captain Elliot Buckmaster posed in dress whites during the ceremony to launch the new USS Yorktown *(CV-10) at Newport News, Virginia in 1943. The black arm band is in memory of those who perished in the sinking of his previous ship, USS* Yorktown *(CV-5).*

ers' evasive maneuvers and anti-aircraft skill beat back this attack without a single defensive airplane. The oiler *Neosho* was not so fortunate. A massive attack from the Japanese fleet carriers damaged the oiler, which sank four days later, and immediately sunk the escort destroyer USS *Sims*. But the action of May 7 was not complete. *Yorktown* was sighted by a spotter plane at dusk and Takagi launched a risky night attack.

What the Japanese sorely lacked, shipboard radar, the U. S. Navy had and used to their advantage as bad weather covered TF-17. The American CAP splashed 21 of 27 Japanese at-

tackers, including planes that mistakenly joined the circling F4F Wildcat fighters above *Yorktown*. The carrier and aircraft losses made the Japanese the losers in the day's battle. The Invasion Group turned back after the loss of *Shoho*.

The fighting ramped up as expected on May 8. Roy was in the process of making a shipboard documentary when the Battle of the Coral Sea thrust itself into his plans. "I was going to make a movie for a morale booster [for the men below deck]. You hear a lot of thumping, banging and explosions but they don't have any idea what's going on. So here I was making this movie to be later shown at movie time. I had permission to be on the bridge from Captain Eliot Buckmaster, Naval Academy guy. And his only admonition was 'Stay out of my way.' And he was in a flash suit. I had a dungaree shirt, dungaree pants, no helmet, no hat. My shirt is stuffed full of cans of film. I'm shooting a movie camera and I got a backup still camera stowed somewhere close by. I had done preliminary shots of looking through binoculars, compasses and things like that of Admiral Fletcher and Captain Buckmaster."

Roy was about to get a crack at filming many action shots for his documentary. Both sides sent out search planes in the early morning from their positions in the middle of the Coral Sea. The Japanese used floatplanes as their land-based aircraft were grounded in wet weather. Fitch dispatched eighteen dive bombers to search for Takagi's partially obscured strike force but once discovered, the two navy carriers launched 60 bombers with a fighter escort. Again, the lack of radar would hamper the Japanese as they kept their Zero interceptors on deck until search planes spotted incoming aircraft. A cloud cover shielded *Yorktown*'s dive bombers but their mission resulted in zero hits. A windshield fogging issue when nosing over from 20,000 feet was the culprit in the poor performance, but the issue would soon be rectified. An hour after the unsuc-

cessful run by the *Yorktown* planes, torpedo bombers also attacked *Shokaku*; but the fleet carrier evaded the

A Japanese aircraft passes over an American destroyer at Coral Sea during the May 8 attack on U. S. carriers.

fish. Just when the mission appeared to be a bust, three bomb hits tore up *Shokaku*'s deck.

Though both sides lost planes in the attack over the Striking Force, the situation could have been worse for the Japanese. *Zuikaku* was hidden under a rain storm and most of the Japanese bombers were away on a mission of their own. After a false alarm generated by ships' radar sent CAPs aloft from both American carriers, the real attack began at 1055 hours when the first CAP was back on deck. A new CAP of Wildcat fighters and Dauntless dive bombers was put up and splashed 3 of 18 attackers. Kate torpedo bombers dropped down to make torpedo runs on *Yorktown*, but evasive action by Buckmaster avoided them.

Roy remembers the scene from his perch on the bridge.

"One of the exciting things, coming down the port side of the *Yorktown* was a Japanese torpedo plane that had come in, dropped his torpedo and missed us, being shot up. The airplane's on fire, burning. And he turns - Kamikazes were not known in those days, in '42. He was going parallel to the port side and was going down and I got an almost three-quarter inch image on a 35mm film. I'm shooting black & white with a Bell & Howell camera. And just as I was shooting, he [the Japanese pilot] shook his fist and about that time the airplane just exploded right beside the ship and plunged right in the water. And we were haulin' ass, we were going pretty fast when he turned, came along, then blew up and crashed. I got his picture."

During the Battle of the Coral Sea USS Lexington *was bombed by Japanese planes and rendered unusable. She is shown here still burning furiously after the crew abandoned ship. Some of the aft planes had not yet caught fire when this photo was taken.*

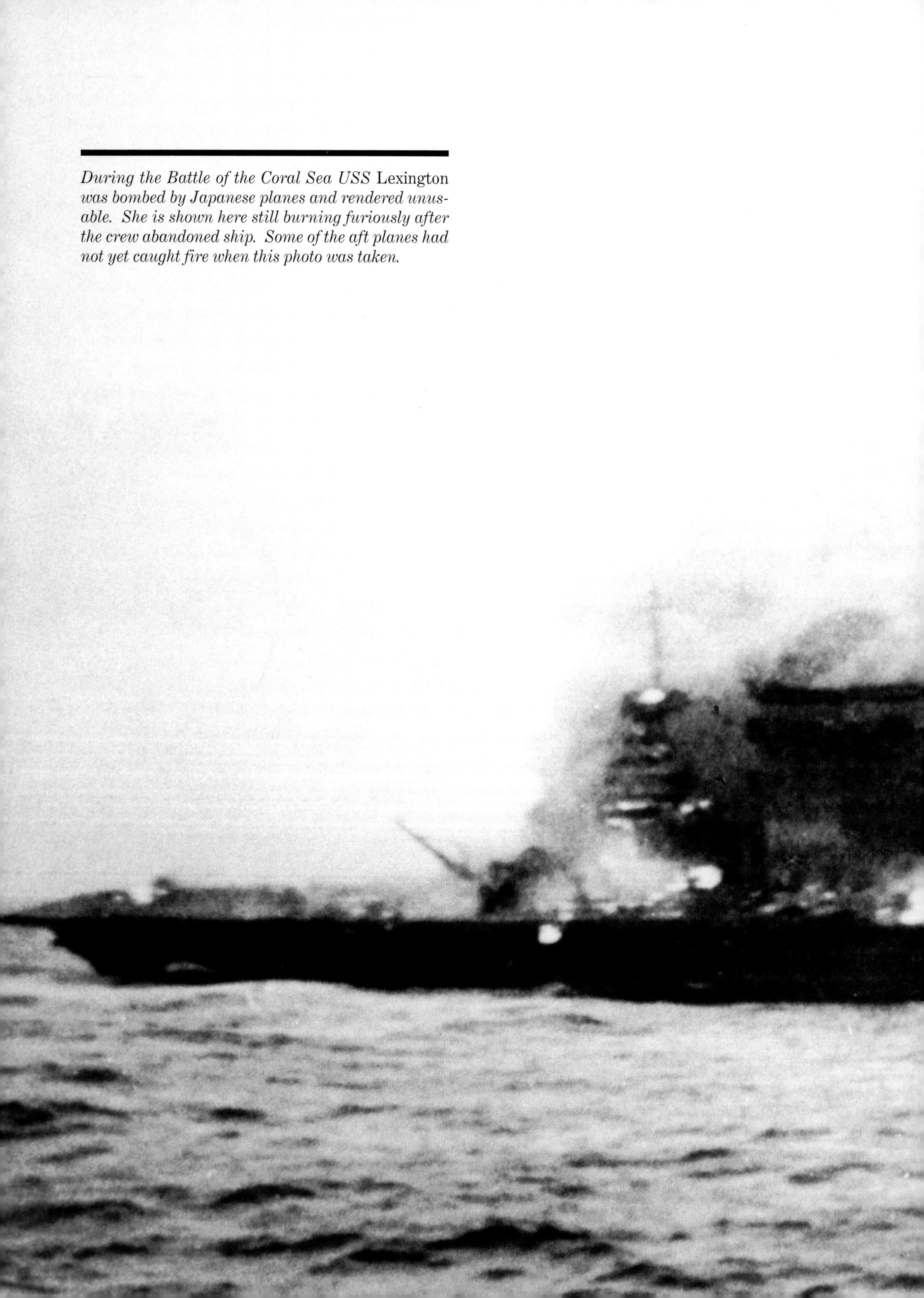

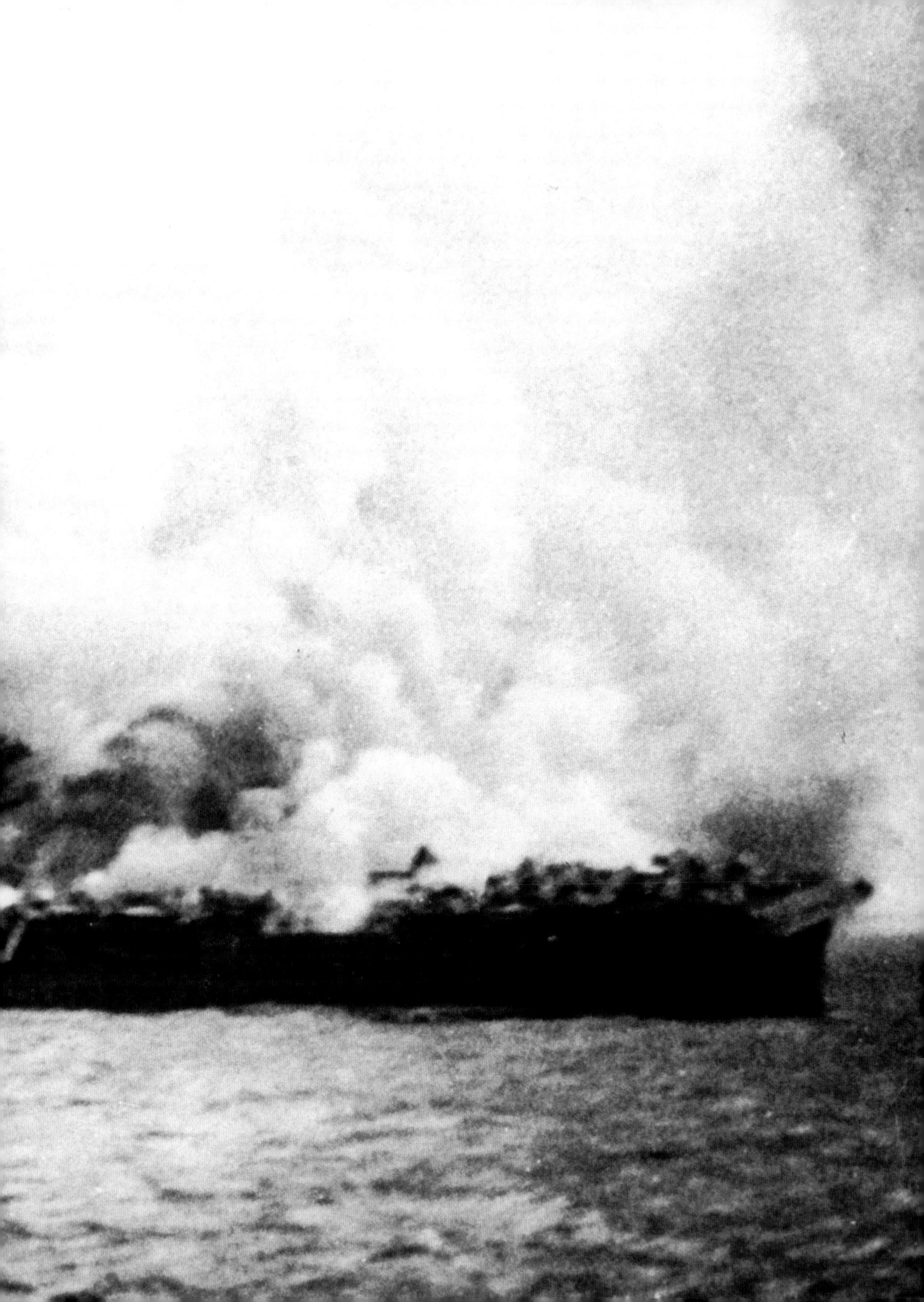

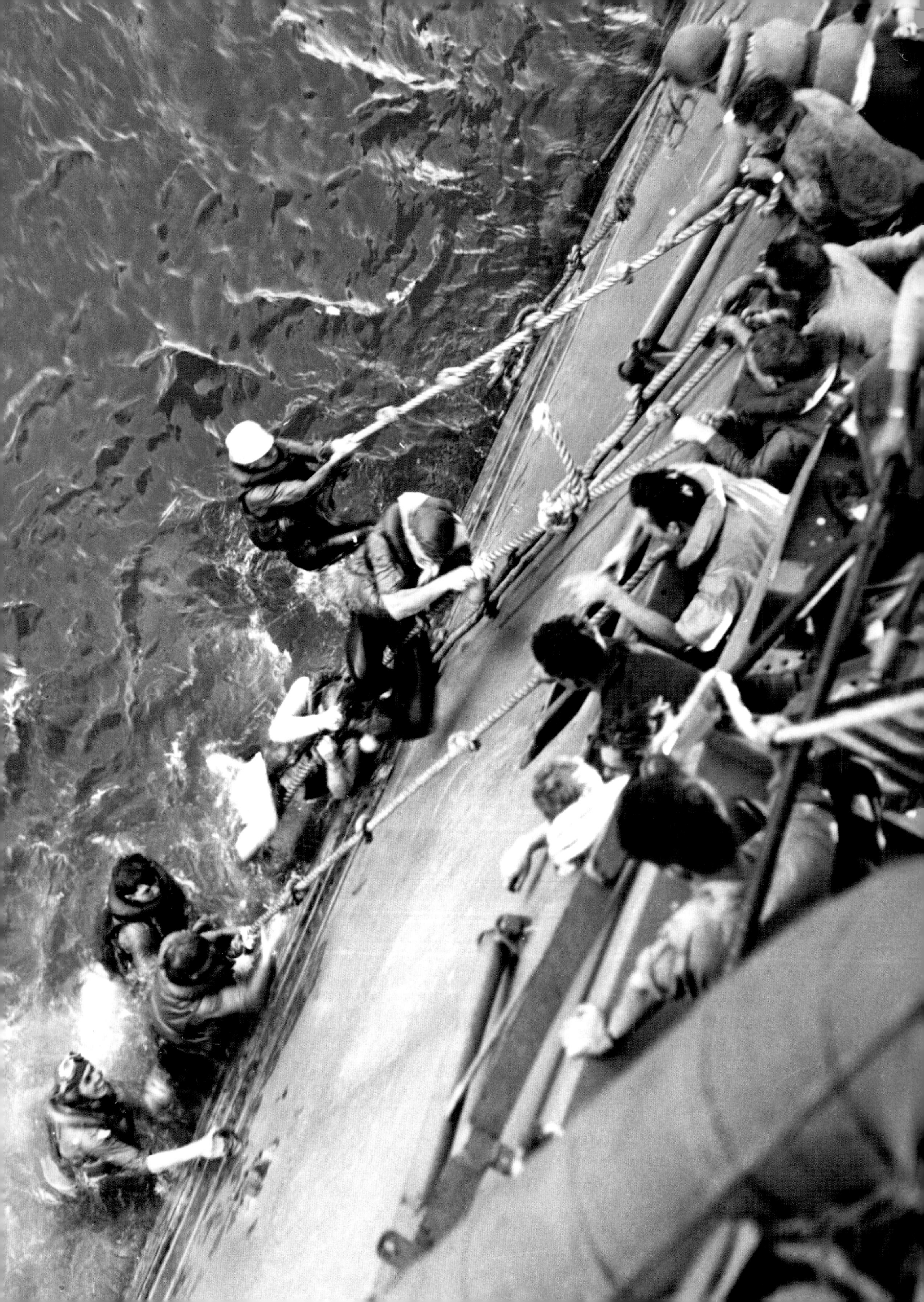

Lexington was not as fortunate. One of the longest ships in the world at that time, she was slow to respond to the helm. Captain Frederick Sherman avoided one torpedo spread but the second yielded one hit forward and another amidships for the Japanese Kates. Val dive bombers followed those scores up with two more hits and other near misses. Fires on *Lexington* were burning out of control. "The gas system was not purged and the gas line broke and a fire started," explains Roy. "And the airplanes caught on fire and I took a picture of an airplane flying off the deck when the ship exploded. The airplane catapulted right up through the light clouds off the bow. Then the ready torpedoes were a hazard and Captain Sherman elected to abandon ship."

The Vals also scored a direct hit on *Yorktown*, a 250-pound bomb that dropped four decks through the flight deck and killed most of a 42-man damage control party near the storeroom where the explosive detonated. This hit led the Japanese to report to the Combined Fleet commander that both American carriers had been sunk. That was taken as good news. The actual bad news was the Japanese lost 31 planes and only 39 of the survivors remained operational. Bomb damage to *Shokaku* precluded any air launches and Takagi began to withdraw north in the afternoon. A later futile attempt to find TF-17 went for naught, and finally Yamamoto was forced to abandoned operation "MO."

Fletcher ruled out a second attack as well, given the American losses. *Lexington*'s planes were transferred to *Yorktown*, which was fortunate considering another large explosion occurred on the carrier in mid-afternoon. Fletcher dispatched *Yorktown* and escorts south while two cruisers and three destroyers oversaw the aban-

Survivors of Lexington *go over the side after the order to abandon ship was given.*

donment of *Lexington*. At 1841 hours, when all that could be recovered was taken from *Lexington*, the destroyer *Phelps* sent five torpedoes into the hull. The great ship flopped over and disappeared. So ended May 8, 1942 and the first naval battle in which opposing ships never came within sight of each other.

Operation "MI"

As disastrous as operation "MO" turned out to be for the Japanese, operation "MI" would be more devastating. Even though the Japanese would try to take Port Moresby later by land, the disruption of the timetable and change of plans forced on Yamamoto greatly impacted future events. Therefore the U. S. Navy had its first strategic victory of the Pacific War by sinking one carrier and severely damaging another, destroying enough planes to put two Japanese fleet carriers out of business – one for two months and the other for 30 days – at the cost of *Lexington*, one destroyer and an auxiliary. Nimitz ordered *Yorktown* to refuel at Tongatabu and return to Pearl Harbor. He became concerned again about threats to the Midway-Hawaii defense line in the Central Pacific and ordered the carriers to prepare for a new mission.

Besides the direct hit, concussion and shrapnel from near misses had done structural damage to *Yorktown*. Bill Roy humorously tells the tale of what the crew thought and what happened on their return to Oahu. "So we expected to be in the shipyard at Pearl Harbor for temporary repairs and then go to Bremerton, Washington for six months. Instead Admiral Nimitz came aboard and said, 'You have 72 hours. Get out.' And so we did."

Nimitz had reason for concern. Admiral King, disappointed when Nimitz cancelled a May 16 Halsey raid, nevertheless stood by his subordinate. In fact it was King's successful raiding strategy that was behind Nimitz's worries. Yamamoto was desperate to put a stop to the raiding. Although his plan to secure Midway as a means to cut raiding in the Central Pacific was opposed by the Naval General Staff, that abruptly changed when the Doolittle raid shamed the naval strategists by exposing the emperor's life to American bombs. Still not sure where the April 18 bombing attack originated, the high command was taking no chances. In a prophetic aside, Yamamoto remarked that successful or not, operation "MI" would keep the Central Pacific quiet for some time.

Midway atoll, although known as Midway Island, was two small pieces of land in close proximity. There was a Naval Air Station at Midway with navy and Marine planes in May of 1942. As long as that airfield operated, reasoned Yamamoto, Japan's eastern buffer was not secure. Of less concern apparently was the security of Japan's communications. The relatively tight security maintained throughout the Pearl Harbor operation was starting to spring leaks. Besides mastering the Japanese diplomatic "Purple" code, American code breakers, including the inspired operation maintained by the navy in Hawaii, were making great progress with the J-25 Japanese naval code. One mystery term kept appearing in enemy chatter, prompting the code breakers to fabricate a test. They concocted a message, sure to be intercepted, that the Midway garrison was running low on fresh water. When the message was repeated by the Japanese with the same code word used in more ominous messages, the navy team confirmed that Midway was the Japanese target, reporting the breakthrough up the chain of command. It went all the way to Nimitz.

Lieutenant Joseph P. Pollard, of the U. S. Navy Medical Corps, reported to *Yorktown* just as it was returning from the Coral Sea battle. He articulated his version of the urgency to return to sea some years later. "On 27 May 1942, I was detached from Commander, 14th Naval District

(Oahu), and at 2000 reported on board USS *Yorktown* for duty. She was alongside Pier B-16 in Pearl Harbor. On 28 May the ship moved into dry dock for hull inspection where she remained all day and night, meanwhile loading stores and ammunition. On the morning of 29 May, the ship was still in dry dock. I visited friends, particularly Lieutenant Commander Garton E. Wall, MC, USNR, at the Old Naval Station Dispensary and bid goodbye to Dr. James R. Martin. The latter expressed a strong desire to go to sea with us. Doctor Wall came down to the ship to see me but at that time we were moving back to Pier B-16. Scuttlebutt in the ship was that we were sailing in the morning.

"On 30 May USS *Yorktown* put to sea at 0800 and took a course said to be towards Midway at a speed of about 15 knots. There was gunnery practice most of the morning using both towed sleeve and high speed sled. The gun crews seemed good. Morale was excellent. On May 31 we spent a busy but uneventful day at sea. Our escorts were the *Portland, Astoria* [cruisers], *Hammann, Hughes, Russell* and *Balch* [destroyers]. The ship's company was informed that when this mission was completed, the ship was scheduled for a complete overhaul. This would mean perhaps a month's leave. Since the crew had just returned from the Coral Sea and had spent 102 days without liberty, this was welcomed news. We felt somewhat uneasy at going into battle in our condition as the watertight integrity of the ship was said to be considerably reduced as a result of damage received in the Battle of the Coral Sea."

Yorktown, Enterprise and *Hornet*, the three available carries, would all be defending the Hawaii-Midway line together for the first time. The two carriers of TF-16 set out on May 28 with a rendezvous set later for *Yorktown* and her escorts. Because Halsey was ill, command of TF-16

fell to Rear Admiral Raymond A. Spruance, a capable officer. Fletcher, still in command of TF-17, had overall command of the expedition. King knew the risks in leaving Australia without sea-based air cover, but he was also confident in Nimitz's decisions and was getting a handle on the strengths and weaknesses of his opponent.

As usual, Yamamoto's design was grand and complicated. The Japanese force, an awesome armada of 165 ships, was assembled in May. Two main forces were set to lure the U. S. Navy into a trap over Midway; one was the Mobile Force (Kido Butai), Vice Admiral Chuichi Nagumo's four carriers of the 1st Air Group that were not engaged at Coral Sea, *Akagi*, *Kaga*, *Soryu*, *Hiryu* and their screens. The follow-up punch was to be delivered by a Main Force in which Yamamoto planned to maintain on-board headquarters on the super battleship *Yamato* along with six other battleships, cruisers and a light carrier. Always optimistic of success, the Japanese had assembled a formidable armada that included an occupation force and supporting elements.

Another force completed the grand plan. A Northern Area Force, commanded by Vice Admiral Boshiro Hosogaya, sailed for the Aleutian Islands to attack the American naval base at Dutch Harbor, Unalaska Island and occupy Kiska and Attu in the island chain. The thrust into the furthest west reaches of North America had a dual purpose - to prevent staging of long-range bombers there that could pound the Home Islands, and to create a diversion for the attack on Midway. Armed with the excellent intelligence obtained, Nimitz was not fooled by the diversion. He did, however, send a sturdy force of ships to the Aleutians under Rear Admiral Robert Theobald and positioned the serviceable battleships and a light carrier in the Eastern Pacific under Vice Admiral William Pye.

Both opposing commanders envisioned trapping each other's ships in a scissors attack; the Japanese forcing the American carriers between the Mobile and Main forces, with planes they hoped to launch from occupied Midway; the U. S. Navy squeezing Yamamoto's force between air strikes from Midway and the carriers. Not only the advance intelligence from the code breakers was working for the Americans - other elements of preparation and luck would also frame the Battle of Midway.

The combined task forces of Spruance and Fletcher, fifty ships with 221 aircraft, steamed on parallel courses to the northwest and escaped detection by the Japanese submarine screen which did not reach station at French Frigate Shoals until June 1. Medical officer Pollard noted activity on *Yorktown* during the first three days of June.

"On 1 June we spent a very busy day making preparations for battle. Anti-flash clothing, gas masks and steel helmets were issued to all hands. We broke out and rechecked our emergency medical equipment. On 2 June our scouting aircraft were out morning and afternoon. Excitement was running high in the ship and morale was excellent. We were told that our submarines had reported a Jap invasion force [battleships, cruisers, destroyers and transports] off Midway Island. We rendezvoused with the *Hornet* and *Enterprise* and their escorts in late afternoon and remained with them overnight. On 3 June scuttlebutt was thick. A Jap task force was reported to have bombed Dutch Harbor today. A Jap carrier force was reported northwest of Midway consisting of three carriers and their screen. We were said to be heading towards them."

The Battle of Midway

Early on the morning of June 4, 1942, the Japanese launched an air attack on Midway with half their available aircraft, 108

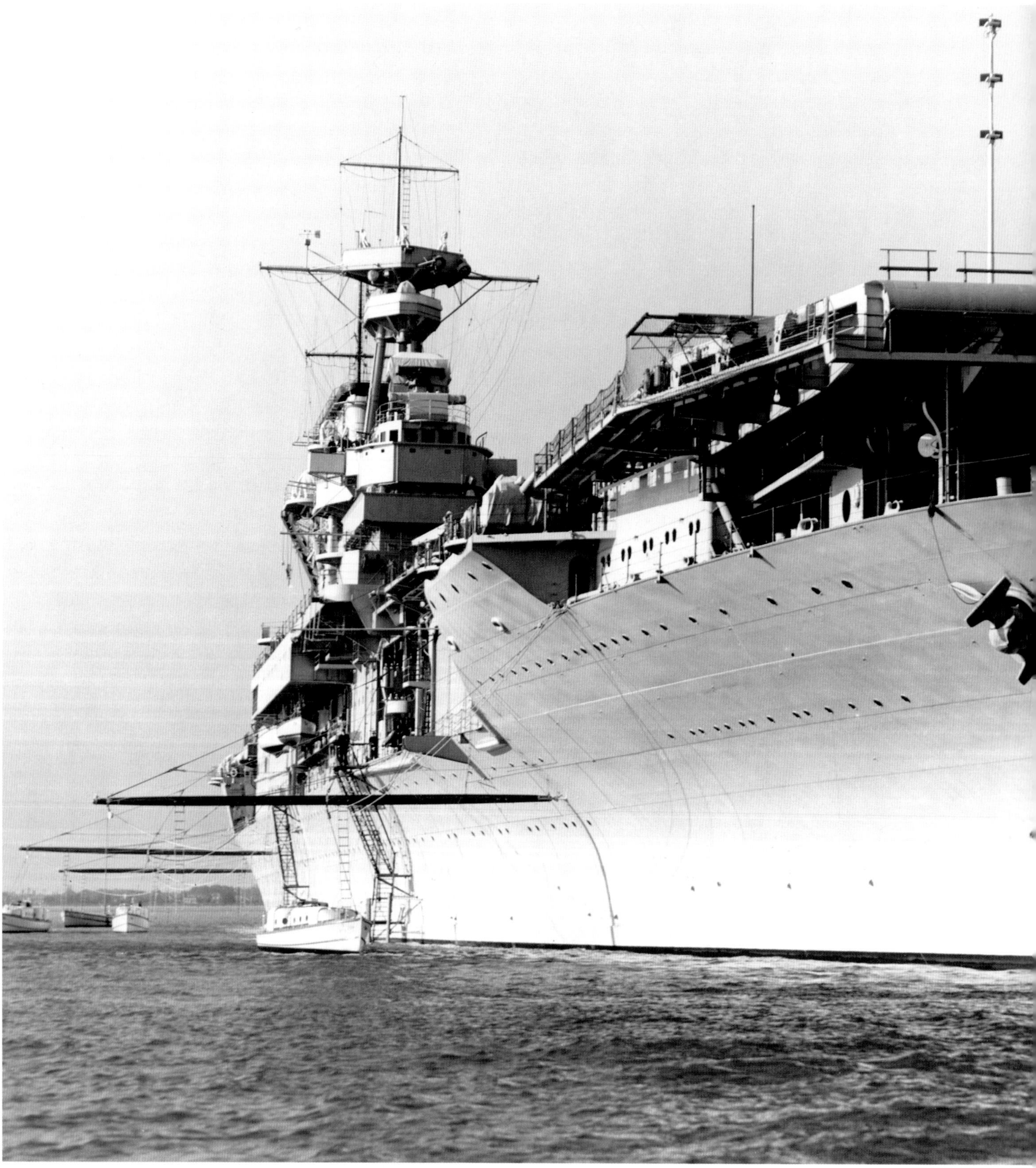

planes, divided between fighters, dive bombers and torpedo bombers. They also sent up float planes to scout to the east. But the Americans on Midway knew they were coming. Navy and Marine bombers, as well as B-17E Flying Fortresses from Hawaii, were heading for the Japanese fleet. A Marine interception force of eighteen F2A-3 Buffalo fighters and six Wildcat fighters met the Japanese bombers thirty miles out but were bested by the emperor's eagles. But, between losses in the air battle and those from anti-aircraft fire, the Japanese defeat of the Midway defenders was incomplete. Not one American plane was destroyed on the ground. Leaving the runways unscathed, the Japanese flight leader radioed back to the carriers that a second strike would be necessary.

This began a series of ill-timed decisions on the part of Nagumo. Yamamoto warned Nagumo to remain prepared for the appearance of American ships; but since none had yet been spotted, Nagumo began to rearm his bombers with high explosives for another strike at Midway. The decks of the four carriers had to be cleared for the returning planes. Then, at 0728, Nagumo received a report that American ships were 235 miles northwest of Midway — but there was no mention of U. S. carriers. Nagumo retracted his earlier command and ordered the armor-piercing bombs reloaded for a run at the ships. The fact that American bombers of all types had been over the Mobile Force since 0700 seemed to be insignificant in the admiral's plans.

Perhaps Nagumo and his staff, which included the outstanding air strategist Minoru Genda, were lulled into a false sense of security by the

USS Yorktown (CV-5) is a majestic sight anchored in Hampton Roads, Virginia in October 1937. Initially assigned to the Atlantic, the aircraft carrier was assigned to the Pacific Fleet following the attack on Pearl Harbor.

THE BATTLE OF MIDWAY

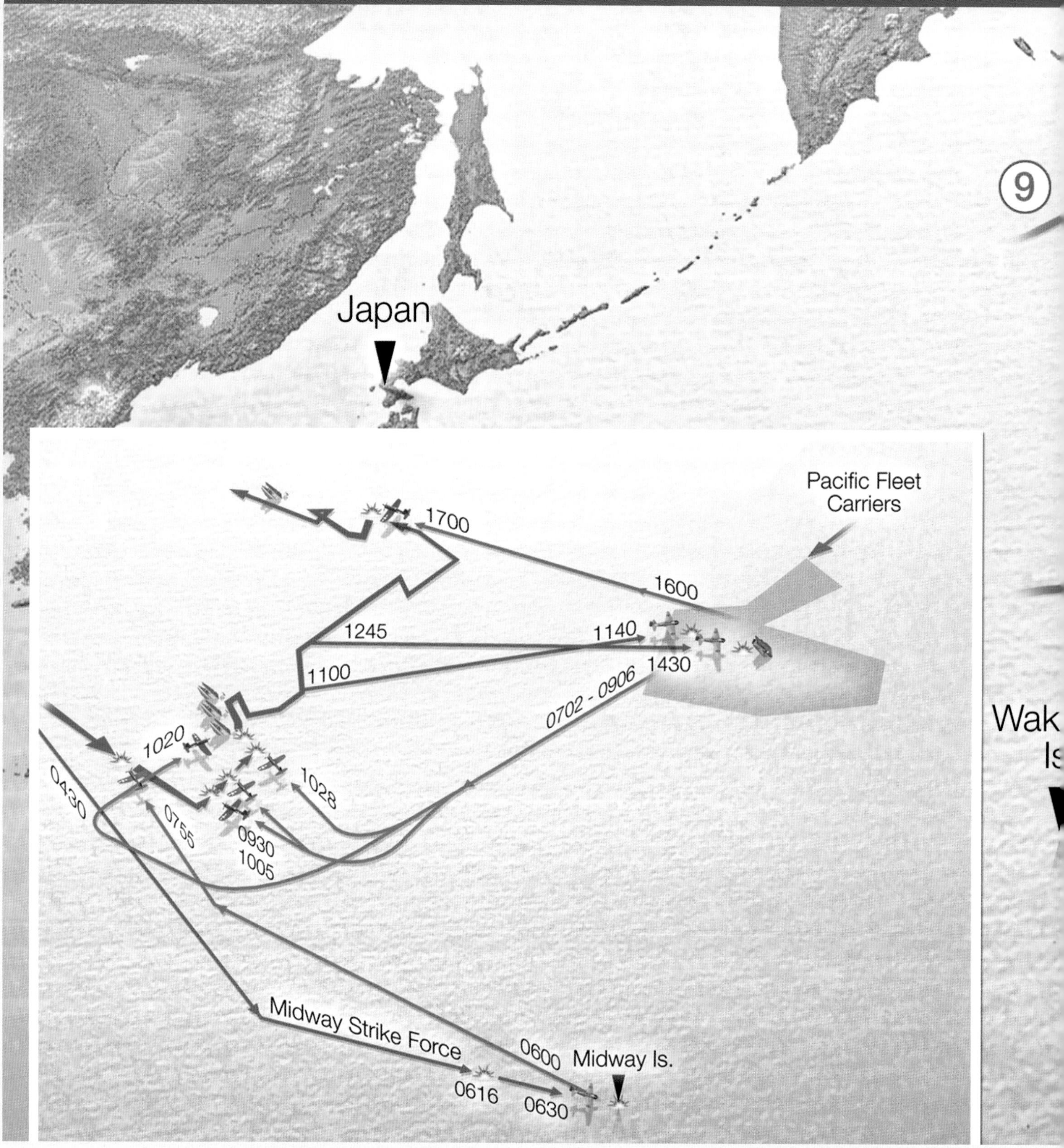

Japan
9
Wak
Is
Pacific Fleet
Carriers
1700
1600
1245
1140
1100
1430
0702 - 0906
1020
1028
0430
0755
0930
1005
Midway Strike Force
0600
Midway Is.
0616
0630

The Japanese plan in operation "MO" was a complicated naval operation involving many individual ships of various types. Principal ships in the operation were the Mobile Force (1) which was the carriers (*Kido Butai*) and the Main Body (3) which contained Admiral Yamamoto's best surface warships. Other task forces had specific roles. The 2nd Fleet Covering Group (5) was designated to guard the Occupation Force (5) as these transports staged landings on Midway. A Mine Sweeping Group (7) would assist the landings and pave the way for a Seaplane Covering Force (6). The rest of the surface ships were involved in the operation to the Aleutian Islands. The Northern Area Force (8) handled the initial attack paving the way for the Attu Occupation Group (9) and the Kiska Occupation Group (10). Following the landings would be the supply and auxiliary ships of the Aleutian Support Group (2). The Japanese submarines provided a screen off the Hawaiian Islands which failed to intercept

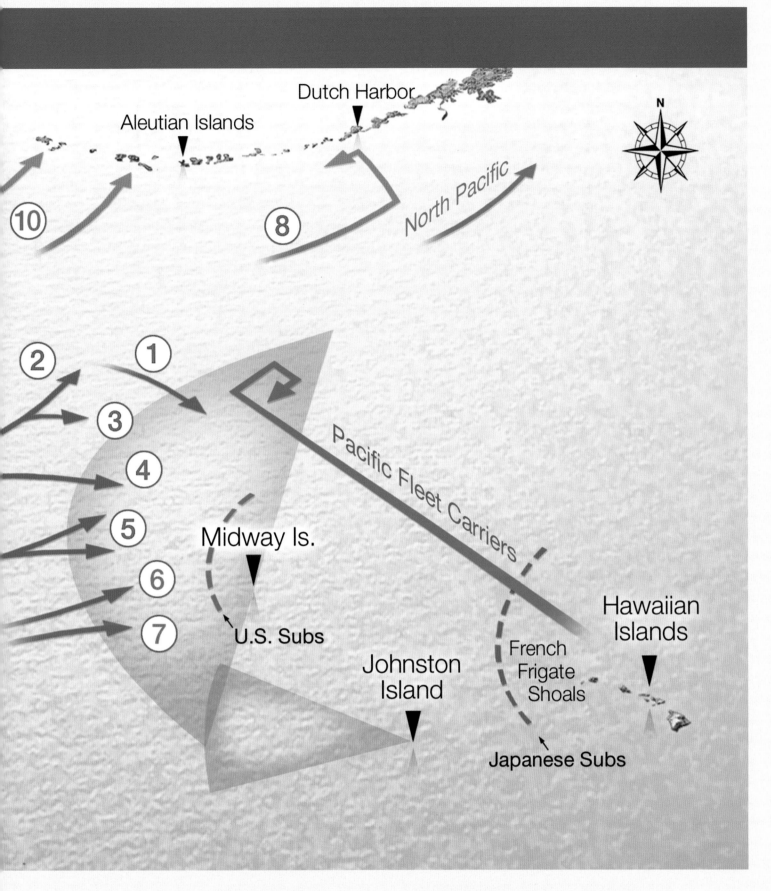

Dutch Harbor

Aleutian Islands

N

(10)   (8)   North Pacific

(2)   (1)

(3)   Pacific Fleet Carriers

(4)

(5)   Midway Is.   Hawaiian
                     Islands
(6)
        U.S. Subs
(7)   French
            Johnston Frigate
            Island   Shoals
                     Japanese Subs

the U. S. Pacific Fleet carriers. USN submarines provided a screen west of Midway but no Japanese ships got close enough to the atoll to be intercepted by the subs.

Inset map: The first action on June 4, 1942 was the short air battle between the Japanese bombers headed to Midway and the islands' defensive air patrol. The American bombers (USMC and USAAF bombers including B-17Es from Hawaii) took off on their own mission a half hour before the Japanese bombed Midway. The times of other missions staged by both sides' carrier planes are indicated, as well as locations of air-to-air combat and ship sinkings. The major blow was the three Japanese carriers sunk by *Enterprise* and *Yorktown* SDB attacks at 1020-1028. Two air strikes from *Hiryu* severely damaged *Yorktown*. Finally *Enterprise* planes sunk *Hiryu* in the last air strike of the day. Midway was the largest air/sea battle of the war at the time.

futility of the Midway-based air attacks. The inexperience of these flyers was telling; torpedo bombers missed or dropped duds, the dive bombers came in too low and were shot down and the B-17 bomb packages missed the maneuvering Japanese ships. The Midway attackers lost eleven dive bombers while downing one Zero and causing no damage to the Imperial Navy ships. But when Nagumo's intelligence was updated to include the fact that the Americans had at least one carrier, his alarm rose. One subordinate suggested an unescorted attack by dive bombers on the American ships. However, the failure to secure Midway coupled with the distraction of dealing with the land-based American planes caused Nagumo and the staff, including Genda, to delay until a massive escorted strike could be launched at 1030 hours. That would prove to be one of the worst decisions of the war for Japan's Combined Fleet.

Fletcher separated TF-16 and TF-17 by twenty miles to avoid creating one massive target; but close enough to provide mutual support. He assumed the Japanese had located his force. He readied his bombers but the overanxious Spruance launched his strike first, failing to coordinate the bombing run of the 116 planes from *Enterprise* and *Hornet* with those from *Yorktown*. Although the Mobile Force had been spotted, finding it exactly on the vast space of the Pacific was difficult. *Hornet* dive bombers passed beyond the Japanese carriers without finding them. They returned to the carrier and Midway when low on fuel and lost most of their fighter escort which was forced to ditch.

At 0920 torpedo bombers from both of Spruance's carriers located the Mobile Force, sailing in a diamond-shaped box, a carrier at each point, preparing for their 1030 hours strike. The superiority of the Type-O fighter over all other aircraft at the time in the Pacific Theater was demonstrated as 25 of the 29 unescorted Avenger tor-

pedo bombers were shot down without dropping a single effective torpedo. Just when the planes from TF-16 seemed to reach the height of futility, Lieutenant Commander "Wade" McClusky's dive bombers from *Enterprise* arrived over the Mobile Fleet at 1000 hours. They had followed a straggling Japanese destroyer back to the carrier formation. McClusky's Dauntless dive bombers went after *Akagi* and *Kaga* at the south and west corners of the box, scoring six hits on the two carries, then packed with planes and ordnance on their decks. At the same time, the 39 fighters, dive and torpedo bombers from *Yorktown* under Lieutenant Commander Maxwell Leslie arrived from the east and headed for *Soryu*. Though the torpedo bombers did no damage, the dive bombers scored many hits and *Soryu* was abandoned within a half hour.

Captain Takahasi Amagai was air officer aboard *Kaga*. He was also an observer during the attack on Pearl Harbor and was interviewed by U. S. officials shortly after the war. He confirmed the effectiveness of *Enterprise* dive bombers and also added an interesting aside.

"There were four hits on the *Kaga*. It was hit by dive bombers two or three hours after sunrise, 4 June. It was hard to see because of smoke, but I believe that the battleship *Hyei* just astern of the *Kaga* was hit by dive bombers and a fire started on the stern of the *Hyei*. I saw torpedo planes but do not think *Kaga* was attacked. No torpedo hits were made. However, while swimming in water several hours after attack [I] saw torpedo apparently fired from submarine strike side of ship at angle and bounce off, didn't explode. Torpedo went bad."

American submarines, like their Japanese counterparts, were lurking in the battle area, but little has been written about their missions. In-

effective torpedoes were a common problem for the U. S. Navy in 1942 and a solution to this became a top priority.

The remaining Japanese carrier, *Hiryu,* launched 18 escorted Vals at 1045 and nine Kates with a small fighter escort an hour later. The Japanese dive bombers followed aircraft returning to *Yorktown* and flew under the carrier's radar. Although Fletcher waved off returning bombers and put up a CAP which splashed 11 of the Vals, the carrier took hits from the other seven. Lieutenant Pollard sets the scene on *Yorktown* before the enemy planes arrived.

"I was called to the flight deck to relieve Doctor Dobos and sick call was suspended. Our bombers

In this battle photograph by Bill Roy, Yorktown *has already sustained hits by three aerial bombs in the Battle of Midway on June 4, 1942.* USS Astoria *maneuvers in the background while the 5-inch/38 guns in the foreground are still being manned.*

were loaded with 1,000 pounders; TBDs with torpedoes, and planes spotted for take-off - fighters, then bombers and lastly the TBDs. Everywhere there was an undercurrent of excitement. At any moment the word might be passed to begin our attack. At any moment we might be attacked. Word came over the bull horn, 'Pilots, man your planes.' We put off our bombers, torpedo planes and half dozen fighters for their protection. Then we put up more fighters for our protection. We sat tight with no news for awhile. There was a great deal of tension. There were small groups of people everywhere talking in low tones. Everyone was wearing anti-flash clothing and steel helmets. All was quiet, too quiet. Battle Dressing Station #1, my duty station, was

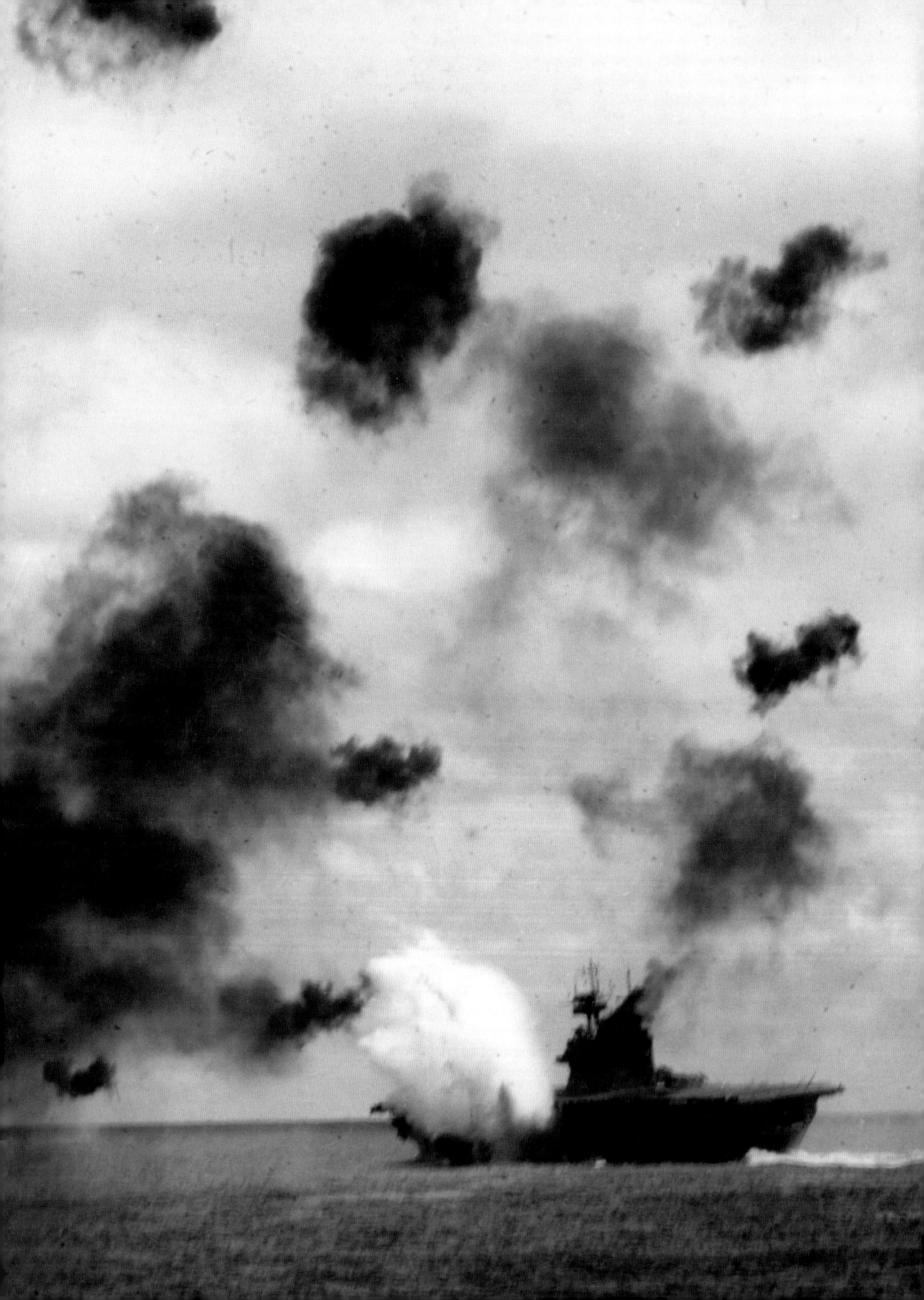

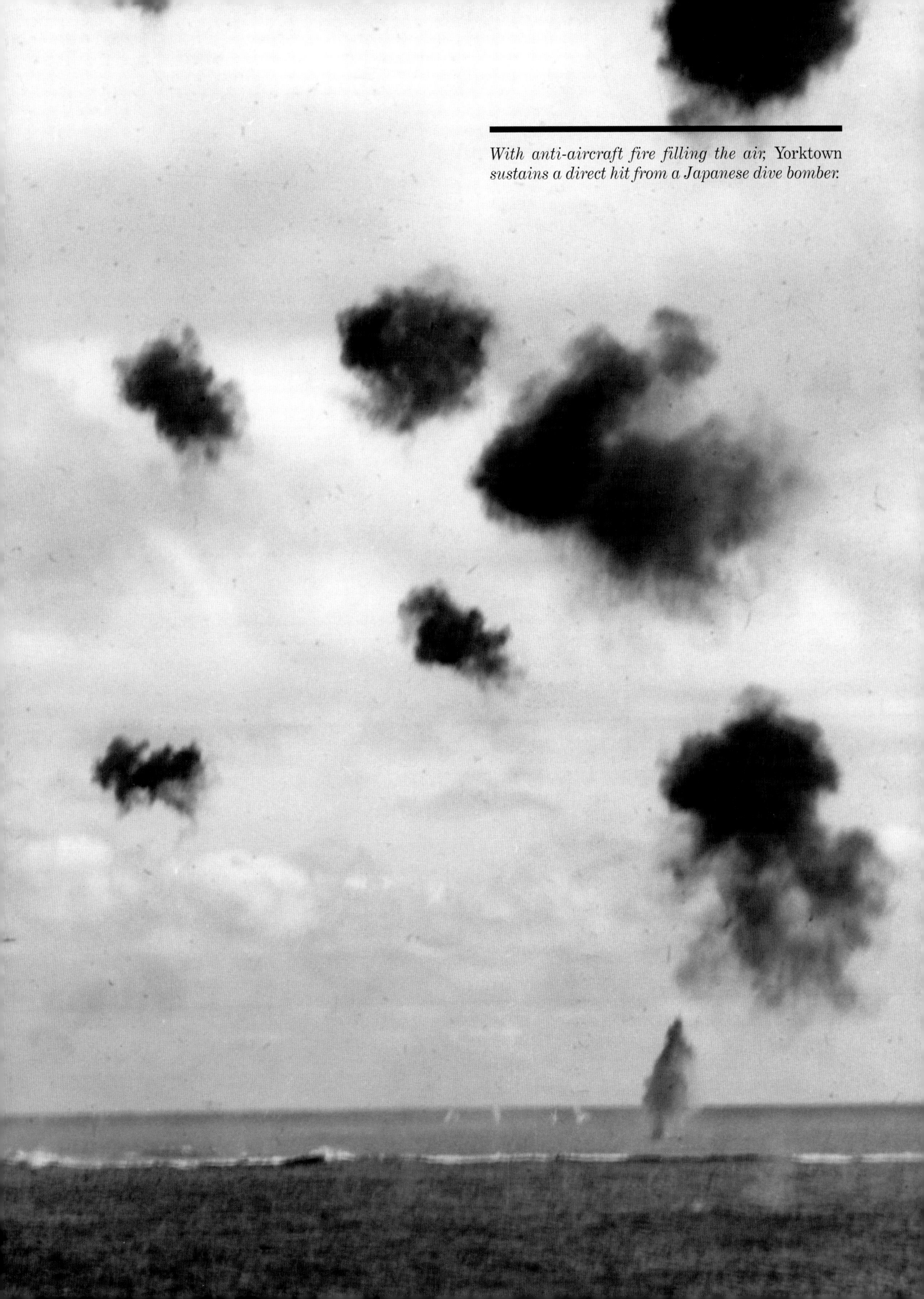

With anti-aircraft fire filling the air, Yorktown *sustains a direct hit from a Japanese dive bomber.*

manned and ready. The morning wore itself away and the afternoon began. I became hungry and went down to the wardroom for a sandwich.

"About 1400 our planes began returning. They had been out a long time and were low on gas. A couple of well-shot-up SBDs made their crash landings. Then the fighters started coming aboard. Many were riddled with holes. We landed about five and then one came in too hot and too high. He began to float over the deck and it looked like trouble. The pilot recognized that he was in trouble and made a dive for the deck. He somersaulted and skidded away on the deck. I made a quick dive under the wreckage but the pilot was unhurt and got out of the wreckage before I could get to him. I began to run across the flight deck to my station but before I arrived there general quarters sounded. Jap planes were upon us. I dived down the ladder for Battle Dressing Station #1 and on my way saw one of our fighters fall on one wing and like a shooting star hit the drink. There was a puff of black smoke and that was all.

"Upon arriving at #1 I lay flat on the deck and hoped that we would not get a bomb in the crowded dressing room or anywhere for that matter. By this time our AA [anti-aircraft fire] was in full bloom. I had never before heard such a roar. First the 5-inch, then the 1.1s and 20 mm's, the .50 cal, and finally the hastily set up .30 cal. machine guns along the rail. I knew then they were upon us. Then all hell broke loose. I saw a burst of fire, heard a terrific explosion and in less than ten seconds was overwhelmed by a mass of men descending from the gun mounts and flight deck into the dressing station. An instantaneous 500 pound bomb had struck just aft of the starboard side of the middle elevator and shrapnel had wiped out nearly all of the men from AA mounts #3 and #4 [1.1] and also my corpsman who stood on the aft island ladder platform where I usually stood."

Bill Roy talks about the situation Pollard was faced with that changed the situation on the deck of *Yorktown* in the blink of an eye.

"Here's a lieutenant, never been on a carrier, now he's got all these responsibilities, all these dead people, all these chopped up people. And when you walk over and take a picture that's never been published, you see the torso and legs and the top's gone, and the belts holding just the legs in the trainer's seat of the gun mount and all of that. And inside the tub are parts and pieces of bodies and everything. And there's one picture I took, nobody knows what it is, in this bucket, but it's a guy's head. But it's just a bucket sitting there."

That was the situation after the dive bombers got through the CAP and dropped their loads on *Yorktown*. The flight deck was quickly patched up and repairs from two other hits were made as well, explains Bill Roy.

"Dixie Keifer was the executive officer, he supervised it [the repairs]. They trimmed up the hole, knocked off some timbers, a metal plate goes out on the timbers and started flight operations in 20 minutes. We took one right down the stack that burned the photo lab, the executive officer's office and the first lieutenant's office. This bomb exploded and blew out all nine boilers. And they were working feverously to get some of them back online and get up some steam. The third bomb went down the bow, to the 4th level, and exploded. We had taken on a couple of truckloads of rags to wipe the engines. And they were scalding and burning. And the danger was they were burning

Crew members of Yorktown *repair damage after a direct hit by a "Val" dive bomber at 1330 on June 4. Bill Roy was the photographer for this and other dramatic* Yorktown *photographs during the battle.*

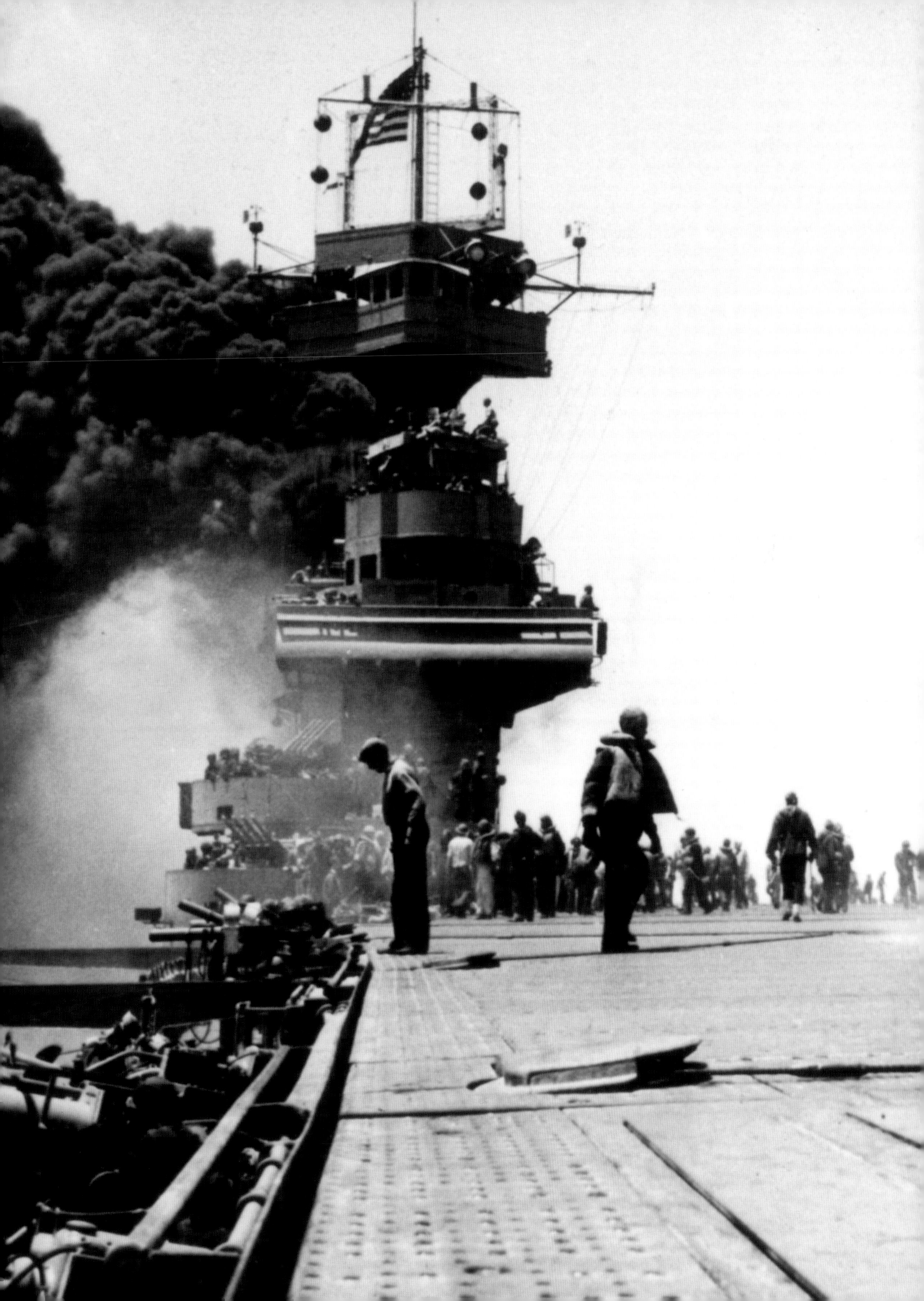

near 150,000 gallons of aviation gas, torpedoes and the 1,000 lb. bomb storage. So it was very precarious, you tiptoed around."

At Battle Dressing Station #1 Dr. Pollard was dealing with the casualties from the dive bomber attack.

"I was overwhelmed with work. Wounded were everywhere. Some men had one foot or leg off, others had both off; some were dying - some dead. Everywhere there was need for morphine, tourniquets, blankets and first aid. Battle Dressing Station #1 rapidly overflowed into the passageway, into the parachute loft and into all other available spaces. I called for stretcher bearers to get the more seriously wounded to the sick bay where they could receive plasma, etc., but the passageways had been blocked off due to the bomb hits. So we gave more morphine, covered the patients with blankets, and did the best we could. Many patients went rapidly into shock. There was no smoke in Battle Dressing Station #1, which was fortunate. Water hoses were dragged into the passageway in an attempt to control a fire somewhere forward in the island. The hose had been perforated by shrapnel and sprayed water all over the deck and on some of my wounded who were lying in the passageway."

By this time Admiral Fletcher and his staff had transferred the Task Force flag to USS *Astoria*, a heavy cruiser. *Yorktown* was given orders to head home, but then radar picked up the Kate torpedo bombers from *Hiryu*. Bill Roy was topside again with his camera gear.

"So, we're just getting up eight knots, and we have some fighters on the deck that had landed, and after we patched up the ship, they had landed. They only had 23 gallons of gas, most of them. And so, they were launched. They tried to refuel them, and they said no we don't want gas in the fuel lines. We have to purge them, so we don't have a fire like the *Lexington*. And they engaged the enemy and it was a torpedo attack. We just got up speed, didn't have enough speed to maneuver the ship very well, and here came the torpedo planes. And we shot them down, most of them, coming in. And two of them got through and dropped their torpedoes on the port side, amidships. And when I was up on the signal bridge and looked down in front of me at the .50 [7.7] calibers, during the torpedo run, they were trying to fire and come in. And this machine gunner right in front of me was just shot out from behind his gun and blood spurting everywhere. I didn't get frightened, I just kept shooting my pictures. And I thought, 'Well, that's a close one.'"

Pollard also vividly remembers the torpedo plane attack.

"We were just hitting 22 knots but they [the fighters mentioned by Roy] took a long run and made it off. Just as the last one left the deck I made a dive for Battle Dressing Station #1 and again the AAs began as before. By the time I could find an unoccupied place on the deck there was a sickening thud and rumble throughout the ship and the deck rose under me, trembled and fell away. One torpedo hit had occurred. My thought was that we could take this one and get away with it perhaps but not any more. Then another sickening thud and the good ship shuddered and rapidly listed hard to port. I knew we were completely helpless but did not want to admit it. Just then word came over the speaker, 'Prepare to abandon ship.' I was dumbfounded. It was incomprehensible. A man lying beside me with one foot shot away and a severe chest wound turned his head towards me and asked, 'What does this mean for us?' and turned his head away. He knew that he would have no chance in the water. This

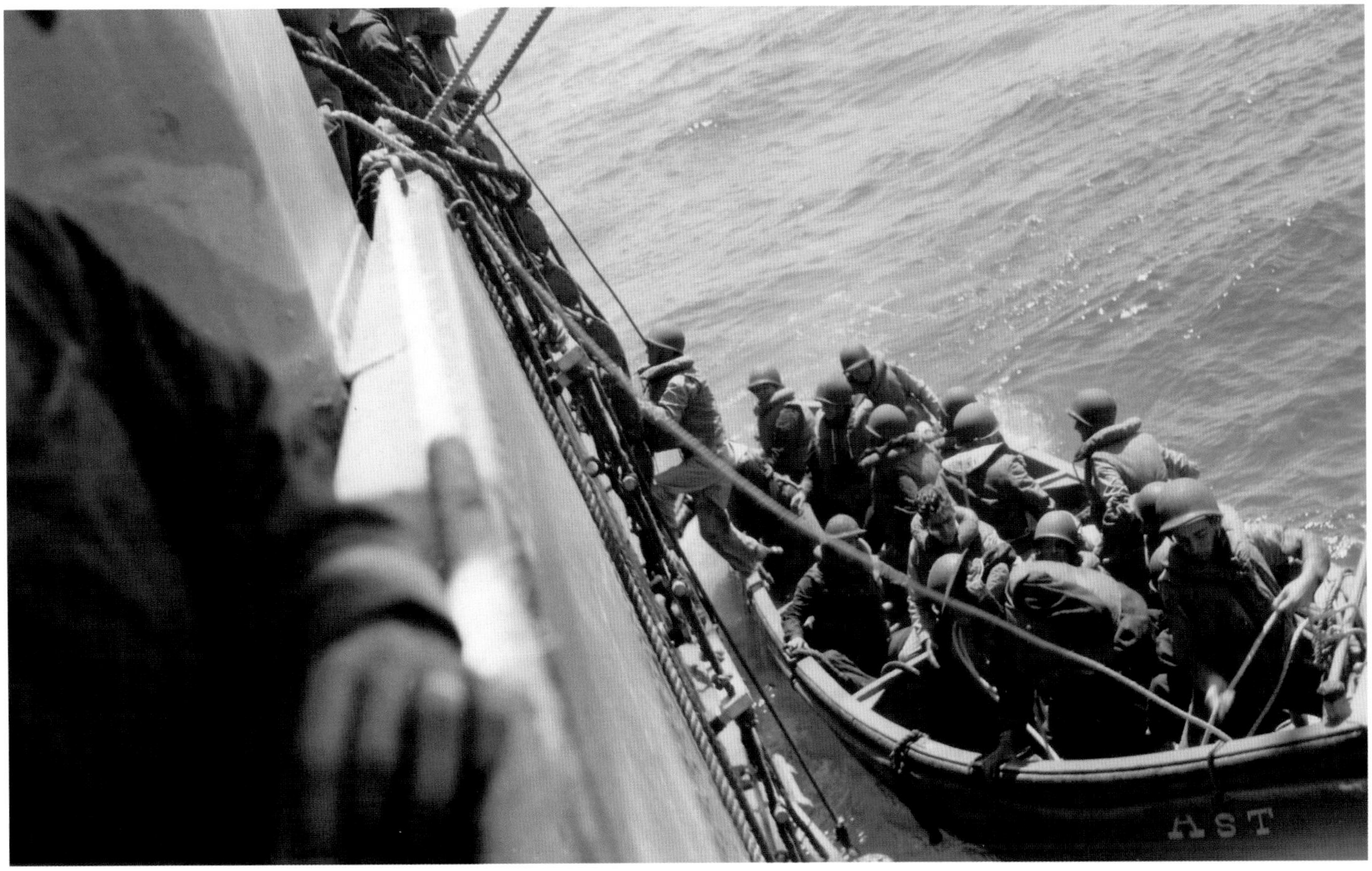
AST

Rear Admiral Fletcher, task force commander, leaves his flagship, Yorktown, *with other crew members. Fletcher transferred his flag to the cruiser* Astoria.

man was later seen in the naval hospital in Pearl Harbor on the way to recovery."

"So we took two torpedoes," explains Roy. "The ship stopped, went over 28 degrees, the hanger deck is in the water on the port side, and I went off the starboard side. I went over the life lines, and there's a mess attendant. He said, 'I can't swim, I can't swim.' So I got hold of him on the lines. They're all tangled up. Problem is, the lines were cut to the ship's [height] on an even keel. When it rolls over to port the lines come up 10 or 12 or 15 feet. And everyone had a problem; you have to come down and you can just make it to the armor plate and stand on it for a bit, and then you jump in the water. Hold on tight with that old Kapok lifejacket, you just had the line around your waist. So it'd bubble up under your chin.

"Anyway, I got him down in the water, got him to a life raft, and then I found out that the boats could not be lowered with the wounded. So they lowered people down in the water with their open wounds. Ghastly wounds they were. Put them right in the salt water and oil – there's oil everywhere. They put them in life rafts and consequently those of us who could swim a little bit, who weren't injured, just had to hang on to whatever we could hang on to. The side of the ship, basically. Well the wind and waves keeps you against the side of the *Yorktown*, and it's rough, it's rusty, it's got all kinds of crap on it, even though it had just come out of the navy yard but they didn't polish it up. So, here we are, trying to survive now in oil. And the first thing you do is get it in your eyes and nose and

ears and hair and all of your clothes and it sticks to you. Then you start swallowing it, then you start throwing up. And that's where I tore my diaphragm. Probably throwing up the oil down in your stomach and your stomach rejects it. And it's burning your eyes and nose, and Lieutenant Potter wrote about that because he experienced the same thing. And he's trying to work with the wounded in the water."

TOP: An American torpedo bomber in flight during the Battle of Midway. RIGHT: A photograph of the Japanese carrier Hiryu *on the morning of June 5, 1942. She was the last of four carriers bombed and destroyed by U. S. Navy planes in the Battle of Midway on June 4.*

Like Roy, Pollard observed the same mess attendant who couldn't swim, but Captain Buckmaster who, as custom dictates, was the last to leave the ship went to the attendant's rescue.

"Our destroyers were weaving back and forth about 300 yards away picking up survivors. Captain Buckmaster swam alongside the raft that I was holding on to but would not come aboard as we were so overcrowded. Instead he swam to a nearby raft and hung on to it. A passing motor whaleboat threw his raft a line and was towing it to the *Russell* but with too much speed and a mess attendant was pulled off. Instead of treading water, he began screaming and wearing himself out. Captain Buckmaster turned loose of his raft and swam to the mess attendant. They were both about gone when a man from our raft swam out and helped keep both of them afloat. We took the mess attendant aboard but the Captain preferred to swim."

"We're in the water for a long time," Roy says,

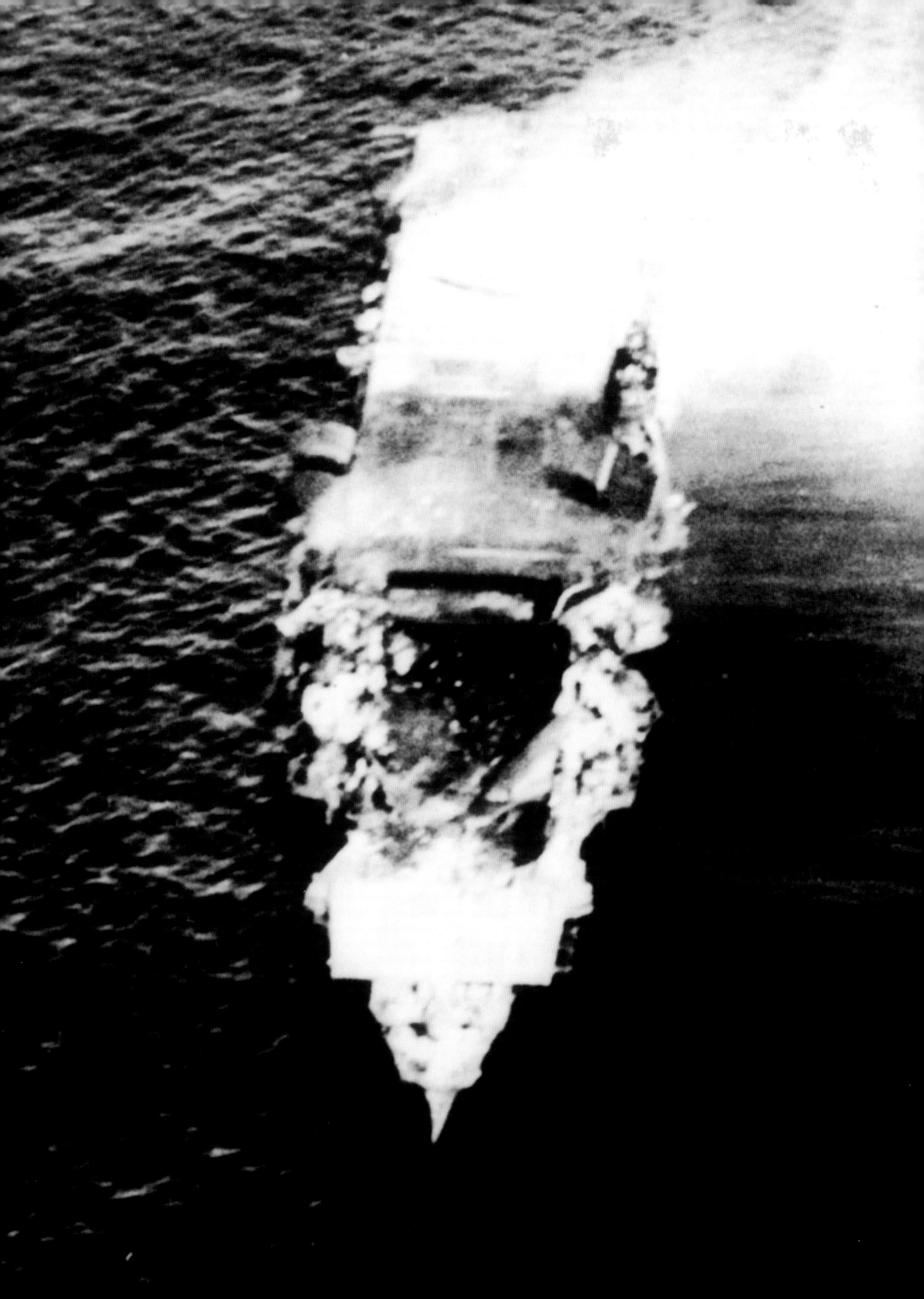

In uniforms that were often oil-stained from going over the side, survivors from USS York- town *are checked in on USS* Fulton (AS-11) *in preparation to be taken to Pearl Harbor.*

"and now it's getting a little dark. And so I worked my way to the stern of the *York-town*. So I'm right at the stern of the *Yorktown* and it's getting dark and I think, 'Oh, my God, if I pass the stern of the *Yorktown* I'll be in the open Pacific. They'll never find me.' So I closed my eyes and said a prayer of hope. I opened my eyes, and I never heard it, because my ears are all clogged up with oil, but I saw this flash in the water, and it was the end of a rope. So I did a few strokes and grabbed the rope with my right arm. And they slowed down by then when they saw me. And then they took off to the *Hammann* [DE-412] and dragged me through the water, cold, still wet and thoroughly exhausted."

While *Hiryu*'s planes were out bombing *York-town*, it was one of the American carrier's spotter planes, ironically, that located *Hiryu* 100 miles north of TF-16. Admiral Spruance launched forty unescorted bombers from *Enterprise* and *Hornet*. *Enterprise* bombers arrived first, while *Hiryu* was trying to launch one more air strike at twilight. Captain Susumu Kawaguchi, air officer on *Hiryu*, described what happened next in his post-war interview.

"The *Hiryu* was hit six times during the fourth attack by dive bombers. One on forward elevator. Two just aft of forward elevator. Three just forward after elevator. Lifts damaged. Fire. Many engineering personnel killed. The floor of the lift flopped against the bridge; we were unable to navigate."

It was the Dauntless dive bombers that did the job once again. They earned the fear and respect of the Imperial Japanese Navy in a few short months. By the time the planes arrived from *Hornet*, the ship was already in flames and the Japanese planes returning from *Yorktown* had no place to go.

"That night [June 4] I slept on sacks of potatoes," remembers Roy, "and the next morning I went down below and some sailor had some kerosene and some rags, and I got in the shower; he scrubbed the oil and I scrubbed the oil. I still had film in the pockets of my shirt. I had about four cans of film, I believe. Captain Buckmaster went aboard the *Astoria* to converse with Admiral Fletcher, to see if we could salvage the *Yorktown*. [When *Astoria* came to] I passed those [film cans] up to this sailor I knew off the *Yorktown*; the *Astoria* had a processor for 35mm like we did on the *Yorktown*. He dropped a little bucket over the side and I put it in that.

"So Captain Buckmaster got permission from Admiral Fletcher to form a salvage party. In the meantime, a fleet tug had come out from Pearl Harbor and it was already there when we got to go on the 6th of June. He had a tow line on it and was not making any headway. So he [Buckmaster] came back aboard the *Hammann*, and sat in a chair with a little table and said, 'I want volunteers for the salvage party.' And of course he immediately recognized me and he said, 'Step over here, boy.' And I did. So I went back on the salvage party. One hundred and forty-one enlisted men and about sixteen officers, I believe. Engineering officers and damage control people. So we went back early morning on June the 6th and the *Yorktown* is still floating. It had gone 50 miles

from the time we had abandoned the *Yorktown* to when we went back aboard with the salvage party. The *Hammann* brought us alongside to furnish us electrical, pumps and water for the fire. They tied up real snug. And James Cunningham, a Seaman 1st class, was the line tender to be sure the lines were tight and taut."

Unable to find work in his native West Virginia, James H. Cunningham joined the navy in 1940. As a crewman aboard *Hammann*, he followed *Yorktown* to the Atlantic and back because *Hammann* was one of her escorts. He was at Coral Sea and Midway, where *Hammann* picked up survivors of *Yorktown* including Bill Roy. He talks about taking the salvage party to *Yorktown* on June 6.

"That morning we were tied up alongside *Yorktown*, I walked up to [the] deck and I looked out there a hundred yards or so, and this thing was stickin' up out of the water. And I told a lot of guys that were superior to me, you know, if that's a periscope and they laughed at me and they said, 'Oh no, that's just a swab handle.' The swab, if they was in the water, they would stand up like that. So I run up to the bridge and got a pair of binoculars and looked out there, and the periscope was still goin' – and then I started looking for some officers and I couldn't find any officers to report to, but then I ended up going on watch."

In order to lighten *Yorktown* so the tug had a chance to tow it, all extraneous equipment had to be jettisoned. That included weapons of war such as guns and planes.

"We boarded the *Yorktown*," says Roy, "and the first order of business was to put out the fire. So you go up there where the hold is and pop the nozzle [of an extinguisher] and just throw it down the hole. And then they got water hoses and put them over and we pretty well flooded the area down there to suppress the fire. That was the first thing to do otherwise you never know when it's going to reach something and explode. And about that time, they called me to come down and help get the airplanes pushed overboard. I said to a chief, 'Can't you give me that airplane?' And he said, 'You got it, boy' and over it went. I have an airplane at 30,000 feet on the Pacific floor if I can go down and get it.

"I was called to go up on the flight deck and identify various dead; we're walking along identifying dead bodies there by airplanes. Anyway, we piled dead bodies against the bulkheads and laid them on the deck. We got down to the catwalk and there's an emergency radio system down the cubby hole off the catwalk on the starboard side aft of the island structure. So I looked in there and this sailor's all shot up and he crawled in there to get out of the other dangers and he died right there so we had to pull him out. So we take all of their identification and watches and rings and wallets, any personal effects and put them in a brown envelope the pharmacist's mate had for that purpose for the family. So we identified everybody. We put them down on the hanger deck. The ship's listing already. Well when we were torpedoed by the submarine, all of them [the envelopes] went overboard. So we don't know exactly who all was dead on the ship."

While this was going on *Hammann* was still next to the stricken carrier. Jim Cunningham continues, "I had to stand watch up on the forecastle of the ship that day, and I sit up there from about noon until about 3:30 or so, and got relieved and then when I got relieved – it was hot, you know – I went down to mess hall and got me a drink of water. When I came up from the mess hall and walked by CIC [the ship's command center], I looked – the door was open and I looked in there – and there's a torpedo that says

'*Hammann*' on it, and I looked at that thing and I took a couple steps and I turned around and I looked at it again. About that time, that's when they hollered 'torpedo' and said, 'It's headed your way.' I went back to the stern where my gun station was, you know, and that's when I stood there on deck and the torpedo hit and everything, and I got in the water and swam. I think I remember seeing Roy up there on the flight deck taking pictures, you know, of course he took pictures of my ship sinking, and of course, he logged up the pictures, and he's got the pictures, too, Roy does, of my ship sinking."

"I grabbed my still camera, 4-inch x 5-inch Speed Graphic," details Roy, "went down the hanger deck, crossed, just in time to see the *Hammann*. The port turbine was reeling – a boatswain was trying to cut with a fire axe these big lines. [He] cut 'em and a sailor was running back and he checked the depth charges and there was a confusion about whether they were armed or not. The first torpedo hit right up aside of the *Hammann*, killed 12 of the 16 officers. The second was almost to amidships and the stern went back because of the thrust of the port engine started up to pull it away from the *Yorktown*. But it kept drifting back because nothing was operating. When it was broken in two everything went out. Some *Yorktown* sailors [on the *Hammann*] were knocked overboard at that time. I made three pictures of the stern going back. The first one is at an angle, with people hanging on for their lives. Seventy-seven were injured severely, and in the water."

Jim Cunningham describes his time in the water in these first crucial minutes.

"I'm swimming out to a life raft, and I felt a couple bumps on my leg, but don't know if they were sharks or what, but anyway, I got to the life raft and I couldn't get aboard the life raft be-

USS *Yorktown* PhoM2/C Bill Roy operates a Fairchild K-20 aerial camera from the back of a plane in April 1942.

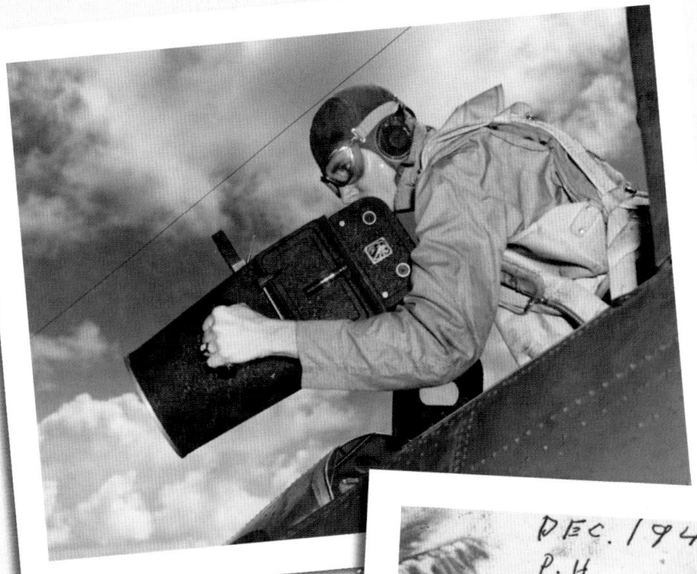

Ray Richmond and other sailors pose with Honolulu socialite Bam Sperry on her family's plantation. Richmond, who was recovering from the wounds he suffered in the Peal Harbor attack and other sailors from the hospital were invited to the plantation during their rehabilitation period in early 1942.

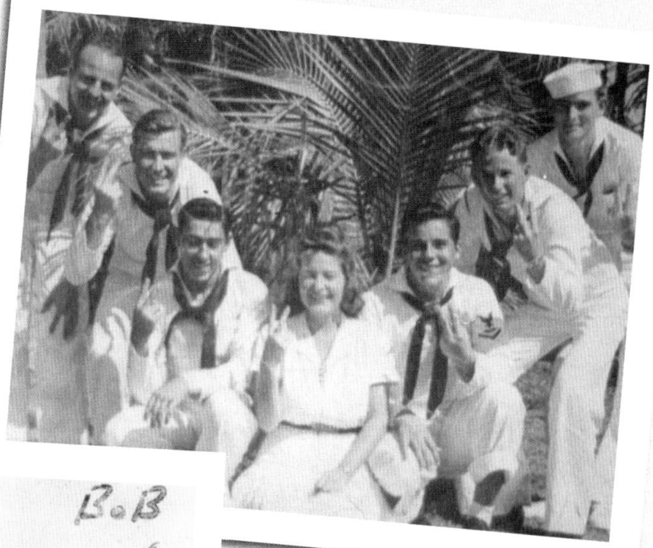

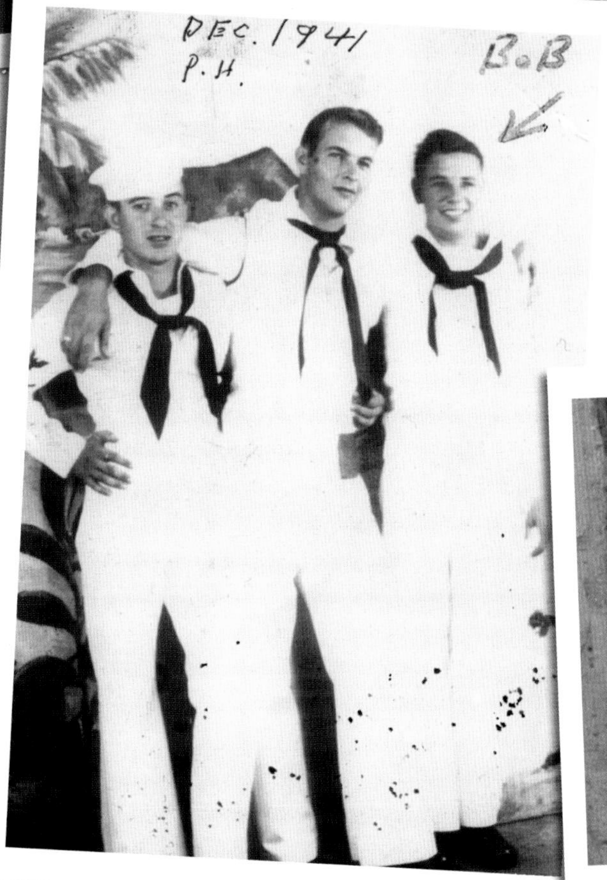
DEC. 1941
P.H.
BoB

Bill Roy is pictured holding a Bell & Howell Eyemo 35mm during his photography school training. The virtually indestructible silent movie camera yielded Roy some dramatic footage during attacks on *Yorktown*.

Bob Ruffato and two friends pose for a picture in Pearl Harbor in December 1941. Ruffato escaped from *Utah*, a decommissioned battleship that was nevertheless a Japanese target on December 7, and began 1942 assigned to the cruiser *Honolulu*.

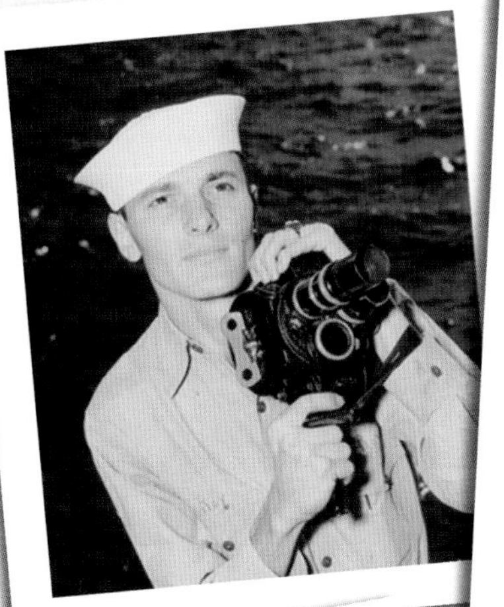

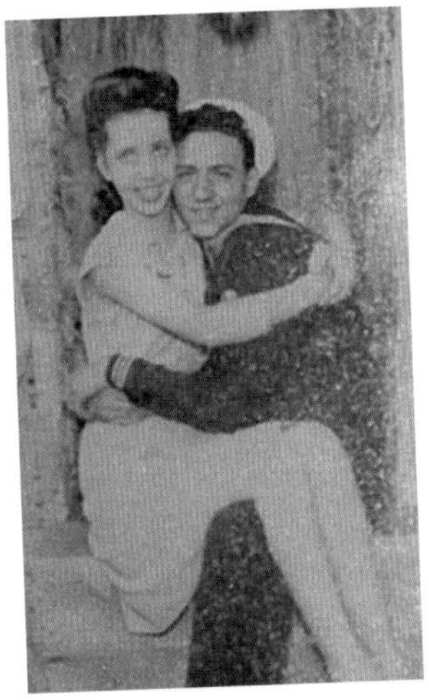

A popular item with sailors stationed in Hawaii in World War II was to purchase a picture postcard of themselves posed with a local beauty. The few seconds embracing the lovely model was part of the package price.

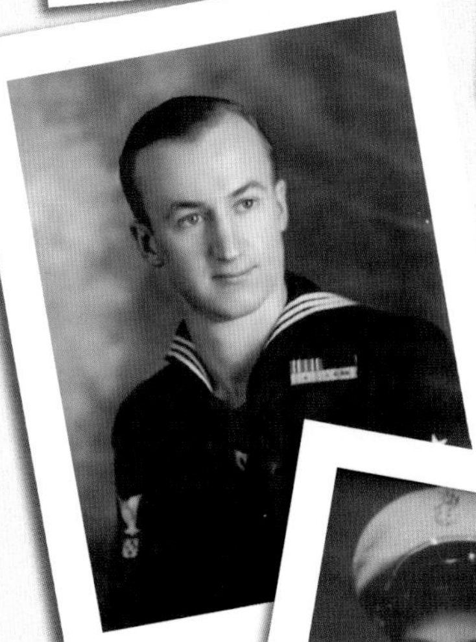

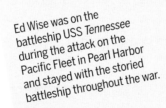

Ed Wise was on the battleship USS *Tennessee* during the attack on the Pacific Fleet in Pearl Harbor and stayed with the storied battleship throughout the war.

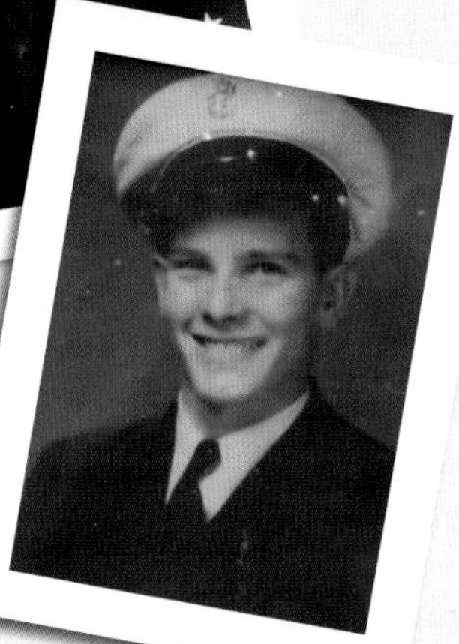

Wilson Derby began his long career aboard USS *Nevada* in 1939 and was very active in shipboard athletics. He was a forward on the ship's basketball team that won the fleet championship in 1940.

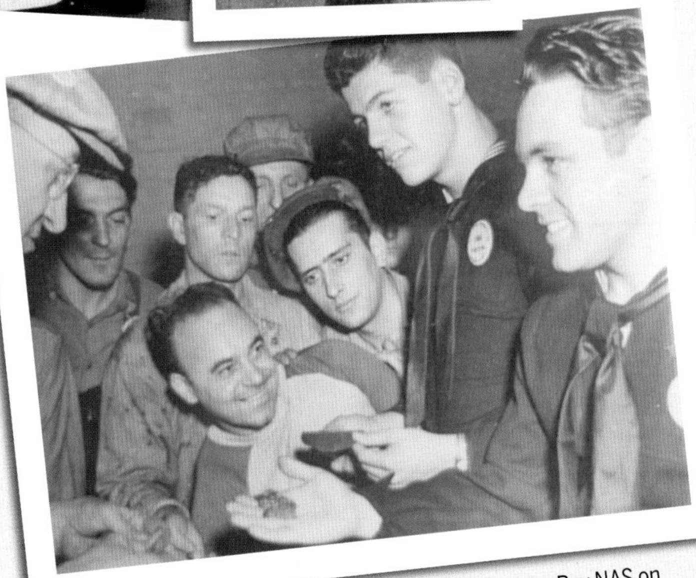

Gordon Jones (second from right), who was at Kaneohe Bay NAS on December 7, is seen participating in a War Bonds rally when he returned to the states for training at aviation instrument school in 1942.

cause it was filled up already and heck, one guy was sitting in the center of the life raft, and blood was coming out his mouth just like a fountain. So then I grabbed a hold of the life raft and two other people grabbed a hold of the life raft alongside of me, on each side of me. I looked around and I seen the stern of our ship go in the air, going down, you know, and I knew that there was going to be explosions when the ship went down, and so I pulled myself up a little bit on the life raft and that's the only thing that saved my life. Later on at a reunion I found out that the two guys on either side of me died because they didn't do the same thing I did. The people were so excited on our life raft, they wouldn't get in the water and I kept yelling at them to get the paddles in the water and so then

Admiral Chester Nimitz and staff members wait on a Pearl Harbor dock on June 8 for the arrival of the submarine tender Fulton *carrying* Yorktown *survivors.*

we got to the other ship and I had to get somebody's hand to help me aboard ship because I was so weak."

While the crew of *Hammann* struggled in the water, another torpedo spread was fired from the Japanese submarine, *I-168*, which headed right to the now exposed *Yorktown*. Bill Roy continues with that part of the story.

"The next two torpedoes hit the *Yorktown* on the starboard side which is the high side. It lifted the *Yorktown* up, and Captain Buckmaster describes it in his after action report. It broke the rivets of one of the legs of the tripod mast which is huge. It collapsed airplanes from the overhead, broke the lines, dropped the planes on the deck. I was hurled back into a bulkhead, cut my finger, hurt my left shoulder. So I got up, and made a last picture of the *Hammann*. It's gone. Now the water's clear. And some sailors were knocked off the *Yorktown* into the water when the *Hammann* was hit. So anyway, the tug cut the tow, came around and we crossed over on some lines on this little tug boat and went out to the *Balch*.

"And we lingered all during the night, with the hope we could still go back and salvage it the next morning. When we were salvaging I picked up a Fairchild K-1 aerial camera with a Zeiss lens and handed it over to the *Hammann* people and the paymaster had passed over a satchel with 100,000 dollars in it to pay the crew. And that went over, and some records and all the confidential things to be destroyed to be sure it wasn't captured. [Before leaving the *Yorktown* the second time] I went back to the burned out photo lab and in the corner, we kept a K-20 aerial, 5-inch x 7-inch. So I took that with me, it's the only thing I had. The next morning at daybreak, the *Yorktown* is still on an even keel. And I'm making a picture, but it's not quite daylight. So shortly after that, I hear over the loudspeaker '*Yorktown* photographer to the bridge on the double.' So I went hauling ass up to the bridge and the officer of the day said, 'I think the *Yorktown*'s gonna sink. You got your camera?' And I said, 'Yes, sir.' I took 19 pictures with that K-20. As the *Yorktown* rolled over and sank, we circled it twice. And cut through the flotsam. And the [intelligence officer] said take pictures of the flotsam. He said come about, take me through the flotsam this way. And he starts to come about and he says take me through the third time and the captain says 'I'm taking it back to Pearl.' 'Cause all we saw was a bunch of broken down crates and rags and whatever would float from the ship."

On June 7, concerned that American bombers based there could strike Japan's Home Islands, the Japanese landed on Attu and Kiska, the former at the extreme west end of the Aleutian Islands. This followed the bombing of Dutch Harbor where the Navy had an important PBY base. The occupation of Attu and Kiska by the Japanese was a sorrowful experience for the Aleutians' peaceful natives (converted to Christianity by Russian Orthodox missionaries, they had begun adapting to American influence over the previous seventy years). Their ordeal was another in the early war period that stoked a determination for liberation among Americans.

It took news of the *Hiryu*'s destruction to finally jolt Yamamoto into realizing that Operation "MI" was a disaster. He had hampered his chance at seeing the overall situation by operating from the Main Force, rather than from his Combined Forces headquarters in Japan. In what seems now like a rage-influenced decision, Yamamoto set a course east intent on forcing the U. S. fleet into a surface engagement. Spruance had meanwhile shaped a course back to Hawaii. Then Yamamoto thought better of a further thrust east and reversed course. So did Spruance, and on June 5 and 6 he pursued the Japanese surface ships, striking from the air and sinking the 8-inch gun cruiser *Mikuma* and disabling her sister *Mogami*.

The toll for the Japanese at Midway was staggering. Four flattops and a heavy cruiser sunk, a number of other ships damaged, 275 planes splashed - 143 more than all aircraft losses for the Americans - and most tellingly, 3500 men killed in action. The U. S. Navy lost 307 men killed. Other than the sinking of *Yorktown* and *Hammann*, the loss of life and number of wounded, the Battle of Midway proved to be a decisive victory for the United States Navy. As the ships made their way into Pearl Harbor over the next several days, many of the sailors, officers and airmen were greeted personally by Admiral Nimitz. A grateful president and nation wished they could have been there to do likewise.

"*I Sank the* Yorktown *at Midway*"

The most severe loss sustained by the U. S. Navy as a result of the Battle of Midway was the two warships sunk during the June 6, 1942 salvage of the carrier *Yorktown*. The flattop and USS *Hammann*, the destroyer responsible for bringing the carrier's volunteer salvage crew to the crippled ship, fell prey to the only Japanese submarine to have an impact on the battle, *I-168*. When Lieutenant Commander Yahachi Tanabe of *I-168* brought *Yorktown* into his periscopic sights, he knew he had an opportunity to sink the ailing ship, but was aware of the danger posed by escorting destroyers. The moment of decision and what happened next were recounted by Tanabe twenty-one years later in an exclusive interview with a U. S. Navy journalist. "I Sank the *Yorktown* at Midway" first appeared in *Proceedings Magazine* of the U. S. Naval Institute in 1963. A portion of Tanabe's comments are excerpted here.

"An odd series of events had put *I-168* where she was on June 6, 1942, deep inside the *Yorktown*'s protective circle of American destroyers whose crews were listening for a Japanese submarine. Of the 160-odd ships that gathered from all parts of the Empire to strike at Midway, and the Aleutians, *I-168* had the simplest assignment of all — scouting.

"*I-168*'s task was to scout to the southward of Midway, and report on as much of the enemy's activities as we could observe. We would be near when the troops landed, but by then, our job would have been done. We were the van ship of the entire operation, coming in sight of Kure [Atoll, 55 miles] west of Midway, on May 31, 1942. Part of the over-all strategy called for seizing this island, too. It was to be a seaplane and midget submarine base. After radioing a report that nothing appeared to be happening on that island, I proceeded to Midway, and spent the first three days of June making observations there. Our observations made us think that the Americans were expecting imminent attack. The four carriers of our striking force, although detected at the last, got near enough to launch planes against the island. *I-168* had a front seat, or at least I did, at the day periscope, when 108 of our planes hit the island. My crew grew more and more excited as I described the action to them, and a great cheer went up as I described some fuel tanks being blown sky high.

"By midnight of June 4, the Midway Battle was lost, though we did not know it yet. The next time our radio antenna poked above the waves fright-

ening news came through it. [Japanese aircraft carriers] *Soryu* and *Kaga* had gone down the evening before. *Akagi* and *Hiryu* had followed them. One of the messages gave *I-168* a new role to play. Scout planes from Japanese cruisers had sighted the American aircraft carrier *Yorktown* lying dead in the water about 150 miles northeast of Midway. My orders came through quite clearly: 'Submarine *I-168* will locate and destroy the American carrier.' So it was that, at 0530, on June 6, the 12- mm binoculars of my best-trained look-out picked up *Yorktown*. She was a black shape on the horizon, about 11 miles distant.

"Our screws were barely turning over, and I hoped they were not giving off enough turbulence for the American ships to detect us. I had sighted one destroyer ahead of the carrier with a towline out to her, and another destroyer nestled close to *Yorktown*'s side. Three more kept station on the side I was approaching, which made me feel certain there must be at least two more on the opposite side. This meant seven of them against one of us. It never occurred to me to do anything except continue my approach and attack, in spite of the odds.

"Each time I took a sight, the sun was higher in the sky. *Yorktown* appeared to be making just a little headway. I kept making minor changes of course to keep *I-168* headed at her amidships section. We might get sunk in this action, but before that happened, I meant to do the maximum possible damage to this ship. I wanted my torpedoes to plow into her midsection, not her bow or stern. All *I-168* men limited their movements to the most necessary ones only, fearing to create some sound which the American detectors might pick

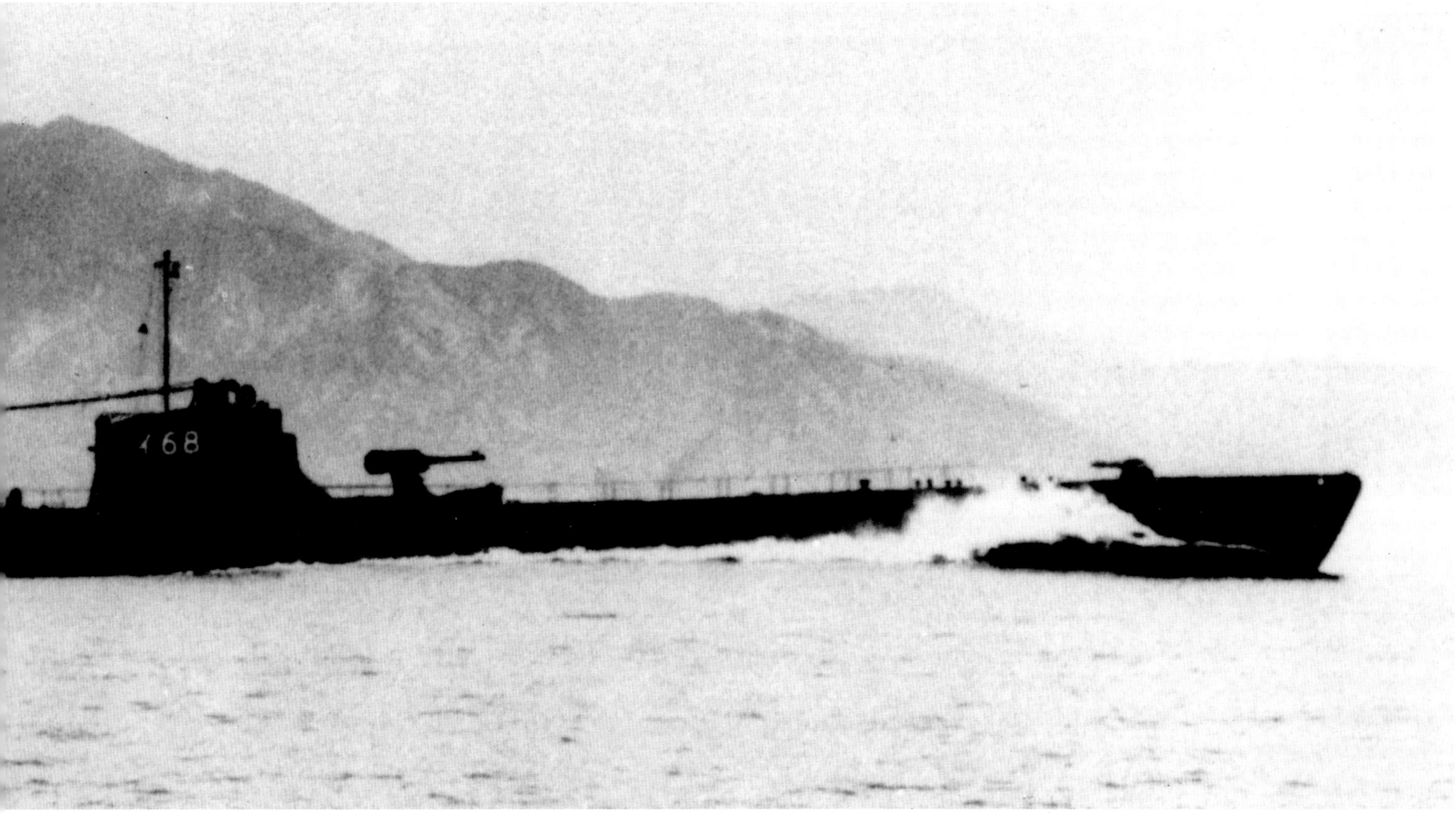
I68

Japanese submarine I-68 *(later* I-168*) in March 1934, probably during her trials. She was renamed* I-168 *in May 1942, a month before she torpedoed USS* Yorktown *and USS* Hammann. *She was sunk in 1943.*

up. By 1100, I had decided that the enemy equipment was not very sensitive. This gave me confidence as the range shortened; I kept moving in. Suddenly my sound operator reported that the Americans had stopped emitting detection signals. I couldn't understand this but, since it was now nearly noon, I tried to make my voice light and told my crew, 'It appears the Americans have interrupted their war for lunch. Now is our chance to strike them good and hard, while they are eating!' Abaft my beam, each about 1,000 yards distant, were a pair of American destroyers, one to port, one to starboard. *I-168* had safely pierced the protective screen of escorts; I could now give the order to fire.

"Then I took another look. *Yorktown* and her hugging destroyer filled my periscope lens. I was too close! At that moment I estimated my range at 600 yards or less. It was necessary to come around and open up the range. What I had to do now was try to escape detection by those destroyers above us and get far enough away so that my torpedoes, fired from a 60-foot depth, would have enough running space to stabilize themselves at a 19-foot depth for hitting. Whatever was the reason, enemy sound detectors could no longer be picked up by our equipment. I knew the destroyermen above were not asleep. I kept *I-168* in a right-hand circle, easing the rudder a little so that I could return to my original track at a point about one mile from *Yorktown*. I didn't dare put up the periscope until the compass showed us back on our original course. I intended to limit my salvo to a two degree spread. I would fire No.1 and No.2 first, then send No.3 and No.4 in their wakes, on the same courses. That way, I could achieve two large hits instead of four small ones. I could thus deliver all my punch into the carrier's midsection, rather than spread it out along her hull. At a range of 1,200 yards, my periscope up, I sent my four torpedoes away as planned. I did not lower the periscope then, either. The wakes of my torpedoes could be seen, so their source could be quickly established. And, if *I-168* was going to die, I at least wanted the satisfaction of seeing whether our fish hit home.

"'Take her down to 200 feet!' By that time we were where I wanted to be, directly beneath the enemy carrier. I didn't think she would sink at once, so had no fear of her coming down on us. And one of our torpedoes had run shallow and hit the destroyer alongside *Yorktown*. There would be men in the water. Her destroyers wouldn't risk dropping depth charges for awhile, for fear of killing their comrades. My plan didn't work. The American destroyers were on us in no time, dropping depth charges. They had *I-168* pinpointed, and took turns making runs, according to my sound operator. We had torpedoed *Yorktown* at 1330. By 1530, the enemy had dropped 60 depth charges at us, one or two at a time. I took advantage of this by trying to keep an opposite course to whichever destroyer attacked us. The tactic worked a number of times, many depth charges dropping well astern of us as the enemy passed directly overhead. One of the destroyer captains must have estimated that I was doing this though. The last depth charge of the two-hour barrage landed just off my bow, putting out all lights, springing small leaks in many places, and causing the danger of chlorine gas forming in my forward battery room. Torpedomen finally plugged the leaks with wedges, however, and everything came under control. By now we had taken on enough water to weigh the bow down considerably. I ordered all crewmen possible to move aft a counterweight. This did not remedy the situation, so I employed a tactic used by other Japanese submarines in the war. Every man walked forward again, picked up a sack of rice from our supplies, and carried it aft. This helped considerably, and *I-168* was on an even keel by the time full electrical power was restored.

"It was still daylight when I ordered 'Surface!'

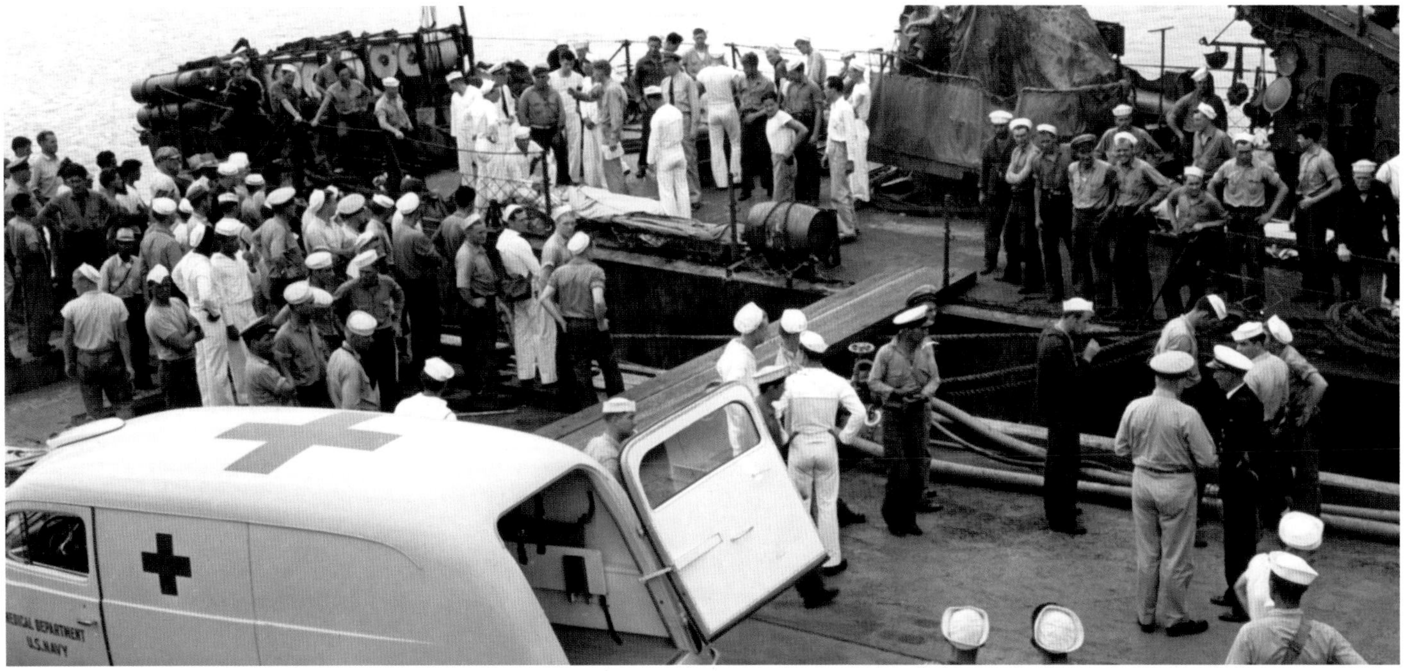
MEDICAL DEPARTMENT
U.S.NAVY

Survivors of USS Hammann, *the destroyer caught in the middle of* I-168*'s destruction of the venerable* Yorktown, *arrive at Pearl Harbor aboard USS* Benham *(DD-397).*

We were not long on the surface before two of the three ships swung about in pursuit. I estimated their distance at about 11,000 yards. We ran west at 14 knots, the best speed I could make while charging batteries and taking in air. I ordered smoke made, using the heavy black clouds for cover. When they closed to about 6,500 yards, they opened fire and not long afterward *I-168* was straddled. All a good gunnery officer had to do now was 'walk' across me a few times and all would be over. 'Stand by to dive!' I shouted, and cleared the bridge. I followed all hands into the hatch, ordering *I-168* swung about for a dive into her own smoke. The tactic worked. Both destroyers over-ran us. They soon had our location fixed again, but dropped only a few charges before breaking off the action and making toward the east at high speed. *I-168* was going to get out of this now. We surfaced a little while after sunset. Assuming that patrol planes from Midway would be seeking us out, we headed north. I hoped they would think I had set a course for Truk, and thus be thrown off the scent. After a few hours, we changed course for Hokkaido, our northernmost island, it then being the nearest to us on a great circle course. *I-168* cruised at her most economical speed. By practicing severe economies we were able to set Yokosuka, then Kure, as our final destination.

"A great crowd greeted our arrival. There were cheers, music, congratulations, and speeches in abundance as we tied up. A special news broadcast had told earlier how *I-168* had torpedoed the carrier *Yorktown*, and that she had sunk the following morning. A special report of the exploit was rendered His Majesty, The Emperor — something done only when the war news was of great magnitude. But all I could think of that day at Kure, while being hailed as a hero, was that as yet no news of *Kaga*, *Akagi*, *Hiryu*, and *Soryu* had been released to the public. All the Japanese people thought we had scored another Pearl Harbor at Midway. They didn't know that four of our fighting carriers, together with hundreds of Japan's best planes and pilots, were gone forever. My sinking of the USS *Yorktown* was small revenge for that loss."

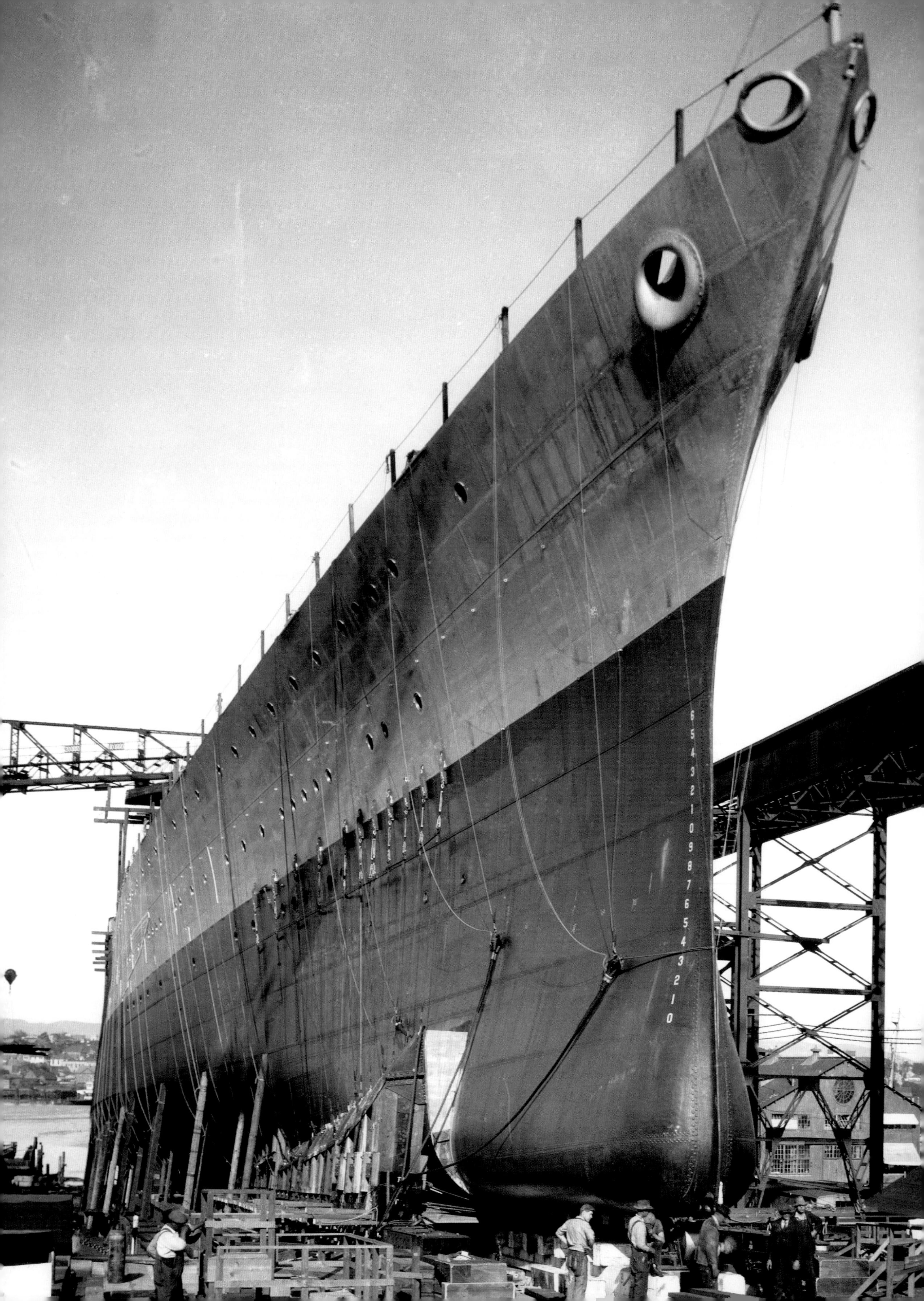

CHAPTER 5

Rest
and
Refitting

Gearing Up for Total War

The impact of the Battle of Midway was immediately realized by both sides. Not only did the American public celebrate it as retribution for Pearl Harbor, U. S. military leadership used the victory to forward war plans outlined earlier in the year. But, while General George C. Marshall, Army Chief of Staff, and other army leaders in Washington continued to study the way to beat Germany, Admiral King realized that the Midway victory allowed his Pacific war plan to move into phase two. Blocking and raiding was no longer the only or best option open to the U. S. True, thanks to priorities that relegated defense of

the Aleutian Islands to a secondary concern and bungling on the part of Admiral Theobald, two islands in what would eventually become America's 49th state were temporarily occupied and another U. S. naval base (Dutch Harbor) was bombed. But this turned out to be an acceptable price for nearly wiping out Japan's once all victorious Kido Butai. King's blueprint next called for landing on Japanese occupied islands – it was just a question of where to start.

For the Axis powers, the impact of Coral Sea and Midway rippled through commands from the Pacific to Europe. Although he would live another ten months, Isoroku Yamamoto's influence over Imperial Navy decisions was reduced after the Midway disaster. Personally, he probably found some inner peace in the idea that, although he had lost the gamble, the die was cast and the direction of the war was clearly determined. Beyond the Combined Fleet and Tokyo however, the impact of

USS Chicago *(CA-29) as it is readied for launch on April 8, 1930. The heavy cruiser was in the middle of key Pacific sea battles.*

From his Washington, D. C. office, General George C. Marshall had the unenviable task of balancing the wants and needs of American and Allied politicians and leaders of other service branches while managing U. S. Army operations on six continents.

Japan's loss was also felt. The Soviets, no longer feeling a threat at their backs, threw all their resources into defeating Germany at Stalingrad and elsewhere along the Eastern Front. Hitler saw the Japanese defeat, along with Mussolini's poor showing in the Mediterranean, as evidence that his tripartite partners could not be counted on.

While the United States was cranking up its industrial might and military force for offensives in the Pacific, logistical problems would dampen the speed and effectiveness of operations. The Navy was developing what one historian calls "its own army" by forming and training divisions of Marines capable of mounting amphibious operations on a par with (or better than) what the army could do at the time. But moving masses of men, equipment and supplies to staging areas in the Pacific was risky business. The Japanese still had an effective fleet of submarines and land based planes on islands from Kiska and Wake to Rabaul and Tulagi. In order to shelter this build up, the U. S. began to assemble and train three combat divisions in Australia and New Zealand.

Manpower, however, was not a problem. The U. S. Navy, with only a little over 337,000 men and women in the branch in December 1941, saw that

TOP: Admiral Ernest J. King photographed at the navy department during the height of the war. King, the man who it was said was so tough, "he shaved every morning with a blow torch," was not afraid to defend his "Japan first" strategy with other members of the Joint Chiefs of Staff or Washington politicians. RIGHT: Four bombs miss their targets and fall harmlessly into the bay at Dutch Harbor during the June 3, 1942 attack. A ship in the background staved off a determined machine gun attack.

number triple over the next year. The Marine Corps also welcomed a large influx of recruits to fill the expanding responsibilities. Whether for patriotic motives, the desire for adventure, or simply to avoid being drafted into the army, young men flocked to recruiting stations after Pearl Harbor. Basic training of recruits was still handled, with rapid efficiency, at the navy's Norfolk, Great Lakes, Illinois and San Diego centers. Recruits were turned into Marines by drill instructors (DIs) at San Diego and Parris Island, South Carolina. Edwin Cole Bearss grew up on a ranch in eastern Montana and developed an interest in history and world affairs early in life. He followed the events in the European war long before America became involved in the conflict. At supper on December 7, 1941 he announced to his parents that he was going to join the Marines. Though they were disappointed, they could hardly have been surprised – his father and cousin Mike had both been in the Corps and Cousin Mike was one of the most decorated Marines prior to World War II.

"Boot camp, because of the emergency, had been cut from twelve weeks to seven weeks. Boot

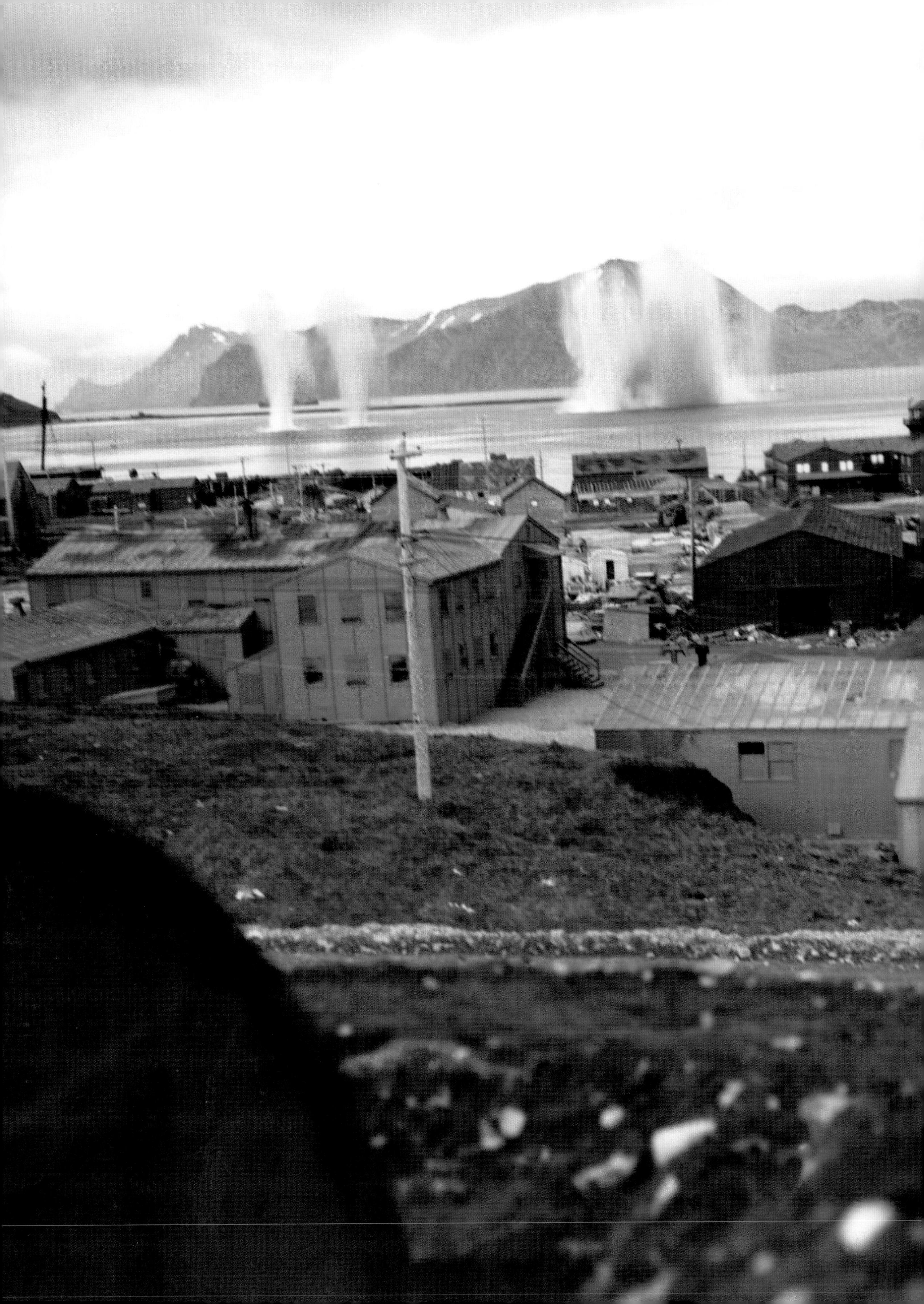

camp at that time was three weeks at the recruit depot at the San Diego Marine Base where you spent most of the time doing close order drill and having the DI's take you down to the very nadir of your ego. And at the same time they build you up, in [the image of what] the motto of the Marine Corps wants you to be. The Marine Corps is the best organization of any military service in the world. If you fail the Marine Corps you have now disgraced all those men who've been in the Marine Corps beginning at Tur Tavern in Philadelphia in November 1775. And the next three weeks are on the firing range. Then you spend the last week when the DI's treat you half-way like you are a Marine – at least you're a half-assed Marine – and then at the end of the sev-

Cadets learn knot tying at the U. S. Merchant Marine Cadet Basic school in San Mateo, California. Merchant seamen were part of the massive war effort, operating freighters and other ships that were necessary to the military's success, but also targets of submarines and other enemy fire.

enth week you get your initial assignment and you're a Marine. You all shake hands and in those days you – they don't do it now – you also bought your DIs watches. I was worried that the war was going to be over because Yamamoto was running wild as far to the east as Pearl Harbor, as far to the west as the Bay of Bengal. We were still in boot camp when the tide turned with the Battle of Midway. Things were going bad the week which I got out of boot camp for our allies; both the Soviets and the British. The Wehrmacht launched a drive that led to the recapture of Rostov on the Don and in North Africa the Afrika Korps stormed Tobruk."

Other facilities were opened or expanded for

specialized training and to fill the officer corps. The American military reached out to the educational com-munity. Colleges and universities across the nation began to offer courses to enlisted and officer students under the military's direction. Many of these institutions of higher learning were also engaged in active research projects to further the war effort. The educational mobilization of the country, like the industrial one, would be a key factor in Allied success in the three years eight and a half months America was at war. The training and education of U. S. military personnel would be an important factor in how the huge production of material could be used to achieve victory with less loss of life than that experienced by other combatants.

The U. S. Navy's blocking and raiding strategy

Marines reach the final stages of training at Parris Island, South Carolina in this 1942 photograph.

was a stop-gap measure that was rushed into service with existing resources. It was a necessary step to success in the Pacific, but it also emphasized the weaknesses of the pre-war navy's equipment and methods. Though the loss of two American carriers and other ships at Coral Sea and Midway was more than offset by the greater destruction inflicted on the Japanese, necessary changes were already being implemented to make the navy more effective and capable in supporting the amphibious operations to be mounted by the Marine Corps.

On land, in the air and on the sea, American ingenuity and technology would introduce better and more efficient weapons for use by those in the field. The first of the new *Essex* class carriers (CV-9) was launched shortly after the Battle of Midway. Shipyards from Bath, Maine to Bre-

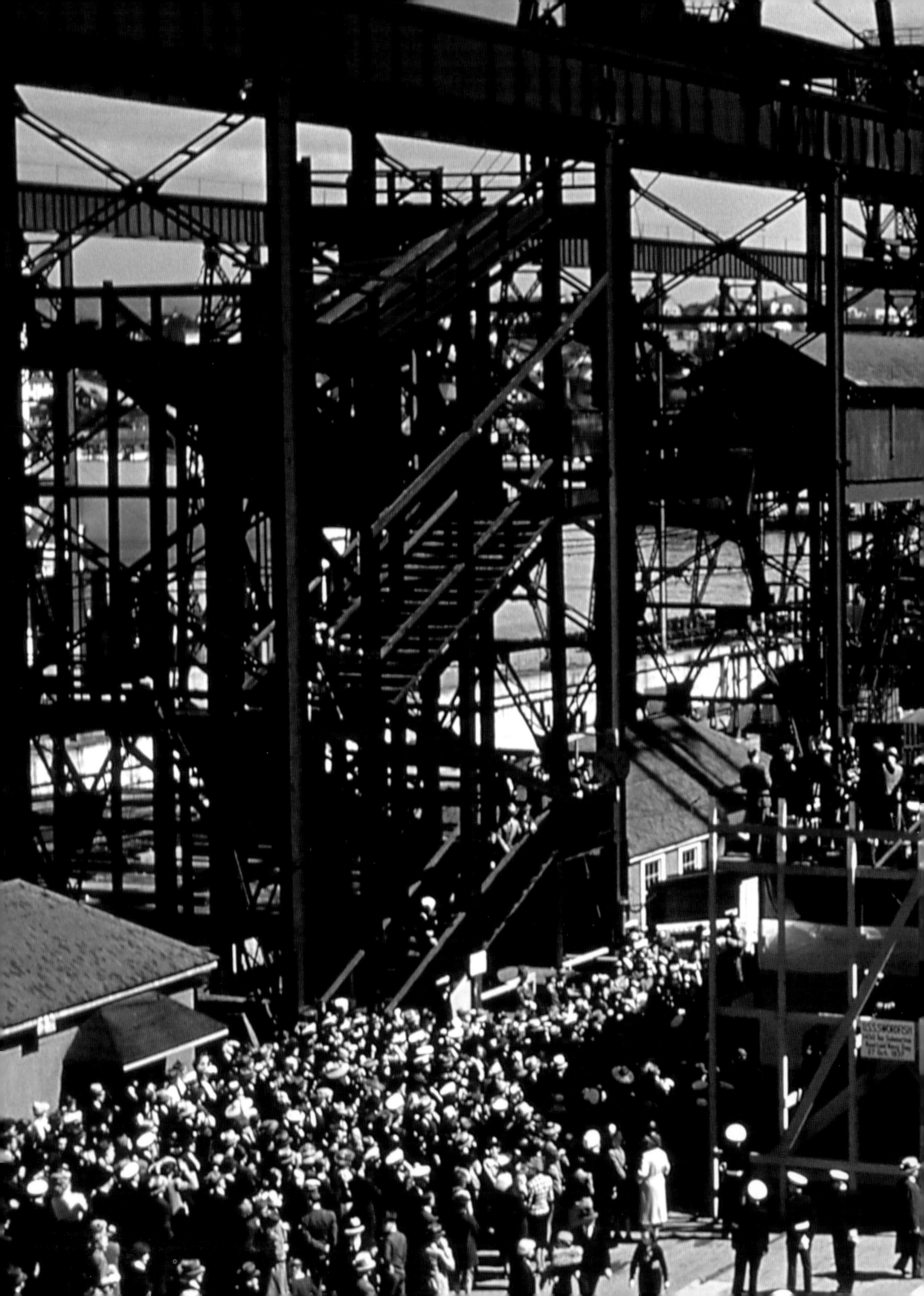

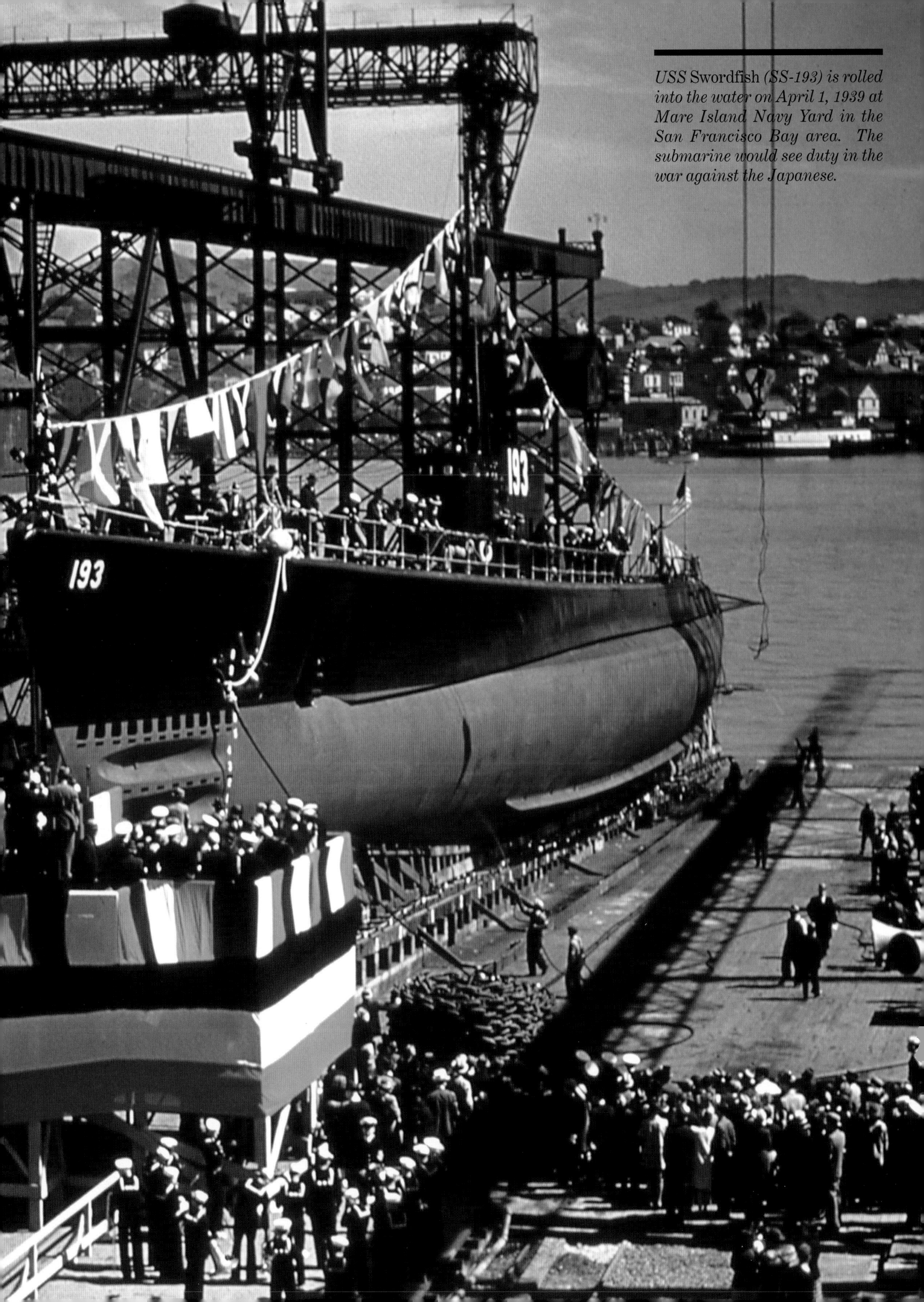
193
193

USS Swordfish *(SS-193) is rolled into the water on April 1, 1939 at Mare Island Navy Yard in the San Francisco Bay area. The submarine would see duty in the war against the Japanese.*

merton, Washington; from Pittsburgh, Pennsylvania to Pascagoula, Mississippi, were turning out all shapes and sizes of craft that could be built on a steel keel. Even the old battleships of the Pacific Fleet – all but two were back in action by war's end – were being repaired, modernized and refitted. USS *Nevada* was raised from the mud of Waipio Point and temporary repairs made at Pearl Harbor enabled her to get to Bremerton, Washington as Woodrow Derby remembers.

"[*Nevada*] was raised February 12, 1942 and went into dry dock at Pearl then back to Bremerton for complete repair, where it was rebuilt. It looked like a brand new ship except that it was still slow; the most speed it could make was 18-19 knots at full speed and that wouldn't keep up with much of anything. There they took off our old ship 5-inch guns on the boat deck and put in four twin-mount 5-inch 38's on both sides of the ship and they were power controlled and they worked very well."

USS *Pennsylvania, California, Tennessee* and *West Virginia* made similar refitting calls to Bremerton, as did USS *Maryland*, only lightly damaged in the raid. The addition of new, better suited anti-aircraft guns, as mentioned by Derby, was a major part of the upgrades on the battleships and pre-war carriers. All the new ships and those that were refitted, including cruisers and the latest pre-war destroyers, benefited from the "twins" and "quads," the smaller caliber anti-aircraft guns capable of putting up flak at an incredible rate. With their radar controlled directors they could operate in all lighting and climate conditions.

Not only the guns – and the ships and planes that mounted them – were improved. Ordnance was upgraded as well. Surface ship, submarine and aircraft torpedoes, which were a disappointment in early Pacific battles, were a top priority for redesign. Undersea operations in particular were frustrating. Steam torpedoes went out the

window, replaced by self propelled models that worked so effectively for the Imperial Navy. Even the newer models had the problem of running ten feet deeper than set and fuzes that would not ignite in head-on collisions with targets. Eventually these problems were worked out. Wire guidance and improved warheads with better fuzes were developed. Even traditional shells, fired from big shipboard guns, were upgraded to carry more explosive punch. A radio-electric timed fuze with a number of applications was the product of university research under contract with the navy ordnance department.

Policy Issues East and West

By contrast, the Japanese could not replace their losses in warships quickly or completely even though they retained a sizeable surface and undersea fleet in mid-1942. And they were quickly outdistanced in new ship construction, increasingly so, by the U. S. In 1943 America built five times the number of warships commissioned under the Rising Sun. But easier to

TOP: USS West Virginia *in a Pearl Harbor dry dock in June 1942 when it was undergoing repairs from the attack there. Stuart Hedley and Crosin, his friend, were in turret Three on* West Virginia *on December 7. Hedley explains the origin of the unexploded shell in the photograph below and the mess it caused. BOTTOM: "The shell did not explode. It hit the recoil cylinder which is on the top of the gun. Our feet were back up underneath us. When the explosion took place in the left gun the real explosion came from when the shell hit the recoil cylinder (about twice the size of a couch and filled with glycerin). Well, it split that casing and the glycerin flash fired — killing twelve men in that left gun. It blew the hatch right off past my legs underneath the elevating screw and across Croslin's legs and hit against the barbet. It simultaneously picked both of us up and threw us back eight feet where the elevating screw came out of the deck."*

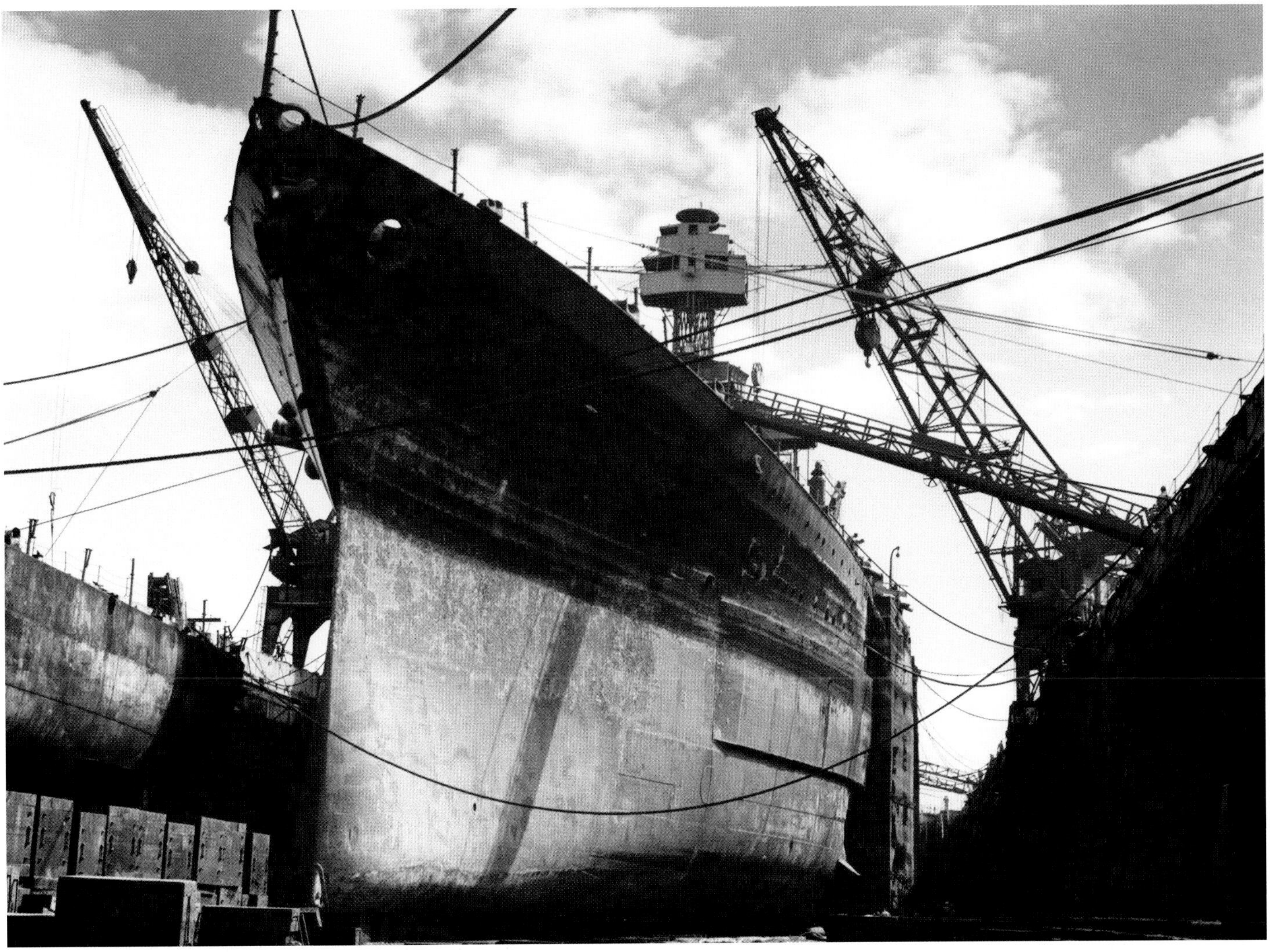

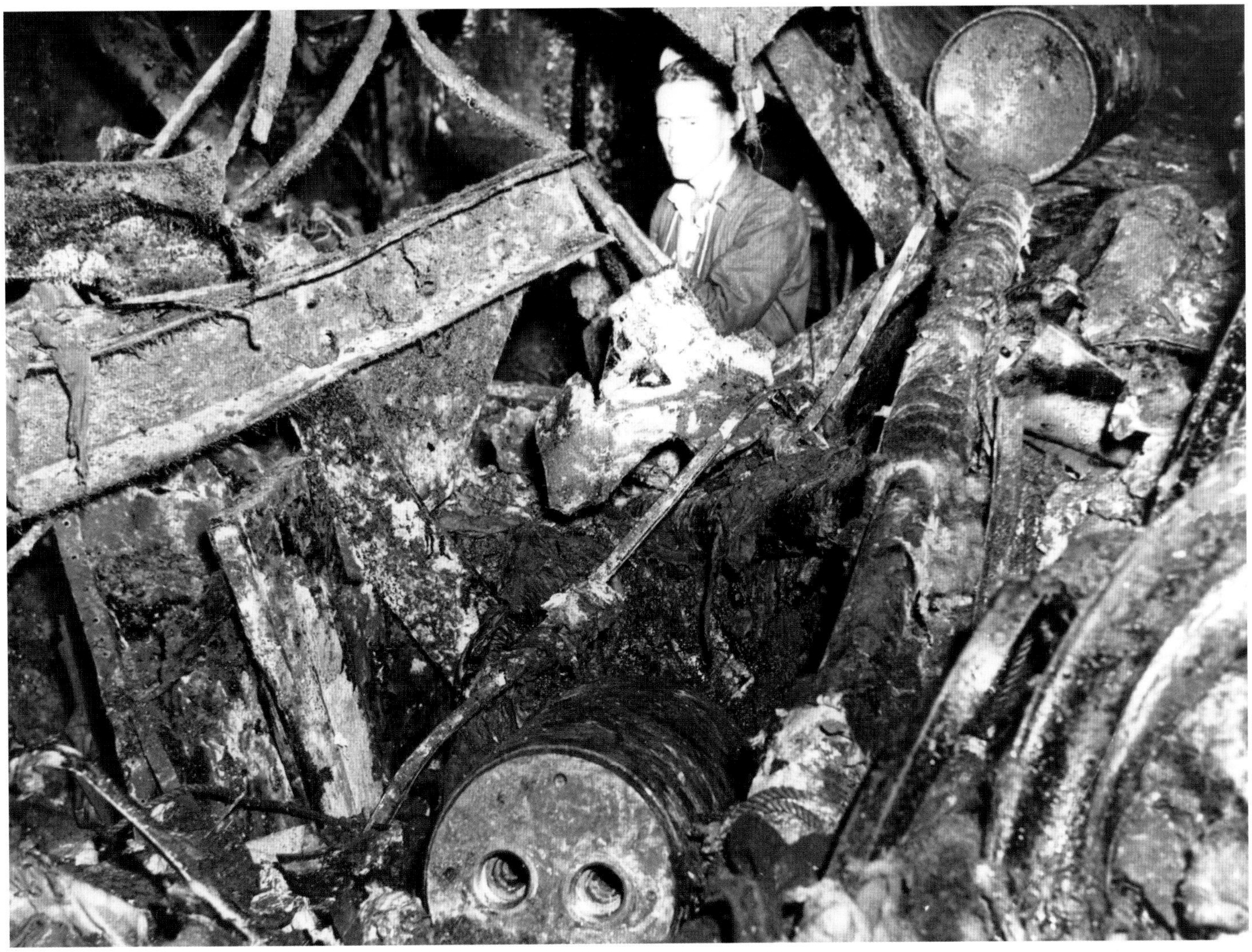

solve problems were also missed by the high command in Tokyo. The espionage effort which had so effectively prepped the Imperial Navy for the attack on Pearl Harbor never repeated the same success. Radar equipment entered shipboard use very slowly and nothing augmented Japan's over-reliance on float planes for reconnaissance. Worse still was communications security. The U. S. was only a few steps behind in decrypting any changes in the JN-25 Imperial Navy code. The Japanese did little to protect ship to ship and sea to land communications. As a result, U. S. military intelligence knew many of the enemy's strategic and tactical decisions before the Japanese executed them.

A major problem that hampered Japanese operations early in the war was a need to hammer out an agreement between the Army General Staff and Navy General Staff in Tokyo and the Combined Fleet Staff. In the first six months of the Pacific war when victory allowed Japanese leaders to think big, there were wide disagreements on strategy. The army wanted to return the focus of operations to Asia, particularly toward defeating the Chinese and looking for an opportunity to invade the Soviet Union, and they took steps in that direction. The Navy wanted to expand the perimeter further to the east and southwest; the Combined fleet staff went so far as to propose an invasion of Hawaii, while other navy planners saw the future empire extending to South Seas islands and even an invasion of Australia.

On the question of Australia, modern scholars place occupying that continent high on Japan's wish list and some veterans insist they discovered hard evidence to back up the idea. Clay Albright from Birmingham, Alabama joined the Marines as part of that patriotic rush felt by young men after the Pearl Harbor attack. He and other veterans reported one of the items found on the few Japanese prisoners taken during the fight on Guadalcanal. "They had special money printed up, occupation money," says Albright, "We captured a bunch of it."

Occupation money may have been printed and issued, but the army was not enthusiastic to invade Australia in an operation they estimated would require ten divisions. And given the resistance they encountered in the Philippines where the original plan of two divisions proved to be woefully insufficient, ten divisions may have been an underestimate. But the service branches in Tokyo at last reached a compromise. The army agreed to the joint invasion of New Guinea and the navy would continue to expand in the region using the resources of the Fourth Fleet based at Truk. It was a cheap commitment for the army because the Japanese Special Naval Landing Force (SNLF) combat battalions with the Fourth Fleet would do most of the work in the initial amphibious landings. SNLF units already had tremendous successes in places like Guam, Wake, New Britain and Tulagi. If opportunity presented itself, Japan's military leaders still looked to invading New Caledonia, the New Hebrides and Ellice Island, Fiji and Samoa to isolate the important eastern Australian coast where most of the country's population lived, as well as New Zealand.

On the other side of the Pacific, across the breath of a country bustling with troop and war material trains, the situation was quite different. Admiral King was in a policy tug-of-war with General Marshall, his companion on the Joint Chiefs of Staff. And policy was not the sole providence of either of these men. Each was however, an advocate for what direction this two front war should take. Marshall, with the agreement of President Roosevelt who was in turn pressed hard by Winston Churchill, wanted the war with Japan to take second place. Ironically, the vic-

TOP: Maintenance workers in Rabaul wave goodbye to flight crews taking planes out on a night sortie. BOTTOM: A crew readies a Japanese Air Force-97 flying boat headed for a bombing sortie on Port Moresby from Rabaul in 1942.

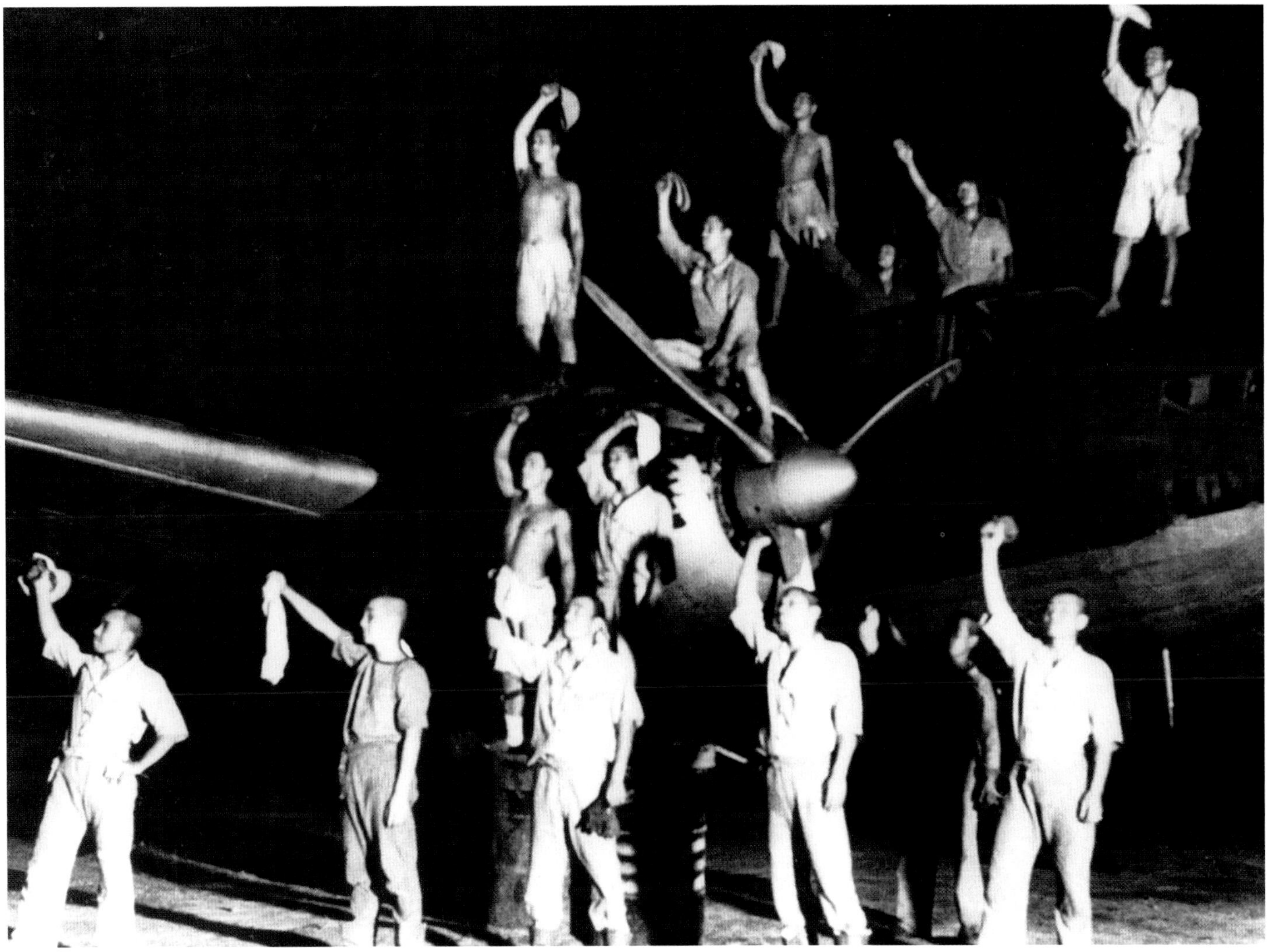

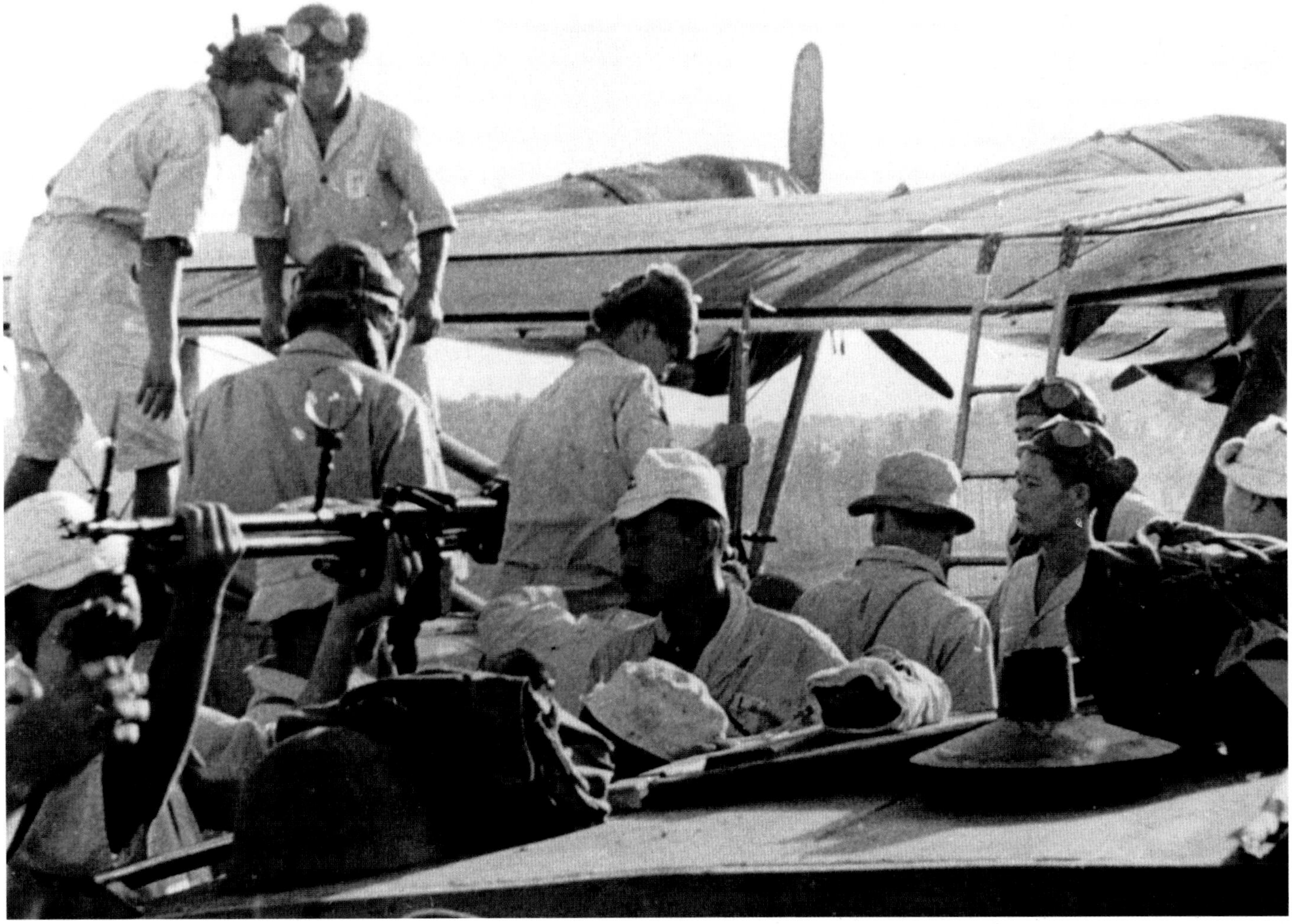

Pacific Theater in May 1942

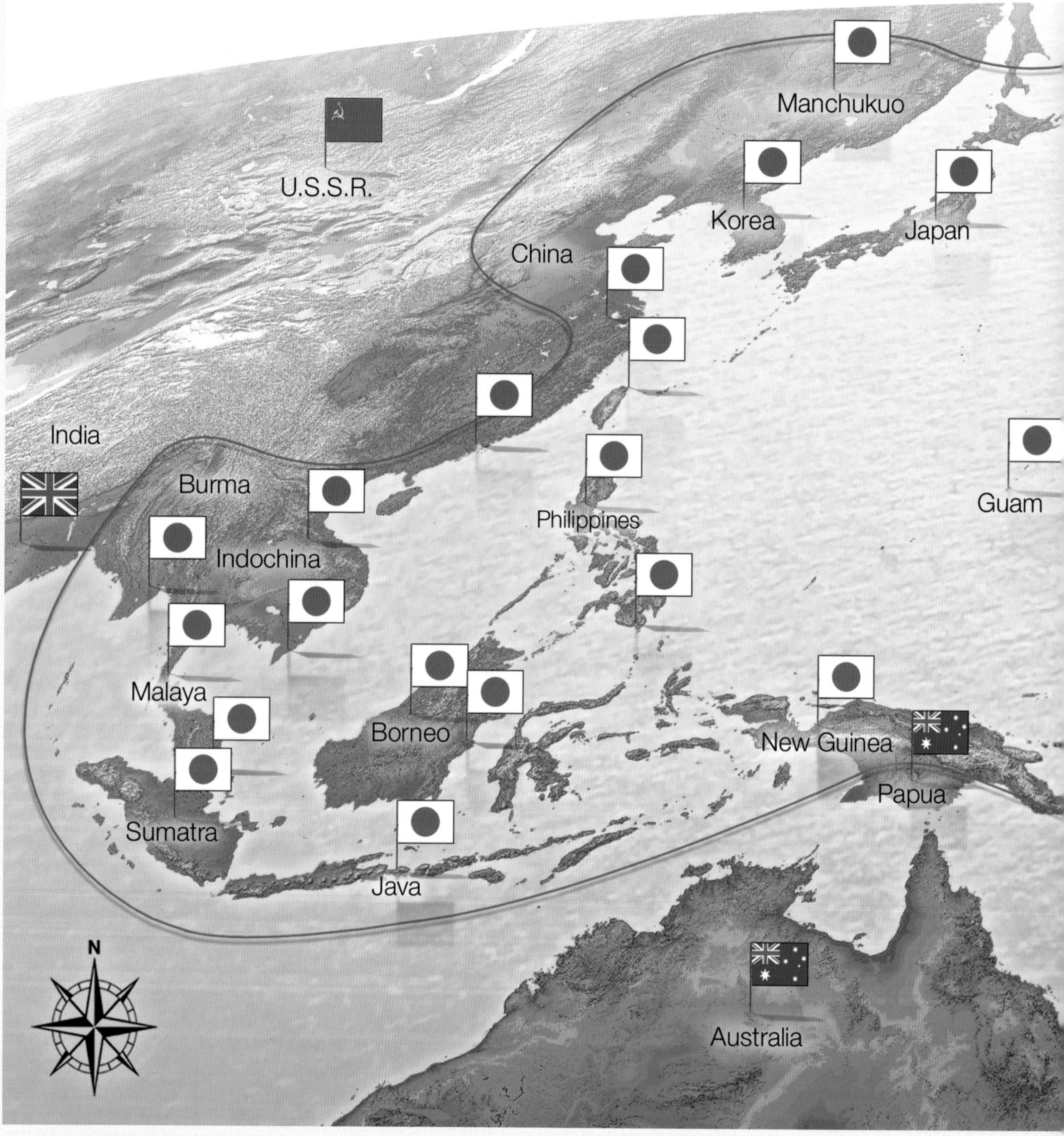

Manchukuo
U.S.S.R.
Korea
Japan
China
India
Burma
Guam
Philippines
Indochina
Malaya
Borneo
New Guinea
Papua
Sumatra
Java
N
Australia

In nearly five months of determined aggression the Japanese army and navy did much to establish military control of East Asia and the Pacific. Well-planned efforts gained them places distant from the Home Islands; Singapore, Burma, Wake, New Britain and the Solomon Islands, though at times this expansion was paid for with blood. However, the incursion into the Aleutian Islands as part of Operation "MI" was to be their last successful invasion. After the Battle of Midway the Allies began an unending push to win all that territory back.

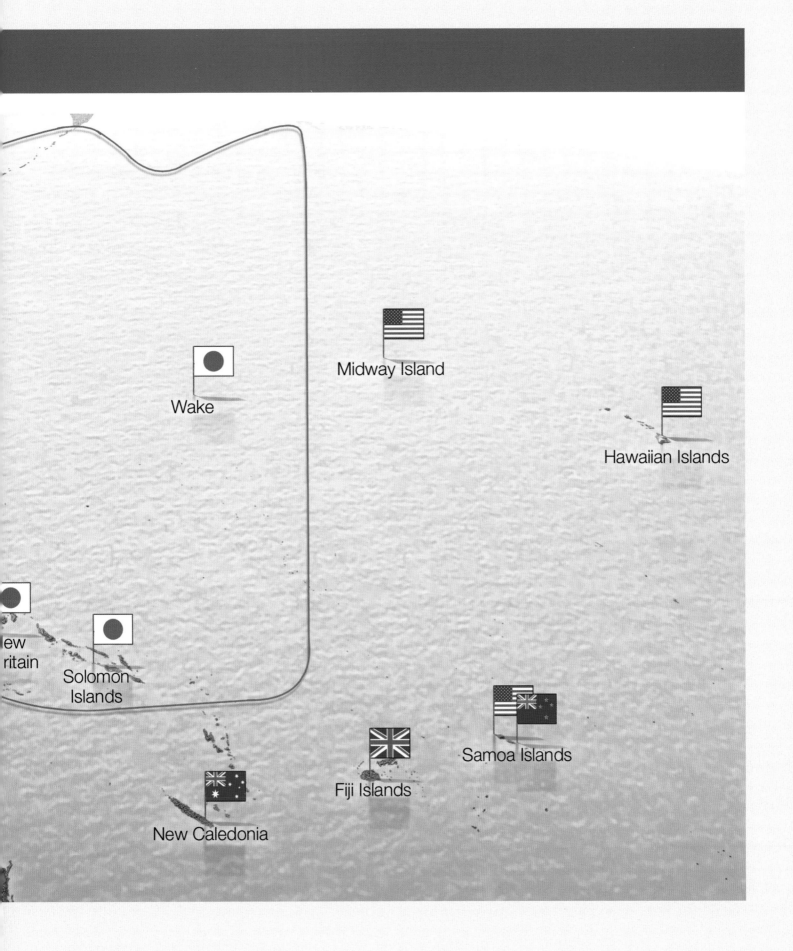

Wake

Midway Island

Hawaiian Islands

New Britain

Solomon Islands

New Caledonia

Fiji Islands

Samoa Islands

Japanese Marines march through a Shanghai street in 1937. The China operations, getting resistance from both Nationalist and Communist Chinese forces, kept Imperial Army leaders from making a large commitment of troops to the Southwest Pacific.

tory at Midway may have given Marshall reason to argue that some degree of progress already had been made in the Pacific. King, pugnacious from the beginning, wanted to land a knockout blow on Japan while the foe was woozy from the Midway pummeling. The reality would be neither senior officer getting what he wanted, but the balance might have tipped slightly to Marshall as an invasion of North Africa was being looked at to augment the air and sea operations in support of Britain. Churchill, consumed with Britain's European war against Hitler, made no commitment to the Pacific war on the part of the commonwealth. However a rift developed between Britain's war leader and Prime Minister John Curtin of Australia over Aussie divisions being drained at Tobruk and elsewhere in North Africa while Curtin's homeland was dangerously exposed to the rampaging Japanese. And in this view he would find an ally.

Operations in the Southwest Pacific

Characteristically, General Douglas MacArthur was not going to wait for Washington's juggling act to end. He had his eye on one thing; returning to the Philippines. He had suffered personal embarrassment in "fleeing" to Australia, as his detractors described his early exit from the islands. It was in his character to feel personally responsible for the American and Filipino soldiers and friends left behind

as prisoners of war. All this made him impatient, even impetuous. When his requests were not well received in Washington, MacArthur enlisted Curtin's help in his appeal. At one point he even sided with King against the emphasis the army and the president gave to Operation Bolero, the code name for the U. S. military build up in Great Britain in preparation for invading Europe and defeating Nazi Germany.

When the Joint Chiefs of Staff did look at the Pacific situation in the summer of 1942, they developed three objectives. First, landing at Tulagi and Santa Cruz in the Solomon Islands, where King had decided the island hopping counteroffensive in the Pacific should begin. Second, to push through the Solomons and Papua, eastern New Guinea, where the Japanese were launching their second attempt to capture Port Moresby.

Japanese sailors wear gas masks during Pacific Ocean maneuvers in late 1942.

The final objective, to which the first two were preparatory, was the capture of the strategic Japanese base at Rabaul on New Britain.

MacArthur favored a direct route to Rabaul and promised a speedy two-week campaign that would trump King's planned island by island advance through the Solomons. For this prize, MacArthur was willing to risk everything; but everything was not at his disposal. He wanted control of the fleet aircraft carriers but Admiral King would never permit any army commander, especially MacArthur, to direct the navy's most valuable asset. In order to protect them, King assigned control of the carriers to the Joint Chiefs of Staff, meaning himself. King was fast making enemies with MacArthur (even bypassing the South West Pacific Area commander in chief to communicate directly with navy officers subordinate to MacArthur), while he continued to try the patience of Marshall and the president.

President Roosevelt's steadfast support of British plans even as Churchill and company were showing little respect for the ideas of the Joint Chiefs allowed King to bring Marshall an acceptable plan. The first objective would be assigned to Nimitz and the navy, including the Marines who would stage the first landing – not just on Tulagi as planned, but also on the larger and previously ignored island, Guadalcanal, across Sealark Channel. The reason was a reliable air reconnaissance reported in early July that the Japanese were building an airstrip on Guadalcanal. The plan's second and third objectives would be carried out by MacArthur and his command. The line between Nimitz's Pacific Ocean Area theater and MacArthur's South West Pacific Area was even redrawn to make sure Guadalcanal was included in Nimitz's command. The compromise seemed to have merit and would determine the direction of the Pacific war for many months. There was no time for further infighting on the part of any of the American commanders in the drive to defeat the Japanese.

MacArthur was a stern task master and pushed subordinates as hard as he pushed himself. Even as he began the Papua operation with Australian reserve troops, the Japanese were moving south across the formidable Owen Stanley Range from Buna on the north coast of New Guinea. Both forces were on a collision course in the unusually rugged and jungle covered peaks of the only north-south trace between the Japanese landing and Port Moresby. But in contrast to the situation in the Philippines six months earlier, MacArthur now had a potent and increasing air presence with land-based planes in Australia. And the airmen, the Fifth Air Force of the U. S. Army Air Forces (from August 1942 under its superb commander, General George Kenney), had already been testing their abilities to go up against Japanese fighters and find available targets in the region.

TOP: This Japanese two-man submarine entered Sydney harbor and was sunk by the Australians. She is seen here in November 1942 when she was ferried between Sydney and Melbourne to raise money for the naval relief fund. RIGHT: During the Japanese attack on Dutch Harbor in June, 1942 smoke rises from bombs dropped on a navy warehouse and oil tanks. American fuel oil, lifeblood of the navy, was stored all over the Pacific. Japanese oil was hauled to the Home Islands for refining and then transported to bases in tankers which became the prime targets of U. S. Navy submarines.

Vernon Main started his Army career at Barksdale Field outside Shreveport, Louisiana with the 13th Attack Squadron. He volunteered for service after the Nazis invaded Poland in 1939 and, though he knew how to fly, was passed over for flight school. Instead, he learned how to repair airframes and engines and became a flight engineer. After flying anti-submarine missions in the Atlantic from Savannah, Georgia, Main and the 13th were shipped across country to Oakland shortly after the Pearl Harbor attack.

"We loaded up about the middle of January, I guess, 1942 and shipped out tentatively for the Philippines; they were still trying to get rein-

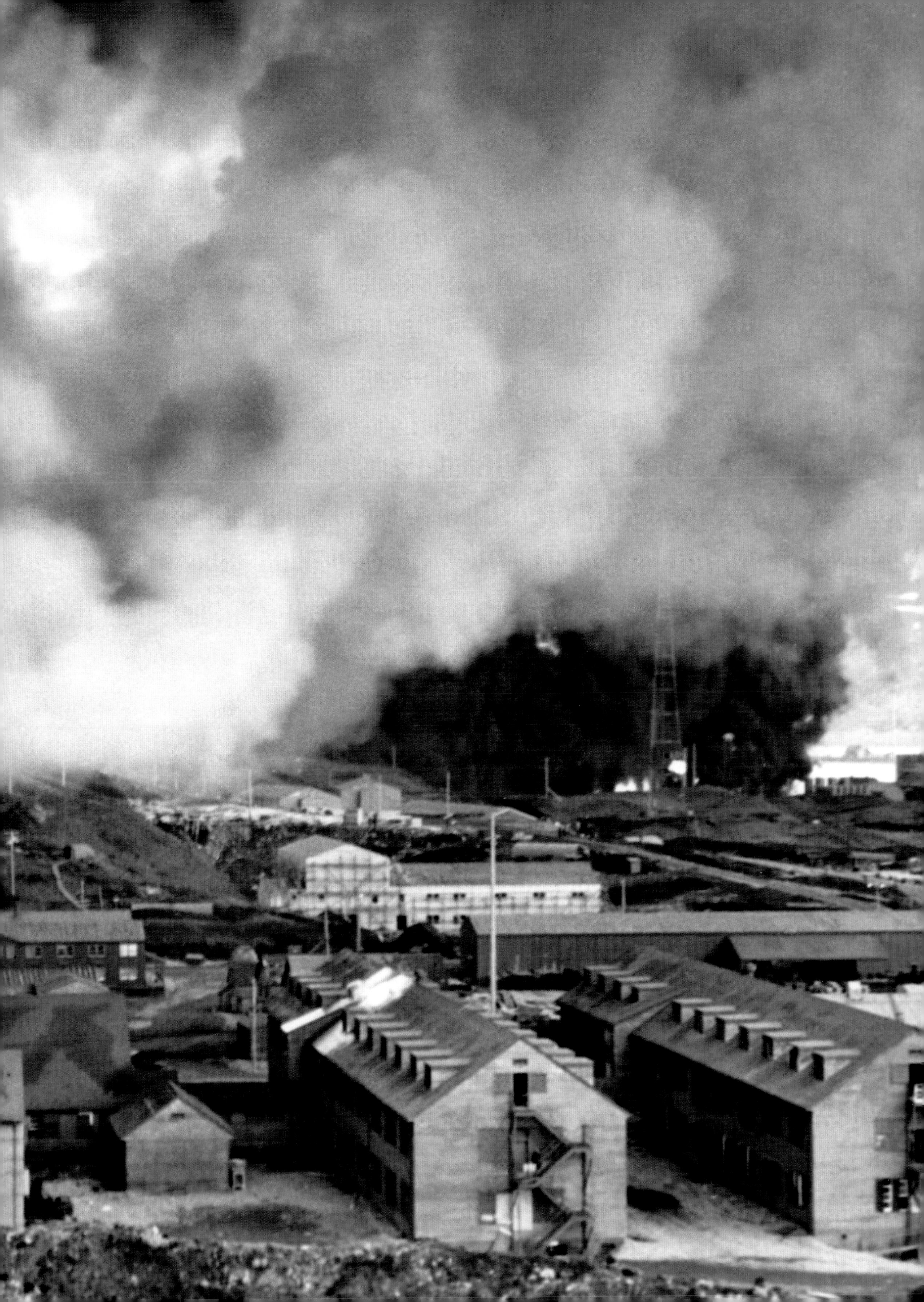

forcements to MacArthur. As a result, our orders changed several times during that journey and it took us 33 to 35 days to get to Australia. We landed in Brisbane off the *Ancon*, the vessel that took us over. It had been a very stately luxury liner and was confiscated by the Army transportation department. We off loaded there, went to a racetrack, Ascot racetrack, in Brisbane to build tents on the infield of the racetrack. Not allowed to go into Brisbane or go to town or anything else but an awful lot of people scaled the fence and did just exactly that. Five or six days later we boarded a train and headed to Charters Towers, [Queensland] Australia. We had to change trains three times because there was no uniformity of the size of the railway tracks in Australia at that time. We arrived at Charters Towers which was an old gold mining town of the turn of the century, and they

A row of Douglas A-20 Havoc attack bombers sit on an Australian airfield. They belonged to the 89th Bombardment Squadron, part of the 3rd Bombardment Group that was an instrumental combat unit for the USAAF in the Pacific.

had the Australian equivalent of the CCCs [Civilian Conservation Corps public works project] here in the United States and they built these cute runways at Charters Towers, four or five thousand feet long. They were good for us, for our type of airplane but they had one real shortcoming. They sloped them down from the center of the field where the two runways crossed each other. It was a fifteen foot drop from the middle of the runway to the end of the runway in each direction. It caused two serious accidents later on because people landed on the nose wheel without realizing they were going up slope instead of down slope."

The 13th Attack Squadron became the 13th Bomb Squadron of the 3rd Bomb Group, U. S. Fifth Air Force. The Fifth's commander, George Kenney, was an imaginative airman who had great

The M-1 Helmet

While images from Pearl Harbor, Wake Island and early Philippine actions show American GIs wearing the "doughboy" World War I-style helmets, the U. S. Army Quartermaster Department quickly initiated a new helmet design, the M-1, so that field forces would have more comfort and protection when they entered combat in 1942. The M-1 contract was originally let to the Westinghouse Electric & Manufacturing Company and, along with other suppliers, the company turned out millions of these helmets during World War II, subsequent conflicts and peacetime through the 1980s.

The beauty of the M-1 is that it is actually two helmets in one. The protective outer shell, rounded in shape, is made from one pressed piece of non-magnetic steel with a stainless or magnesium steel rim all the way around. Inside the outer steel helmet is a removable fiberboard helmet liner manufactured to contour exactly to the steel outer. Even during the war, the fiberboard construction was quickly replaced by emerging types of plastic – forerunners of contemporary construction hard hats. The liner had adjustable cotton webbing to fit the wearer's head and included the all important leather sweat band as part of the webbing design. The liner and steel helmet both had chin straps – the liner strap made of leather and the steel helmet strap made of cotton webbing. In combat only paratroopers wore the chin straps consistently.

(Paratroopers used a special modification of the standard helmet designated M-1C). The theory was that an approaching enemy could seize the helmet's thin brim from the back and with the helmet strapped on, could pull the head back, exposing the throat and vital organs. A pressure release strap was developed, but World War II movies and pictures accurately display what most GIs did with the straps – let them hang down or buckle them across the back of the helmet.

Not only did the army use the M-1 helmet prolifically, the Marines did the same, and the navy also issued them to topside shipboard gunners who would be subject to strafing and

Private John Ziaja of Massachusetts models the new M-1 helmet on a duty location in Great Britain in June 1942.

enemy shell bursts. USAAF bomber gun crews also had specially designed models that allowed for the accommodation of earphones. Army M-1 helmets were painted olive green on the outside with olive or brownish liners and tan webbing. Medics had the Red Cross in a white circle painted on the front. Officers had the appropriate rank insignia on the helmet front when they weren't concerned about rank recognition in combat. The Marines by late 1943 began wearing a forest green/coral brown camouflage cloth cover over the steel helmet. The navy's shipboard helmets were painted battleship gray, while all service branches used and continue to use chrome and painted M-1 helmets in ceremonial applications.

Another addition to army versions of the M-1 helmet was a net webbing to go over the outer shell, to reduce shine and provide a way to place leaves and other camouflage on the headgear. British Commonwealth troops continued to use the old saucer-shaped helmets but often also used the outer webbing as well. Before war's end an M-2 model was also introduced to U. S. forces with modest modifications.

GI's referred to the outer part of the M-1 as the "steel pot" and, though cooking in them was discouraged to keep the metal from getting brittle, used it as such; for washing, food gathering, for sitting on during a ten-minute break during a "hump" or, in an emergency, excrement. But the most important use of the M-1 helmet was keeping them as safe as possible during combat.

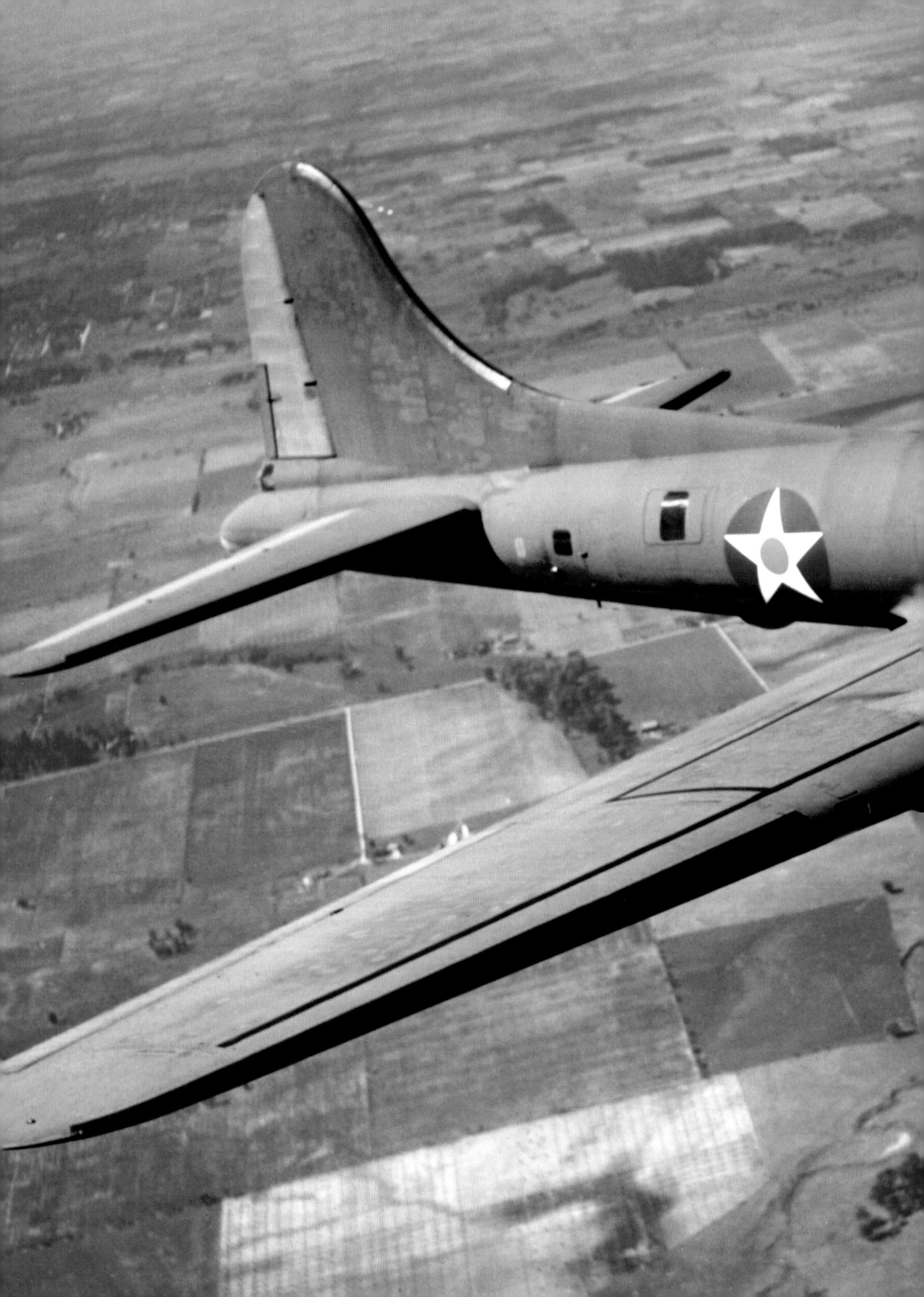

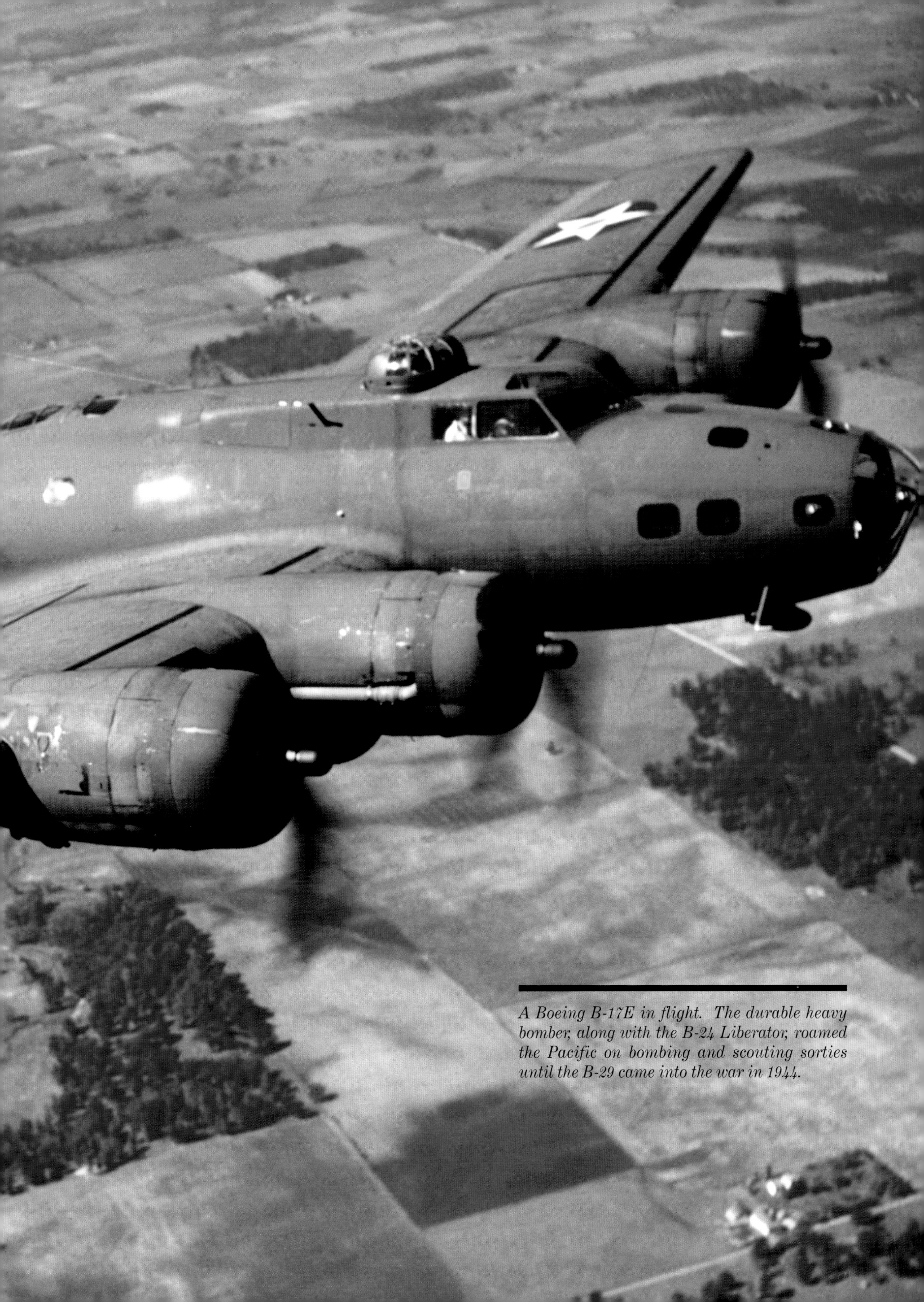

A Boeing B-17E in flight. The durable heavy bomber, along with the B-24 Liberator, roamed the Pacific on bombing and scouting sorties until the B-29 came into the war in 1944.

admiration for MacArthur and would be his air chief for the remainder of the war. However, those logistical issues which were to prove difficult for American forces in the Pacific during the war's first year were felt early on by the four combat squadrons of the 3rd Bomb Group, called *The Grim Reapers.*

"When we got to Charters Towers," explains Main, "that was when we found out they had left all of our airplanes on the dock in San Francisco. We had no airplanes! So we were immediately turned into infantry to dig foxholes right across the northern half of Australia because they knew the Japanese were coming. The commanding officer of the 27th Bomb Group had just gotten out of the Philippines [by submarine] and they were trying to get their airplanes back to the Philippines and the Philippines went down. So they stayed in Australia and he became our CO. Somewhere he found out about the B-25s all gassed up and ready to go because the Dutch had ferried them from the United States to Australia intending to bring them to the Dutch East Indies where they were fighting. The Dutch East Indies were falling faster than snow and as a result, they sent all of the flight crews back to England and they became expatriates. They left their airplanes there all serviced up and ready to go and that's where we went and literally raided them. And it took just a day or so to get them back up to Charters Towers."

Though not as colorful as the "midnight appropriation" story about the acquisition of the medium bombers, another history advises that the planes were ordered and paid for in the U. S. by the Netherlands Purchasing Committee and, lacking ready crews for their new 18th Squadron, they were handed over to the USAAF, delivered to Australia in crates and assembled and flown to Charters Towers. But Main was in the C-39 cargo plane that flew to Brisbane on April 1 to get the planes and so the "raid" idea persists. In any case, four days later Main was flying with the 13th in the B-25s on their first combat mission.

"We pulled our very first action, the raid on Gasmata on the island of New Britain, from Port Moresby. We flew into Port Moresby, fueled up and went over the Owen Stanley Range and bombed Gasmata on Easter morning 1942. We came back to Charters Towers that night and we were told there was something really big in the mill and we [were] getting ready to go off on a very important mission. We later found out after we got the airplanes all ready to go we had to put the 500 gallon bomb bay tanks in – which were not [self] sealable – in order to reach the Philippines. When we were told we were going to the Philippines everyone, including the top management, knew it was a one way trip because it was 1100 miles to Darwin from Charters Towers and 1800 miles to Mindanao in the southern half of the Philippines. As a result, we left on April 11, 1942 and went to Mindanao, [landing at] a Del Monte Plantation. The air base they were building there wasn't finished; they were building it and we stayed three days, bombing three times a day for three days, Cebu City and Davao, which were ports of embarkation for the Japanese troops that were coming into the southern Philippines. We saw we were going to run out of fuel – it was the only thing we didn't have enough of – and General [Ralph G.] Royce who led the mission, brigadier general, he decided we'd had enough and we were going back to Australia. And we did. We landed back in Darwin. We fueled up again and were back in Charters Towers before Doolittle took off from the aircraft carrier. We didn't lose an airplane or lose a man and we shot down two interceptors on one of our missions and Doolittle lost every airplane. And of course he went in [to the Chinese mainland] and everyone bailed out and everyone came back that made it into China. As

The Marine mounted patrol at Kaneohe Bay, Oahu. Even though sabotage was a great concern at the rugged and expansive naval air station, the base did not experience a serious security breach during the war.

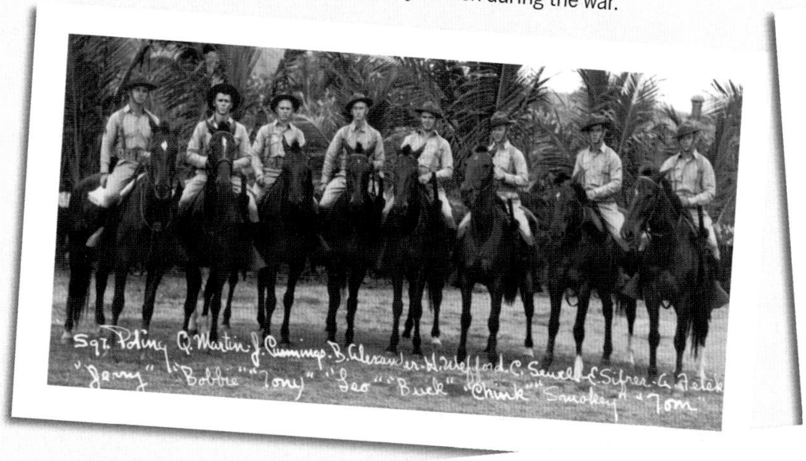
Sgt. Poling Q. Martin J. Cummings B. Alexander
"Jerry" "Bobbie" "Tony" "Leo" "Buck" "Chink" "Smokey" "Tom"

Recruit John Lovas at the Marine Corps training center, Parris Island, South Carolina in the summer of 1941. After Lovas attended sea school in Portsmouth, Virginia he was assigned to a new cruiser, USS *Columbia* (CL56) that was launched on July 29, 1942.

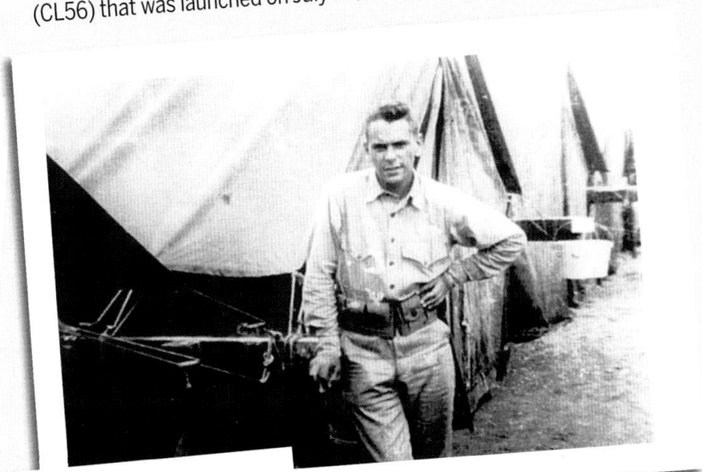

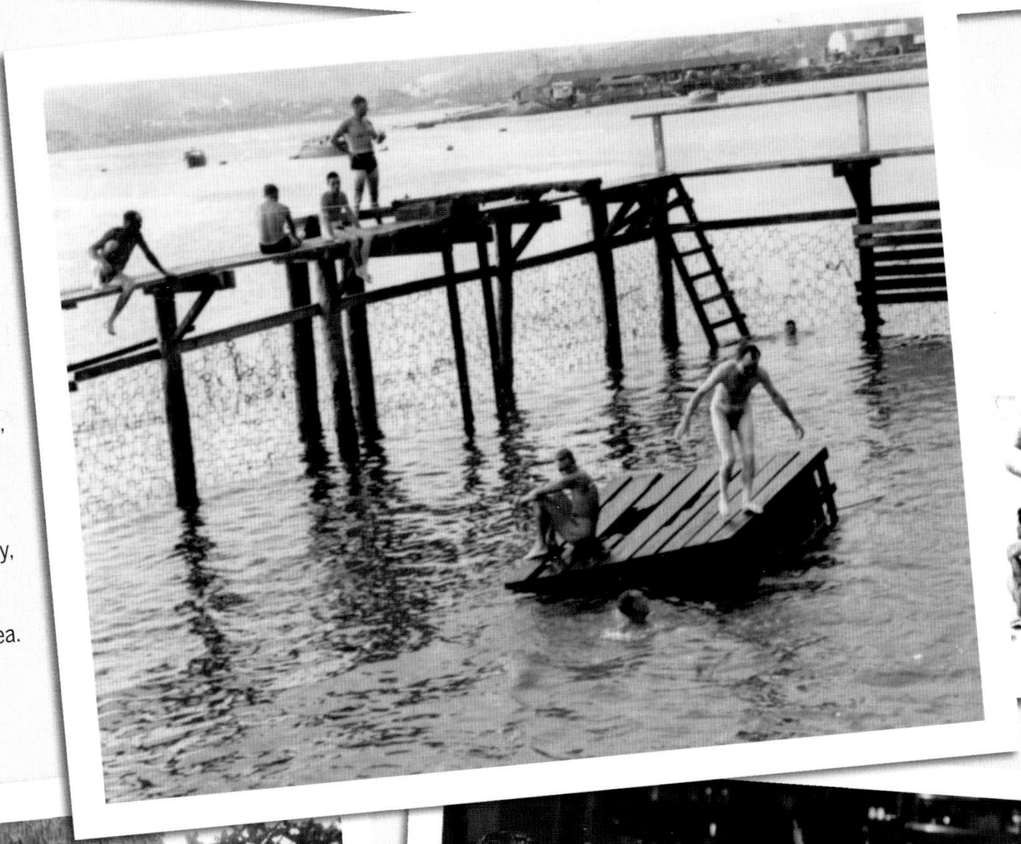

American GIs enjoy some old fashioned "skinny dipping" at a swimming area in one of the lagoons at Port Moresby, Papua. Shark netting surrounds the area.

Back in Hawaii Marine Jim Evans and two Marine friends pose on an Oahu beach.

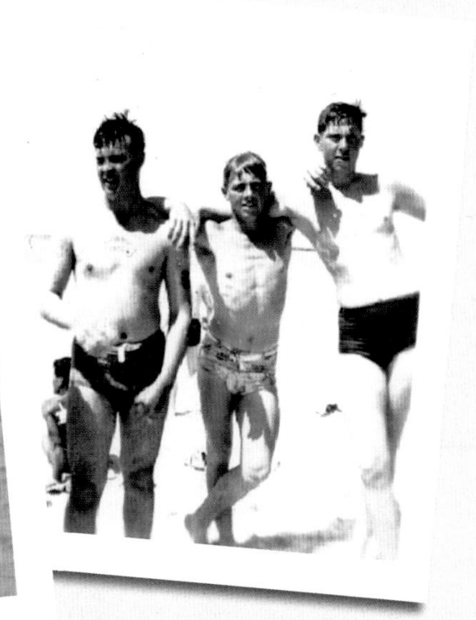

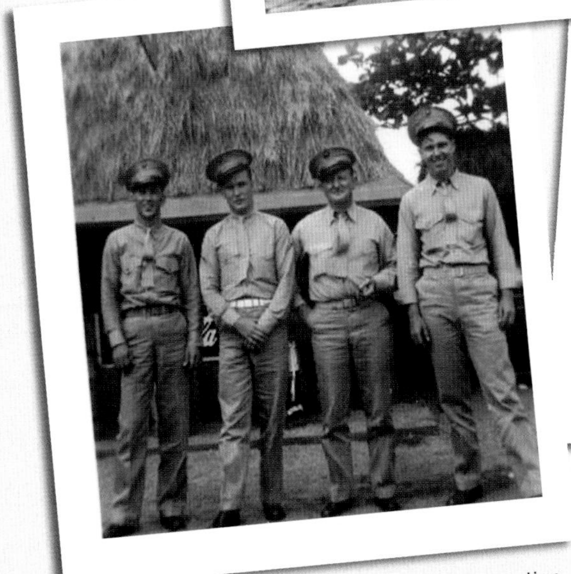

Kaneohe Bay Marines in front of a local tourist attraction.

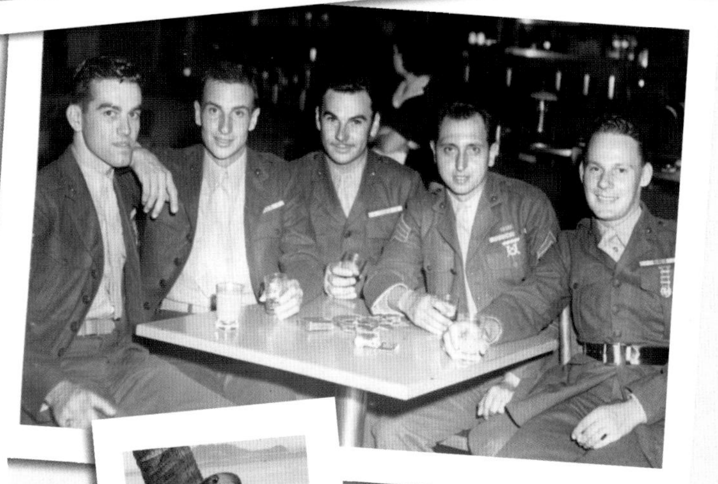

Marine buddies of Jim Evans enjoy liberty at the Lau Yee Chi Waikiki nightclub in Honolulu.

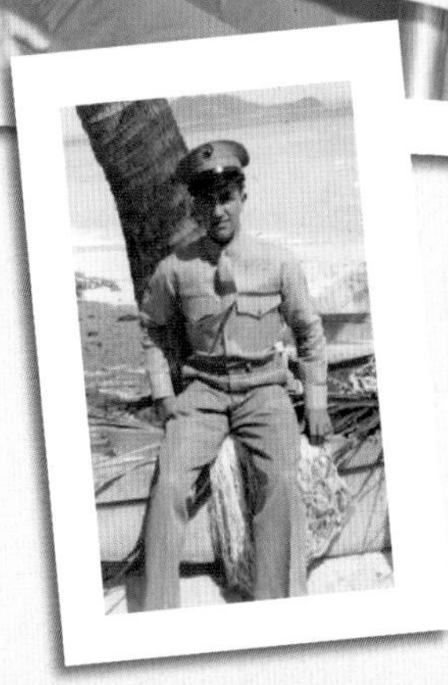

Jim Evans's friend Walt Koziol strikes a pose surely to please family and friends – underneath a palm tree on a Hawaii beach.

"I was a captain's orderly. And by that time I had made corporal and we took the ship (USS Columbia) out on what they call a 'shakedown cruise' and tried to break everything on it, including removing the paint that came with the ship. Why put the paint on in the first place if you're gonna scrape it off? But then later on I understood it was to keep us from getting too bored and it gave us something to gripe about." – John Lovas

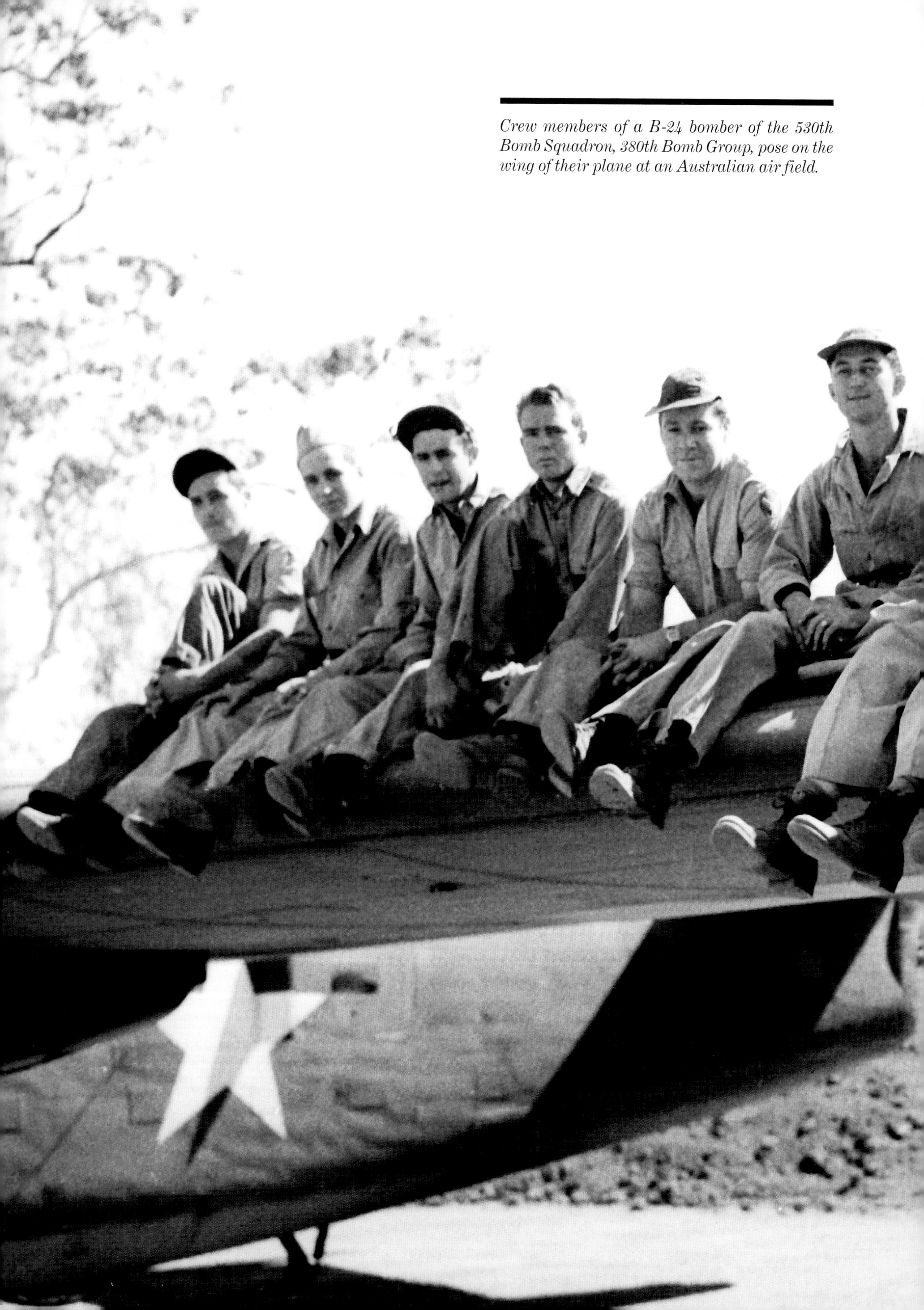

Crew members of a B-24 bomber of the 530th Bomb Squadron, 380th Bomb Group, pose on the wing of their plane at an Australian air field.

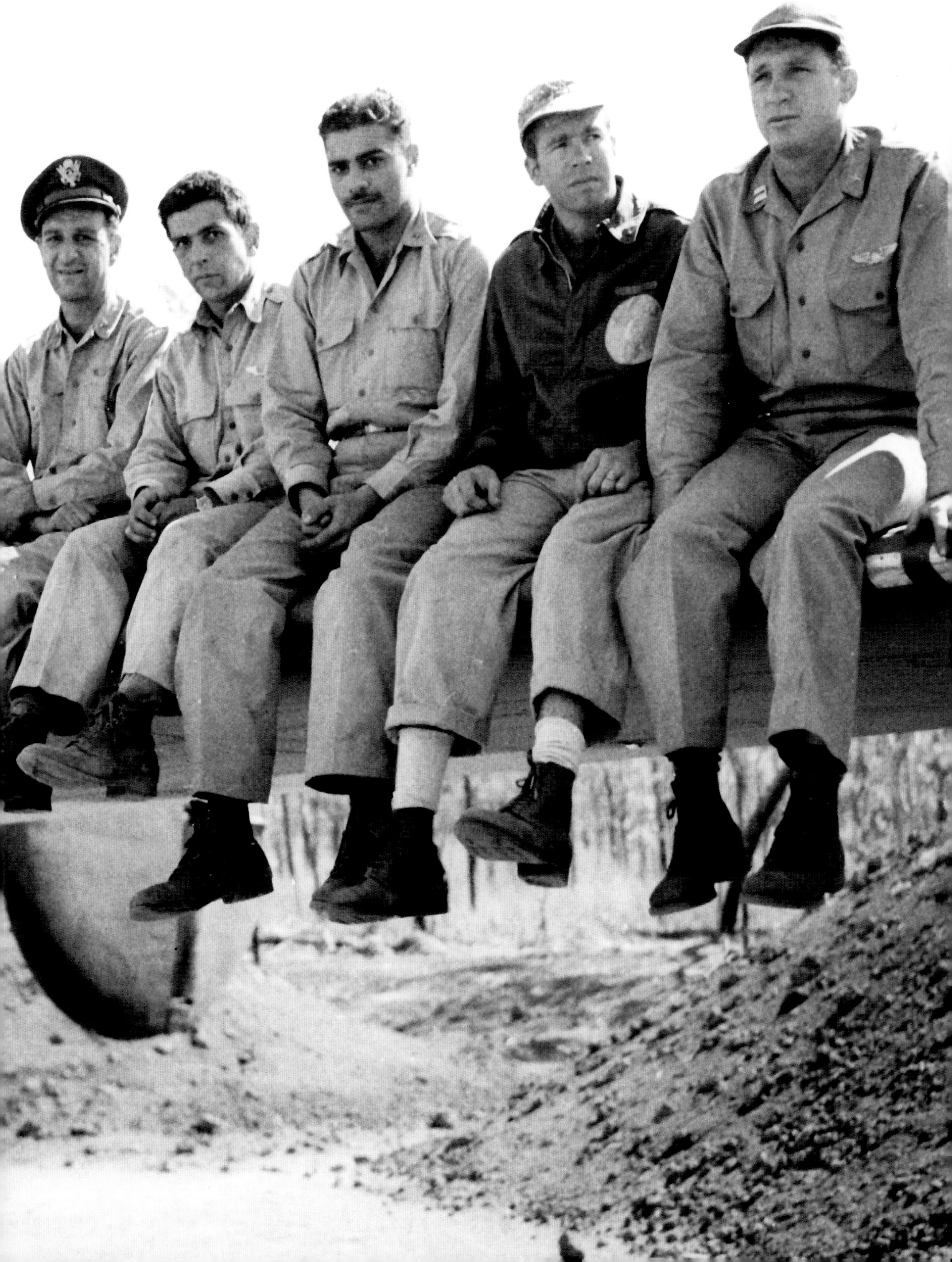

a result, he received a Medal of Honor from the President and we didn't even get recognized. Nobody heard of the Royce Raid."

From this improvised beginning the U. S. Fifth Air Force went on to have a remarkable combat record in the Pacific Theater operating first out of Australia and then from New Guinea. The early air missions against Japanese strongholds such as Rabaul, Imperial Army redeployments, as well as transport and supply convoys and operations were handled with mostly seamless overlap among the three U. S. service branches. Air units from allied nations joined navy, Marine and army air force flyers in important reconnaissance missions and the rescue of downed airmen.

The airmen were aided in their reconnaissance by the Coast Watchers, an organized group of Australian civilians and reservists who had familiarity with and worked from isolated locations in the region's islands. Most were plantation managers or others who resided in these remote areas before the war. They operated radio sets from hidden outposts with the help of sympathetic islanders. The Coast Watchers would report Japanese ship and plane movements and spot downed Allied airmen, often at substantial risk to themselves.

Submarine Operations

One other aspect of U. S. operations cannot be overlooked during the early war period. While American and Filipino soldiers were falling back on the Bataan Peninsula, while Japanese task forces were making a seemingly unstoppable parade through the islands of the Pacific, while American carriers were jockeying for their first crack at the Combined Fleet – even while Vernon Main and the other Fifth Air Force flyers were carrying out their first missions – U. S. Navy submarines were quietly seeking targets of opportunity in the Pacific Ocean and other nearby waters of the region.

The difference between U. S. and Japanese submarine operations was that the American boats concentrated on merchant craft and shipping, particularly tankers. The Japanese focused on capital ships and other warships. The Imperial Navy also experimented with the two-man submarines, carried piggyback on the larger I-class boats and then released near harbors for destructive (and probably suicidal) operations. The launch of five two-man subs at Pearl Harbor was the largest operation of that kind. Another mission was aimed at Sydney harbor in early May 1942, but no ships were damaged and one two-man sub was lost.

One of the strategic errors committed by the Japanese military was in the handling of arguably the most important asset gained in their expansion, the oil of the Dutch East Indies. British and Dutch operators of refineries in Borneo, Sumatra and Java, when all hope was lost, sabotaged those facilities. But rather than restoring the refineries and providing a ready fuel supply for expanded operations in a large region far from Japan, the Japanese continued to refine all petroleum in the Home Islands. The decision played into the hands of American submariners who sank tankers carrying millions of tons of precious crude oil during the war. Oil was one of many vital commodities necessary for the coming violent, time-consuming and desperate struggle for Guadalcanal.

TOP: USS Swordfish (SS-193) in San Francisco Bay in 1943. When attached to the U. S. Asiatic fleet, the submarine under the command of Lt. C. C. Smith was responsible for evacuating key American and Filipino officials from the Philippines in February 1942. Roving the Pacific and Indian oceans and surrounding waters in 1942, Swordfish also had a distinguished record in the destruction of Japanese shipping. BOTTOM: Japanese submarine I-5. These mammoth underwater boats trolled the Pacific and other waters looking for military targets. Some were able to accommodate partially assembled scout planes within their hulls.

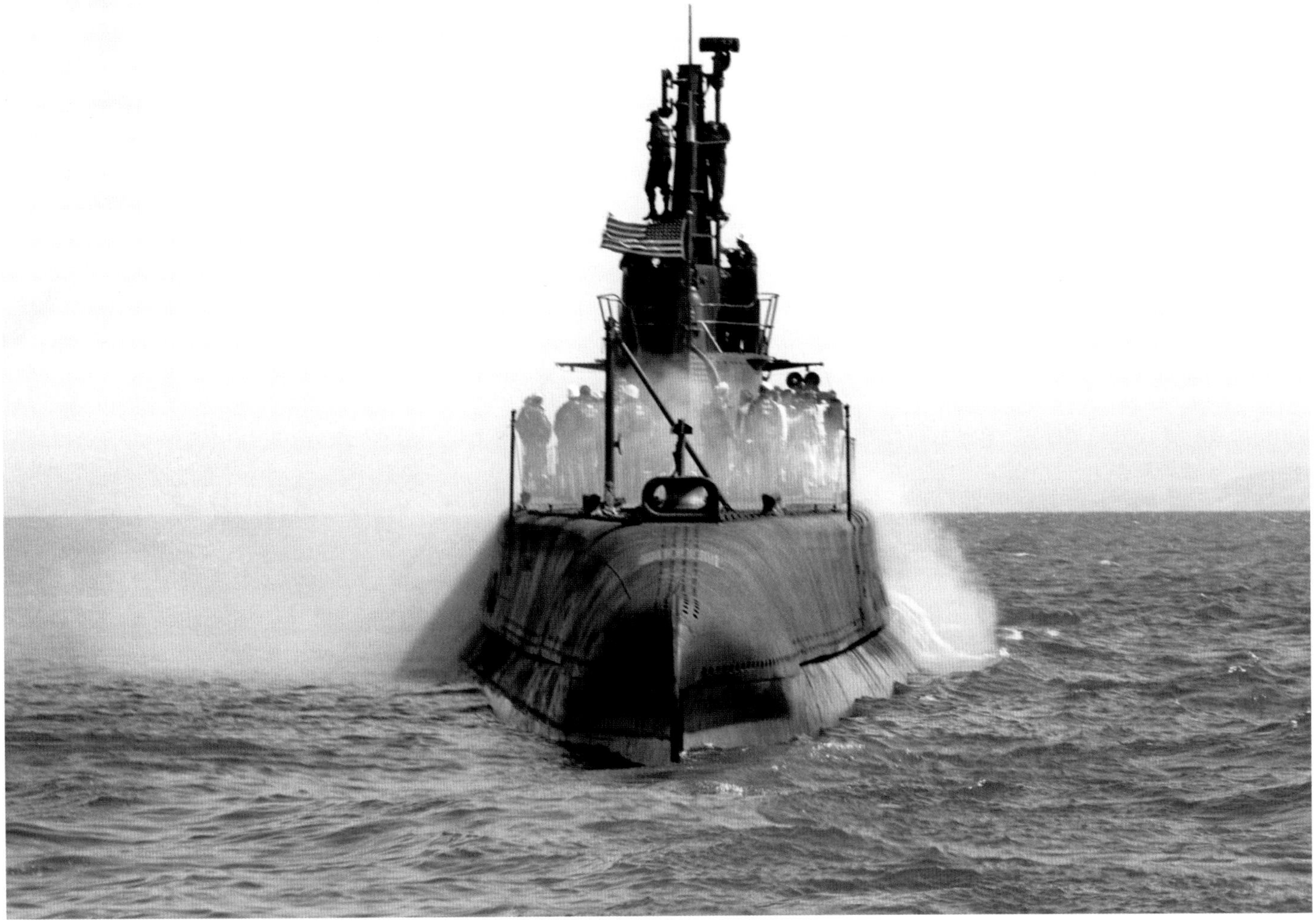

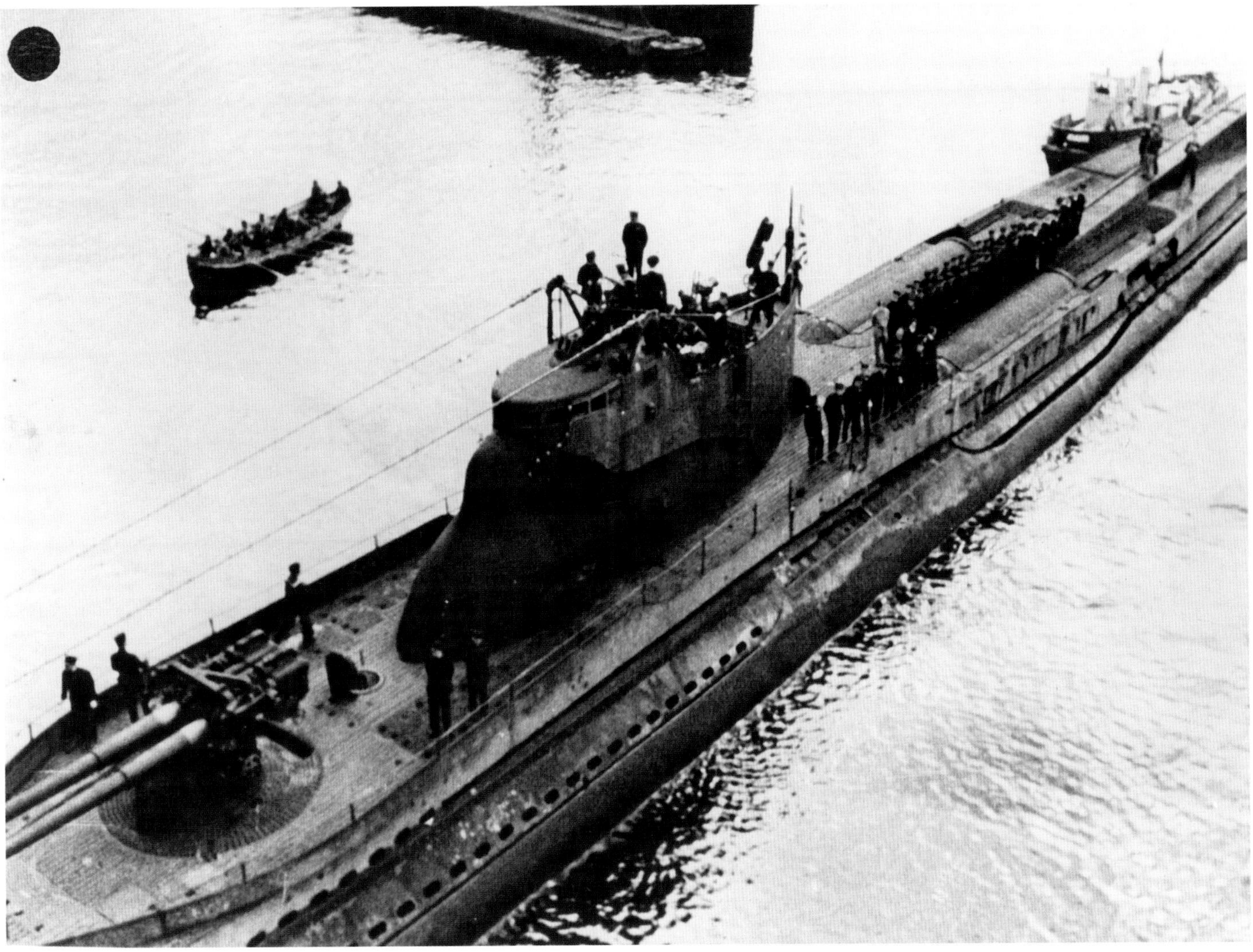

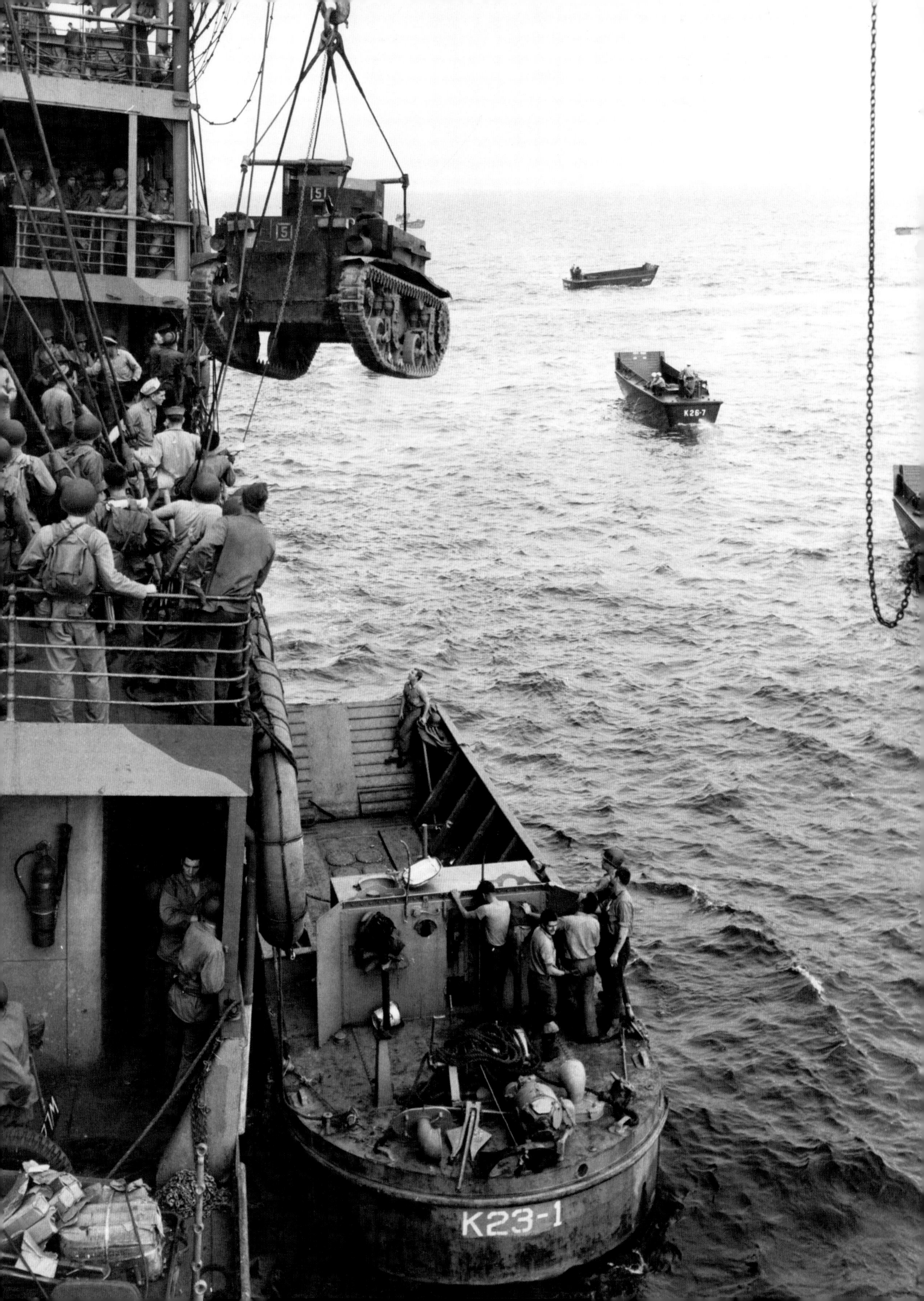

15
K26-7
K23-1

The Struggle for Guadalcanal and Papua/New Guinea

The Old Breed

Anything with "first" in its name almost always means something special, perhaps even exceptional or revolutionary. In history, the first is often an event or entity that starts a trend, movement or timeline of action. Military history is full of "firsts" - 1st Continental Army, First Seminole War, First Manassas, to name a few American history examples. It is no surprise, therefore, that two of most storied U. S. divisions in World War II were "firsts." The U. S. Army 1st Infantry Division, the "Big Red One," first onto Omaha Beach on D-Day; and the 1st U. S. Marine Corps Division, "The Old Breed," the unit that began the amphibious war against Japan at Tulagi and Guadalcanal.

The 1st Marine Division was also the Corps' first division-size unit and was specially trained to spearhead the amphibious war in the Pacific. It was formed in 1940 and trained at places like Quantico, Virginia and Guantanamo Bay in Cuba. The division's flood of incoming recruits joined a core of pre-war career enlisted men and officers who gave the unit its enduring "Old Breed" nom-de-guerre. The latter group included shipboard Marines, guard company men, Marines stationed in China and those who fought in small units in places like France in World War I, Haiti and Nicaragua. They were tough, profane and fearless. They were the Marines who had made the Corps' superb reputation. The 1st Division was led by

A large crane moves a Stuart light tank from a freighter to a tank landing barge at Guadalcanal. After the island was fully wrested from the Japanese in early 1943 it became a major U. S. base for operations in the South Pacific.

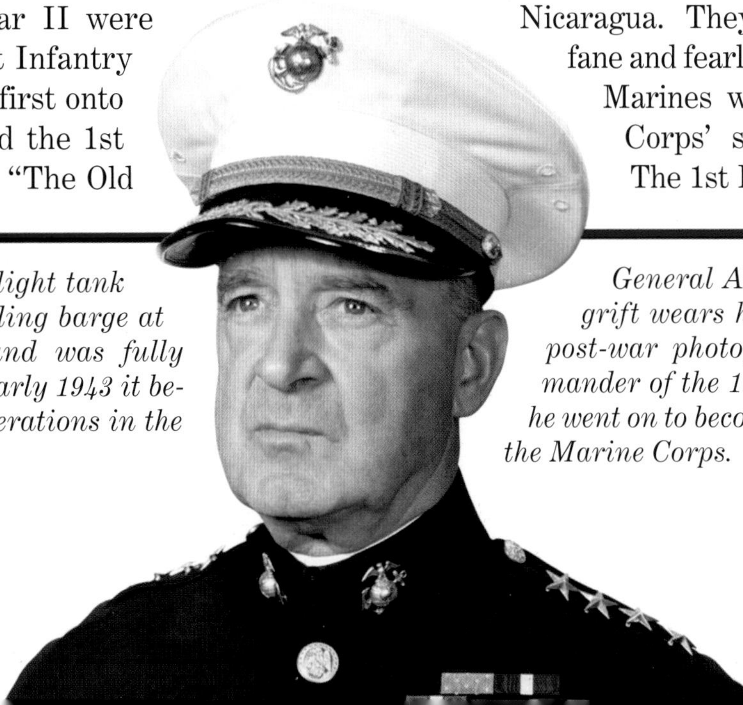

General Alexander A. Vandegrift wears his dress blues in a post-war photograph. From commander of the 1st Marine Division he went on to become Commandant of the Marine Corps.

An amphibious tractor designated LVT by the U. S. military and nicknamed "alligator" by American GIs demonstrates its capabilities. It would play an important part in the jungle and lagoon fighting of the Pacific islands.

Major General Alexander A. Vandegrift, an officer who got a good dose of jungle warfare in Nicaragua and Haiti, and had seen duty in China and Veracruz, Mexico. A quiet leader, clever tactician and organizer, some have compared him to "Stonewall" Jackson, or perhaps his ancient Macedonian namesake, Alexander the Great. Vandegrift had a subtle yet effective way of cooperating with superiors and equals; and a deep but unpronounced caring for his men.

The preparations for redeploying the 1st Marine Division were extensive and began in earnest in the spring of 1942. The division was split up for the journey to and across the Pacific. Gathering in units from Quantico, Cuba and elsewhere, two-thirds of the men were sent by ship through the Panama Canal and the other third went by rail to the west coast where they were loaded onto transports for the trip Down Under. Arthur Farrington was a recruit from Washington, D. C. who, as a member of the 1st Regiment, completed training at Quantico and boarded a train west.

"So then, they put us on a train. Leave Union Station, Washington, D.C. Down across [Francis Scott] Key Bridge, I think it was Key Bridge, and away we go. We were goin' to San Francisco. The 7th Marines [less its 3rd Battalion], they had gone through the [Panama] Canal but they told us we were going across country by train. Every time the train stopped we had to get off and we did close order drill and everything. And a lot of the civilians, they loved that. The officers had us sing

the Marine Corps hymn when we were off the train. I got a map. It shows where we went, through the towns and everything. We did not pick up other Marines along the way. The 1st Division was all by itself."

Another vehicle widely used in the Pacific War was the DUKW, called by everyone the "duck." The amphibious truck was first built in 1942 by General Motors and its partners and was invaluable in numerous island campaigns.

Farrington and those with him left San Francisco on a passenger liner taken over by the military transportation authorities.

"We were on a ship, we call it the *Manura* [actually the MS (motor ship) *John Ericsson*]," Farrington says. "It was manufactured in Sweden. Down in the dining room where they had the balls, swastikas were the decorations and we couldn't believe it. And the waves! We were hitting rough seas and the bathrooms flooded.

And people were sick. So we called ourselves – it was a motor ship – the motor ship *Manura*. On the way to Wellington.

"Wellington was fun. We ate ice cream and everything. The automobiles, these were taxis usually, they had something on the back bumper. And the driver would get in there and he [would] put stuff in there and light it. And tend the fire. It manufactures a gas that the things run on. We'd get in there and we'd take off. It would never make the hills there and the drivers hated them. We would make fun of them."

No major disasters befell the 1st en route to Wellington, New Zealand, the first overseas stop on the way to the beaches of Guadalcanal. No disasters on the way; but one was narrowly averted when they arrived. And it took ingenuity and a lot of what would normally be un-soldierly effort to overcome it. Vandegrift had wanted a year to prepare the division for the first amphibious campaign by United States troops in almost fifty years. He would not get that, not even close; more like forty days. That was cut short by the less than neighborly reception on the part of some of the locals. Dillon Gaulding was another Marine recruit who was getting his first look at a foreign land in New Zealand.

"I was with L Company, which was part of the tank battalion. We sent about half the division through the Panama Canal and the other half across the country to San Francisco. That's where I went, to San Francisco, and from there by transport to New Zealand where we stayed for about four weeks until we went to Guadalcanal. There's really a nasty story about that. Many of the people who were in the 1st Marine Division there were just out of boot camp, and of course they had already gotten their mission which was Guadalcanal. The commander [General Vandegrift] had received pretty short notice and he asked for a few more weeks to train troops in New Zealand and they gave it to him but he lost it. We had our ships loaded just to get the equipment there and we had to unload all of them, [to create] what we called a combat load. The New Zealander dock workers were on strike. And they would not let us use their equipment nor would they help us. It took us two weeks to unload all that and they had to send the New Zealand army down there to get the dock workers off the dock. We didn't get any training. We worked eight hours on and eight hours off for two weeks to get all our ships unloaded and loaded again."

The exhausting work of acting as stevedores did not crush the morale of the well trained Marines. They knew what was at stake. As the first regiments of the 1st Division were at work in Wellington, others were making their way across the Pacific, including the unit Ed Bearss was assigned to.

"We're out of boot camp, we're initially assigned, most of us are assigned to the Double Deuce [22nd Marines]. It is a newly organized unit formed around a cadre of men from the 6th Marines. Most of the NCO's and senior officers are 6th Marines from Iceland with their sea stories. The others are guard company Marines, and the rest are like me, boots. When we arrive at Camp Linda Vista we find that the 1st Battalion of the Double Deuce has already gone to Samoa and we're to join them in Samoa as soon as possible. On the 19th of July [1942], four weeks to the day after we get out of boot camp we board the transport *Lurline* with the 2nd and 3rd Battalions, Double Deuce. I was in company E of the 2nd Battalion. We cast off and the second sailing day there's rough weather and most of the people were sick. I'm queasy and I remember our sergeant, Gunny Sergeant Cleo Via. In a Marine Corps unit, the Marine's Marine is the gunnery sergeant. The 1st sergeant ranks the gunnery sergeant, but the 1st sergeant is an administrator. So Gunny Via gets us all out on the open deck just below the boat deck. We're standing up and he comes down the line and wherever he sees a guy who's real pale he gets in their face and says, 'Boy do you know what we're having for dinner today? Greasy pork chops!' And he'd laugh like hell as the guy headed for the rail. Since my father had been in the Marine Corps I was smart enough to sleep in the top bunk; the top bunk is the one you're not going to get puked on.

"We arrive in Pago Pago Harbor [American Samoa] on the 29th. As we approach the island the Japanese do something they don't do often. Their submarines are designed to operate with their fleets. They are not going to use them primarily to destroy shipping as us and the Germans do. The Japanese submarine fires, according to the log, we found out later, two torpedoes but they didn't hit. We picked up speed and zigzagged; then stopped to drop the mail in American Samoa and sailed that afternoon to Apia in Western Samoa. There the Double Deuce will remain 'til the autumn of 1943."

Bearss did not wait that long to get into the action and in September he volunteered to join the 3rd Raider Battalion. When the 22nd Marines arrived in Western Samoa, other 1st Division units were in the final stages of preparation for the Solomon Islands invasion. Even with the shortened training schedule, cut thinner by the need to act as dock workers in New Zealand, Vandegrift still wanted some beach landing exercises for his men. The next stop was the Fiji Islands. However, the Japanese, seemingly carefree about where all these Marines might be headed, had plans of their own. They were headed back to Papua and, having failed to take the town, Port Moresby, on the southeastern corner of the big island by sea, they were now determined to take it by land.

In the Land of the Fuzzy Wuzzies

Port Moresby, Papua in World War II was much like Vicksburg in the American Civil War. While the climate and topography were quite different, the strategic importance was pivotal to plans for both opposing forces. Having been turned away in May after the naval Battle of the Coral Sea, the Japanese high command ordered on June 12, 1942 that Operation "MO" be revitalized with an overland advance from the north coast of Papua. The main topographical feature of this slender finger of land is the Owen Stanley Range, an extraordinarily high range of jungle-covered mountains bisecting the penisula. A new Seventeenth Army under the command of Lieutenant General Harayoshi (Harukichi) Hyakutake was formed from nine infantry battalions and supporting forces and assigned to strategic areas surrounding Rabaul. The South Seas Detachment under Major General Tomitaro Horii, supported by the Sasebo 5th S N L F, was given the task of crossing the mountains to take Port Moresby.

Though Port Moresby was already serving Allied air operations, General MacArthur saw the importance of strengthening it as a base for his approved (as of July 2) drive on Rabaul. Unlike most of New Guinea, which was an Australian Mandate after it was rested from Germany following World War I, Papua had been a part of Australia for generations. It had its own militia made up of the native Papuan population but was also eligible to be protected by Australian militia units. The Australians playfully called Papuans "fuzzy wuzzies" because of their wiry, out of control hair. With most of the country's 2nd Australian Imperial Force (AIF) committed to North Africa in defense of the empire, the militia was the first available force for Papua while a new AIF division was being formed and two U. S. Army units, which arrived on the continent in May, were being trained. Not only did MacArthur have plans for the defense of Port Moresby, he sought other areas of the peninsula for landing strips to improve air operations in the region.

One of those places was Buna on the Bismarck Sea, north across the Owen Stanley Range from Port Moresby. Initially, Allied planners deemed Buna unsuitable for a landing strip, but a nearby location was found. Operation Providence was launched to take Buna by a south to north march over the mountains by Australian militia. Too late. Hyakutake's initial force, a company of engineers reinforced with infantry called the

Yokoyama Force, landed at Buna on July 21. The Japanese, though bombed by Allied aircraft, got a foothold at the marshy delta of a creek and beat back local resistance. Lacking maps of Papua, the Japanese relied on aerial reconnaissance which showed a road over the mountains. But the Kokoda Track was hardly a road – it was only a delicate foot path that forced tough going for Japanese soldiers carrying 100 to 160-pound packs. Motorized vehicles were out of the question. Bicycles were the only wheeled vehicles capable of negotiating the rugged trail.

As difficult as the going was, in five days Horii's vanguard made it to the inland government station at Kokoda, where the north/south trail intersected with one running west over the range. Even though Hyakutake had only planned for this force to be a reconnaissance unit, their trail-blazing operation became much more. The trail was rendered all but impassable by fast-flowing streams cutting through the thick jungle at inopportune places. Rain fell almost constantly, swelling these streams and making them a constant challenge. However, resistance was light. Only a few attempts were made to slow down the Japanese advance by the combined militia and native force that often scattered in the face of the night- and rain-shrouded attacks the Japanese preferred. The reason for the paltry resistance on the track was that MacArthur had ignored intelligence warnings that the enemy would try to take Port Moresby with an overland march. Consequently, the Japanese occupied Kokoda in the third week of August. They were on track for a push through the range toward Port Moresby but could not take the objective alone; a second force was to advance on Moresby from Milne Bay on the eastern tip of Papua.

To the Japanese soldiers occupying Kokoda in late August the enemy they encountered in Papua must have validated the words of their training manual which stated, "Westerners - being very haughty, effeminate, and cowardly - intensely dislike fighting in the rain or mist or in the dark. They cannot conceive night to be a proper time for battle - though it is excellent for dancing. In these weaknesses lie our great opportunity." Their opinion would likely change soon; first at Milne Bay and later along the Kokoda Track as battle-hardened Aussies returning from North Africa entered the fray.

Early on, General Hyakutake planned an amphibious landing at Milne Bay as part of the operation. The area was already bristling with Allied military operations. The former Lever Brothers coconut plantation was being shaped into an air operations center by U. S. Army engineers. By the time the proposed Japanese landing occurred on August 26, two Australian battalions were occupying the bay and guarding the airstrip under construction. Bad luck began to unwind this operation for the Japanese. Heavy cloud cover hampered air reconnaissance, causing the Japanese to underestimate the force that would oppose them. The army troops earmarked for the operation were diverted to meet the growing threat at Guadalcanal. The force was then limited to naval and Special Naval Landing Force units under Commander Shojiro Hayashi and was split between a group sailing down the coast in barges from

TOP: Natives train on Florida Island in the Solomons to fight against the Japanese. Nearly all the Pacific island and New Guinea aboriginal people were unsympathetic to the Japanese occupation and many fought against them or aided the Allied troops as guides, porters and litter bearers. BOTTOM: Damien Parer, official AIF cinematographer, reunites at Kokoda with his brother Cyril, who had already been fighting the war in Papua. The Kokoda Trail over the Owen Stanley Range that took the Japanese toward the key Papuan town of Port Moresby was full of natural obstacles and occasional Allied resistance.

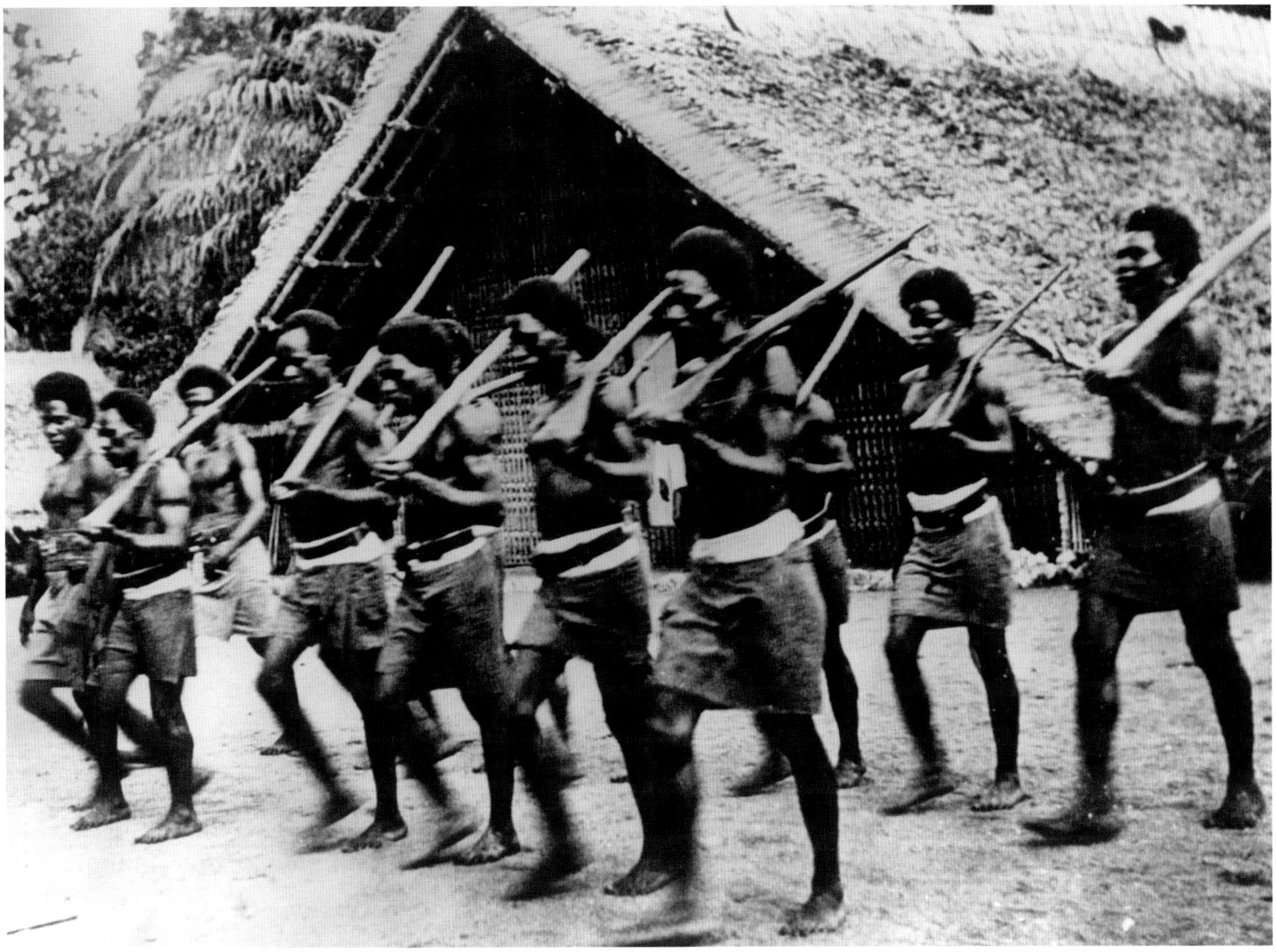

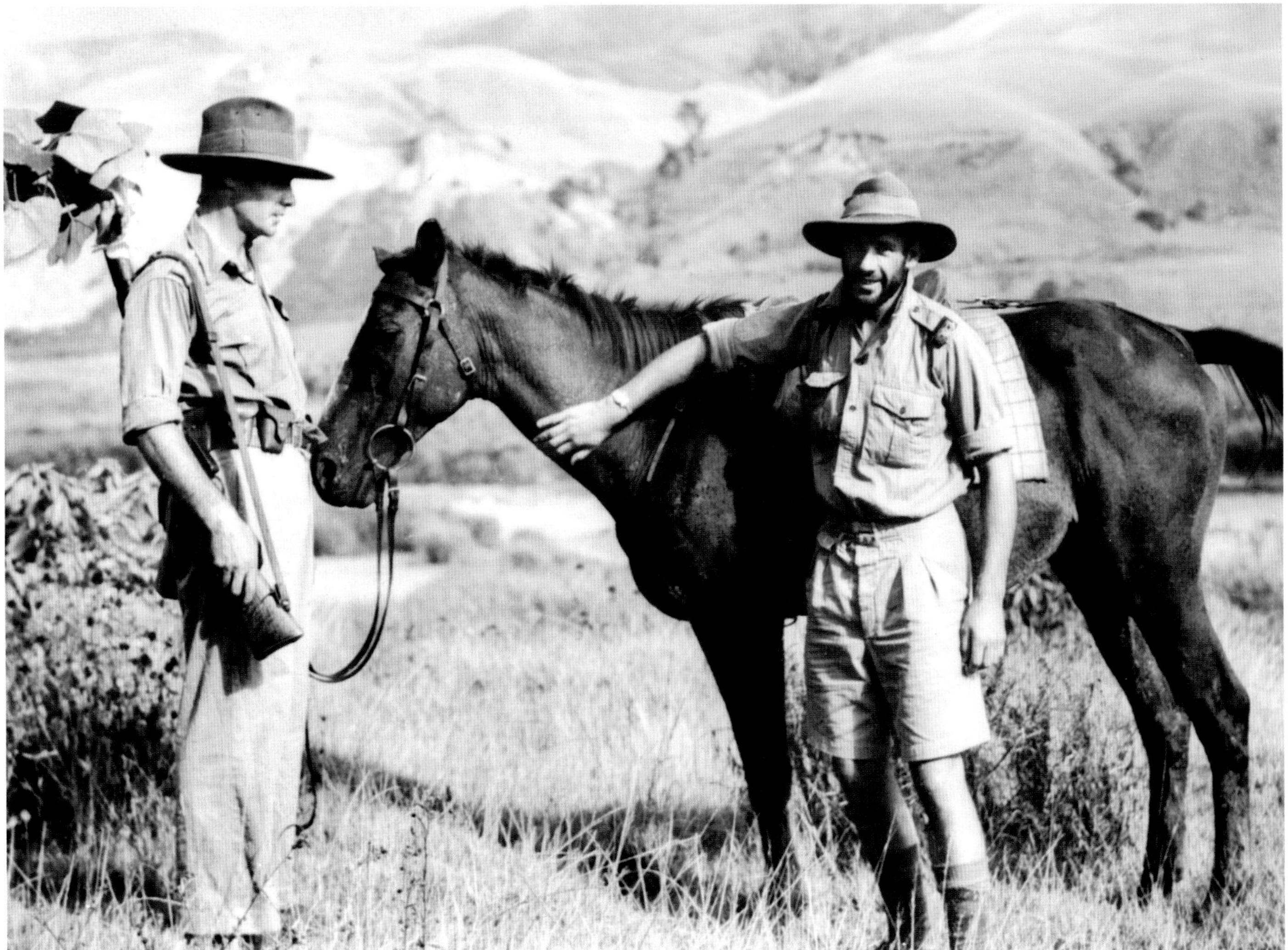

Japanese Invasion of Papua
OWEN STANLEY RANGE
Gona
July 21-22
Buna
Kokoda
July 28
HORII
July 23-27
Efogi
Sept. 8
Ioribaiwa
Sept. 17-26
Australian Counterattack starts on Sept. 23
Port Moresby
Rabaul
Solomon Sea
Milne Bay

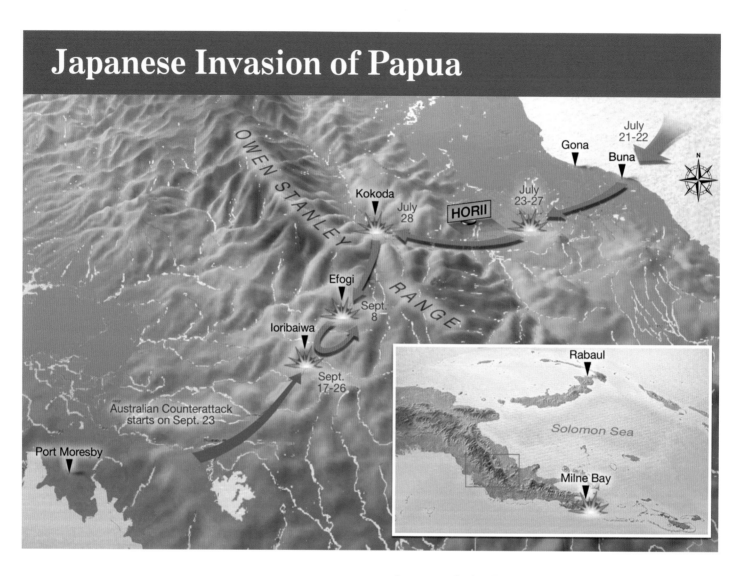

Having been turned away from Port Moresby by sea as a result of the Battle of the Coral Sea, Japan decided to take the key town and air base by overland march. The physical conditions of the march through the jungle and over the rugged Owen Stanley Range proved to be more difficult than enemy fire for the Japanese expedition. The Australian Imperial Force (AIF) finally stalled the advance of their foe at Ioribaiwa in September.

Buna to mount an overland approach and another to land in the bay.

A coast watcher discovered the Sasebo 5th SNLF creeping down the coast and twelve Australian P-40 fighter aircraft were called in. They destroyed the barges while the Japanese were ashore eating lunch, stranding and effectively putting this force out of action. To make matters worse for the Japanese, the seagoing operation, lacking charts, late on August 25 landed in a downpour seven miles east of their proposed landing site. They had to fight along a narrow track to approach the airfield being constructed at Gili Gili. Despite receiving additional marines, tanks and an officer who outranked him (Commander Minoro Yano) Hayashi advanced slowly against a stubborn foe.

By the time Yano, then in command, launched an all-out attack on the airstrip shortly after midnight on August 31, the Australians had a perimeter

defense set up and answered all aspects of the Japanese attack. On September 1, the Aussies counter-attacked and drove the Japanese back east past the initial point of resistance at K. B. Mission. With Hayashi dead, the wounded Yano received permission to evacuate his troops on September 6. The Milne Bay operation was the first land operation in the Pacific that was a failure for the Japanese and an early victory for the Allies.

John Virgo from Cadell in South Australia was a corporal in 2/10 Battalion, AIF and fought in North Africa before his unit was reassigned to New Guinea. He was killed on August 27 as the

Two Australian Imperial Force officers examine a Japanese Type 95 light tank captured in the fighting at Milne Bay as it sits on a rail car in October 1942. When AIF soldiers turned back the Japanese landing at Milne Bay it helped place the entire Japanese campaign against Port Moresby in jeopardy.

Australians contested and slowed the Japanese advance to Gili Gili on Milne Bay. His commanding officer, Captain G. R. Miethke, took the time to write a letter to John's parents which gave a glimpse into the battle and John's role in it.

"By now you will have received the official advice of the sad death of your son in action August 27. John was young, keen and intelligent and one of the promising NCOs in my company. On August 27 we bumped into a much stronger enemy force unfortunately supported by tanks. Your son was in the forefront of the company which stood the brunt of the attack. However, he fought magnificently, despite tanks being within five yards all round his section.

"A burst of machine gun fire killed him instantly. If it is any consolation to you, the thickest of the enemy dead were piled in front of John and his section. We exacted a toll of 10 for every man we lost. The whole company mourns his death and I feel that I have lost a personal friend. Please accept my deepest sympathy for your loss."

Things were going better for the Imperial soldiers on the overland operation, but not nearly as well as before the combat-experienced Australian troops entered the fighting. At Iurava, General Horii and his force met the first of the Australians of the 2nd AIF, the 21st Brigade, and the fighting reached a new intensity. After three days of hard combat, the Japanese were able to continue their advance toward Port Moresby. However, a new foe was introduced as the force crossed the summit of the Owen Stanley Range. The jungle, rain and most significantly, the mud heaped additional misery on the Imperial Army soldiers. Yet, they scrapped and sloshed their way down the mountains and came face to face with the Australians making a stand at Ioribaiwa, 30 miles from Port Moresby.

Reinforced by the 25th Brigade of the 2nd AIF, but still outnumbered, the Aussies battled the Japanese — sometimes in hand-to-hand combat — until they were forced on September 19 to withdraw to Imita Ridge, the last high ground above the city. Horii, however, did not pursue. At Ioribaiwa he was ordered not to advance until the other force made their thrust from Milne Bay, an advance which never came. Japanese soldiers had the opportunity to rest, rejuvenate and raid local gardens to build up their meager food supply. As the Australians watched warily from the nearby ridge, a period of relative inactivity ensued. Horii ordered his engineers to create a log

stockade for defense while he waited for supplies and air cover to make the final push. But something was seriously delaying these additions. Something happening a few hundred miles to the east in the Solomons was disrupting Japanese plans.

Throughout the months leading up to and beyond the Allied operations on Papua and in the south Solomon Islands, airmen of the USAAF and Australia's RAAF flew missions toward Rabaul and other strategic places in the region to support land operations and disrupt enemy movement and supply. They even bombed Horii's force on the Kokoda Track, although without much success. The Fifth U. S. Army Air Force continued operations started shortly after its April arrival at Charters Towers and other Australian bases. Port Moresby was the necessary refueling stop on the way to these targets until more advanced positions were secured. Vernon Main remembers the Papuan town, a place to which he has no particular desire to return.

"We started flying missions out of Charters Towers to Port Moresby, New Guinea. And we staged out of Three-Mile airstrip [Port Moresby] for six months or more, flying back and forth because the Japanese held Lae, they held Buna, they held the whole north side of the island and they were over Three-Mile strip every day at the crack of dawn.

"They just shoot up the runways, and shot up the place, and killed a lot of people who got caught on top of the ground. So, we had to go in there before daylight, fly our missions, and get outta there, come back there late in the afternoon and hope that we could land because they dropped bombs on the runway and made big holes, but then we'd go back to Australia every day we could. We never left the airplanes on the ground in Port Moresby very long — in February, March,

April, May, June of '42 because the Japs controlled the air. Anti-aircraft crews carried one or two guns around Moresby at the time. It got better as the war went on, but in the beginning, boy it was bare knuckles."

Rear Adm. Richmond K. Turner (foreground) plans the invasion of the Solomons with Maj. Gen. Alexander A. Vandegrift. Turner took the unusual step of flying his flag on a transport ship, USS McCawley.

Moment of Truth – Guadalcanal Invaded

While MacArthur was managing ground, air and sea forces in the South West Pacific Area, other American commanders were beginning the long campaign of island-hopping that defined much of the Pacific war. As Gen-

eral Vandegrift loaded his 1st Division leathernecks for the trip to Guadalcanal and Tulagi, the navy was positioning ships for their role in the invasion called Operation Watchtower. But as the mission developed, not all of Vandegrift's problems were caused by those taking their orders from Tokyo. He also had to deal with a cast of characters with stars on their shoulder boards in a cumbersome navy chain of command.

Admiral Nimitz was in overall area command in his Pearl Harbor headquarters, but with Vice Admiral "Bull" Halsey still recovering from the debilitations that kept him from the battle at Mid-

U.S. Marine Landing on Guadalcanal & Tulagi
Savo Island
Tulagi Island
Tanambogo & Gavutu Islands
Florida Island
Route of U.S. Marines Landings
Cape Esperance
Aug. 7
Aug. 7
Airfield under construction
Landing Zone Beach Red
Lunga Point
Taivu Point
Lunga River
Tenaru River
GUADALCANAL ISLAND
Mt POPOMANASU

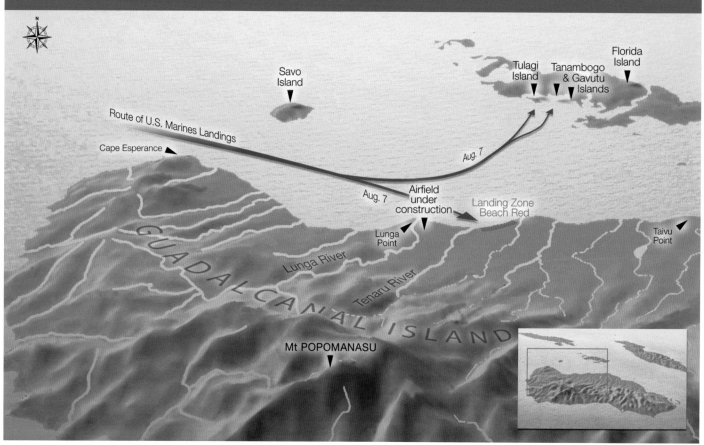

The landing of the 1st Marine Division and other USMC units on the lower Solomons island of Guadalcanal (large island in the inset map) and the small islands leeward of Florida Island (upper right) represented a major step forward in reversing earlier gains by Japan. After separating from the carrier force, Rear Adm. Richmond Kelly Turner's transport force split in Sealark Channel to land the Marines at Beach Red on lightly defended Guadalcanal and the more contested Tulagi and Gavutu & Tanambogo Islets.

way (Halsey suffered intermittently from dermatitis which caused a severe rash, painful itching and necessitated hospitalization), the naval command in the region cascaded through seven admirals. Vice Admiral Robert L. Ghormley commanded what was designated the South Pacific Theater — which kept the Solomon invasion in the navy's control and away from MacArthur — and Rear Admiral Frank Jack Fletcher, the "blackshoe" (a surface ship officer, as opposed to "brownshoe", a moniker for naval aviators based on their footgear) skipper who fought at Coral Sea and Midway, was the expedition commander flying his flag on *Saratoga*. Fletcher had these rear admirals immediately under him; Leigh Noyes commanded the Air Support Force (carriers and escorts) and the carrier *Wasp* and Thomas Kincaid commanded *Enterprise*.

Ghormley placed Rear Admiral John S. McCain in charge of all land-based planes and seaplanes in the region, part of a cumbersome

U. S. Marines charge ashore from a Higgins boat during the invasion of Guadalcanal.

command arrangement that would impact the expedition. Having already lost two carriers in the Pacific, Fletcher was guarding his flattops like a mother hen watching over her chicks. Fletcher's nervous concern would impact the campaign in its first days. Also under Fletcher was Rear Admiral Richmond Kelly Turner, in command of the amphibious force of transports and escorts. Turner was an experienced seaman and air officer whose bushy black eyebrows accented an animated face. Rear Admiral Victor A. C. Crutchley, Royal Navy, lent by Britain to their Commonwealth partner, came with the Australian ships in the force, and Rear Admiral Norman Scott commanded squadrons under Turner. General Vandegrift was subordinate to Turner until his Marines landed and therefore received orders from Fletcher and Ghormley through him.

With an impressive armada of carriers, cruisers and destroyers, the navy transports made their way from New Zealand toward the Solomon Islands. The sailing direction was designed to give the enemy the false impression that this was a convoy headed for Australia. Dillon Gaulding recalls the scene:

"We had carriers and maybe ten to fifteen heavy and light cruisers and twenty to forty destroyers with us. On the way there, it's kind of interesting; Vandegrift decided he'd do some practice landings at the Fiji Islands. The day we were going to do it we didn't have LSTs [Landing Ship-Tank], the slower ones for tanks which were much more effective in making landings later, all

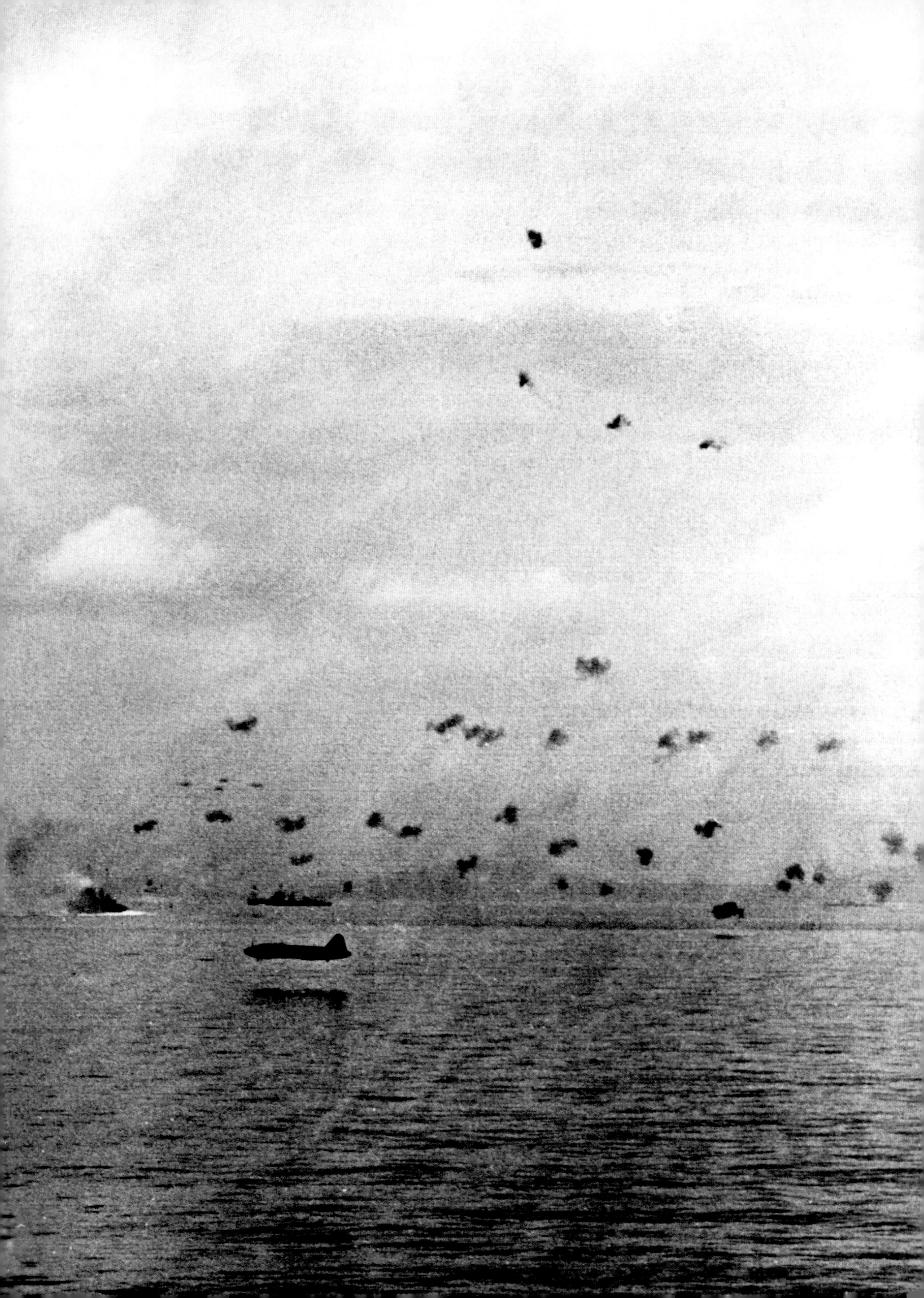

Four Japanese bombers fly low over the waters off Guadalcanal on August 7, 1942. They brave a gauntlet of anti-aircraft fire to target U. S. transports unloading Marines and supplies.

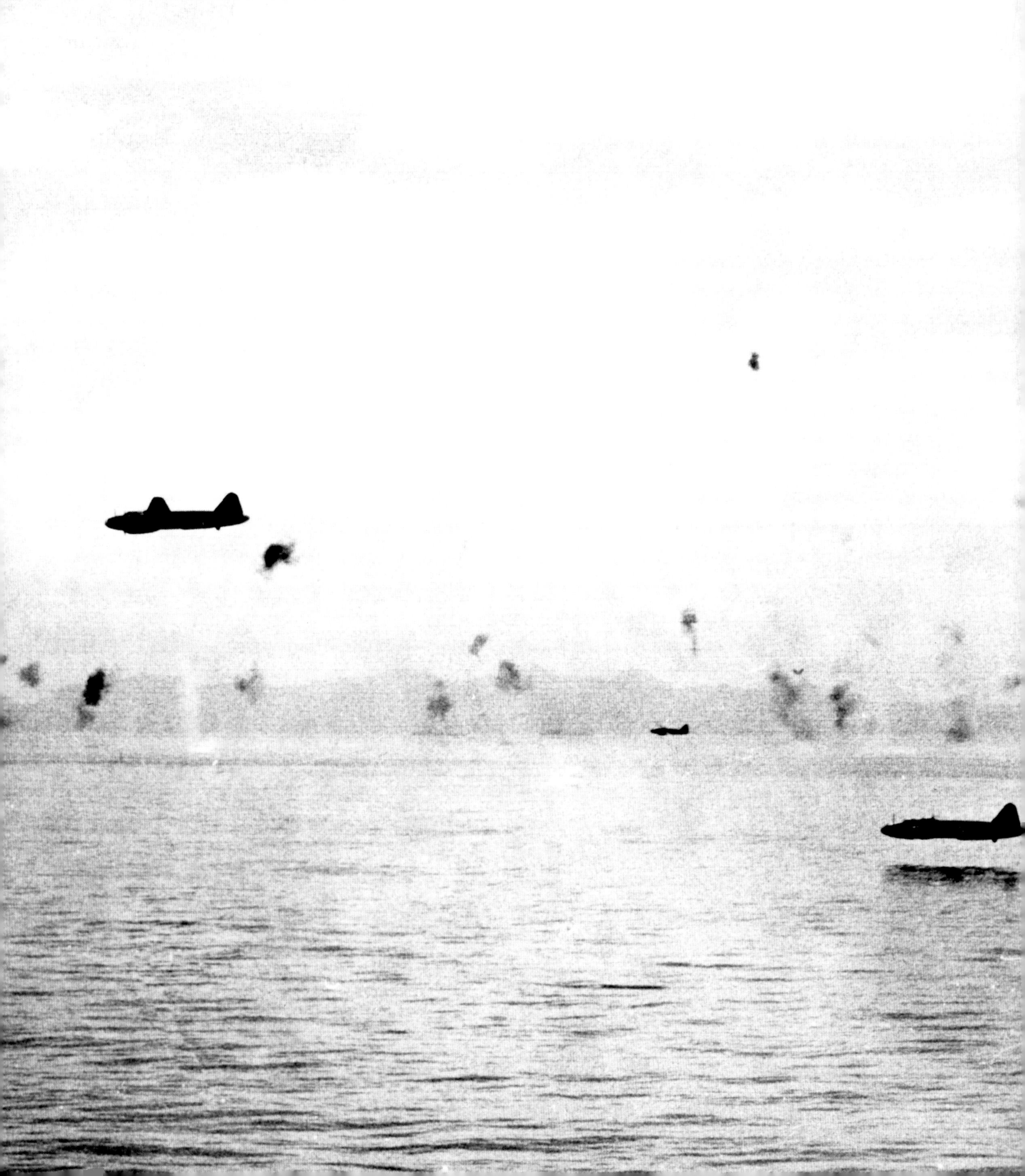

we had were Higgins boats which were about thirty feet long. You got your troops in there and maybe trucks or whatever and you go ashore that way. When we started putting the Higgins boats over in the water at Fiji, the weather got pretty bad so he [Vandegrift] decided not to practice and we put everything back on board and sailed out. Something interesting they told us — it shows how far the primitive world was removed — they said there were still head hunters and cannibals on the Fiji Islands but look what they are today."

The short landing drills at Koro, Fiji were termed by the 1st Marine Division commander as "a complete bust." It didn't matter. The Marines were going in and they would make the best of it. Beginning on August 5, the ships set a heading due north. Cloud cover obscured the largest naval force yet assembled by the U. S. for an amphibious invasion from the prying eyes of Japanese air reconnaissance. The convoy split southwest of Guadalcanal; the carrier force remaining in open waters southwest of the big island while Turner's ships approached from the west. Part of Turner's command, those transports in Group Yoke, maneuvered north around Savo Island toward Florida and Tulagi islands where they would land Marines to overrun the Japanese headquarters, while Group X-ray took the southern channel toward their assignment, landings on Guadalcanal. The channel between Guadalcanal and Florida Island was called

TOP: *This 40mm gun emplacement on Guadalcanal attests to the importance the Marines placed on defending against Japanese aerial attacks. RIGHT: The American flag is raised on Guadalcanal Island in August 1942. The first land campaign to retake the Pacific islands from the Japanese was underway.*

Sealark Channel by the British who, until recently, ruled the area. The western portion of Sealark Channel opened into an ominous bay that would soon take on a telling moniker, Ironbottom Sound.

Early on August 7, 1942, the Marines transferred from navy transports to Landing Craft - Vehicles and Personnel (LCVP) – the Higgins boats — without incident. F-4-F Wildcat fighters from *Wasp* pounded the seaplane base on Tulagi. The main force headed for Guadalcanal and a landing on Beach Red west of Lunga Point with their objective the nearby airfield under construction. These Marines were not fired upon while landing, bolstering their rookie confidence.

Clay Albright, the six-month recruit from Birmingham, Alabama, was assigned to the 1st Pioneer Battalion and went ashore on Guadalcanal on the first day of the invasion. The battalion was responsible for unloading and stowing all of the supplies that came ashore.

"Before the Solomons the Japanese had whipped us in every [land] battle. They thought they couldn't be beaten, and they were halfway right at some spots. Anyhow we were in what looked like a Hollywood scene, dozens and dozens of ships of all kinds lying off the island of Guadalcanal. We went in on August the 7th of '42. I was on the boat; most of our crew were going in about 10 o'clock. In the meantime we set out there in

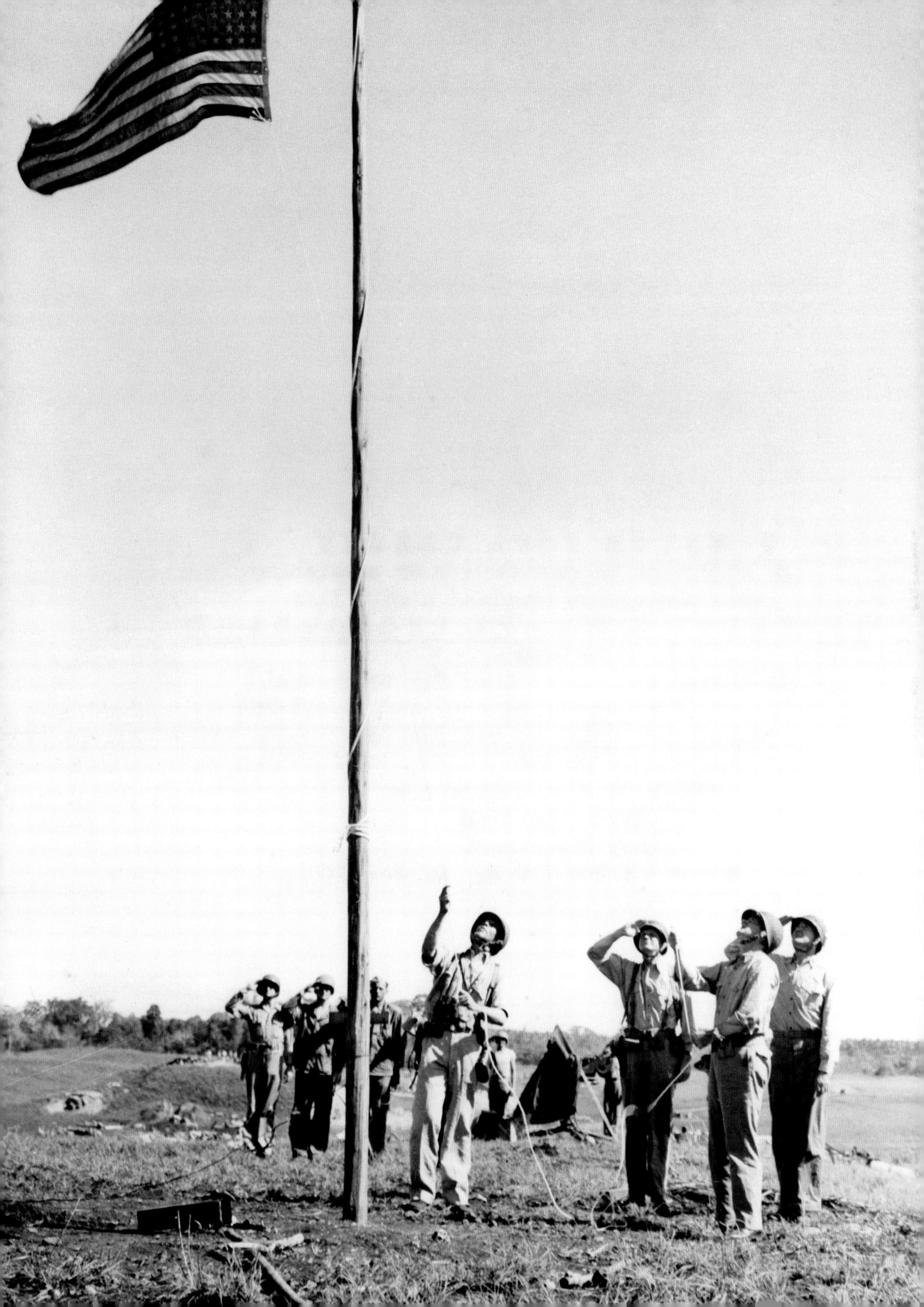

the harbor getting all the supplies ready. We didn't have [landing craft] like we had later on in many places. We didn't have the Japs — who saw our ships and they were scared to death and they ran for the hills. We went in and didn't have much resistance. Our objective was to get the airport and hold — that's what we wanted because the Japs were too close to Australia. We were there until sometime in December."

In the first 48 hours of the Guadalcanal campaign Marines unloaded supplies from Higgins boats and other small craft that navy coxswains shuttled back and forth from the large transports. Despite the rapid pace of the deliveries, many of the 1st Division's supplies never reached shore before the transports pulled out on August 9.

him everything he would need to know to fight in the jungles of the South Pacific. He landed on Guadalcanal on the first day as a member of the 3rd Battalion, 11th Marine Regiment, the 1st Division's artillery.

Herb Allebaugh was a seventeen-year-old kid when he joined the Marine Corps just before the Pearl Harbor attack. His training at Parris Island and New River (now Camp Lejeune) taught him to be a Marine, but didn't necessarily teach

"We left the 22nd of July for Guadalcanal, we had no idea where we was going and we had no idea about Guadalcanal, we had never heard of it before. It was the night before that they told us where we were going. That's when we got out our clean bayonets and we made sure our ammo belts were full and our rifles were clean and everything. We got up bright and early in the morning and had what we call a battle breakfast. We always had steak and eggs before goin' in. Then we started hearing the warships — destroyers and cruisers — bombard the place. When it got daylight the planes started coming over. We were told we'd only be there a week or two weeks then General MacArthur would have his troops in there to relieve us. We found out later that was a fairy tale. We had about seven or eight days of C rations in our pack. On the 7th, we went in there. There was a bunch of poor-ass kids to put it bluntly and we were all pretty well scared. Tryin' not to get in there with wet and dirty pants, I'm not ashamed to say that one bit. Of course, everybody was trigger happy and that night we got firin' at the damn moon, because tracer bullets were flying all over, everything we thought was a tracer.

"It was about the third night there we had what they called the Condition Red on the Canal, you expected an invasion. At that time we had taken the airport and we were lined up along the beaches, and it was pouring. We have rain here in Florida but it's nothing like we had over there. I was able to find one of the trucks and I was underneath the truck with another fellow from Miami and we were just watching; waitin' for what was gonna happen. All of a sudden I saw this boat out there floundering around and yelled to whoever would listen to me, 'There's something out there.' It so happened some guy came over, he stumbled over me and like a durn kid I went up on him and spoke to him in some kind of foul language that I wouldn't use today and I found out he was my colonel, [Lieutenant Colonel James J.] Keating.

"Thank God he was the man that he was and he realized we were just scared kids and he forgave us. He said, 'Can you still see him?' I said yes. And he said, 'Do you have a tracer?' I said yes. He said 'Put it in and fire at him.' I fired the tracer — it was one of our own LCVPs, landing boats, which we didn't know at the time and he gave the order for everybody to fire on him. So we sank him. One of the guys come ashore and we found out it was one our own navy boats.

And he said the guy with him must of got shot because he couldn't find him in the water. Not until the next day, we found him about a mile up the beach and he said that the other guy was dead. [Both LVCP crewmen survived] It's just one of those things you don't know what's going on, your left hand doesn't know what your right hand's doing."

Jay Baker was an officer who commanded a platoon in Company I, 3rd Battalion of the 5th Marine Regiment during the initial landing. The 3rd Battalion was part of Combat Group B, which landed at Beach Red, east of Alligator Creek, with the 1st Regiment.

"I was growing up in Worcester Massachusetts and I knew that something was going to be happening as far as the war was concerned. We were having problems in Europe and then all of sudden the Japs showed up, and so there were problems for us in the South Pacific. I had always wanted to be in the Marine Corps so I joined up. Because of my background I got to serve as an officer. I went through basic school in Quantico, Virginia, and became a second lieutenant and all of a sudden found myself on Guadalcanal at the beginning of the battles of the Solomon Islands."

Baker would soon find himself locked in the struggle for the ridge line inland from Henderson Field, where many of his comrades lost their lives. Meanwhile, Dillon Gaulding was landing with his Recon company.

"We went to the island of Guadalcanal where I landed. We had very little resistance in Guadalcanal—there were very few Japanese troops there but about 450 construction workers. About all they had done was clear the place for the airfield they were building. But on the islands across the sound, Tulagi, Florida, and Gavutu, they met very

A Marine operates an anti-aircraft machine gun emplacement from a sandbag-lined foxhole. The large side magazine kept the gun filled with lead.

strong resistance — they were part of the 2nd [Regiment]. We did not take the 7th Regiment with us because they had sent them to Samoa earlier to defend [it] and they took a lot of our best people out of the division when they went to Samoa. We took the 2nd Regiment out of the 2nd Marine Division [which was based at Camp Elliot, near San Diego] to go with us to replace them. Some of the 2nd Marines were over there on Tulagi [and Florida Island] but it was mostly paratroopers and the raider battalions."

Besides infantrymen, artillerymen and later, Seabees, the Marines landed trained personnel of all types to handle the complex occupation of the large hostile island and establishment of a well-sited airfield. Louis J. Bacher was a telephone wireman attached to 1st Regiment headquarters.

"I was a corporal when we landed on Guadalcanal. I was with the regimental headquarters. Actually, during the landing there, I landed on the Guadalcanal side and there wasn't any problem there. Except my job was to lay wire from the beach on in to the regimental area and the wire didn't get laid very well because the amtraks and, I think we had a couple of halftracks, chewed it up. But anyhow, the communication wasn't that good. We did have radios and that was before my experience with radios, so I was strictly a wire-

A machine gunner wades through a jungle stream ahead of fellow leathernecks. It was a familiar scene in the war in the Solomon Islands.

man at that time. We got strafed a couple of times with Japanese airplanes the first day and the second day. And we got a heck of a lot of shelling from everything from a submarine to battleships. I think they had a 5-inch [4.7-inch] or smaller gun on the sub. There was a destroyer type thing that would just plop them in every once in a while. He was far enough out there so nobody could get him with anything. You may have had some mention of a guy, I can't even think of his name now, but he was a mortar man [Lou Diamond, a China Marine and World War I vet]. He tried to hit a ship with a mortar, but it was too far out. Some claim that he hit it and all that, but I don't think he did."

The nervous quiet that permeated Guadalcanal on the first day of the invasion masked a variety of emotions in the Marines on the beaches. Concern for their comrades fighting and dying across Sealark Channel was one of them. The elements of the 2nd Marines, 2nd Battalion of the 5th Marine Regiment, 1st Raider and 1st Parachute battalions that landed on the island of Tulagi, the Japanese headquarters and the two islets held together by a spit of land, Gavutu and Tanambogo, found the defenders ensconced in caves and fortifications and ready to "defend to the last man," according to an official communication.

As patrols from the 1st Regiment ventured

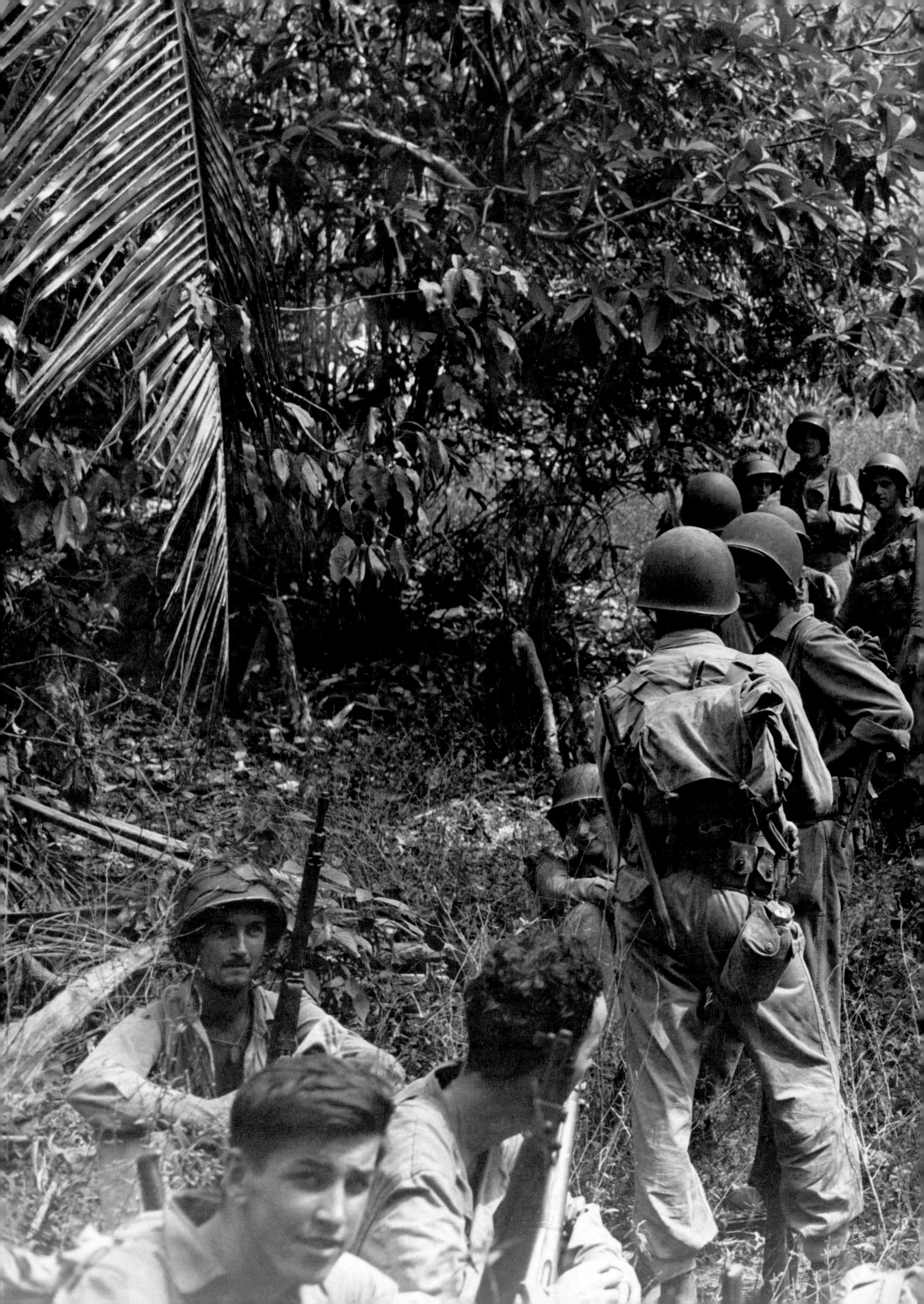

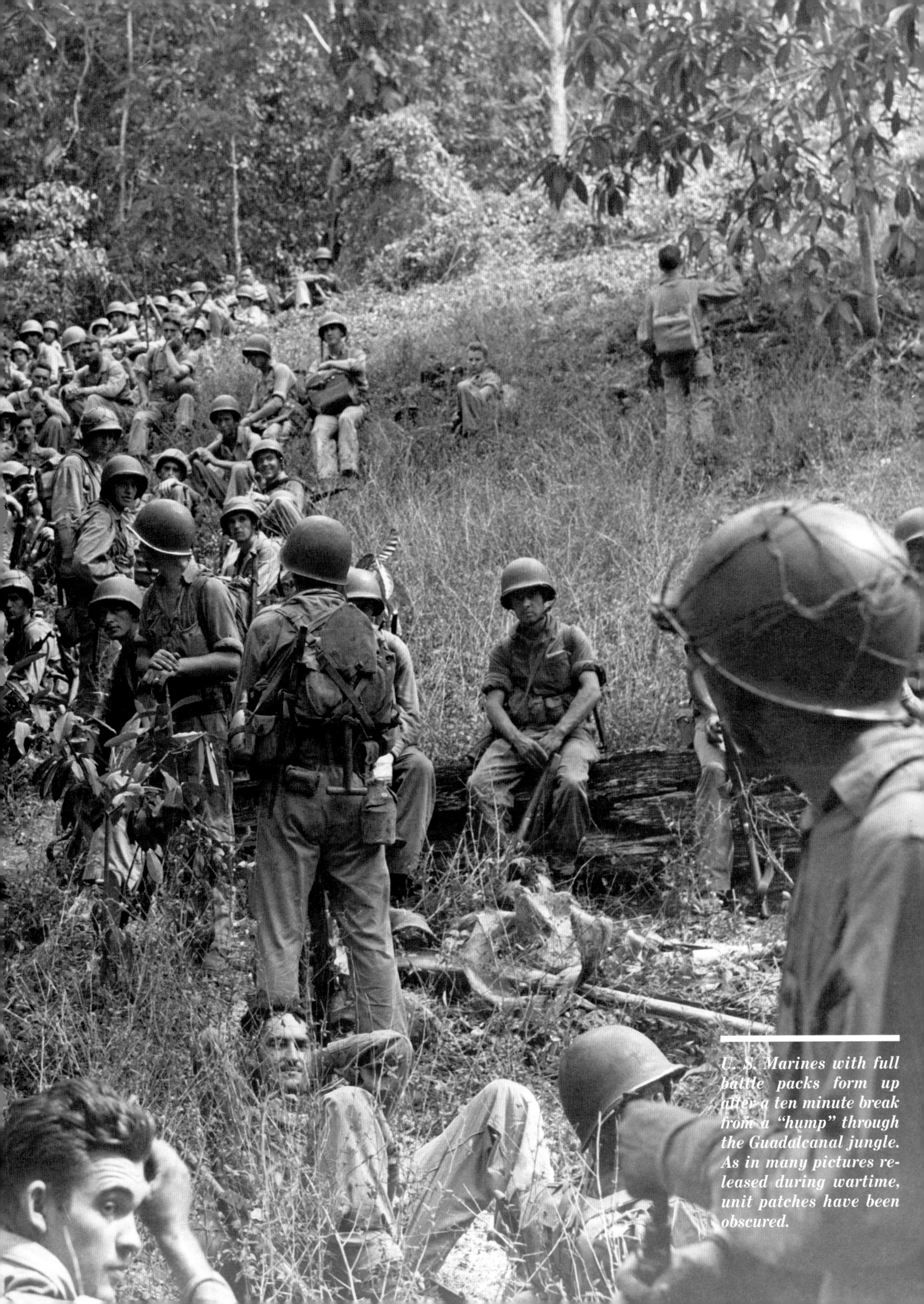

U. S. Marines with full battle packs form up after a ten minute break from a "hump" through the Guadalcanal jungle. As in many pictures released during wartime, unit patches have been obscured.

Japanese prisoners pose for the camera after being rounded up on Guadalcanal. Some may have been Koreans, pressed into slave-like service working on airfield construction.

cautiously inland, surprise might have been the emotional reaction as these men encountered a dense, dark, mosquito-infested jungle. Most of them had never seen or been trained for anything like it. There was probably also much frustration. The race to unload supplies delivered by impatient navy coxswains in a traffic jam of landing craft produced a jumbled mass of materials on the beach. The mess overwhelmed the 1st Pioneer Battalion and those assisting them and allowed Japanese bombers that came over in the afternoon of August 7 to turn apples into apple-sauce and create other more serious losses. The naval part of the Guadalcanal operation smacked of high anxiety. Within thirty-six hours the anxiety would be rewarded with a spectacular surprise encounter with a Japanese task force, and a stunning defeat.

The Battle of Savo Island

As soon as the alarm came in from Tulagi the Japanese high command sprung into action. Admiral Yamamoto, still in firm command of the ships and planes in the far-flung outposts of the Pacific, ordered immediate and decisive action at Guadalcanal. The commanders in the area were happy to oblige. At Rabaul, the facility was overloaded with bombers and fighters for a planned mission to bomb the new Allied airfield at Milne Bay. The commander of the 25th Air Flotilla, Rear Admiral Sadayoshi Yamada, immediately dispatched "Betty" two-engine bombers and long-range "Zeke" Zero fighters to oppose the American landing in the lower Solomons, 565 miles away.

Even though a coast watcher gave warning of the Japanese air force approaching Guadalcanal, the Americans' Wildcat interceptor aircraft were not deftly handled by Noyes and his officers. Both sides lost planes in the afternoon raid on August 7 that destroyed much of the Marines' supplies. The navy flyers finally gained the edge on August 8. However, with the end of air operations on the second day, Admiral Fletcher made the decision to withdraw the carriers from the area, citing as his reasons evidence of Japanese torpedo bombers, a loss of fighters in the first two days and fuel considerations. Though he had previously warned Admiral Turner and General Vandegrift that he would only allow the carriers to operate in the Solomons for four days, the abandonment of air cover for the transports, still unloading men and materials, was a serious setback for the campaign.

It was inevitable that the Imperial Navy would respond to the invasions with everything it had. The IJN was not going to allow the defensive perimeter Japan had established to be broken without an all-out fight. The right man for the job, the aggressive Vice Admiral Gunichi Mikawa sat in command of the Eighth Fleet at Rabaul. Seeing that air attacks alone would not dislodge the Solomons landings, he quickly assembled a surface flotilla to sail southeast through a channel in the Solomons from Bougainville to Guadalcanal that American seamen would name "the Slot." Mikawa had five heavy cruisers, two light cruisers and a destroyer in his task force. At 1628 on August 7, the force got underway, Mikawa commanding from his flagship, the heavy cruiser *Chokai*.

There was no doubt in the minds of the U. S. Navy brass that the Japanese would use all means available to dislodge the Guadalcanal landings, and that included submarines and surface ships. Even before the first Marines got ashore, Admiral McCain had set up a network of seaplane tenders capable of servicing a number of PBYs for reconnaissance. Among the most reliable navy scout aircraft were a pair of seaplanes: the two-engine PBY Model 1 and 5 Catalina; and the four-engine PBY2 Coronado. These planes also served as bombers, haulers, ambulances and rescue aircraft. Before long the navy introduced a PBY version of the B-24 bomber, which is described by aviation mechanics mate Gordon Jones, who stayed in the Pacific Theater after surviving the Japanese attack on Kaneohe Bay, Hawaii.

"PBY 4-1's they called them, big old bomber. The Y stood for Consolidated, they were made by Consolidated [Aircraft Corporation] right here in San Diego. We had two squadrons down there. Then I went up to Guadalcanal and for many months was on Guadalcanal. Of course the Japanese came down and bombed us once in a while and that was kind of hairy. One funny thing, we had the plane and the officer in charge of the plane, he was a senior pilot, and he had authority to do some things. He had the authority to put what we called nose art, a drawing or something on the side of the plane. And of course at that time they had half naked girls and stuff, and he had one also on our plane. But anyway, he heard that Eleanor Roosevelt was coming up to our base. They got the painters out and put sweaters on those girls."

McCain's plan called for fan-shaped reconnaissance flights to the northwest. Fletcher and Turner asked for additional reconnaissance runs. In addition, Australian Hudson scouting planes and B-17 bombers from MacArthur's South West Pacific Area command also scanned the skies. With all these planes in the air, one would think it would have been hard to miss Mikawa's ships, but that's what happened. Ironically, the first concrete evidence of the Japanese ships came from those not looking for them; brief mentions from B-17 bombers on their way to other targets and the U. S. submarine *S-38* that reported destroyers and cruisers passing over it at high speed. Poor decision making by commanders and pilots in the air rendered the information gathering useless. The shifting cloud cover of the Solomons also spoiled the opportunity for a truly early warning of the Japanese column of ships. One patrol plane missed the opportunity to spot the ships on August 7 by sixty miles.

Late on the night of August 8, word finally reached Admiral Turner from Australia that Japanese ships were on the move. As a means of guarding against any surface ship or submarine attack, Turner had divided his escort ships, eight cruisers and eight destroyers, into three sector watches; Northern and Southern Forces guarding the passages on either side of Savo Island, and the Eastern Force, sealing off the eastern entrance to Sealark Channel. The transports continued to work through the night. At 2032 hours Turner summoned Admiral Crutchley and General Vandegrift to his flagship, the transport *McCawley*, for a conference. Crutchley took his flagship *Australia* out of line to steam to Lunga Point where *McCawley* was. He placed the Southern Force under the command of Captain Howard D. Bodie of *Chicago*.

Vandegrift, away from his command post when the call came, arrived at the meeting 45 minutes after Crutchley. When both officers were present, Turner expressed his concern about the situation. With the departure of the carriers no air cover was available and Turner interpreted the belated information received about the Japanese surface force — that it included two seaplane tenders — to mean the Japanese were planning to return with bombers in the morning. Due to the fighting on Tulagi, the disposition of supplies there was way behind schedule. Turner hoped that Vandegrift's Marines would complete the job overnight so all transports could leave early on August 9. Turner got the Marine general's word that they would try. To Crutchley's concern about a possible surface attack, Turner expressed confidence that preparations were adequate.

The reality was something less than adequate. A rain squall added to the darkness of the night and Mikawa's column passed by two picket destroyers set out from the rest of the Allied ships on either side of Savo Island. These destroyers had SC radar which did not pick up the approaching Japanese task force. Meanwhile, Captain Bodie did not place *Chicago* at the head of the column as would be normal procedure for the command ship. He turned in thinking Crutchley would return *Australia* to its position shortly. The British admiral did not and *Australia* was far off when at 0143 on August 9, Japanese float planes dropped flares over the transports and the battle was on.

Surprised and overwhelmed in the dark and rain, cruisers *Canberra* and *Chicago* took a terrible beating as the Japan-

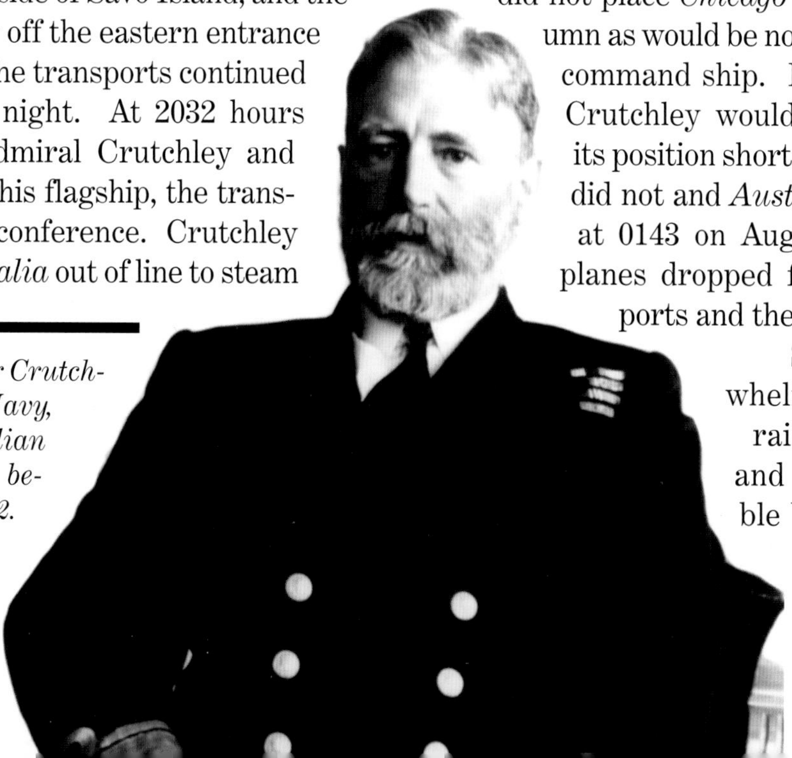

Rear Admiral Sir Victor Crutchley, VC DSC Royal Navy, commanded the Australian Squadron for two years beginning on June 13, 1942.

USS Chicago *fires torpedoes during a drill. She would be on the receiving end of surface ship torpedoes in the Battle of Savo Island.*

ese column entered the sound from south of Savo Island and engaged these ships first. The two cruisers fired wildly and with scant effect on their foe while their escort destroyers had little success in the fight. The Japanese column then made a course correction to the northeast and went after the Northern Force with equal ferocity. Although the destroyer *Patterson* had sent out a radio warning at 0143, communications and command decisions were in a state of confusion and the ships in the Northern Force were caught off guard. USS *Quincy* was caught in a crossfire as Mikawa's column broke up, and the other two cruisers in the Northern Force were hard hit as well.

The captains of the transports reacted to the appearance of parachute flares and distant gun flashes by stopping the unloading process and getting underway. With poor visibility and inadequate radio communication, Turner could do little but watch and wait. By 0230, having crushed the two columns of Allied ships patrolling near Savo Island, Mikawa led his ships back out to the open sea. He would return up "the Slot" without completing his primary assignment from Ya-

The Battle of Savo Island and Ichiki Offensive

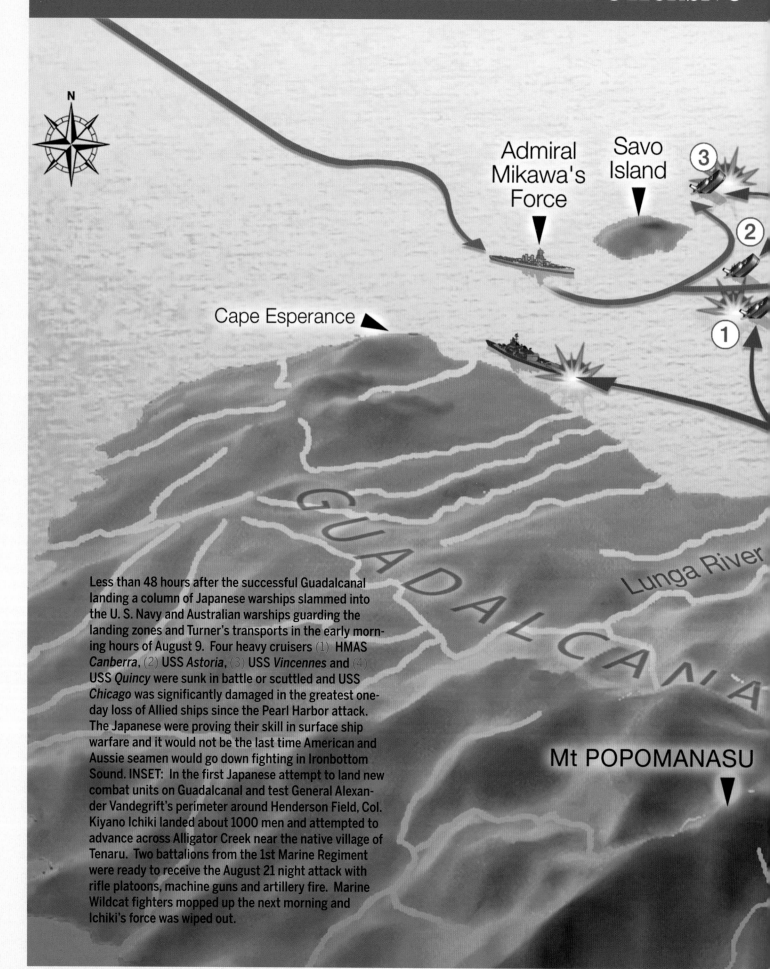

Admiral Mikawa's Force

Savo Island

Cape Esperance

Lunga River

GUADALCANAL

Mt POPOMANASU

Less than 48 hours after the successful Guadalcanal landing a column of Japanese warships slammed into the U. S. Navy and Australian warships guarding the landing zones and Turner's transports in the early morning hours of August 9. Four heavy cruisers (1) HMAS *Canberra*, (2) USS *Astoria*, (3) USS *Vincennes* and (4) USS *Quincy* were sunk in battle or scuttled and USS *Chicago* was significantly damaged in the greatest one-day loss of Allied ships since the Pearl Harbor attack. The Japanese were proving their skill in surface ship warfare and it would not be the last time American and Aussie seamen would go down fighting in Ironbottom Sound. INSET: In the first Japanese attempt to land new combat units on Guadalcanal and test General Alexander Vandegrift's perimeter around Henderson Field, Col. Kiyano Ichiki landed about 1000 men and attempted to advance across Alligator Creek near the native village of Tenaru. Two battalions from the 1st Marine Regiment were ready to receive the August 21 night attack with rifle platoons, machine guns and artillery fire. Marine Wildcat fighters mopped up the next morning and Ichiki's force was wiped out.

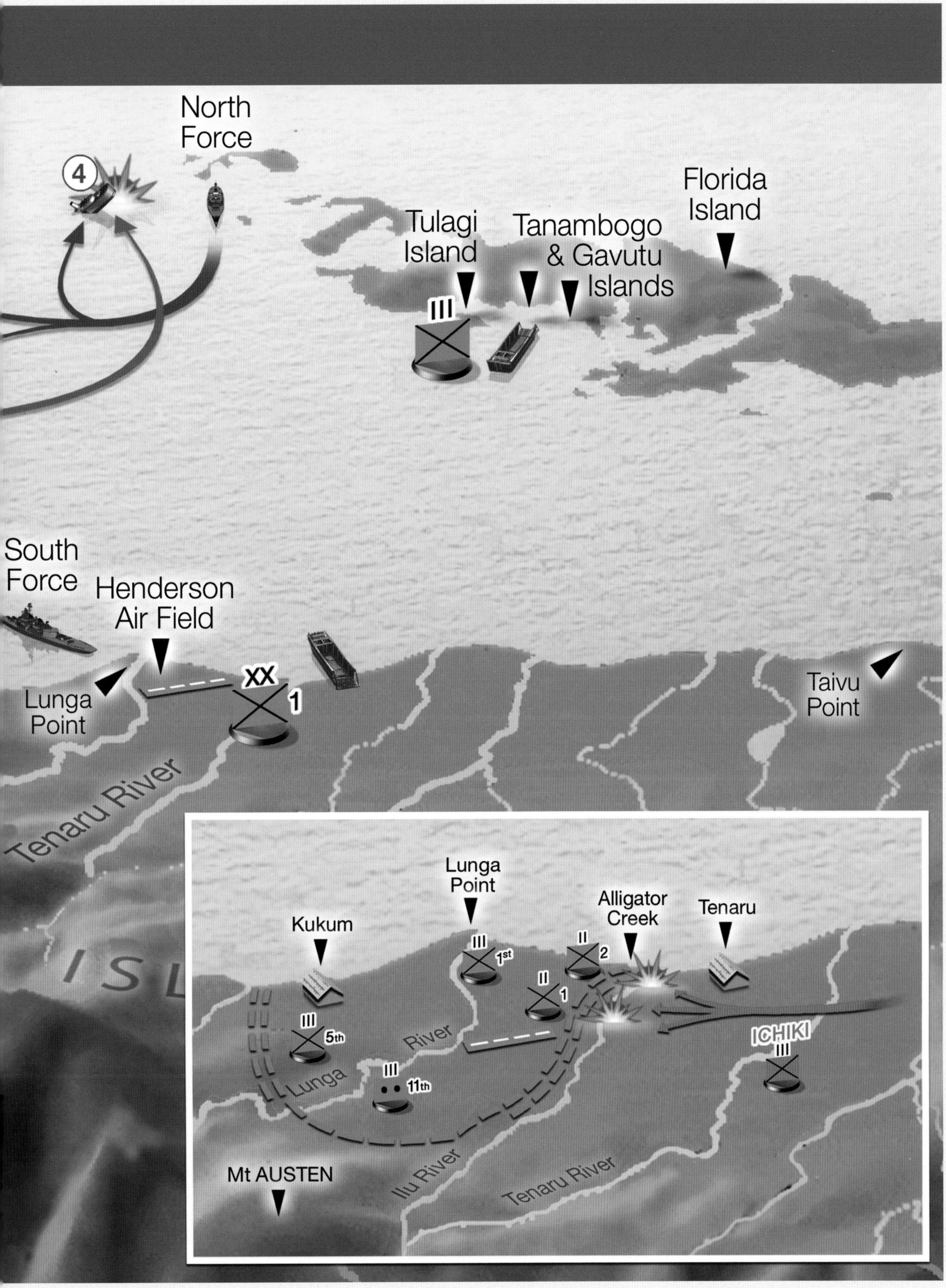
North Force
4
Florida Island
Tulagi Island
Tanambogo & Gavutu Islands
III
South Force
Henderson Air Field
Lunga Point
XX
1
Taivu Point
Tenaru River
ISL
Lunga Point
Alligator Creek
Tenaru
Kukum
III
1st
II
2
II
1
III
5th
River
Lunga
III
11th
ICHIKI
III
Mt AUSTEN
Ilu River
Tenaru River

mamoto, the destruction of the transports, but he left Turner's amphibious escort force in shambles.

Clay Albright remembers his impressions of the Battle of Savo Island from his location on shore. In the salvage operation after the battle he also learned a little about the military maxim, "never volunteer."

"I don't know how far we were from it but we saw the battle at night and found out later that we got beat, that's what the scuttlebutt was. It was a wonderful sight with ships exploding way over the horizon, we thought they were all winners for us but found out it wasn't. Nothing happened to me but I had a buddy that volunteered to stuff I didn't agree with, he liked to got us killed but that's another story. I don't remember what kind of ship it was but anyhow it was floating going out from shore and they wanted volunteers to keep the Japs from getting on the ship. My buddy volunteered he and I and we got ready to go about 10 o'clock that night and found out that ship sank, so we were still ashore. That was just one little incident; it wasn't fun."

Even though Admiral Fletcher was long gone (he audaciously wired Turner, handing over the expedition command to him), the exhausted skipper decided not to pull out just yet. He would allow the transports to continue unloading through the day of Au-gust 9. Several attempts were made to salvage the wounded cruisers, and jumpy gun commanders on the destroyers working on *Canberra* and *Astoria* fired salvos at friendly ships on more than one occasion. By the end of the day all remaining transports and surface warships were gone and the Marines were "marooned" on Guadalcanal.

The staggering loss in the Battle of Savo Island was another wake-up call for the U. S. Navy. Cruisers USS *Vincennes* and *Quincy* sunk during the battle. The loss of the venerable HMAS *Canberra* was a sad day in the history of Australia. It was intentionally sunk on August 9 while *Astoria*, another storied cruiser, met the same fate. The destroyer *Jarvis*, damaged in the air attacks, was pounced on by Japanese torpedo bombers on the way back to Sydney for repairs. All aboard were lost. *Chicago* and some of the destroyers were damaged. American and Australian servicemen killed in the action totaled 1077 (not counting the crew of *Jarvis*) and 700 wounded. Add to the total dead one navy captain, Howard D. Bodie, who took his own life after the investigation panel looking into the defeat questioned him in the United States months later. Perhaps Admiral Nimitz expressed best the epitaph of the Allied defeat at Savo Island in characterizing what he believed to be the causes of the disaster, concluding with the "probability that our Force was not psychologically prepared for action."

TOP: USS McCawley *as seen in February 1941 during Caribbean landing exercises. Admiral Turner met here on his flagship with Admiral Crutchley and General Vandegrift as Japanese ships crept toward his task force late on the night of August 8. RIGHT: The transport USS* George F. Elliot *was severely damaged by Japanese bombers on August 7 off Guadalcanal and continued to burn throughout the day and night of August 8. It became a beacon for attacking Japanese ships to locate American transports after rounding Savo Island.*

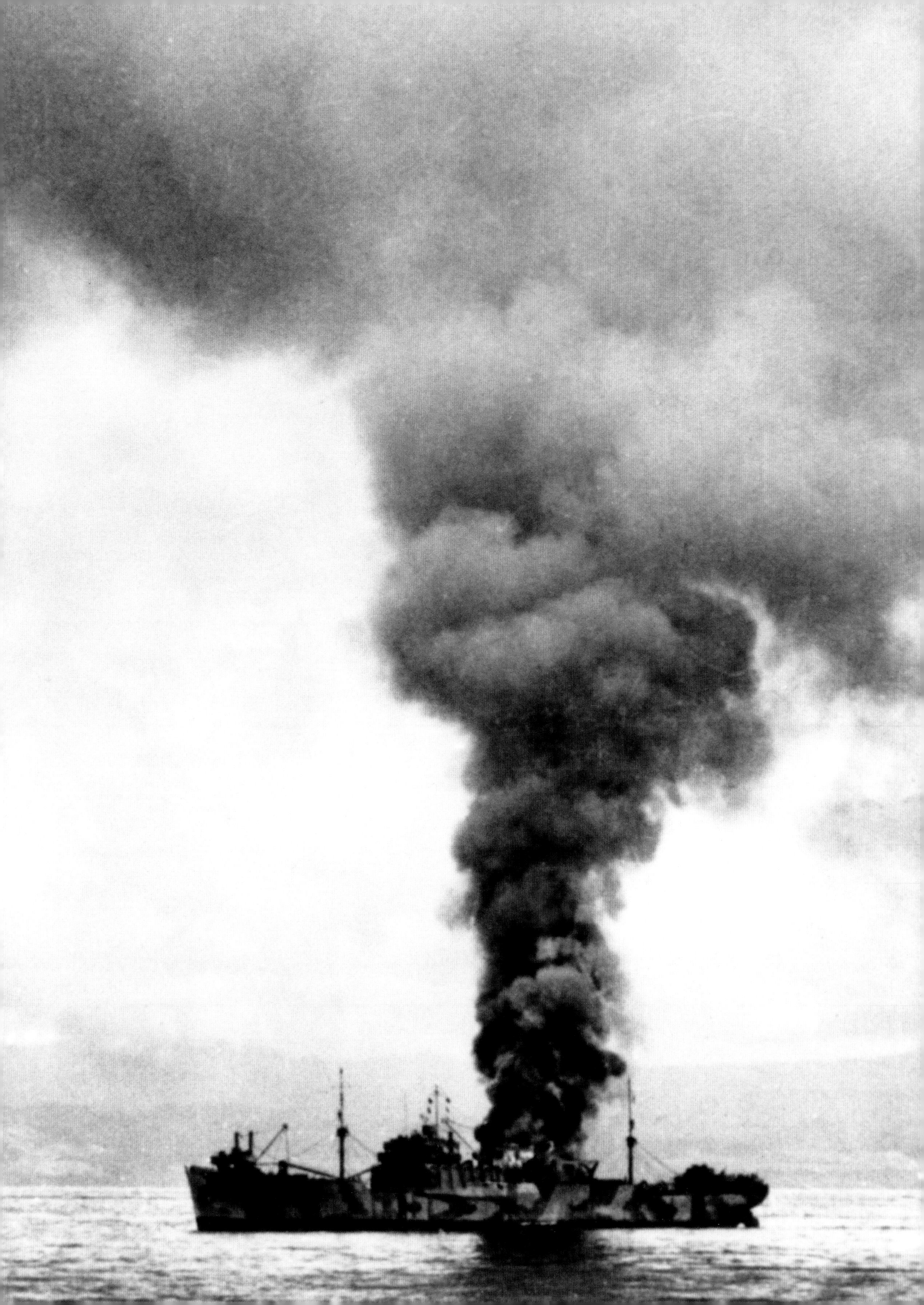

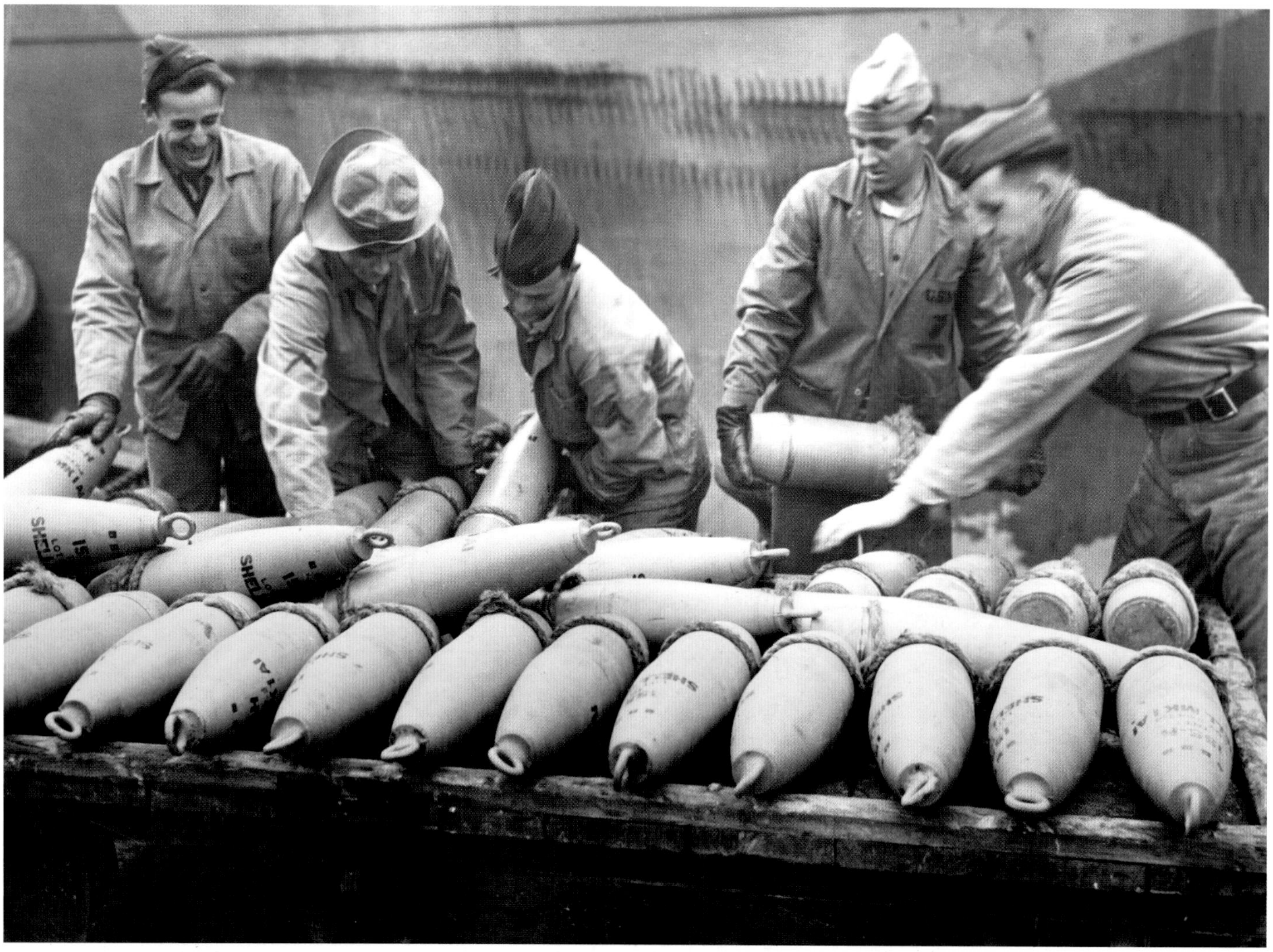

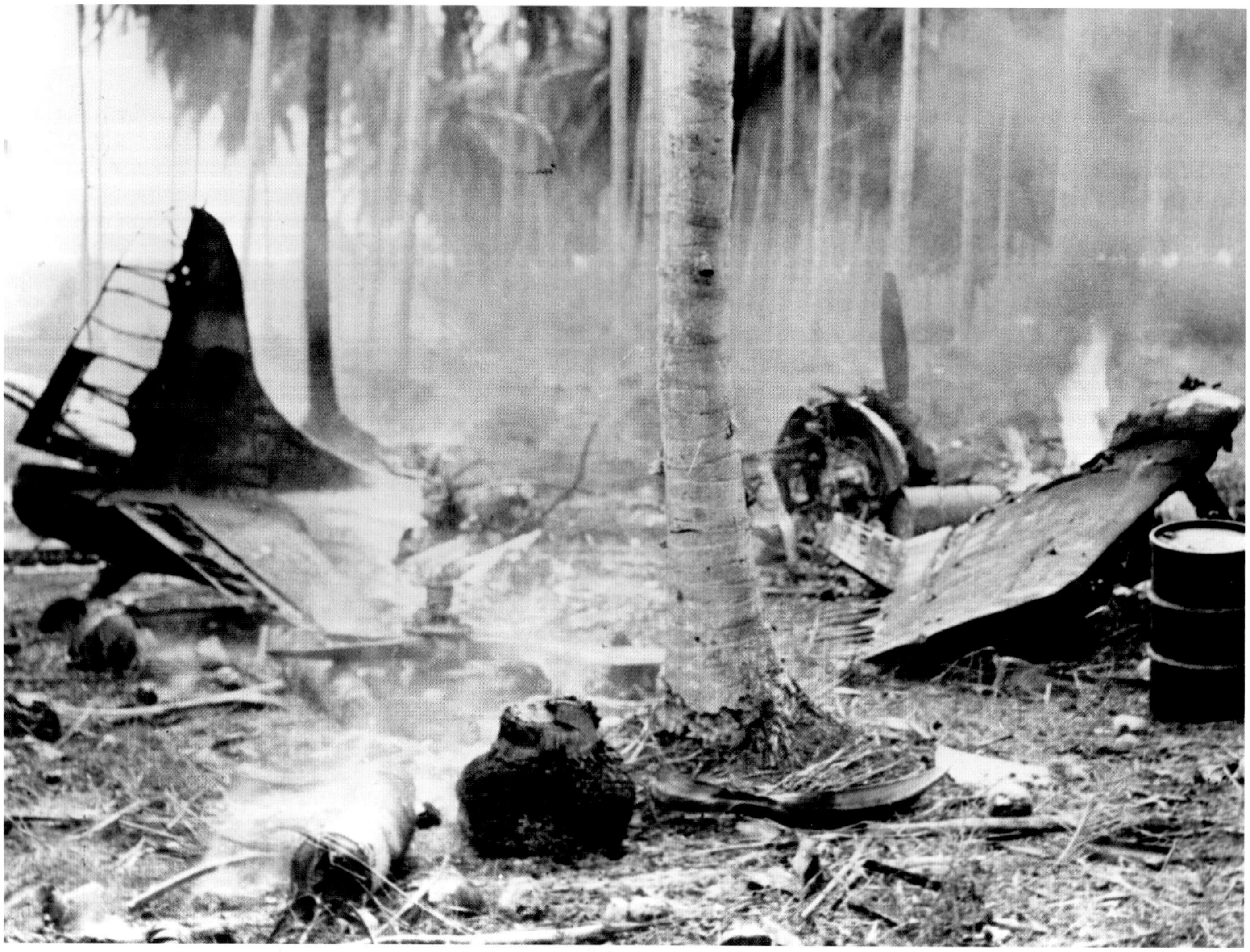

The Marines Dig In

The success of the naval operation on August 8 prompted the Japanese to reinforce Guadalcanal. Mikawa lost no ships in the Battle of Savo Island and his combined casualties were only 214 sailors. However, he also failed to destroy the Allied transports, which Yamamoto reasoned incorrectly would cancel the invasion. Therefore, Guadalcanal now needed Japanese ground units to contest the Marines and their slim claim to part of the island's coastal plain. This soon occurred with the beginning of an organized and efficient shuttle of army and SNLF units from Rabaul and Guam to Guadalcanal. When perfected, this shuttle effort was nicknamed the "Tokyo Express" by Americans in the region.

With only thirty-seven days of rations and an even shorter supply of ammunition, Vandegrift's men nevertheless began to plan for a long campaign. Exhausted from three days of non-stop activity, as were the sailors who just departed in Turner's ships, the 1st Marine Division men had to continue their duties. Paramount to the plan was defense of the airstrip. The Marines established a defensive perimeter around the field, determined to hold it against all comers. All abandoned Japanese material — trucks, guns and especially rations — was appropriated to make up for the shortages from the unloaded transport ships. The one thing that couldn't be replaced, however, was the reserve force of Marines that never disembarked from Turner's convoy.

The few Japanese soldiers, most involved in supervising the airfield construction, headed for the hills when the Marines landed. The construction workers, in half uniforms that sometimes made them hard to distinguish from Imperial Army regulars, were Korean. They were forced labor brought in for construction of the airfield. Some escaped to the hills where they probably starved to death. The lucky ones were captured by the Marines, as Dillon Gaulding describes.

"We took all the construction workers prisoner and we had them penned up in barbed wire. Later we sent them out when we got a little more control of the sea. On Guadalcanal we immediately sent forth. We had the Seabees with us [beginning on September 1] and boy they were efficient; it was amazing. They put that airstrip together in no time and they used heavy wire matting for the runway. We had our first big battle, what they called the Battle of the Tenaru, August the 21st."

Engineers made a hasty job of readying the airstrip for planes. Upon completion, the airstrip was named Henderson Field in honor of Marine Major Lofton Henderson, shot down and lost in the Battle of Midway. By August 18, the runway at Henderson Filed was ready to receive planes. Two days later, a pair of Marine squadrons flew in from the escort carrier USS *Long Island*. One squadron was composed of Wildcat fighters and the other of Dauntless dive bombers. They would be needed to oppose the first Japanese offensive coming up very quickly — on the same day the airfield was completed, the enemy's 28th Regiment from Rabaul landed east of the Marines' position.

The Japanese landing party from the 28th Regiment scrambled ashore east of Lunga Point under the command of Colonel Kiyano Ichiki. These troops were from Hyakutake's 17th army, but only 1000 soldiers of the approximately 2500 in the regiment came ashore at first. Underestimating the Marines' response, Ichiki attacked on

TOP: Marine aviation ordnance men take care of a wagon load of bombs that would eventually be delivered to Japanese targets. BOTTOM: Japanese bombing scored a direct hit on this American dive bomber parked near the runway at Henderson Field.

the night of August 21 across Alligator Creek, the eastern limit of Vandegrift's defensive perimeter around the airfield.

The Marines shredded the Imperial Army soldiers with machine gun, rifle and canister fire from well-placed artillery pieces. In the morning, the mop up operation was aided by tanks and strafing fire from the newly arrived Wildcats. Eight hundred Japanese soldiers died in the battle (called the Battle of Tenaru River by the Marines because they switched the names of the two rivers in the area). Ichiki committed suicide and the Japanese Army leadership realized it would have to rethink its approach if Japan wanted to get the leathernecks off Guadalcanal.

Even as 1st Division Marines continued to secure the perimeter around Henderson Field, 400 Seabees from the 6th Naval Construction Battalion arrived on September 1 to improve and expand the facility. It was the first of many times the Seabees would be used in a combat zone. Bernard Bonnecaze, who arrived on Guadalcanal a few months after the beachhead was established, was assistant to the engineering officer for one of the Marine squadrons operating from Henderson Field. He describes the way the field construction was improved by the Seabees' advanced techniques.

"They [the Japanese] had about a one foot depth of debris which was I guess you'd call just an accumulation of the soil, and then underneath that was I mean probably layers and layers of coral that accumulated on that so-called coastal plain. What we did though was tamp it down with rollers. We had something called Marston Matting. It was metal strips which [were] locked together and you built the hard surface, and a permanent surface, with those strips of metal. It was like a screen, you know. It had [open] circles in the [metal] strips. In other words, it was like a holey-looking piece of metal that locked together and you would place them on the surface and it would make a flat, smooth surface of metal. And that's how we landed our planes on there. The only thing about that was that the strips, when we got a lot of rain at times, you wouldn't have much traction, so your tires on your plane when you landed [would slide], and you'd slip without control. It could be detrimental to that plane's operation."

On Papua, despite the qualms Australians had about MacArthur, and they claimed to have many, the country's soldiers were motivated to fight for what they considered to be home territory. And they soon had one of their own commanding on the ground. General Thomas Blamey was a veteran staff officer who served in World War I and more recently with the AIF in the Middle East. When the AIF brigades and militia managed to hold the Japanese at bay within hailing distance of Port Moresby, with some unintentional help from the Imperial army and navy commanders, the Australians seized the opportunity for a counter-attack back over the Kokoda Track toward Buna. That's exactly what General MacArthur had in mind as August rolled into September 1942.

The struggle for Guadalcanal and Papua/New Guinea was to continue well beyond the Christmas holidays when many Marines and AIF soldiers dreamed of being home. Whether for strategic importance or national pride, the Japanese were determined not to lose one inch of their territorial conquest without a fight. So much blood was spilled on the beaches and in the jungles of the Solomons and Papua that the winding streams there ran red with it at times. Places with names and peoples unfamiliar to most citizens of the United States or the Home Islands became pin points on a thousand maps; places that would have to be held or lost as pieces in the giant puzzle that was this violent, heart-wrenching war.

From left Pfc. Dale E. Bordner, 2nd Lt. Marvin C. Hughes and 2nd Lt. Eugene Wallace stand on the dock just after arriving in Port Moresby following their dramatic rescue from enemy territory in New Britain.

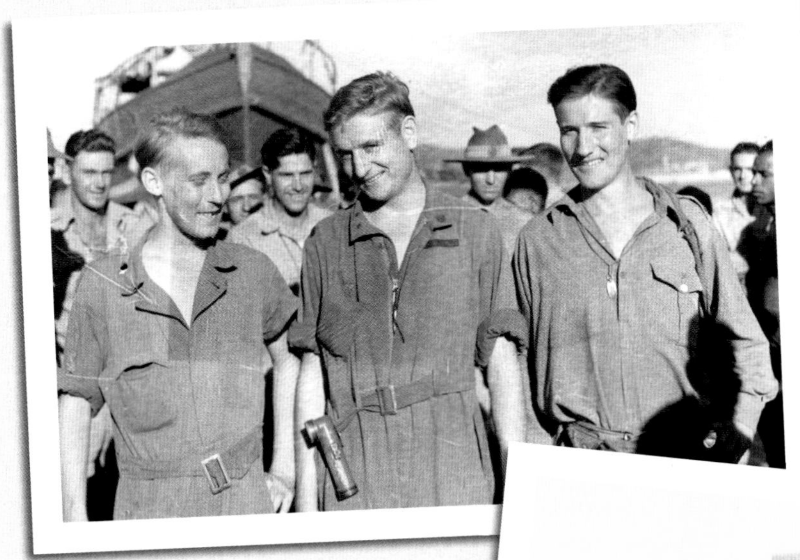

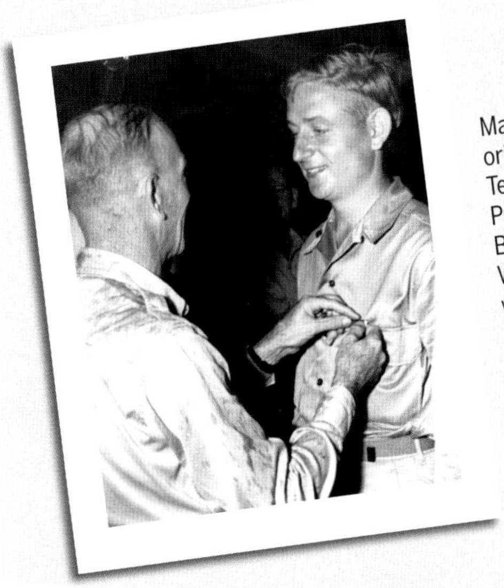

Marvin C. Hughes, originally from Baird, Texas, received a Purple Heart from Brig. Gen. Ennis Whitehead for the wounds he suffered in the crash and ten-month ordeal that lasted from May 1942 to March 1943.

Second Lt. Eugene Wallace is pictured here in his dress uniform in the early days of his U. S. Army Air Force career.

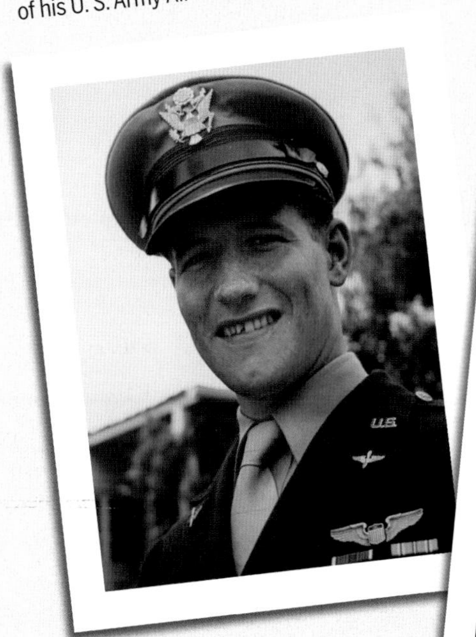

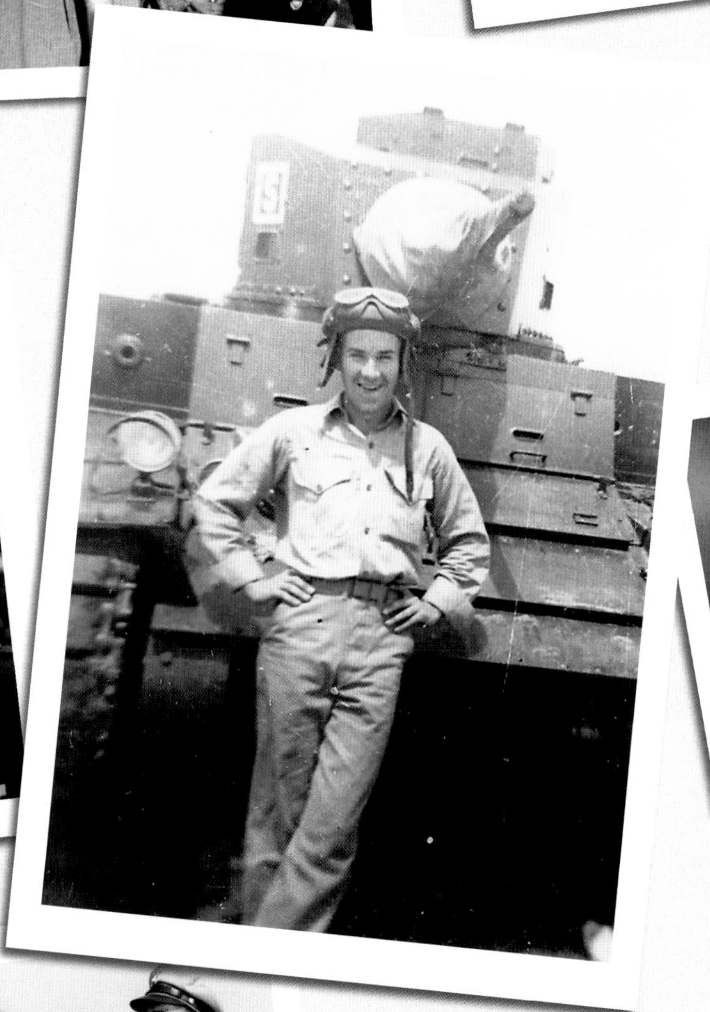

Lloyd Kingston seems a happy chap as he stands in front of his light tank on Guadalcanal. He was a radio operator/machine gunner in the Stuart tank.

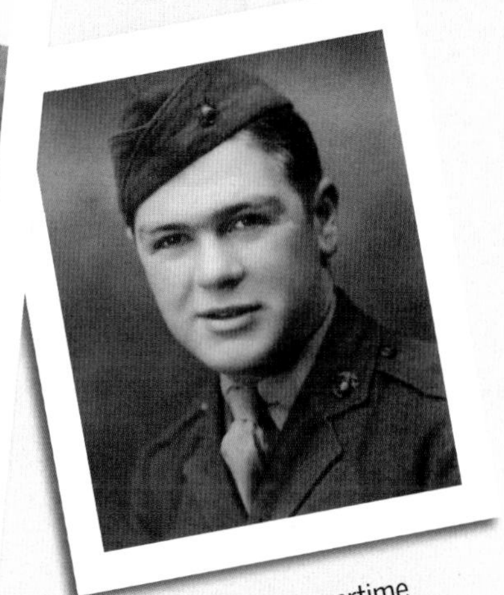

Herb Allebaugh in a wartime photograph. As a young Marine recruit he got his first taste of war on August 7, 1942 at Guadalcanal.

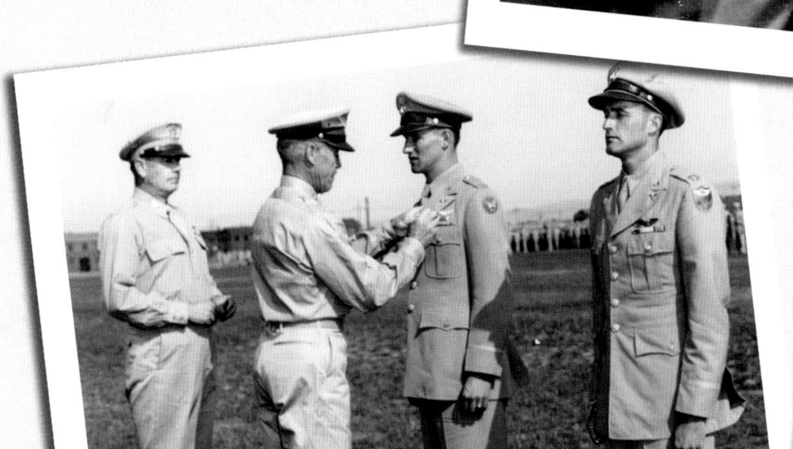

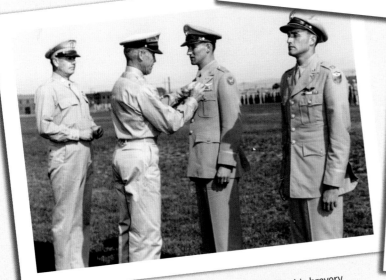

Eugene Wallace received a Purple Heart and a Silver Star for his bravery in the New Britain mission and subsequent ordeal. This medal ceremony took place at the Santa Ana Army Air Base in Southern California.

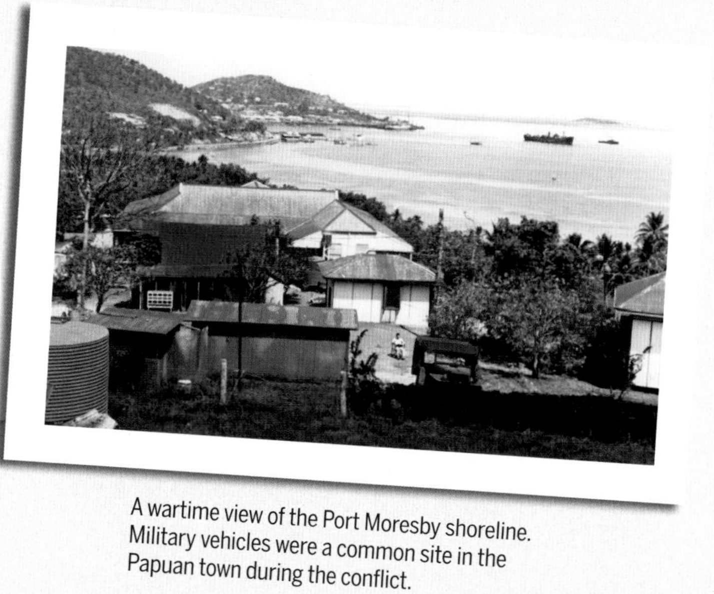

A wartime view of the Port Moresby shoreline. Military vehicles were a common site in the Papuan town during the conflict.

Status of the Pacific War–September 1942

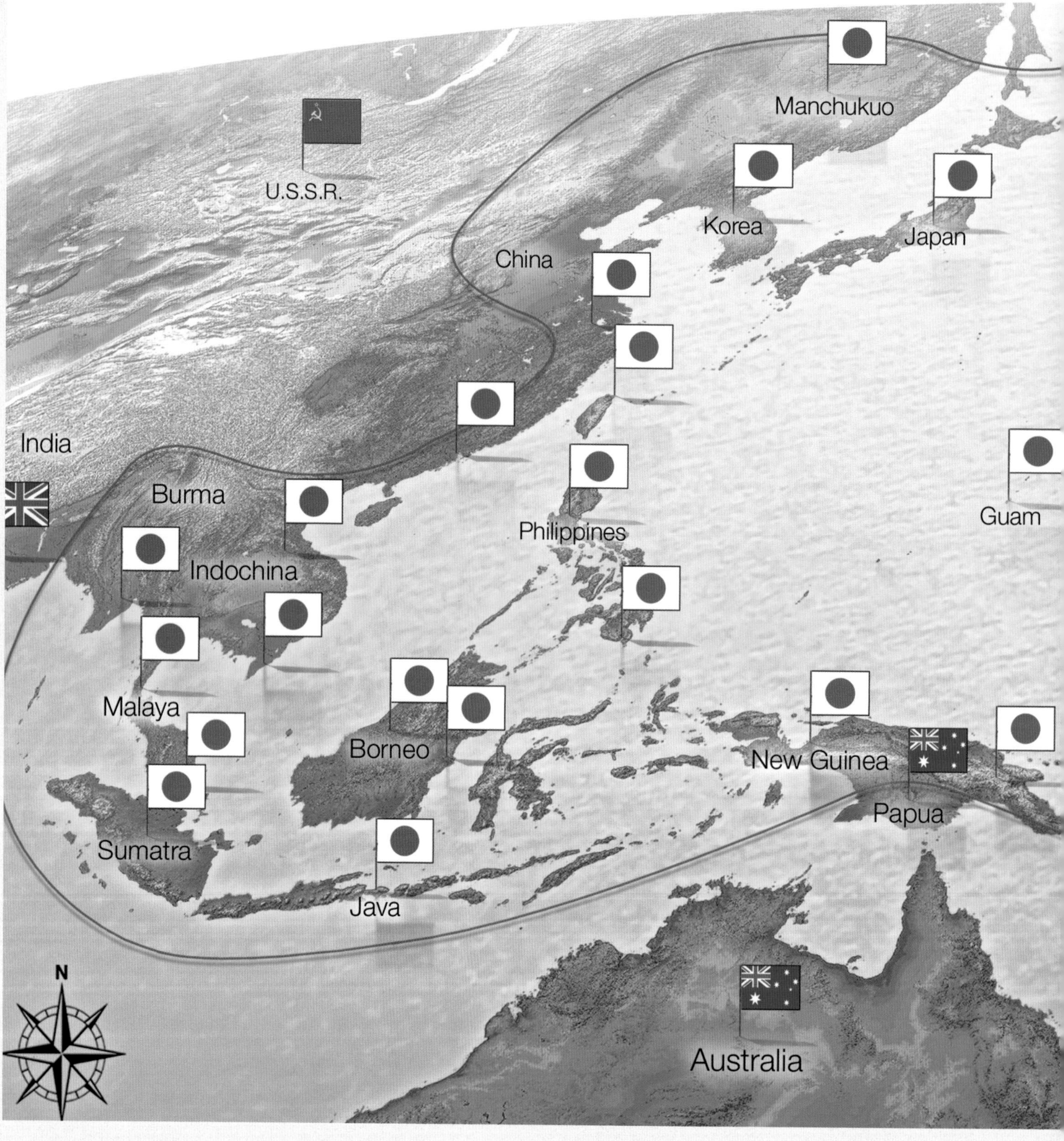

Manchukuo
U.S.S.R.
Korea
Japan
China
India
Burma
Philippines
Guam
Indochina
Malaya
Borneo
New Guinea
Papua
Sumatra
Java
N
Australia

By August and September 1942 the map of the Pacific began to change. U. S. Marines landed on Guadalcanal, Tulagi and other nearby Solomon Islands. And while the Imperial Navy and supporting land units were determined to make life difficult for the Marines and the navy supporting them, the foothold into Japan's security buffer of Pacific Islands was secured. Meanwhile to the west, the Japanese overland advance in Papua was halted by the AIF and hampered by Allied air strikes. The strategic initiative in the oversized island of New Guinea was about to change also.

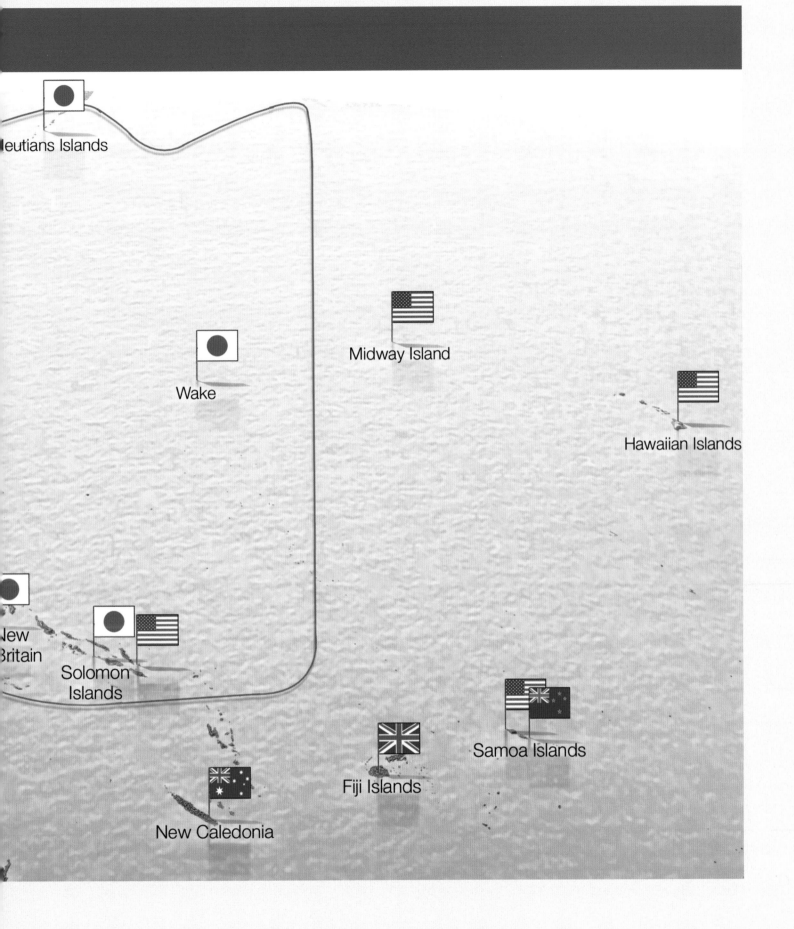

Aleutians Islands

Wake

Midway Island

Hawaiian Islands

New
Britain

Solomon
Islands

Samoa Islands

Fiji Islands

New Caledonia

On the Edge of Danger: Ten Months in the Jungle

To say bomber crews of the 5th Air Force and other units flying in the South Pacific Theater in 1942 faced incredible danger is perhaps to imply soldiers, sailors, marines and airmen of all forces in combat zones were any more safe, which was certainly not the case. But these bomber crews were facing a daunting foe, well prepared for interception of enemy bombers in the air and from the ground. Japanese Zero fighters ruled the air and could fly circles around accompanying Allied fighters, if there were any. In the early days of the war there were not and Allied crews had to rely on their own onboard defenses and flying skills during missions to Rabaul and other important targets.

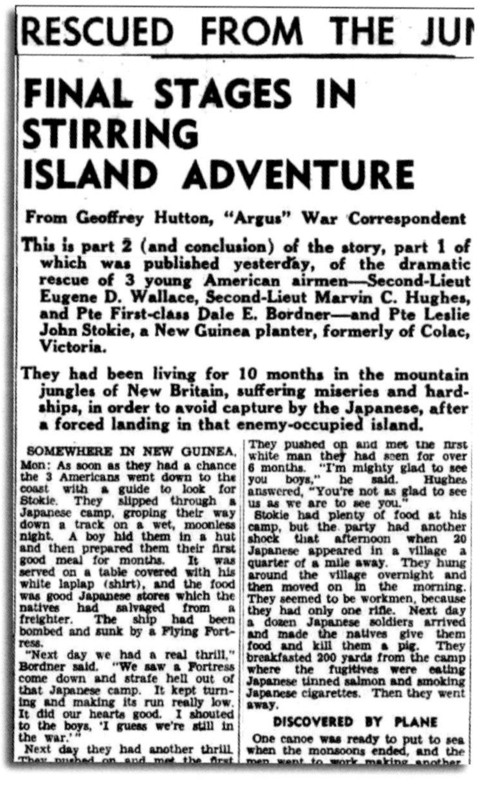

RESCUED FROM THE JU[...]

FINAL STAGES IN STIRRING ISLAND ADVENTURE

From Geoffrey Hutton, "Argus" War Correspondent

This is part 2 (and conclusion) of the story, part 1 of which was published yesterday, of the dramatic rescue of 3 young American airmen—Second-Lieut Eugene D. Wallace, Second-Lieut Marvin C. Hughes, and Pte First-class Dale E. Bordner—and Pte Leslie John Stokie, a New Guinea planter, formerly of Colac, Victoria.

They had been living for 10 months in the mountain jungles of New Britain, suffering miseries and hardships, in order to avoid capture by the Japanese, after a forced landing in that enemy-occupied island.

SOMEWHERE IN NEW GUINEA, Mon: As soon as they had a chance the 3 Americans went down to the coast with a guide to look for Stokie. They slipped through a Japanese camp, groping their way down a track on a wet, moonless night. A boy hid them in a hut and then prepared them their first good meal for months. It was served on a table covered with his white laplap (shirt), and the food was good Japanese stores which the natives had salvaged from a freighter. The ship had been bombed and sunk by a Flying Fortress.

"Next day we had a real thrill," Bordner said. "We saw a Fortress come down and strafe hell out of that Japanese camp. It kept turning and making its run really low. It did our hearts good. I shouted to the boys, 'I guess we're still in the war.'"

Next day they had another thrill. They pushed on and met the first white man they had seen for over 6 months. "I'm mighty glad to see you boys," he said. Hughes answered, "You're not as glad to see us as we are to see you."

Stokie had plenty of food at his camp, but the party had another shock that afternoon when 20 Japanese appeared in a village a quarter of a mile away. They hung around the village overnight and then moved on in the morning. They seemed to be workmen, because they had only one rifle. Next day a dozen Japanese soldiers arrived and made the natives give them food and kill them a pig. They breakfasted 200 yards from the camp where the fugitives were eating Japanese tinned salmon and smoking Japanese cigarettes. Then they went away.

DISCOVERED BY PLANE

One canoe was ready to put to sea when the monsoons ended, and the

The story of the crew of Imogene VII, a Martin B-26 Marauder twin-engine medium bomber, is one of those marvelous human-interest stories that captures the imagination and touches the heart not only about war, but about life. On May 24, 1942, the eight-man crew on Imogene VII included First Lieutenant Harold L. Massie, pilot, Second Lieutenant Eugene Wallace, co-pilot, Second Lieutenant Marvin C. Hughes, navigator, Second Lieutenant Arthur C. King, bombardier, Pfc. Dale E. Bordner, radio operator, Corporal Stanley Wolenski, flight engineer, Private Joseph Dukes, tail gunner and Staff Sergeant Jack B. Swan, photographer.

Wallace, a 22-year-old from Los Angeles, was an aviation enthusiast early in life. After civilian flight lessons, he joined a government sanctioned flight cadet program. In his class was another cadet who would also join the Army Air Corps, Gene Roddenberry, creator of *Star Trek*. Wallace wrote to his family in early December, 1941, as the class course was ending.

"Dear Family, I finished my flight training and have been waiting for graduation this Friday, the 12th, and Saturday morning we will most likely receive our assignments. It almost looks as if none of us will be able to get home for Xmas. I will know more when I am definitely assigned to a new post and learning just what the commanding officer has planned for the immediate future."

His future was in Australia with the Army Air Corps, which shortly thereafter became the U. S. Army Air Forces. As a member of the 5th Air Force, Wallace had to quickly put his training into combat experience. He describes a typical mission for planes of the 22nd Bomb Group of which he was a member.

"There were times when we got to Buna [a target in Papua] and at times we refueled in New

Guinea and we would proceed on up to Rabaul; then drop our bombs on Rabaul and then proceed to return to Australia to our base there which was very rudimentary and reload and stand by going up to New Guinea and another load of bombs."

On May 24, 1942 with the crew noted above, Imogene VII took off from Seven-Mile Airstrip

LEFT: A headline in the newspaper Argus *announces the rescue of three American airmen who endured ten months eluding Japanese soldiers on the dangerous island of New Britain. ABOVE: The first picture taken of rescued airmen Bordner, Hughes and Wallace, along with John Stokie who sheltered them, in the gun blister of the Catalina flying boat that picked them up off the shore of New Britain on March 25, 1943.*

near Port Moresby. The Marauder was in the starboard position of a typical three-bomber sortie and was carrying incendiary bombs. Massie was on his first operational mission in the pilot's chair. Gunner Dukes had never flown in any aircraft before that day. He was an early draftee who learned all he knew about being a tail gunner in training school. Wallace was on his third combat mission. Swan was along to photograph the results of the bombing run, a plane-laden runway in the large Rabaul complex of military installations. To Wallace, time flew by during the bombing runs.

"It all went very quickly in terms of the bombing attacks and for instance the time we got shot down, we proceeded out from Port Moresby over the mountains and then on up to Rabaul. We had three airplanes and this particular time we experienced [enemy] planes that had taken off from Laguna Canal. They came out as we were going in. We proceeded beyond Laguna Canal and we proceeded parallel up the coast and then inland."

Imogene VII dropped its load of bombs and Swan photographed a successful hit, but as Massie banked the plane for the return a burst of anti-aircraft fire tore into one wing and damaged an engine. The first indication of trouble came to the pilots when Hughes staggered into the cockpit saying he was hit. As Wallace administered first aid, Massie ordered the crew to jettison weight as he struggled with a rapid loss of altitude. Eventually it was obvious that Imogene VII was going down. Massie guided the plane into a flat landing on the rough seas, an incredible feat to accomplish with a large wounded bomber. Wallace explains:

"When we hit the water we were all thrown forward and I actually hit the airplane itself inside and I knocked some of my teeth out and split my lip. Basically [the plane] didn't tear up all that much but we landed in the water and as I recall, the pilot, I could see his hands on the throttle, and he was beginning to pull back to get ready to slow up the airplane and get ready to land in the water."

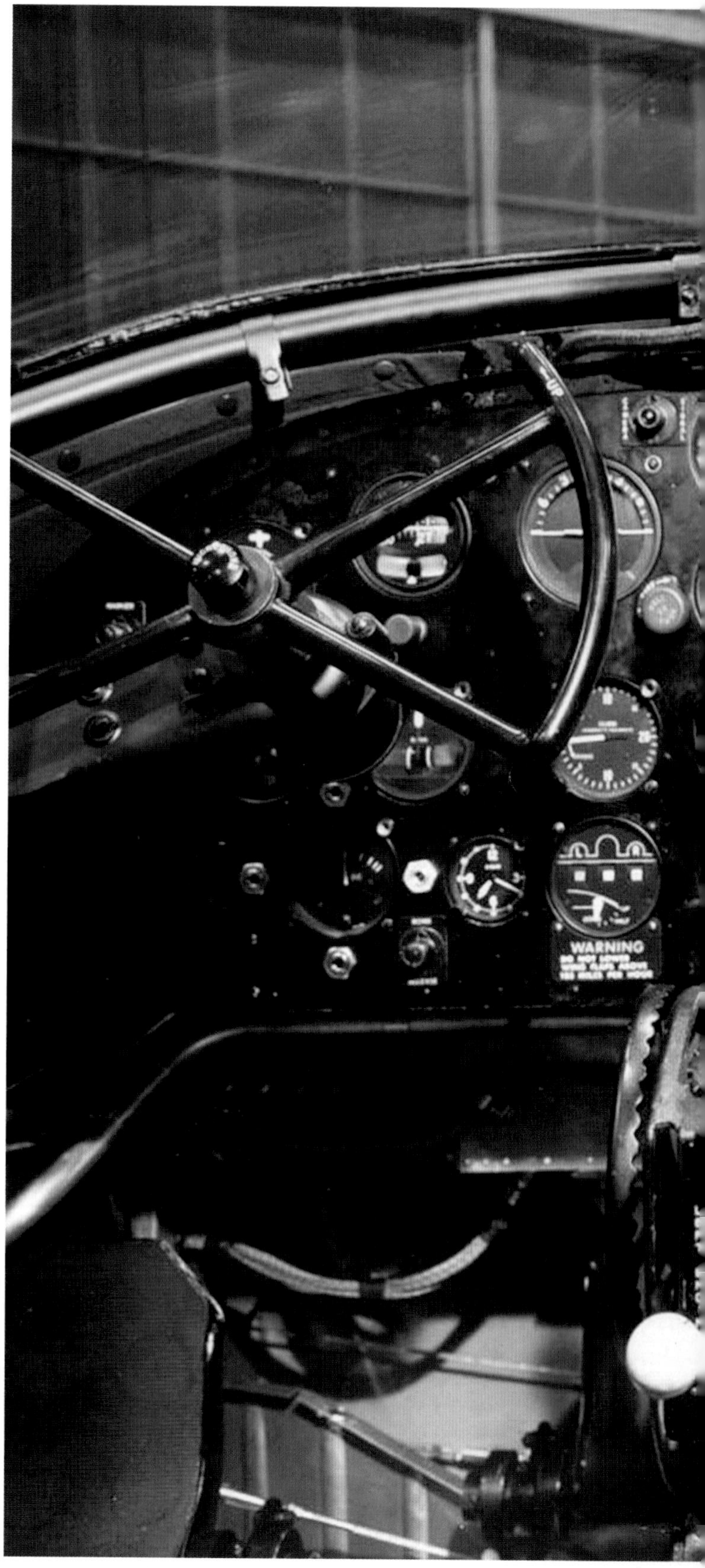
WARNING

The cockpit of a Martin B-26 bomber in a photograph from 1941. Co-pilot Gene Wallace would have been in the right seat.

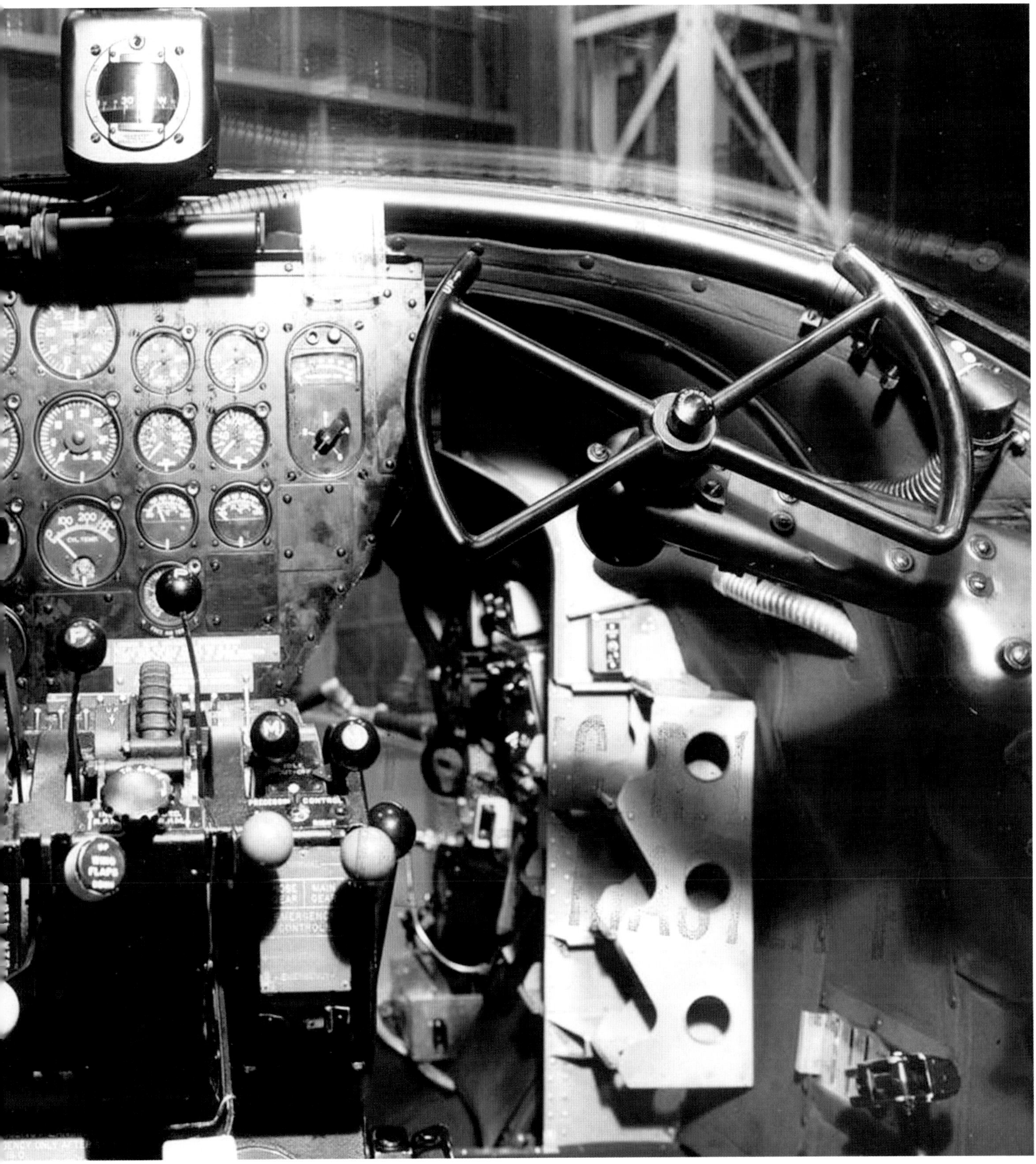

Shortly after the crash landing, six bloodied heads bobbed around in the water, five in the safety of their life jackets, most with serious wounds. The plane began to submerge nose first and the six airmen in the water had to endure the terrified cries of the two men trapped inside, Dukes and Wolenski, as they vainly tried to get to them.

"The plane turned up and I had heard earlier yelling for help, 'Help me, please help me,' and I got out in the water and swam around. I could tell it was the rear of the airplane and I'd been swimming to get around to the rear and I could hear the people yelling for help inside the airplane. I didn't actually get into the airplane from the rear as you would expect to lend a hand."

The plane soon disappeared in the water taking the two crew members to an undersea grave. Massie, a strong swimmer, shunned a "Mae West" life jacket; he took off for the shore, three-quarters of a mile away, in the direction of a group of thatched huts. The airmen were on the Japanese controlled island of New Britain, a scant fifty miles south of Rabaul, and they didn't know what to expect.

"The question was, are these natives going to be a threat? We saw a couple of the natives slide out a canoe and begin to paddle so at that time we recognized that they were friendly. There were three of them, two or three, got out in the water so they were joining us."

In good time Massie returned with the dark-skinned island natives and the outrigger canoe. The most seriously injured of the six airmen were put into the canoe while the young male natives and the other airmen swam alongside. The rapid talking of the young men with a few words of pidgin English made King think they were cannibals bringing home dinner. This produced a weak laugh from his comrades, the first break they had from terror since trouble developed on the plane.

Upon arriving on shore, the whole village turned out and the men were shown and carried to a thatched hut in the village set aside for guests, including being provided a houseboy. Finding from the natives' conversation that it was good to be English, the crewmen elected not to explain to the village the difference between Englishmen and citizens of Britannia's former colonies. Soon, it was communicated to Wallace that there was another white man in the area and, despite the ordeal of the day, he left with escorts for a meeting. After a three hour walk he encountered the man.

"It was the Austrian. When I approached him, both of us coming together and held out our hands to say hello, he was talking to us but I was aware that he was speaking broken English with a German accent. Basically he escorted us to the mission and his quarters which were nearby. Then he pointed across the bay there from his mission and explained how the Japanese engaged him. Japanese came up to him and he then showed his passport and it was in German."

Because of the German passport, the Japanese left the missionary to his business, but obviously he would not be able to shelter six American fliers. After treating Wallace to a meal he gave him a blanket, disinfectant and some bandage cloth to take back. Wallace returned the same day. The next day the missionary came to the village.

"He showed up the next morning and he was trying to tell us the lay of the land and what we were facing and all that sort of thing, where the Japanese troops were and so forth. The natives of the village were all interested in us and they called

us master, 'Hello master,' et cetera, so obviously they were willing to help, not that they could do much to help us physically or medically."

While the stronger ones, Wallace, Massie and King, looked after their injured comrades, Hughes, Bordner and Swan, the natives looked on with interest. Swan had a broken shoulder and was in the worst shape of the six. They observed the village leader, the luluai, conduct a town meeting and make it known to the village members not to reveal the presence of the airmen to the Japanese in the area. After Massie made a long trip to see another white man in the bush, he returned with supplies and tips to improve relations with the natives. He suggested, "Sing to

Wallace and Bordner wave from a native canoe as a B-24 Liberator does a flyby over Stokie's compound at the village of Ea Ea on March 6. After Stokie flashed a mirror to get the attention of the American bomber crew additional flyovers were needed to insure the discovery was not a Japanese trap.

them, humor them; let them see you bathe and wash your clothes frequently (cleanliness is an eccentricity they expect of white people); the natives hold three things sacred – their "marys" (wives), pigs and gardens; the controlling emotion in (their) lives is fear."

Wallace and the other able airmen took the advice. They sang (*Rambling Wreck from Georgia Tech* was a favorite among the villagers), taught them simple games like hopscotch and bathed in the ocean in sight of the natives. The white man sent along tobacco sticks for trade. Food was running low in the coastal village the airman adopted as home and danger was still in the air. Thirty-eight days after the crash – Wallace carved notches in a coconut shell for a calendar – he, King and Massie moved on. They headed in the direction of the white man – an Australian – who Massie had visited earlier.

Massie became ill with an unknown ailment. He was carried in a blanket sling by natives hired for the job and paid in tobacco sticks. Sores on his leg wounds worsened and he almost died, but with the help of the Australian and his friends, he regained his spirit and some of his strength. By July 17, Wallace's 23rd birthday, they were reunited with Hughes, Bordner and Swan, who were delivered by natives in an outrigger canoe. The Japanese knew they were there and were closing in; so they had to get out.

It was decided they would have to get to the other side of New Britain. The trip overland through the dense jungle was difficult. Disease was in the air and the natives of the interior were less friendly and communicative. At one point Wallace, Hughes, Bordner and Swan became incapacitated. King and Massie decided to forge ahead. Wallace and his three companions continued to have individual difficulties at various times. One or two would forge ahead leaving the others behind for a time. A sympathetic native called "doctor boy" shared his home in the mountains with the refugees. Sometime toward the end of the year, Swan died of his wounds and the natives brought word that Massie and King had been captured by the Japanese. They were never heard from again. Wallace became sick with malaria and stayed behind for a time.

Then Hughes and Bordner brought the best news they had received since they left New Guinea. A white man sent a message offering to take them into his camp after hearing of the airmen's presence through the native grapevine. Under the circumstances, they had to put their trust in John Stokie.

"Well, John Stokie was at Rabaul when the Japanese attacked and he was in the hospital with his gun," says Wallace. "He was willing to give us information and advice and so forth and some medical attention, bandages and stuff."

Stokie was a former plantation owner who became a private in the New Guinea Volunteer Rifles. Stokie always included the phrase NGVR 239, his service number, with his signature. When the volunteer force in Rabaul was overwhelmed by a much large force of Japanese and the city fell in early 1942, Stokie took to the jungle and became a one-man guerilla force. From his camp near Ulamona on the west coast he was skilled at hiding from the Japanese. Stokie took the three airmen under his wing when native guides loyal to him made contact with Wallace and the others in the jungle and brought them to the coast. It was February 1943.

Stokie unveiled a plan of escape. He had a seaworthy dugout canoe with a sail hidden and would have his native allies build another. When the trade winds shifted to the southeast, they would sail down the coast and over to New Guinea. It was quite an ambitious journey they wouldn't have to make. On March 6 the first B-24 Liberator flew over the camp. Stokie flashed a mirror which caught the crew's attention. On successive passes, Wallace and Bordner put out to the lagoon in a canoe and waved while the villagers danced on shore.

The next day another bomber buzzed the village and dropped a streamer with instructions to identify the organization in the sand. On a later pass, the B-24 dropped a package by parachute with some supplies and specific instructions about communicating a serial number. The American flyers wanted to be sure the party on the land wasn't a Japanese decoy to trap a rescue party. The signals were repeated by Wallace and his companions every day until a B-17 flew over. The communication had been acknowledged because a Liberator then flew over and dropped a package with specific

instructions for a night rendezvous with a PBY.

In the pre-dawn hours of
March 25 Bordner was on
watch. He heard the low
drone of a plane and realized a seaplane was approaching. Catalina A24-17 of the Royal Australian Air Force under the command of Captain
Reg Burrage and a crew of eight undertook the
dangerous mission. Although the rescue was witnessed by the whole village (who were left with
presents of knives and tomahawks for their help)
the commotion did not attract the attention of the
Japanese in the area. The rescued party – Stokie,
the three American airmen and three of Stokie's
native companions – successfully transferred from
canoe to the PBY. Six hours later the plane was
on the ground at Port Moresby, a place Wallace,
Bordner and Hughes had last seen almost exactly
ten months earlier.

*A Royal Australian Air Force Catalina flying
boat piloted by Squadron Leader Reginald
Burrage touches down at Port Moresby at the
end of the dramatic rescue.*

"After we were rescued
they were relaying inter-
views [with us] down to their
[South West Pacific Area]
headquarters in Brisbane,"
Wallace explains. "We eventually were taken out
to our base to say hello to the troops."

After bidding their new friend John Stokie
goodbye, the trio returned to their home base in
Australia where they received Purple Heart
medals. Eventually they would return to the
United States. Gene Wallace made appearances
for the War Bond effort and worked on some of
the Hollywood-produced war films and docu-
mentaries. He made an effort over the years to
keep in touch with colleagues, including Reg Burrage, the man in the Catalina PBY who led the
rescue effort that pulled him out from ten months
in the jungle.

CREDITS

Staff

Bill Breidenstine
Publisher & Marketing

J-C Suares
Creative Director

Dan Smith
Art Director

Jennifer E. Berry
Photography Editor

Gregory Proch
Map Designer

Kevin Johnson
Production Director

Jerry Morelock, PhD
Editor

Edwin Cole Bearss
Foreword and Additional Editing

Virginia Wilson
Administrative Assistant,
Proofreader and Transcriber

Sharon Gytri
Research and Clearance

Patricia Grove
Transcriber

Tara Pelander
Transcriber

Megan Harwick
Research Assistant

Acknowledgements

The author wishes to acknowledge the contributions of the following people and organizations: Ronald A. Abboud, Maria Embry, Jesse A. Thompson, Col. Len Hayes, Sandra Stewart Holyoak, Stuart N. Hedley, Edward E. Wise, Raquel Ramsey, PhD, Jo Davidsmeyer, Claude Griffiths, Regina and the late Gil Martinez, Wallace Wendell, Frank H. Haigler M.D., June Comier, Bud Wharton, Les Miller, Kacey Hill, The National World War II Museum, New Mexico Veterans Memorial, Rutgers Oral History Archives, Wisconsin Veterans Museum, Pearl Harbor Survivors Assn. Inc., San Diego Chapter 3, 1st Marine Division Association, Stephen Petranek, Barbara Justice, Gerald Swick, William Horne and Rob Wilkins.

Kelly Davis and Robert Garcia interviews courtesy of the New Mexico Veterans Memorial; Herbert H. Hanneman interview courtesy of the Wisconsin Veterans Museum; Austin Andrews and Alfred McGrew interviews courtesy of the Rutgers Oral History Archives; Ann Bernatitus, Dorothy Still Danner and Joseph P. Pollard interviews courtesy of the Naval Historical Center, Department of the Navy

Letter to John Virgo family from G. R. Miethke courtesy of Don Virgo

"I Sank the Yorktown" Excerpted from Proceedings with permission; Copyright © 1963 U.S. Naval Institute/www.usni.org.

"Japan's World Debut: The 1904-05 Russo-Japanese War, p. 27, by Jerry Morelock

About the Interviewed Veterans

As of the publication of Volume I of *War Stories: World War II Firsthand*, I have personally interviewed 150 men and women for this project and the interviews will continue until the series is completed and the important work of preserving these veterans' experiences is done. I am grateful to the veterans, who often allowed me into their homes and shared their experiences and mementos with me; and also to the family, friends and organizations who have allowed me to gain access to these individuals. I am also deeply in debt to those organizations and individuals who have provided oral histories of veterans whom I could not interview myself.

I cannot express my appreciation enough for the opportunity to learn from these veterans how they handled war and military service. Regrettably, since this project began some of those veterans interviewed have passed on. John William Finn, USN, Medal of Honor Recipient, died in May 2010 at the age of 100. His story is in this volume. James L. "Jim" Evans, past national president of the Second Marine Division Association and whose contributions are included in this and future volumes, died in February 2010. Frank Tuttle, USMC, died in November 2009 and Hans Enderle, Afrika Corps, died in December 2009. Their stories will appear in future volumes.

Bibliography

Ambrose, Hugh,
The Pacific: Hell Was An Ocean Away, New York, New American Library, 2010

Collins, James L. Jr.,
consultant editor,
The Marshall Cavendish Illustrated Encyclopedia of World War II, Vol. 10, New York, Marshall Cavendish, 1972

Flanagan, E. M.
Corregidor, the rock force assault, New York, Presidio, 1988

Frank, Richard B.,
Guadalcanal, New York, Random House, 1990

Goodenough, Simon,
War Maps, London, Macdonald & Co. Ltd. 1982

Marston, Daniel,
editor, *The Pacific War: From Pearl Harbor to Hiroshima,* London, Osprey Press, Inc., 2001

Morison, Samuel Eliot,
History of United States Naval Operations in World War II: Vol. II, The Rising Sun in the Pacific, 1931-April 1942, Boston, Little, Brown & Company, 1947

Morison, Samuel Eliot,
History of United States Naval Operations in World War II: Vol. V, The Struggle for Guadalcanal, August 1942-February 1943, Boston, Little, Brown & Company, 1947

Prange, Gordon W.,
At Dawn We Slept, New York, Penguin Books, 1991

Ramsey, Edwin Price and Stephen J. Rivele,
Lieutenant Ramsey's War: From Horse Soldier to Guerilla Commander, Dulles, Va., Potomac Books Inc., 1990

Tenney, Lester I.,
My Hitch in Hell: The Bataan Death March, Dulles, Va., Potomac Books Inc., 2007

United States Strategic Bombing Survey, Interrogations of Japanese Officials, Vol. 1, Washington, D. C., Government Printing Office, 1946

Willmott, H. P., Robin Cross and Charles Messenger, *World War II,* New York, DK Publications, 2004

More information including references used in this work and other selected readings can be found at:

www.WWIIWarStories.com

A sample of websites elevant to this volume:

www.history.navy.mil
www.history.army.mil
www.history.usmc.mil
www.nationalww2museum.org
www.usmcmsuem.org
www.militarymuseum.org
www.nmvetsmemorial.org
www.nps.gov/nwwm
www.nps.gov/valr
www.nsa.gov/about/cryptologic_heritage/museum

Image Credits

Veterans and U.S. Government sources graciously provided the vast majority of the images in this book. Image references below are listed by page number and position (t-top, m-middle, b-bottom, l-left, c-center, r-right).

The National Archives and Records Administration Collections:
9, Office of War Information; 10, U.S. Army; 16(t), U.S. Navy; 29, Office of War Information; 30-31, U.S. Navy; 33, U.S. Navy; 38, U.S. Navy; 41, U.S. Navy; 43, U.S. Navy; 47, U.S. Navy; 49, U.S. Navy; 50-51, U.S. Navy; 54, U.S. Navy; 57, U.S. Navy; 60(t), U.S. Navy; 61(t), U.S. Navy; 64, Office of War Information; 69, Office of War Information; 70, Office of War Information; 71, U.S. Army; 77, U.S. Army; 79, U.S. Navy; 80-81, U.S. Army; 84, U.S. Navy; 88, U.S. Army; 89, Office of War Information; 92, U.S. Army; 95, U.S. Army; 97, U.S. Army; 100, U.S. Army; 101, Dorthea Lange/Department of the Interior/War Relocation Authority; 104, U.S. Army; 105, U.S. Army; 106, U.S. Army; 107, U.S. Army; 108-109, U.S. Army; 111, Office of Government Reports; 112, Office of War Information; 115, Office for Emergency Management/War Production Board; 116, U.S. Navy; 124, U.S. Army; 127, U.S. Navy; 129, LT Paul Dorsey/U.S. Navy; 130-131, U.S. Navy; 133, U.S. Navy; 136-137, U.S. Navy; 138-139, U.S. Navy; 140, U.S. Navy; 145(b), U.S. Navy; 146, U.S. Navy; 147, U.S. Navy; 150, U.S. Navy; 159, U.S. Navy; 160-161, U.S. Navy; 163, U.S. Navy; 165, U.S. Navy; 166, U.S. Navy; 168, U.S. Navy; 171(tl), U.S. Navy; 172, U.S. Navy; 177, U.S. Navy; 180, U.S. Navy; 181, U.S. Navy; 184-185, U.S. Navy; 187(t), U.S. Navy; 195, U.S. Navy; 202-203, U.S. Air Force; 205(b), U.S. Navy; 206, U.S. Navy; 208, U.S. Army; 209, U.S. Army; 217, U.S. Navy; 219, U.S. Navy; 220-221, U.S. Navy; 222, U.S. Marine Corps; 224, U.S. Marine Corps; 226, U.S. Navy; 227, U.S. Marine Corps; 228-229, U.S. Navy; 230, U.S. Navy; 233, U.S. Navy; 236, U.S. Navy; 238, U.S. Navy; 241(tl) (tr), U.S. Air Force; 245, U.S. Air Force; 249, U.S. Air Force; 251, U.S. Air Force.

U.S. Naval History and Heritage Command: 18; 32; 37; 39; 55; 59; 60(b); 72; 96; 117(mc); 126; 128; 135(t); 148-149; 154-155; 167; 174-175; 178; 187(b); 205(t); 207; 223; 237.

The Library of Congress: 2, Farm Security Administration/Office of War Information Photograph Collection; 12, Hiroshige Utagawa; 13, Chadbourne collection of Japanese prints; 14, Mathew Brady; 15, Japanese Prints and Drawings Collection; 16(b), George Grantham Bain Collection; 17, Detroit Publishing Company Photograph Collection; 27, Ryōzō Tanaka; 182, Farm Security Administration/Office of War Information; 183, Alfred T. Palmer/Office of War Information.

Getty Images: 67, Photo by Peter Stackpole/Time Life Pictures/Getty Images; 76, Time Life Pictures/Getty Images; 192, Three Lions/Getty Images; 193, Keystone/Getty Images; 197, Keystone/Hulton Archive/Getty Images; 213(t), Keystone/Getty Images.

U.S. Air Force: 93; 135(b); 196, The 3rd Wing History Office; 198-199, National Museum of the United States Air Force; 246-247.

Images from other sources:
Edwin C. Bearss: 7; The National Cryptologic Museum: 19; State of Hawaii Department of Transportation: 25; Guy Aceto: 28; The Congressional Medal of Honor Society: 61(b); James L. Evans: 63(tl), (tc), (ml); 201(tl), (mr), (bl), (bc), (br); Don E. Lester: 63(tr); Raymond Richmond: 63(mc); 171(tr); John W. Finn: 63(mr); Joseph M. Kawka: 63(br); The Franklin D. Roosevelt Library, Hyde Park, New York: 65; Masahiko Homma: 73; William Alfonte Collection/General Douglas MacArthur Foundation: 75; Felipe A. Fernandez: 117(tl), (br); Lester Tenney: 117(tr); Angelo Borruano: 117(bl); Austin Andrews: 117(bc); Edwin P. Ramsey: 119; 123; © John Solie: 120-121; Kure Maritime History and Science Museum: 145(t); William G. Roy: 171(ml); Bob Raffato: 171(mc); Claude "Cosmo" Griffiths: 171(mr); Edward E. Wise: 171(bl); Woodrow W. Derby: 171(bc); Gordon E. Jones: 171(br); U.S. Army: 179; Mainichi/Aflo: 189; Australian War Memorial: 194, P03932.002; 213(b), 013159; 215, 013453; 232, 305286; John J. Lovas: 201(tr); The Estate of O. Howard Davidsmeyer Sr.: 201(ml); 241(br); Eugene Wallace: 241(ml), (bl); Lloyd Kingston: 241(mc); Herb P. Allebaugh: 241(mr); The National Library of Australia: 244.

Endpapers: Veterans supplied their own images unless otherwise noted. Jay Wertz: left side-1, 4, 5, 7, 11-13, 15, right side-1-5, 7, 9, 11, 14; James L. Evans, Jr.: left side-2; Bob Loveday: left side-14; Kim Townley: right side-16.

Index

INDEX

From top left to right

1. Edwin Cole Bearss
2. James L. "Jim" Evans
3. John J. Lovas
4. Glenn Boeck
5. Woodrow W. Derby
6. Felipe A. Fernandez
7. John William Finn
8. Dillon R. Gaulding
9. Stuart N. Hedley
10. Bernard F. Bonnecaze Jr.
11. Herbert A. Franck
12. Gordon E. Jones
13. Joseph M. Kawka
14. Lloyd R. Kingston
15. Arthur A. Kowalski
16. Herb P. Allebaugh